REALIZING HUMAN RIGHTS

REALIZING HUMAN RIGHTS

Moving from Inspiration to Impact

Samantha Power
and
Graham Allison
Editors

St. Martin's Press
New York

Portions of chapter 2 in this volume, from *The Courage to Stand Alone* by Wei Jingsheng, translated by Kristena M. Torgeson, copyright © 1997 by Wei Jingsheng. Used by permission of Viking Penguin, a division of Penguin Putnam Inc.

ISBN 0-312-23494-5

Library of Congress Cataloging-in-Publication Data

The future of human rights / edited by Samantha Power, Graham Allison.
    p. cm.
  Includes bibliographical references and index.
  ISBN 0-312-23494-5
    1. Human rights. 2. United Nations. General Assembly. Universal Declaration of Human Rights. I. Power, Samantha. II. Allison, Graham T.

K3240.F88 2000
341.4'81—dc21   00-038238

Book design by Acme Art Inc.

First edition: October, 2000
10 9 8 7 6 5 4 3 2 1

CONTENTS

PART III

Human Rights Policy Ideas, Institutions, and Instruments

PART IV

Afterword: The Challenges Ahead

THE CARR CENTER FOR HUMAN RIGHTS POLICY

The Carr Center for Human Rights Policy is a research, teaching, and training center that critically examines the policies and actions of governments, international organizations, and independent actors that affect the realization of human rights around the world. Located at Harvard's John. F. Kennedy School of Government, the Center focuses principally on evaluating the means and processes that can be used to advance human rights. Drawing upon the methods adopted by other research centers at the Kennedy School, the Center is developing programs that empirically and analytically address central issues in human rights policy and practice. The Center was formally established in June 1999 through a gift from Kennedy School alumnus Gregory Carr.

The Center has organized its work into four substantive program areas: national and international responses to mass atrocity, including the use of force and transitional justice; the effectiveness and accountability of nongovernmental organizations; domestic human rights policy—constituency-building and compliance; and perspectives on changing norms. These topics, simultaneously overlapping and complementary, create an integrated research agenda that reflects the Center's links to both the academic and policy communities.

Among the Center's current projects are a research project on the dilemmas of when and how to intervene militarily to protect human rights, and a domestic training and research project with state and local government officials in Idaho working to promote human rights and diversity. The Carr Center is developing a variety of training tools that can be tailored to other national and international needs, including those of governments and human rights organizations.

In the division of labor among human rights organizations, the Center hopes to occupy a unique niche. Because the Center is not an advocacy organization, it will offer a forum to engage diverse views about human rights. In particular, the Center is eager to integrate disciplines and professions not traditionally associated with the field of human rights. By drawing new voices to the table, the Center seeks to extend and deepen the understanding and analysis of human rights. With this publication, the Center initiates its book series.

ACKNOWLEDGMENTS

We are grateful to our contributors for taking the time out of their active lives to reflect on these human rights policy questions. The authors worked with Carr Center editors and researchers for more than a year sharpening and supplementing the essays so they complemented one another, filled in historical gaps, and responded to potential challenges. This effort is reflected in their fine contributions.

Two individuals made extraordinary contributions to this book. Teresa Lawson, a lawyer by training and now an editor by profession, worked deliberately and delicately with each author sharpening this book. Though her expertise lay in international security, she developed a ready grasp of and interest in human rights and helped press the authors to satisfy her curiosity as well as the book's needs. Ingrid Tamm Grudin, a dedicated young scholar with a promising future in human rights, guided the production of the book from its inception. She helped identify authors, prepared detailed memos on the kinds of chapters the book required, and then undertook indispensable editing, writing, research, and author-prodding along the way. We look forward to watching her research on domestic human rights policy take shape in the years to come.

Thanks are also due to Jasmine Friedman, who keeps the Carr Center running at all times; Diane Curran and Alison Smith, who provided invaluable research assistance on questions of law and policy in the book's early days; the mayors and councilmembers of Idaho, who have launched a statewide human rights campaign and taught us lessons about achieving impact at home; Sarah Chalfant and Liza Walworth of the Wylie Agency, who believed in the project from the outset; and Karen Wolny, our editor at St. Martin's Press, who has run with it.

Lastly, we would like to thank Greg Carr, whose commitment to human rights and faith in the Carr Center team make all things seem possible.

We dedicate this book to Frederick C. Cuny, Leah Melnick, Miguel Gil Moreno de Mora, and Kurt Schork, who devoted-and then gave-their lives to the cause of realizing human rights.

S.J.P. & G.T.A.

INTRODUCTION

In 1948 Eleanor Roosevelt predicted that human rights would creep like a "curious grapevine" into public consciousness around the globe.[1] Dismissed at that time as utopian fantasy, her forecast has proven more prescient than the skepticism of her critics. The proposition that all human beings—whatever their nationality, culture, or location—possess specific inalienable rights simply because they are human is now almost universally acknowledged, if still erratically heeded.

Even less expected and more striking is the extent to which post–cold war international affairs has been forced to confront the human rights challenge. As America's leading strategist-practitioner of realpolitik, Henry Kissinger has recognized with palpable ambivalence: "human rights has become a central feature of American policy, sustained by Administrations of both parties."[2] Though human rights has not become so central a feature that it overrides interest-based concerns, human rights advocates have managed to push the U.S. government from rhetoric and moral pressure in the 1970s, to economic sanctions in the 1980s, to military action in the 1990s. Indeed, it has become impossible for the Western powers to debate the cardinal issues of foreign policy, from trade to the use of force, without being reminded of their impact on human rights.

Today, while former critics and cultural relativists still can be heard stressing their distinct "local" priorities for human rights implementation or their culturally-specific pace of reform, few have the nerve to take issue with the principles themselves. With the exception of a few outliers like North Korea, Myanmar, and Malaysia, every regime on earth today recognizes at least the need to be *seen* to respect human rights. As Columbia law professor Louis Henkin writes in his chapter in this volume, the Universal Declaration of Human Rights has become "the holy writ to which all pay homage, even if sometimes the homage of hypocrisy."

There is also widespread agreement about the core content of human rights. Individuals are entitled to life, liberty, and personal security, which include freedom from torture and arbitrary arrest, freedom of speech and religion, and equality before the law. Individuals are also entitled to adequate living standards, including basic education, food, and shelter. Great debates continue about the relative priority of political and civil rights as against economic and social rights. Likewise, the precise meaning of and limit to most rights remain hotly contested. Nonetheless, the 1948 UN Declaration of Human Rights and the subsequent Conventions together define "human rights" in a fashion that has secured broad consensus.

As we applaud advances in the recognition of human rights that were barely conceivable fifty years ago, we must simultaneously confront the magnitude of the horrific abuses of rights in the twentieth century. In the first half of the century, two world wars and the Holocaust claimed seventy-five million lives, while Stalin exterminated tens of millions. And, *since* the 1948 passage of the Universal Declaration of Human Rights, we have seen Mao's devastating cultural revolution, Pol Pot's Cambodian genocide, Bosnia, and Rwanda. These are brute facts—impossible to ignore. The past century compiled a record of atrocities unsurpassed in any century in recorded history. Realistic recognition of what men and women have repeatedly demonstrated their willingness to do—and to allow to be done—to fellow human beings counsels caution, and should restrain exaggerated expectations.

While freedom, prosperity, and peace have flourished in parts of the world, acute poverty, disease, and starvation continue to ravage other areas. More than one billion people live on less than $1 per day. Another two billion live on less than $2. Nobel Prize–winning economist Amartya Sen is one of many who challenge scholars, policymakers, and human rights advocates to give greater attention to the economic and social rights so often ignored. He asks, "Why should the status of intense economic needs, which can be matters of life and death, be lower than that of personal liberties?"[3]

Individuals in both the policy and human rights communities recognize that at the same time human rights norms, institutions, and policies have proliferated in recent years, abuses and suffering have abounded. Rather than deterring us, these grim facts should propel thinking men and women into more systematic inquiry about which actions can be effective in advancing human rights under what conditions. The record of the recent past requires careful study by governments, international organizations, nongovernmental organizations (NGOs), and citizens as we all try to fashion more effective strategies for going forward. Too often policies and actions of governments, NGOs, and businesses have been applied inconsistently and implemented ineptly. International actors or groups rarely pause for serious, sustained analysis of human rights policy. In short, if a key challenge of the second half of the twentieth century was gaining universal acceptance of the idea that human rights existed or mattered, *the* key challenge for the decades ahead is to identify the policies and actions that most effectively realize human rights.

In the aftermath of World War II, leaders now revered as the "wise men" conceived new strategies for preventing a third world war. In this book, we have assembled many of the leading policymakers, activists, and analysts from the human rights community and asked them to consider the question that so many are beginning to ask with regard to human rights; namely, "What works?" A remarkable group of experienced activists, diplomats, field workers, journalists, lawyers, politicians, and professors assess the state of human rights in the world today and offer their best judgements about strategies and tactics for advancing human rights in the years and decades ahead. From Chinese democracy activist Wei Jingsheng to the former UN war crimes prosecutor Richard Goldstone, the authors describe the forces and instruments they believe have been effective in promoting human rights and make recommendations stemming from their personal experiences, their institutional preferences, and their specific human rights agendas. Their reflective testimony provides vital clues to anyone attempting to grapple with the new century's challenge.

Among the common threads that tie together these contributions, two deserve special note. The relationship between state power and individual rights, one of the oldest chestnuts of political theory, has emerged in a new form—most vividly in Kofi Annan's concept of a "second sovereignty." The sometimes-competitive, sometimes-cooperative, always-evolving relationship between nongovernmental actors and governmental policymakers also recurs throughout. The chapters in parts one and two take the dawn of a new millennium as an occasion to look backward, identifying some of the forces behind recent progress in human rights policy. They focus on how human rights norms have been introduced and institutionalized and how human rights advocates inside and outside government have been motivated and aided. In the third and fourth parts of this volume, the contributors critically examine the institutions, tools, and actions of governments, international organizations, nongovernmental organizations, and individuals that promote and protect human rights. They assess the legal enforcement bodies, governmental policies, and nongovernmental forces that have recently been put in place or arisen. Together they offer instructive arguments on behalf of instruments as diverse as regional human rights courts, war crimes tribunals, democracy promotion, economic sanctions, and, under extreme circumstances, military intervention.

Despite many recent apparent successes for human rights, a canyon still separates the world's rhetorical and legal commitment to human rights on the one hand and billions of individuals' realization of these rights on the other. The persistence of crimes against humanity, repression, and desperate poverty should propel much more critical analysis of what has and has not worked, of obstacles that must yet be surmounted, and of new ways to better advance the human rights agenda. Before we can grapple with contemporary human rights policy challenges, we must begin by understanding the road we have traveled.

THE ROAD TO THE TWENTY-FIRST CENTURY

One can find origins of the modern human rights movement in early philosophical charters including the English Magna Carta, the French Declaration on the Rights of Man and Citizen, and the U.S. Bill of Rights. While often formulated in universal terms—"all men are created equal"—sovereign states meant these early claims to apply only to their own citizens. In 1648 the Treaty of Westphalia resolved decades of religious wars between Catholics and Protestants in Europe. This helped lay the foundation for the modern state system by fixing territorial claims and stipulating that what occurred within a state's borders was that state's internal affair. This state system anchored the "law of nations" in sovereign prerogative, sovereign immunity, and *raison d'état,* discouraging interventions in the domestic affairs of fellow states.

Although many perceive the North Atlantic Treaty Organization's (NATO's) recent intervention in Kosovo as a radical, modern affront to the privilege of states to be free of outside interference, the sovereignty of states has never been absolute, and concern for rights never entirely absent. For instance, in a nineteenth-century prelude to the humanitarian intervention of 1999, an allied fleet comprised of British, French, and Russian squadrons teamed up in the Battle of Navarino in 1827 to destroy the Turkish-Egyptian fleet, aiding the Greek struggle for independence from the Ottoman Empire. This intervention was humanitarian in the sense that the plight of Greek citizens was prominent in the minds of the interventionists, but, like most humanitarian interventions, not wholly so: Preventing Turkish control of the Aegean was also a paramount consideration. Analysts of the NATO intervention in Kosovo find similarly mixed motives in what was billed as a humanitarian war.

While full-scale military interventions were not undertaken often before the twentieth century, statesmen did occasionally intervene diplomatically in the hopes of ameliorating abuses committed by another state against its citizens. Edmund Burke famously championed the cause of India in the British parliament, while William Gladstone was aided in his successful bid to unseat Benjamin Disraeli in the 1880 British election by campaigning against Britain's tepid response to the "Bulgarian horrors" perpetrated by the Turks against their Christian subjects. In addition, the forces of nineteenth-century nationalism, though muzzled within multiethnic empires and states, helped erode state sovereignty, as leaders of nationalist movements in the Ottoman and Habsburg empires mobilized oppressed minorities, claiming rights under the banner of self-determination.

Human rights and humanitarian law and principles also predate the establishment of the United Nations. Campaigns to abolish slavery and grant women's suffrage were early human rights crusades. Parties to the Geneva Conventions agreed to restrain their own conduct toward their armed foes and toward unarmed civilians and prisoners of war. Though these laws were fortified and refined in 1949, the first Geneva Convention was signed by twelve nations back in 1864, calling for the "inviolability" of medical personnel and the humane treatment of the wounded and prisoners of war. Similarly, though the illegality of aggressive force was later amplified at Nuremberg, it was the Hague Conventions of 1899 and 1907 that first articulated the principle. Though the League of Nations framework made no explicit mention of human rights, Woodrow Wilson's fourteen points pledged to make the world safe for democracy and claimed for colonized peoples across the globe a right of self-governance. The League tentatively attempted to legally enshrine this concept by putting in place a Minority Treaties regime in Poland, Austria, Greece, and elsewhere that obliged signatories to respect at least the cultural rights of their minorities, but enforcement of these collective rights relied on the sovereign's consent, and the Great Powers were left immune from scrutiny.

Whatever the parallels and precursors, it is fair to say that nineteenth–and early twentieth–century inroads into sovereignty bear only scant resemblance to contemporary assaults. Although in the earlier period some states were concerned with the fate of minorities (usually Christian) and were occasionally willing to pry into another state's internal affairs, such intermeddling was rare. Sovereign privilege overrode any conception of natural, higher law.

World War II marked a turning point in the development of international human rights law and, eventually, public consciousness. Immediately after Britain's entry into war in 1939, Winston Churchill declared that the war was being fought "to establish, on impregnable rocks, the rights of the individual." With his 1941 "Four Freedoms" address, Franklin Delano Roosevelt built on this foundation, launching what Henkin calls the modern "rebirth" of the human rights movement. Roosevelt said he looked forward to a world founded on "four essential human freedoms": freedom of speech, freedom of religion, freedom from want, and freedom from fear. In a single stroke, he thus outlined a core set of civil, political, economic, and social rights that remain at the heart of the human rights movement today. Hitler's atrocities highlighted the necessity for recognition of a law higher than that put in place by state authorities. This higher law was needed to check and, in extreme cases, override the will of the ruler even when his actions directly affected only his own citizens. While this recognition stemmed primarily from a revulsion at Hitler's horrors, it also reflected an awareness that abuses committed by states within their borders could undermine the international system. Thus, the events of World War II heightened awareness of not only the rightness but also the utility of standards that held states accountable for respecting and protecting individual rights. Contemporary human rights advocates continue to assert that gross human rights abuses imperil both the universal *values* of individuals and the *interests* of states in preserving global peace and security.

Though the link between the Holocaust and the need for human rights protections seems obvious today, this connection was not apparent at the time. The founding conference of the United Nations at Dumbarton Oaks in 1944 did not initially include human rights on its agenda. Yet as Henkin tells the story here, despite the absence of forethought, the UN Charter casually included eight crucial words in the statement of the organization's secondary purposes: to "promote respect for human rights and fundamental freedom." Though these words would take decades to penetrate public consciousness and practice, the UN charter was the first major international document to include the term "human rights." It was prudentially silent, however, on both the substantive content of the phrase "human rights" and on the philosophical origins of these rights.

The Universal Declaration of Human Rights, which was passed by the UN General Assembly in 1948, marked the first international effort by governments to spell out the rights that all men and women shared. The principles outlined in the Declaration might have amounted to mere words had not courageous citizens around the world chosen to take these rights seriously and demand that they be enforced. Many of the authors in this book were captivated by the human rights ideals and acted to see them realized at home and abroad. The chapters in part two offer clues about ways in which individual beliefs and actions can bring about change.

The chapters written by **Wei Jingsheng, Jimmy Carter,** and **Leonid Romankov** reflect the power of this incandescent idea that each of the six billion individuals around the globe today have basic human rights. Each of these authors has also fueled the propagation of this idea considerably by his activities in the public sphere. The three men could not be more different: one a dissident who was jailed for eighteen years for urging democratic reform in China; the second an American president who used his position as possibly the most powerful person in the world to attempt to elevate human rights in U.S. foreign policy; and the third a Russian intellectual who was fired from his job in Soviet times for circulating forbidden *samizdat* publications, and who has since engaged in politics at the local level. Yet these individuals are united by personal stories that reveal similarities in their regard for the citizens neglected or abused by governments, and in their conviction that international pressure and contacts can produce results.

Wei, Carter, and Romankov offer diverse personal testimonials to the importance of rights. Wei deems these values "objective truths, natural rights." He argues that rights are found in human nature: "the sum of hopes and aspirations that emerge naturally and do not need to be taught." Because of the sheer force of these natural urges, regardless of their circumstance, individuals are destined to claim their rights with or without outside provocation. For Carter, rights are endowed by the Creator, but have advanced as a consequence of human initiatives including decolonization, the spread of information technology, and American leadership. Romankov explains how literary voices inside the Soviet Union captured the imagination of dissidents, introducing them to the possibility of freedom. International exchanges gave them a taste of what lay outside their closed society, and these beacons eventually acquired such force in *glasnost* (openness), and *perestroika* (restructuring) that cold war walls came tumbling down.

What began as personal commitment for these individuals led in turn to public action. An extraordinary lesson of recent decades is the extent to which individuals can make a difference. Often, they take human rights declarations at face value, assume that leaders mean what they say, and claim their rights. By acting empowered they can become exemplars to others, helping generate momentum for broader mobilization.

As they describe how particular human rights actors progressed from words to action, Wei, Carter, and Romankov lay the foundation for the examination of the issues, institutions, and tools that follows in parts three and four. They demonstrate that broad agreement on the importance of respecting individual human rights does not yield consensus about which means should be employed to secure achievement. There remains considerable disagreement, even among the authors, over questions of advocacy, policy, action, and influence. It is thus essential to examine critically the means by which individuals, non-governmental organizations, international or regional organizations, and states have moved beyond mere concern or commitment to impact.

HUMAN RIGHTS ENFORCEMENT: STATE AND INDIVIDUAL ACCOUNTABILITY

States signed the Universal Declaration of Human Rights in 1948 secure in the expectation that they would be able to choose voluntarily which principles to enforce and which to ignore or avoid.[4] Publicly, they committed themselves to strive to respect the Declaration's aspirational standards. But most were comforted by the fact that no international institutions existed that could enforce the norms or force states to live up to their promises.

Over time, that has changed. In the last three decades the European, Inter-American, and African regional systems have developed courts and commissions predicated on universal human rights standards. To varying degrees and at varying speeds, these institutions have begun ever-so-gradually to influence national compliance with human rights norms.

The European system offers individuals the greatest protection from abuse and hope for redress. Indeed, the European Convention on Human Rights and its associated institutions have made the European system the most advanced mechanism for promoting and protecting human rights in the world. In her detailed account of its development, **Shirley Williams**, a Liberal Democratic member of the British Parliament and professor at Harvard's Kennedy School of Government, navigates the maze of European acronyms and institutions to supply a coherent roadmap of the history and achievements of the European human rights system. She explains how multiple European institutions have jointly helped the continent that saw the worst crimes against humanity of the century make the transition to become one of the most progressive in realizing human rights. If European citizens believe their rights are not being enforced or respected at home, and if they have exhausted domestic routes of redress, they can submit individual complaints to the European Commission on Human Rights, which receives between 5,000 and 10,000 applications annually. If the Commission decides the European Convention on Human Rights has been violated, and it fails to broker a friendly settlement, it will pass the case on to the European Court of Human Rights, which may declare a violation. The Court and Commission rely almost entirely on their own legitimacy for enforcement. Nonetheless, the recent record is encouraging, as the advantages of membership in the European "club" and the respect for the Court has led states to comply with most Court judgements. In September 1999, for instance, the European Court ruled that the British military ban on gay men and women violated the Convention, and Britain quickly dropped the ban. The European system also influences those countries interested in securing membership in the European Union by establishing tough admission criteria. Those nations seeking entry must make their domestic laws consistent with the European Convention, which requires, for example, abolishing capital punishment. Although the European system is the envy of human rights advocates on other continents, the story is far from incomplete. The hope is that Europe's member-based institutions will commence a "race to the top" as new democracies follow the lead of their established democratic neighbors. The fear is that they will generate a "race to the bottom," with standards diluted by the premature entrance of shaky transitional democracies.

Juan Méndez, a member of the Inter-American Commission on Human Rights and now director of the human rights center at Notre Dame Law School, describes the human rights system in the Organization of American States (OAS), which comprises the thirty-five politically, economically, and culturally diverse nations of the Americas. Méndez explains that, unlike the Council of Europe, which requires members to sign the European Convention for Human Rights, OAS members retain the discretion to decide whether or not to sign the Inter-American Convention on Human Rights and whether or not to be bound by the jurisdiction of the Inter-American Court for Human Rights. Because these human rights obligations remain voluntary, there are now six different regimes for human rights protection and enforcement mechanisms within the OAS. Still, the inter-American system has managed to make some contributions to the development of both national and international law and standards. For example, in a region where transitional justice and responsibility for past abuses are becoming major factors inside states and in inter-state relations, the Inter-American Court of Human Rights has introduced the concept of *habeas data,* a right of individuals to receive information about themselves that appears in government files, and a "right to truth" that obliges governments to investigate the fates of the disappeared. Despite its successes, Méndez sees much unfinished business in the inter-American system of human rights protection, especially with regard to protecting and enforcing the rights of minorities, women, and the underprivileged. The biggest weaknesses in the system lie in the political encroachments on its independence and the fact that states that ignore rulings currently go unsanctioned. He calls for the creation of a coercive mechanism to force state compliance.

The newest and least-developed of the regional human rights frameworks is the African human rights system, which is critically surveyed by **Makau Mutua,** a Kenyan professor of international law who chairs the Kenya Human Rights Commission and teaches at Buffalo Law School. Since decolonization, most African nations have been run by leaders who were quicker to close ranks behind their abusive neighbors than to critique or sanction them. Yet, despite the slowness of human rights progress on the continent, the institutional mechanisms that might eventually enable change have begun quietly to be put into place. The African Charter on Human and Peoples' Rights, which entered into force in 1986, draws upon the Universal Declaration of Human Rights but also extends it, enshrining not only individual rights, but those of "peoples," to existence, to enjoy self-determination, and to freely dispose of their wealth and natural resources. The Charter also establishes individual and state duties, such as the duty to protect the family and respect and maintain parents. As Mutua writes, "The Charter argues that the individual egoist is not the center of the moral universe." In June 1998, a Protocol added to the African Charter established a new African Court of Human Rights. The creation of the Court marks an acknowledgment of the general ineffectiveness of the African Commission and constitutes an effort to provide individual remedies to Africans and to develop precedents that can be codified in national legal systems. While supporting the Court, Mutua nonetheless faults it for denying individuals an automatic right of access. He also cautions against overburdening the court, urging that it exercise careful selection, accepting for review only those cases that have the potential to make law that would guide African state behavior and human rights culture.

These regional human rights bodies have made states more answerable to universal human rights norms and regional human rights standards. By setting and interpreting human rights standards, these bodies have the potential to raise citizens' awareness of their rights and to provide individuals and states with a forum for complaint. By exposing a state's failure to comply with human rights norms, they can help deter or otherwise modify individual or state behavior. To truly influence national practices, however, such bodies must acquire greater political independence from states, and states must be pressured into heeding court judgments. Both because European national courts begin with a greater deference to human rights and because European states have more to gain (economically and politically) by upholding their commitments to the European Convention on Human Rights, these states have proven the most compliant. While it is important to note the ways in which regional bodies can affect individual rights, it is independent, national legal systems that are the greatest potential guarantors of rights. For the foreseeable future, most individuals will receive remedies at home—or not at all.

This continued reliance on domestic courts for enforcement is most daunting for those human rights advocates who operate in national systems that have refused to respect international human rights norms. **Asma Jahangir**, UN Special Rapporteur on Extrajudicial, Summary, and Arbitrary Executions and former chair of the Human Rights Commission of Pakistan, offers a sobering counterpoint to the essays on regional enforcement. She works as a human rights advocate in Pakistan, where individuals have no regional human rights system to which they might appeal, and where national law is often a tool for oppressing citizens rather than for realizing rights. She describes Pakistan's slide toward rigid Islamist rule; the infringement of the rights of women and minorities; and the counter-efforts of nongovernmental organizations and human rights advocates to maintain a pluralistic, tolerant, and free society. Those who speak out face many tensions. If, like Jahangir herself, they oppose Islamic orthodoxy, they are attacked as "foreign agents" and under constant threat of persecution and even assassination at home. Yet most also maintain serious reservations about Western criticisms of Islam, which, in Jahangir's words, often reveal "deep-seated prejudice against Islam."

National enforcement of international norms often becomes impossible once states have resorted to or permitted certain extreme human rights abuses like crimes against humanity or genocide. Many advocates of international justice hope that a permanent International Criminal Court will be established soon to prosecute individuals who commit gross violations of human rights, but who can not be prosecuted at home. One of the most vocal proponents of such international accountability is **Justice Richard Goldstone**, the former chief prosecutor of the United Nations War Crimes Tribunals for the Former Yugoslavia and Rwanda. Goldstone identifies the need to document human rights abuses, to punish human rights abusers, and, in situations where, for political reasons, abusers can not be apprehended, at least to acknowledge officially that crimes have been committed. He offers a historical analysis that explains why, after fifty years of failing to enforce international laws against crimes against humanity and genocide, the Security Council in 1993 and 1994 created courts in The Hague and Arusha to enforce these laws. Goldstone cautions against a "one-size-fits-all" approach to accountability, arguing that justice, like other foreign policy tools, must be tailored to meet political, financial, and social circumstances. Decisionmakers must assess these circumstances before deciding whether to undertake domestic prosecutions, to set up an international tribunal, to establish a truth commission, or to combine features of these mechanisms. However promising international courts may be, they will fail on all fronts if UN member states do not supply the necessary legal and financial resources, the personnel, and the political cooperation, by gathering and sharing intelligence or arresting indicted war crimes suspects.

HUMAN RIGHTS POLICY IDEAS, INSTITUTIONS, AND INSTRUMENTS

Regional human rights conventions and courts are the most structured, but also the most narrow mechanism for advancing human rights. The last part of this volume reviews seven further ideas, institutions, and instruments that have profound implications for the future enforcement of human rights: human rights organizations, democracy promotion, U.S. human rights diplomacy, economic sanctions, humanitarian intervention, the prevention of deadly conflict, and media-based advocacy.

Kenneth Roth, executive director of Human Rights Watch, and **Morton Halperin**, who, after writing his chapter, became the director of policy planning at the State Department, underscore how contentious the selection of means remains among even those with shared ends. Roth looks at the role of human rights organizations in spearheading human rights advances in the past half century. As he reminds us, when human rights NGOs such as Amnesty International were created, they concentrated on individual prisoners of conscience. They treated the Universal Declaration of Human Rights as "'universal' far more in the breadth of governments [it] addressed than in the range of people [it] protected." In the last two decades, however, human rights professionals have broadened their focus. They have moved beyond pressing to free jailed dissidents, and now lobby to end land mines, violence against women, and armed attacks on city centers. Roth credits human rights organizations with increasing the "cost of abuse" and making "official indifference appear as complicity."

Morton Halperin reflects upon the tensions between institutions committed to promoting democracy and those, like Roth's, that explicitly emphasize human rights. During the cold war, many human rights organizations came into existence to curb abuses carried out in the name of promoting democracy and fighting communism. Tensions persist between the two communities. Halperin argues that the differences are anachronistic and urges the creation of a "unified NGO and intellectual community" committed to the premise that constitutional democracy offers the best long-term promise of human rights protection. "Although the Cold War ended in 1990," he writes, "the U.S. human rights community remains suspicious of all governments, doubtful that democratic reforms will lead to greater respect for human rights, and skeptical both of Western governmental assistance to fellow states or foreign NGOs and of general efforts to design better governmental programs." Halperin argues that human rights advocates must overcome their reflexive suspicion of governments and learn to work with them to tackle the root causes of human rights abuses, not just the symptoms.

This divisive debate, which is virtually unheard of outside the United States, continues to have a negative effect on cooperation between those committed to similar overall objectives. This battle bewilders those like Wei, Romankov, and Jahangir, who are struggling to liberalize their societies and who see the need both for respect for human rights and for democracy. Of course, by "democracy" they mean not simply holding elections, but enshrining the core human rights principles, institutionalizing the rule of law, and entrenching civilian control of the military. While U.S. human rights diplomacy has often focused on democracy promotion, it is essential to distinguish the different brands of democracy. Merely electoral democracies that do not respect fundamental rights, sometimes referred to as "illiberal democracies," should not be immune from criticism. Indeed, electoral democracy and human rights can conflict, for example, when ethnic majorities vote their way into power on a platform of marginalizing or persecuting minorities. The two objectives (thus defined) are both legitimate ends in and of themselves, as well as means to each other. As Louis Henkin argues, democracy is one human right, and human rights set a crucial limit on democracy.

This lingering divide in the United States is also addressed by **John Shattuck**, the former U.S. Assistant Secretary for Human Rights, who is now U.S. Ambassador to the Czech Republic. United States government action to advance human rights, sparked more than two decades ago by Jimmy Carter in the White House and Donald Fraser on Capitol Hill, has come a long way. Shattuck argues that the United States can rarely afford to be "as single-minded" as Roth and other nongovernmental human rights advocates would like. Nonetheless, "human rights diplomacy" has gradually become one mechanism among many used to influence the practice of fellow states. Shattuck sketches the progressive evolution of U.S. executive and legislative attention to human rights. He describes the congressional acts that prohibited aid to gross abusers of human rights and that mandated the creation of the influential State Department *Country Reports* on human rights. One example of a U.S. human rights policy "tool," these reports are increasingly detailed and credible. Since the reports became available over the Internet, foreign organizations and citizens have increasingly relied upon them to criticize their own governments. Whereas the first set of *Country Reports* in 1977 ran 137 pages and only covered the countries receiving U.S. aid, omitting inconvenient details, the 1999 report ran 6000 pages and even-handedly covered 194 countries.[5] Many within the human rights community resent an American approach that tends to criticize others without addressing its own domestic shortcomings or ratifying international human rights treaties. Shattuck acknowledges the tension and expresses pride in having presided over the issuance, in 1995, of the first report that documented U.S. compliance with international human rights norms, which he maintains is an important step toward requiring greater U.S. accountability to international standards.

American selectivity in pressing international norms can make it difficult to secure support for U.S. policies that require multilateral cooperation in order to succeed. Targeted economic sanctions require international cooperation if they are to affect change. **Aryeh Neier**, president of the Open Society Institute, one of the world's leading supporters of civil society, argues that the major powers should not shy from employing the tool of targeted economic sanctions against foreign states that commit human rights abuses. Though sanctions can be "a very blunt instrument" and can yield unfortunate, "unintended consequences," Neier argues, when nuanced and narrowly tailored to meet the particular circumstances on the ground, they can often convince target states to improve their human rights records. He reviews the cases of China, Burma, South Africa, Poland, Argentina, Chile, and El Salvador to present evidence of how sanctions (or the threat of sanctions) can spur specific, small-scale reforms, such as the release of political prisoners or the prosecution of local perpetrators. If sustained and combined with other factors, they can yield outright political transformation. Even when they appear to be making little headway, Neier believes that by signaling international condemnation, they can deter governments from committing abuses. In the heat that accompanies trade debates, Neier reminds us, even those debates that fail to generate sanctions against an abuser of human rights can serve a useful function by drawing attention to the abuses.

The most powerful instrument for preventing or curbing gross abuses of human rights is humanitarian intervention. This fact vexes nongovernmental organizations, regional organizations, and UN member states. UN Secretary-General **Kofi Annan** calls upon international actors to conceive of intervention on a continuum. The international community may intervene by providing technical assistance or by targeting its foreign investment; it may host or participate in disarmament talks; or it may preventively deploy peacekeepers before conflict ignites. In the aftermath of a conflict, it may intervene by supporting efforts at reconstruction and rehabilitation; it may participate in civil administration; or it may perform policing functions. Annan believes neither the member states nor the United Nations should avoid such actions. Indeed, he asks, "Why was the United Nations established, if not to act as a benign policeman or doctor?" But alongside these "soft" forms of intervention, the Secretary-General sees a role for "hard" intervention—the use of military force. The employment of this policy tool in Kosovo in 1999 has stirred major controversy over when, where, how, and under what authority it should occur. Annan dives into this stormy debate on whether a state, or a combination of states, can legitimately intervene to stop crimes against humanity or genocide when the interveners are unable to gain the agreement of the UN Security Council. While he is fearful of states running amok, interfering inconsistently and seemingly arbitrarily in the internal affairs of states, he also issues a challenge to those who are wedded to the legal norm requiring Security Council authorization for intervention. He asks how legitimate it would be to allow this requirement to impede a regional intervention that might curb a genocide like that in Rwanda. The United Nations authorizes the use of force in the common interest. But Annan challenges states to answer the questions begged by this formulation: "What is the common interest?" he asks, "Who shall define it? Who shall defend it? Under whose authority? And with what means of intervention?" In light of the abysmal experience of UN peacekeepers in Somalia, Bosnia, Rwanda, and Sierra Leone, these questions demand ready and brave answers.

David Hamburg, who with Cyrus Vance co-chaired the Carnegie Commission on the Prevention of Deadly Conflict, shows why and how deadly conflict is rendering much of the progress in human rights moot. Civilians are eight times more likely to be killed in armed conflict today than they were at the beginning of the twentieth century. The United Nations' post-war attention to human rights was largely predicated on the assumption that respect for rights and fundamental freedoms were prerequisites to preventing a third world war. Yet, as Hamburg notes, too little attention was paid to internal conflicts, which are now the rule rather than the exception. Should prevention fail, he argues, military intervention may be necessary, intervention that would be greatly facilitated and improved by the creation of a standing, international rapid reaction force.

Media coverage of abuses has increased exposure of deadly conflict and the pressure for humanitarian intervention in recent years. Anna Husarska, a freelance journalist who has covered more than a dozen wars in her two decades of reporting, describes the media role in making human rights organizations effective and in affecting policy choices by government officials. She shows the role of journalists as "conscience triggers," and the power of the media to highlight abuses and to add weight to reports generated by human rights organizations. But she also describes how hard it is for reporters to convince editors of the importance of a story before bloodshed has actually commenced and when it might be averted. Then, once the killing is underway, it quickly becomes old news if it is repeated daily. Husarska sees multiple roles for journalists in improving human rights, but editorial constraints have convinced her that the media alone will rarely serve as the early warning tool that she deems essential to generating preventive governmental action. She sees more hope in organizations like the International Crisis Group, an independent, political NGO that is not hemmed in by the need for advertiser revenue and that can command the attention of senior policymakers with its detailed, prescriptive field reports.

This book does not provide definitive answers to the central questions raised by our authors. Indeed, they often disagree among themselves. But it does provide an essential foundation from which these challenges can be addressed. In the chapters that follow, some of the most capable and credible voices in human rights policy provide their best efforts to help inform serious reflection on issues of crucial importance. Human rights norms now having been firmly recognized, these authors attempt to offer advice as to how these rights can be realized.

Samantha Power
Graham Allison
Cambridge, Massachusetts
June, 2000

NOTES

1. See William Korey, *NGOs and the Universal Declaration of Human Rights: The Curious Grapevine* (New York: St. Martin's Press, 1998).
2. Henry Kissinger, "Single-Issue Diplomacy Won't Work," *Washington Post*, April 27, 1999.
3. Amartya Sen, *Development as Freedom* (New York: Knopf, 1999), p. 64.
4. Mary Ann Glendon, *A World Made New: Eleanor Roosevelt and the Universal Declaration of Human Rights* (New York: Random House, March 2001).
5. U.S. State Department *Country Reports on Human Rights Practices*, available at <http://www.state.gov/www/global/human_rights/hrp_reports_mainhp.html>.

PART I

The Road to the Twenty-First Century

Human Rights:
Ideology and Aspiration, Reality
and Prospect

LOUIS HENKIN

LOUIS HENKIN is University Professor Emeritus at Columbia University, Chair of the University's Center for the Study of Human Rights, and Director of the Human Rights Institute at the Law School, where he previously held chairs in Constitutional Law and in International Law and Diplomacy. He served as law clerk to Judge Learned Hand and Justice Felix Frankfurter, worked at the U.S. State Department as Foreign Affairs Officer, and was Chief Reporter of the Restatement of the Foreign Relations Law of the United States and Co-editor-in-chief of *the American Journal of International Law.* Among his books are *The Rights of Man Today, The Age of Rights, Human Rights* (with others*), How Nations Behave, Foreign Affairs and the Constitution,* and *International Law: Cases and Materials* (with others).

By the end of the twentieth century, human rights, a political-philosophical idea, had become an ideology, the ideology of our times, achieving near-universal acceptance, with little dissent. Ours has been described as the Age of Rights.[1] International human rights—international concern with the condition of human rights within national societies—was conceived during World

War II, and its normative and institutional foundations were established during the decades after the war. In this chapter I trace the development of international institutions and of the international law of human rights, describe the successes and failures of international human rights during its first half century, and suggest how this edifice of norms and institutions has contributed to the human rights conditions of billions of human beings at the end of the twentieth century. Looking ahead, I offer the outlines of an agenda for the new century.

WHERE AND WHEN WERE INTERNATIONAL HUMAN RIGHTS BORN?

The idea of human rights may be seen as an offspring of the idea of natural rights in the seventeenth century, which became a political ideology on the American continent and in France toward the end of the eighteenth century. International human rights might be said to have been conceived on January 6, 1941, the date of the famous "Four Freedoms" message to Congress by President Franklin Delano Roosevelt (FDR),[2] and born on December 10, 1948, the date on which the Universal Declaration of Human rights was proclaimed by the General Assembly of the United Nations (UN).

Speaking after war had begun in Europe, although before the United States entered the war, Roosevelt said: "In the future days, which we seek to make secure, we look forward to a world founded upon four essential human freedoms": freedom of speech, freedom of religion, freedom from want, and freedom from fear.[3] Shortly thereafter President Roosevelt and Prime Minister Winston Churchill expressed, in the Atlantic Charter, their hope to see established "a peace which will afford assurance that all the men in all the lands may live out their lives in freedom free from fear and want."[4]

FDR spoke of *freedoms,* in the language of the U.S. Constitution, but he echoed the ideology of *rights,* found in the writings of John Locke and William Blackstone, in the American Declaration of Independence and the U.S. Bill of Rights, and in the French Declaration of the Rights of Man and the Citizen of 1789. Behind FDR's words were also 150 years of constitutionalism in the United States and the economic and social revolution of his New Deal. Freedom of speech and of religion derived from the First Amendment to the U.S. Constitution; freedom from fear—fear of enemies and tyrants—was doubtless a response to threats such as those posed by Adolf Hitler. Interesting, but not surprising, was "freedom from want," the promise of FDR's New Deal, couched as a "freedom" because he had learned that "a necessitous man is not a free man."[5]

In the next section I trace briefly the odyssey of the human rights idea and the shorter story of international human rights.

THE IDEA AND THE IDEOLOGY OF RIGHTS

"Human rights" is common parlance, but not all agree on its meaning and significance. Human rights are related to, sometimes confused with, "the rule of law," "constitutionalism," or "democracy." Sometimes human rights are seen as one element, a key element, in constitutional democracy; sometimes democracy is seen as one human right, a right of individuals to be represented and to vote; sometimes human rights are seen as limitations on democracy, that is, limitations on the will of the majority or on "the public interest" as it is determined by the majority.

The human rights idea declares that every human being, in every political society, has "rights": recognized, legitimate claims upon his or her society to specific freedoms and other goods and benefits. They are claims "as of right," not by grace, or love, or charity, or compassion: claims that society is morally, politically, even legally obligated to respect, ensure, and realize. Human rights are claims not only against "bad people" or tyrannical government, but even against bona fide, benevolent, representative legislatures and democratic majorities. Human rights are not absolute and may bow to the public interest, but human rights do not bow lightly; rights may "trump" even a public interest duly determined in a democratic society.

The history of the human rights idea is not straightforward or easy to trace.[6] It is accepted that the human rights idea derives from notions of "natural rights" articulated in the writings of John Locke and of the European Enlightenment. An ideology of rights, traced back to the Magna Carta, was maintained in England by the common law. The rights idea and ideology were adopted and adapted in the eighteenth century in the American colonies and in revolutionary France, eloquently articulated in the American Declaration of Independence (and in the Virginia Bill of Rights and early bills of rights of other states), and in the French Declaration of the Rights of Man and of the Citizen. Between 1789 and 1791 an ideology of rights was established by the Constitution and the Bill of Rights as a core of "constitutionalism" in the United States.

After its famous and revolutionary birth, the ideology of natural, universal rights did not flourish widely. In France the ideology of rights was destroyed in the Reign of Terror, and it was not resurrected under Napoleon or his successors or under the French republics prior to World War II. The British historian Lord Acton later declared that the single page of the French Declaration of 1789 had been more powerful than all the armies of Napoleon, but within France, the Declaration seems to have been relegated to historic hagiography.[7] Instead, in time, France moved to "parliamentarism," "progressivism," occasional "socialism," without an ideology of rights; rights were, at best, an indirect, unreliable grant from good government.

England did not embrace an ideology of universal natural rights, having fought the French Revolution and rejected its ideology. Instead, England enlarged its parliamentarism; it maintained its commitment to the rights of Englishmen, protected by the common law but subject to parliamentary supremacy. Although England, like France, abolished slavery, it did so not from any general commitment to an ideology of universal human rights but from a mix of moral and economic motives particular to slavery.

In the nineteenth century, English (and Continental) philosophers rejected natural rights. Jeremy Bentham dismissed them as dangerous "anarchical fallacies," as "nonsense upon stilts." Among philosophers, the ideology of rights was swept by the winds of "positivism" and challenged by utilitarianism, "progressivism," and varieties of socialism. The welfare state was born—an idea, it has been said, not Marx but Bismarck's—with little support from any ideology of natural rights.

There were scattered (and usually temporary) burgeonings of constitutionalism and parliamentary democracy and some respect for rights established by positive law in several countries in Europe and in America, but not much was heard of natural or universal rights.[8]

The United States maintained the commitment to the ideology of rights that had been proclaimed in the American Declaration of Independence.[9] The idea of rights was implied in, and some individual rights were guaranteed by, the U.S. Constitution established in 1789, and rights were elaborated in the "Bill of Rights" added to the Constitution by constitutional amendment in 1791.[10]

But U.S. realization of its avowed rights ideology was hardly complete or exemplary. U.S. constitutional rights suffered "congenital defects": Slavery was maintained under the U.S. Constitution for three-quarters of a century, while racial and gender equality and the equal protection of the laws were not even whispered in the U.S. Constitution until the Fourteenth Amendment in 1868 and were not held to be constitutionally required of the federal government until nearly a century later. By contemporary standards, early U.S. democracy and representative government were less than satisfactory. Only one branch of Congress was a House of *Representatives*. The right to vote was far from universal, and even freedom from discrimination in voting on grounds of race or gender required additional constitutional amendment, in 1870 and 1920. The U.S. Bill of Rights did not govern the individual states until long after the Civil War. "Native Americans" were not part of the constitutional order.

The United States maintained its constitutional commitment to rights into the twentieth century, but the realization of that commitment continued to be incomplete and erratic. Constitutional amendment was required to extend the principle of representative government to include the right of individuals to vote for members of the U.S. Senate (Amendment XVII, 1913), and to this day, the president is not elected directly by the people. Universal suffrage was not effectively achieved until the 1960s, and then not from democratic principles but from those of equality: If one person votes, all must be allowed to vote, equally.[11]

Until 1954 the U.S. Constitution was read to permit racial segregation. For decades U.S. constitutionalism extended the idea of rights to maintain "laissez-faire," to protect business activities from social legislation, and it required constitutional amendment (Amendment XVI, 1913) to permit progressive taxation and make possible some transition to "the welfare state." "Political rights," including freedom of expression, suffered restrictions during the "Red scares" after World War I (and again in the 1950s), and did not see luxuriant development until well after World War II.

Warts and all, however, constitutional rights in the United States were a major—*the* major—realization of the ideology of rights, and U.S. constitutionalism was not without influence elsewhere. But for the United States, constitutionalism was a domestic ideology and not for active export, not even during periods of U.S. expansion beyond its continental borders. World War I—the war "to make the world safe for democracy"—did not mean a war to convert the world to democracy or to rights.[12] Rights appeared early in constitutions in Latin America and in smaller European countries, doubtless due to the U.S. example and, in some instances perhaps, to the influence of the French Declaration of 1789. But before World War II, U.S. influence did not make a sustained contribution to a general, universal ideology of rights.

The ideology of rights was not encouraged in, and did not spread to, the colonies of the British and French empires. In addition, powerful influential governments in Europe spurned the idea of rights during the early decades of the twentieth century. Rights suffered widely and terribly at the hands of national and international socialism and fascism in the Soviet Union, in Fascist Italy, in Franco's Spain, and, needless to add, in Nazi Germany.

From Constitutional Rights
to International Human Rights

In our time, "human rights" commonly suggests "international human rights."[13] The term is a source of some confusion. Strictly, there are no "international human rights": No human being claims human rights against some international body. Human rights—like constitutionalism, like democracy—is a political ideology that applies to national political societies. "International human rights" refers to an international movement to promote and protect and assume and assert international responsibility for *national* human rights, that is, rights within national societies. The international human rights movement has sought to establish an international human rights standard—a minimum standard that national societies are expected to satisfy and by which national human rights are to be judged—and to have states assume legally binding international obligations to live up to the international standards. It has also established and promoted international institutions to encourage, to monitor, and to induce national compliance with those international human rights standards.

The term "international human rights" also calls for explanation of another order. Not long ago it might have seemed contradictory or oxymoronic. Before World War II, how a state treated its own inhabitants was no one else's business. As a matter of principle, in the absence of special undertaking by treaty,[14] the condition of human rights in any country—even in Hitler's Germany—was its own domestic "sovereign" affair, not the concern of international politics or of international law. This attitude has been profoundly, fundamentally undermined. The story can be traced from the war aims of World War II and the Universal Declaration of Human Rights, through the "International Bill of Rights," to what is perhaps the most prominent triumph to date of the international human rights movement: the eradication of apartheid in South Africa.[15]

From War Aims to a New World Order: Dumbarton Oaks and San Francisco

Glimmers of change, from human rights as strictly domestic to human rights as international concern, appeared early in World War II, heralded by FDR's Four Freedoms address. After U.S. entry into the war, all of the states declaring war against Hitler adopted the Atlantic Charter as their statement of war aims. It was not commonly seen as a program for the postwar world but rather as a weapon in psychological warfare. "Realists" probably did not take it seriously as policy for the postwar period; surely few had any clear idea as to what such a policy might entail.

At Dumbarton Oaks in Washington, D.C., in 1944, representatives of the Allied powers met to plan the world order following their victory. Records of the conversations at Dumbarton Oaks contain little evidence that the principal participants, in thinking of the world order to follow the war and in planning a new world organization, thought much about human rights. But eight words appeared among the secondary purposes of the world organization-to-be: "to promote respect for human rights and fundamental freedoms." This was the first use of the term "human rights" in a major international document.[16]

Thus, from the Four Freedoms in wartime manifestos, to "human rights" in the new world order, began what might be described as the subversion of state sovereignty as it had traditionally been conceived. Thus Roosevelt's vision was confirmed and extended. How a nation treated its own inhabitants was to be— as a matter of principle—everybody's business: the business of the international political and economic system, the concern of international politics, a subject of international law. In those eight words, I suggest, lay the idea of human rights and a commitment to its ideology, and perhaps, too, a faint promise of a measure of international responsibility to address gross violations of human rights anywhere.

The faint promises embodied in eight words at Dumbarton Oaks led directly to several sentences in the United Nations Charter adopted in San Francisco in 1945.[17] The Charter, a major international treaty, declared it to be one of the purposes of the new United Nations Organization to promote and encourage respect for human rights; this was the first use of the term "human rights" in a major international treaty, the most important treaty of the century. In Articles 55 and 56, all members of the United Nations pledged to take action for the achievement of "universal respect for, and observance of, human rights and fundamental freedoms for all without distinction as to race, sex, language, or religion."

These few words at Dumbarton Oaks led also to the Nuremberg Charter and the Nuremberg trials, and beyond. The Western Allies, principally the United States, were determined to treat the conquered Nazi leaders not as vanquished, monstrous villains subject to political retribution, but as criminals and violators of law to be tried and punished with due process of law. The Nuremberg Charter established that there existed "crimes against humanity" (distinct from "war crimes," and whether committed in or related to war or not), which constitute violations of international law although not based in any treaty; and that individuals, of whatever rank or office, who perpetrated such crimes might be held personally responsible, brought to trial, and, if convicted, punished and even put to death.[18]

Nuremberg led immediately to the Convention on the Prevention and Punishment of the Crime of Genocide, the first international human rights treaty of the new world order.[19] From Nuremberg one can see a direct line, over long delays and formidable obstacles (principally related to the cold war), to the international tribunals established by the UN Security Council in the 1990s to try crimes against humanity and war crimes committed in the former Yugoslavia and in Rwanda, and to the International Criminal Court launched at Rome in 1998 (discussed further later).

Commitment to human rights in the days of Dumbarton Oaks, San Francisco, and Nuremberg was not unanimous and did not appear urgent. We may assume that President Roosevelt and later President Truman, Winston Churchill, and Charles de Gaulle were firmly committed to human rights; but we need hardly ask about Stalin (or even Chiang Kai-Shek). Moreover, while the United States and the United Kingdom were committed to human rights at home and to imposing them on Nazi Germany and its allies, it cannot be said with confidence that they (and later France) were firmly committed to making international human rights part of the new world order, to giving the term international definition, or to promoting such rights vigorously, everywhere, by all necessary means. Nor were the victorious Allies firmly committed to an international human rights movement: to establishing an international law of human rights applicable to all, including themselves; to assuming international responsibility for human rights violations wherever they occurred; or to creating, and submitting to, effective international monitoring and enforcement.

Dumbarton Oaks and the UN Charter intoned the term "human rights"; they did not define it. To the authors of those instruments, the words doubtless alluded to Hitler's ineffable crimes, to genocide and other "crimes against humanity," perhaps to concentration camps and systematic racial discrimination. These the powers could condemn and even universalize, without fear or concern that they, too, might some day be charged with such atrocities. But the powers probably did not envisage a universal, comprehensive human rights code that might affect their own societies and judge their own political institutions and systems of justice, the conditions in their jails and the acts of their police, their economic and social policies, their racial inequities, even their immigration laws and practices. It seems unlikely that they anticipated that they might be called upon to exercise responsibility for human rights everywhere, even at a cost to themselves in resources and human lives.

And yet, I suggest, one can trace a path from the conversations at Dumbarton Oaks in 1944 to a sturdy, multifaceted international human rights system of laws and institutions at the end of the twentieth century; from human rights as psychological warfare to human rights as the idea and ideology of our times; from ringing rhetoric to law; from the universalization of that idea in the Universal Declaration to its internationalization in "the International Bill of Rights" and in subsequent human rights conventions. The path from Dumbarton Oaks led to international commissions and committees and courts, to the UN High Commissioner for Human Rights and the promise of an International

Criminal Court, to the spreading and growing network of nongovernmental human rights organizations—all striving to induce compliance with international human rights standards throughout the world.

One need not insist that international human rights, as conceived in 1944, has seen steady growth and development. Indeed, one finds already present at the beginning, reluctance, weaknesses in commitment, and resistance to major aspects of international human rights by big powers, including the United States. One must ask what it has all meant for the human rights of 6 billion human beings at the end of the century. Yet by any measure, I believe, international human rights at the end of the twentieth century is a remarkable phenomenon. Central to this history is the Universal Declaration of Human Rights.

The Universal Declaration of Human Rights

The Universal Declaration has claim to be one of the most important international instruments of the twentieth century, second only, perhaps, to the United Nations Charter. The significance of the Universal Declaration lies in four achievements:

1. It helped convert a discredited philosophical idea ("natural rights") into a dominant political ideology.
2. It defined a vague colloquialism ("human rights") in an authoritative code, a triple "decalogue" of thirty articles of fundamental rights.
3. It universalized human rights, promoting a constitutional ideology accepted in a few countries into a standard of constitutionalism for all countries.
4. It internationalized human rights, transforming matters that had been subject to exclusive domestic jurisdictions—"sovereignty"—into matters of international concern, putting them permanently on the international political agenda, and providing the foundation for a sturdy edifice of international norms and institutions.

The Declaration established the human rights idea as the ideology of our times. It is the holy writ to which all pay homage, even if sometimes the homage of hypocrisy. Eschewing—in its quest for universality—explicit reliance on divine inspiration or on natural rights, the Declaration provided the idea of human rights with a universally acceptable foundation, a supreme principle, that of *human dignity*.

The Universal Declaration transformed a phrase and an idea into an authoritative standard and a detailed code. Behind the Universal Declaration were national bills of rights, but the Declaration bettered their instruction. Notably, it established rights to popular sovereignty, representative democracy, and universal suffrage; it married rights in the liberal state to the benefits of the welfare state and recognized and declared them equally as human rights; it rendered "equality" and nondiscrimination a most insistent theme.

A principal contribution of the Universal Declaration has been the realization of its original purpose, to establish a "common standard of achievement for all peoples and all nations." The standard it defined is the human rights standard for the world today, incorporated expressly or implicitly, copied and borrowed from, by new and old constitutions and laws around the world.

The Declaration was the first instrument of international human rights. It is the source of the international law of human rights, embodied in the two international covenants now legally binding on the large majority of the countries of the world and in major international conventions on genocide, torture, racial discrimination, discrimination against women, and the rights of the child, all widely ratified and highly influential. The Declaration contributed to a customary law of human rights that is binding on all states, even on those that have not accepted any relevant human rights treaty. The international law of human rights that the Declaration inspired has also brought about important international human rights institutions. The Declaration remains the authoritative articulation of the international human rights standard: the symbol, the representation, the scriptures.

One might trace a path from the Declaration to historic developments in the second half of the century: to the end of colonialism and the proliferation of new states, to the end of communism and the establishment of democracy as the prevailing ideology for the twenty-first century. One can even see a path—circuitous, not unbroken, but traceable—from the Universal Declaration to what is to date perhaps the most glorious, single, international human rights triumph: the eradication of apartheid and the birth of a new democratic South Africa.

The Universal Declaration is a remarkable, radical achievement, and its successful birth is not easy to explain. It emerged from a new committee, the UN Commission on Human Rights, in a new world organization. The Declaration was completed after the new "One World" was already divided in cold war. The members of the commission and other principal participants included strong personalities of diverse political persuasion: France (René Cassin) and Canada (John Humphrey) vied in claims of parentage; the United States nominated Eleanor Roosevelt, chair of the commission, and keeper of the spirit of FDR; Charles Malik of Lebanon had powerful claims, he and P. C. Chang may have dominated the commission. Other remarkable individuals may have been equally influential: Carlos Romulo of the Philippines, Ricardo Alfaro of Panama, and others from countries later characterized as the "Third World." The representative of the Soviet Union (USSR) was *not* a positive influence, and the USSR and its bloc (along with Saudi Arabia and South Africa) abstained in the vote on the resolution proclaiming the Declaration.

To many in the human rights movement, the Declaration was something of a disappointment. There was disappointment in its uncertain character—a "universal declaration" instead of an international treaty, a "standard of achievement" instead of binding norms—principally as a result of the reluctance and unreadiness of the great powers. "Idealists" who had entered the U.S. Department of State and other Western foreign ministries during the war and had helped plan and implement the postwar order, representatives of smaller countries and of nongovernmental organizations, concerned citizens in many countries—all had hoped for an international bill of rights, a treaty that governments would ratify and that would be legally binding on them, with effective institutions to implement and enforce it. There was disappointment that some important rights were not recognized: The Declaration includes no general commitment to individual "liberty" and autonomy. Some rights were declared in ambiguous terms, with differences papered over. For example, to some, the right to work (Article 23) meant only freedom to choose one's employment if one can find it, while to others it placed an obligation on government and society to provide employment. The right to "receive" and to "enjoy" asylum (Article 14) did not clearly declare that states have an obligation to grant asylum. The Declaration did not even call on states to prepare a bill of rights and to assume human rights obligations, nor did it provide or call for effective means for enforcing the rights recognized.

The International Bill of Rights: From the Declaration to the Covenants

The disappointments of 1948 tended to depreciate the significance of the Universal Declaration when it was adopted; they were not wholly assuaged when—after eighteen years of slow, difficult negotiation—the Declaration was finally converted into binding norms in two international covenants, the International Covenant on Civil and Political Rights (ICCPR) and the International Covenant on Economic, Social and Cultural Rights (ICESCR).[20] Delay was built into the process and into the subject. Governments that were committed to rights and to the Declaration as a "standard of achievement" were cautious about making promises in a binding international covenant. Even governments that did not contemplate adhering to a binding human rights agreement may have wished to forestall the elaboration of a treaty that they could not comfortably ratify some future day, or a treaty that established international norms by which conditions in their countries might be judged morally deficient.

One cause of delay was the gradual end of colonialism and the consequent proliferation of new states, each of which, as it joined the international system, claimed its right to participate in the negotiation process. The new states also sought to develop independent positions on human rights. In particular, they pressed for the addition of a right to self-determination and a right to economic self-determination. (These rights became part of Article 1 of each Covenant.) They chose to emphasize economic and social rights, while the developed states stressed civil and political rights. The result was the bifurcation of what initially had been intended as a single covenant into two, a division that the Universal Declaration had avoided and that continues to trouble international human rights today.

Some provisions in the Covenants were especially controversial, and some rights recognized in the Universal Declaration were not included in either Covenant, notably, the right to property and the ambiguous declaration of a right to receive and enjoy asylum. The Universal Declaration had recognized, in effect, that some limitations on rights in the public interest were inevitable and permissible (Article 29); The Covenant on Civil and Political Rights does not contain such a general limitations clause, but expressly authorizes some limitations on some freedoms, and even requires states parties to prohibit some "free expression" such as war propaganda and "hate speech" (Article 20).

The International Covenant on Civil and Political Rights authorizes a state party to derogate from most rights in public emergency (Article 4), a provision perhaps inevitable but threatening no matter how carefully circumscribed. The addition, at the insistence of developing nations (with Soviet bloc support), of an undefined right of "peoples" to "self-determination" and to "economic self-determination" threatened to discourage adherence by the developed Western powers. All rights in either Covenant were apparently subject to reservations, and there was no provision explicitly barring withdrawal from the Covenant after ratification.[21]

The greatest disappointment was the system of implementation. Governments were unwilling to submit to effective intrusive monitoring or to complaints before impartial bodies. They were unwilling to scrutinize or to complain against others or to expend their political-diplomatic capital and trouble their international relations on behalf of anonymous victims in other countries.

The principal enforcement system that emerged was essentially dependent on self-reporting by states parties, followed by scrutiny of the reports and some cross-examination by the Human Rights Committee established under the ICCPR.[22] Some expressed doubt whether such a system would deter, prevent, terminate, or remedy violations. Provisions for complaint to the Human Rights Committee by another party to the Covenant (Article 41) could be heard only if the state accused had expressly submitted to that procedure in advance, on a reciprocal basis. A procedure for complaint to the Committee by individual victims was relegated to an Optional Protocol, requiring separate agreement.[23]

The International Covenant on Economic, Social and Cultural Rights contained its own disappointments. By that Covenant a state party undertakes only "to take steps" toward achieving the realization of the rights recognized by the Covenant "progressively," and only "to the maximum of its available resources" (Article 2). Understandably, poor countries might be unable to guarantee the full panoply of economic and social rights immediately, but the obligation to do so only "progressively" has lent itself to circumvention and has made bona fide compliance difficult to monitor and to judge. That Covenant does even provide for a monitoring committee comparable to the Human Rights Committee established pursuant to the Covenant on Civil and Political Rights.

Despite their deficiencies, the Covenants were welcomed, although they did not inspire enthusiasm. Ratifications of the Covenants were slow in coming. Major powers, notably the United States, did not hasten to ratify, and many states ratified with important reservations. (When the United States finally ratified the International Covenant on Civil and Political Rights in 1992, it did so with an array of debilitating reservations, understandings, and declarations that collectively amount to unilateral American amendments and interpretations of the text.) The Human Rights Committee had only limited authority, and for years it was cautious and hampered by cold war divisions. Members from the Soviet bloc insisted on the narrowest interpretations of the Committee's authority to interrogate representatives of reporting states, to seek evidence of violations from sources other than the state's reports, or to interpret the provisions of the Covenant. Increasingly, states were delinquent in filing the required reports, and some of the states that filed resisted the Committee's criticism and recommendations for improvement.

Yet the human rights movement survived, and even flourished. As of 1999, some 140 to 145 states (of the near 190 members of the United Nations) have adhered to each of the two Covenants, albeit in some cases with significant reservations. Contrary to expectations and earlier trends, about as many are parties to the Covenant on Civil and Political Rights as to the Economic and Social Rights Covenant. As of early 2000, most of the states party to the ICCPR have adhered to the Optional Protocol, thereby subjecting themselves to the complaints of individuals.

The Human Rights Committee has gained confidence and respect. With the end of the cold war, the Committee has been less fractured and has asserted greater authority to probe for violations. It has scrutinized and criticized the reports of leading countries (including the United States). The Committee has learned to use its authority under Article 40 to make "general comments" as a means of issuing advisory opinions on the meaning of provisions in the Covenant, so as to influence human rights behavior by parties to the Covenant and by states generally.[24] Pursuant to the Optional Protocol, the Committee has issued what are in effect judgments against violating states.[25]

Many states have adhered also to the conventions on particular rights adopted and promoted by the United Nations, including the Genocide Convention, the Convention on the Elimination of All Forms of Racial Discrimination (CERD), the Convention on the Elimination of all Forms of Discrimination against Women (CEDAW), the Convention Against Torture (CAT), and the Convention on the Rights of the Child (CRC).[26] The maturing of the Human Rights Committee and the growing appreciation and experience of other treaty committees—for example, the Committee on the Elimination of Racial Discrimination, the Committee on the Elimination of Discrimination against Women, the Committee Against Torture, and the Committee on the Rights of the Child—have dissipated some of the skepticism that surrounded their birth and have contributed to confidence in "treaty committees" generally.[27]

In addition to "universal" treaties (treaties open to all states), groups of states have developed important regional systems for the protection of human rights. In Europe and in the Americas, regional human rights have had solid growth, including strong normative human rights codes comparable to the Universal Declaration and the International Covenant on Civil and Political Rights, as well as institutions for enforcing the norms, such as commissions and courts, that have had impressive success.[28] The African states have established a Charter on Human and Peoples' Rights with a normative code including civil-political as well as economic-social rights, some people's rights, and a small chapter on individual duties.[29] An African Commission established pursuant to the African Charter on Human and Peoples' Rights has become increasingly "activist," and an African Court is in the making.[30] Regional human rights jurisprudence has enriched international human rights law generally; international and regional human rights also have provided a standard for rights in national constitutions.

HOW AND WHY DID IT HAPPEN?

How, and why, did international human rights emerge, survive, and flourish as a shared ideology in the latter half of the twentieth century? The reasons can be found in national and international political forces, notably in the actions of the

United Nations, U.S. influence, the cold war and its end, the influence of the Third World and of regional organizations, and, finally, what has been called the mobilizing of shame. First, perhaps, the abiding and ineradicable memory of the Holocaust has made it impossible for any state to insist that, in principle, how it behaves toward its own people is no one else's business. The long campaign to end apartheid in South Africa, supported by virtually all states, dealt a fatal blow to attempts to invoke "sovereignty" to defend against charges of gross violations of human rights; no one heeded protestations by the South African government when other states generally cooperated to help end its "sovereign right" to maintain apartheid.[31] By 1993 attempts by China and others to invoke "sovereignty" to prevent international monitoring of human rights rang hollow and evoked little sympathy at the Vienna Conference on Human Rights. In several instances, the UN Security Council found that gross violations of human rights by particular states constituted threats to international peace and security that warranted even military intervention. These political events have virtually swept away "sovereignty" as a bar to international attention to gross human rights violation, at least when the leading powers insist on such attention.

Human rights successes in some countries and in some regions of the world, notably the European human rights system and the inter-American system, also have contributed to the health of international human rights generally. Nongovernmental bodies, unilaterally or in cooperation with one another or with friendly governments and with dedicated intergovernmental bodies, have had growing influence. The press and other information media have brought pictures of terrible atrocities into millions of homes, making it impossible for governments and others to ignore them. The power of the human rights idea itself is difficult to weigh and to appraise, but is not to be underestimated. Institutions and norms have influenced how governments behave, and dominant political forces in the postwar world have helped entrench the human rights idea. Among these, the United Nations, the influence of the United States, the cold war and its end, the Third World, and regional human rights activities deserve particular consideration.

The United Nations

After 1945 the Allies sought to establish their victory and build strong institutions to maintain international peace and security under the control of the great powers, principally through the United Nations and the UN Security Council. But the other institutions and organs they built, notably the General Assembly, included many and increasing numbers of other states. Largely excluded from the Security Council and its concerns with peace and security, the smaller states sought to use those institutions that were under their control to promote the social and economic purposes of the UN Charter, including human rights. Smaller states pressed for an international bill of rights and for stronger UN human rights institutions under the control of the General Assembly and its subsidiary organs. The great powers, reluctant to assume international human rights obligations and responsibilities, did not lead the internationalization of the human rights ideology, but they did not oppose human rights initiatives in the UN forum by others.

Thus, human rights have been on the UN agenda throughout the half century of its existence. Of course, the UN is a political body, and it has reflected the complex politics of the international system, including the politics of human rights enforcement. Especially during the cold war, political UN organs judged and acted politically. The United Nations could not respond early and effectively even to genocide and similar mass atrocities (in Cambodia, Equatorial Africa, Rwanda, the former Yugoslavia). In some cases, UN bodies applied double standards and "selective targeting." For thirty years the Soviet Union and a willing coalition opposed the establishment of a UN High Commissioner for Human Rights; with the end of the cold war, such an office was established, but its mandate was weak and its resources limited. The United Nations has not overcome the reluctance of states to monitor and be monitored. Within bodies such as the UN Human Rights Commission, influential countries still resist international scrutiny, as by the appointment of a "rapporteur" (a UN representative who would report on compliance with international human rights instruments and on alleged abuses). Such resistance often has succeeded, as by China in 1998 and 1999, and again in 2000.

But, for all its inadequacies, the United Nations represents and concentrates international concern over human rights. It put human rights on the world agenda a half century ago and has kept it there. It developed the international law of human rights, including the Universal Declaration, the Covenants, and numerous conventions. It concentrates the world's attention on human rights problems that cry for attention. The very existence of the United Nations—its network of organs, its relations to governments and nongovernmental bodies, and its myriad activities—serves to "promote universal respect for, and observance of, human rights and fundamental freedoms," as the Charter declared in 1945.

The Influence of the United States

The United States has been a major influence in the spread of the human rights ideology and a principal contributor to the international human rights movement. U.S. influence is commonly misunderstood and misconstrued. The United States has been widely—and not unjustly—criticized for crucial failures to support and participate in international human rights. The United States, it has been said, has not been a pillar of the human rights church, but only a flying buttress that supports it from the outside. It is frequently pointed out that by subscribing to the UN Charter and to the Universal Declaration and its progeny, the United States made a broad commitment to promote respect for human rights, not just international human rights for others, and not just when it did not cost the United States much to do so. The United States, we are frequently reminded, has continued to resist ratifying covenants and conventions and has loaded those it has ratified with reservations, understandings, and declarations.[32] It has not yet ratified the International Covenant on Economic, Social and Cultural Rights, nor has it ratified the Convention on the Elimination of All Forms of Discrimination against Women.[33] The United States is almost alone in its failure to ratify the Convention on the Rights of the Child. It is reluctant to lead or to bear the costs of leadership in collective implementation of human rights norms. U.S. resistance to an effective international criminal court has been discouraging.[34] Although human rights are generally protected within the United States, contrary to the international trend, the country has significantly increased the imposition of capital punishment.[35] Prison conditions are some-times bad, police misbehavior is not uncommon, racial equality is still elusive, federal and some state governments have cut back on economic and social commitments to citizens, and U.S. immigration laws and policies are erratic and sometimes inhumane.

Yet, indisputably, the United States has contributed to international human rights in important ways. Principally, perhaps, it has helped to spread the ideology of human rights by its example as a viable constitutional order committed to individual rights. In its international relations—from the Four Freedoms through Dumbarton Oaks, San Francisco, and Nuremberg, and in the United Nations—the United States has supported and promoted the universalization of human rights as well as its internationalization. It played a major role in the preparation and proclamation of the Universal Declaration and of the Covenants and Conventions that followed. The United States proposed—indeed, it imposed—an ideology of human rights on the countries defeated and occupied after World War II and through those states spread the human rights gospel far beyond. The imposition of the ideology of rights on Germany led to contemporary Germany's role as a model of constitutionalism and human rights for other countries in Europe and beyond. The United States used commitment to human rights as an important weapon in the cold war, promoting respect for rights by our allies and would-be allies (although too often it accepted "anticommunism" as a substitute). The United States helped use respect for human rights as the motor of "the Helsinki process" and of its contribution to constitutionalism and democracy, including respect for human rights, in Eastern and Central Europe.[36]

Cold war considerations aside, foreign governments generally have recognized that favorable human rights conditions at home contribute to favorable political and economic relations with the United States and that serious human rights violations threaten those relations. U.S. presidents often have declared that promoting respect for human rights around the world is an important element in U.S. foreign policy. Notably, for example, President Jimmy Carter has been credited with helping to end killings and disappearances during the "dirty war" in Argentina and elsewhere in Latin America. Few would doubt that a desire to improve relations with the United States is part of what impelled China, on October 5, 1998, to sign the International Covenant on Civil and Political Rights, thereby extending the promise of international human rights to almost a billion human beings.

The U.S. Congress has sought to promote respect for human rights in other countries by enacting laws of promotion or of sanction. Congress has, since the 1970s, been responsive to constituencies that are sensitive to human rights in foreign countries generally, or in particular countries. It has maintained sanctions, prohibiting the sale of arms or denying financial assistance to governments guilty of "consistent patterns of gross violations of internationally recognized human rights," and it has required U.S. delegates to international financial institutions to exert influence against international assistance to governments guilty of such violations.[37] At various times, concern over the condition of human rights in particular countries—in Poland or Greece, in the Soviet Union, in some countries in Latin America—has led Congress to impose "country-specific" sanctions; best known perhaps were those against South Africa during apartheid[38] and the Jackson-Vanik Amendment denying trade benefits to the Soviet Union unless it permitted its citizens to emigrate.[39] During the 1970s, Congress mandated the establishment of a human rights bureaucracy in the Department of State, and its detailed annual reports on the condition of human rights in every country of the world have helped establish the human rights ideology in international life.[40] These State Department *Country Reports* have provided a framework for discussion by U.S. ambassadors with foreign governments, mostly confidential but often influential. As a result of one such conversation, a foreign government discontinued police torture; in another instance, a foreign government improved conditions in its prisons and kept them clean. Sanctions imposed by Congress have led to the cancellation of U.S. assistance to foreign security forces charged with gross violations of human rights.[41] In October 1998 Congress enacted the International Religious Freedom Act, which its proponents believe will contribute to respect for religious freedom in many countries.[42]

U.S. courts, too, have exerted some influence against human rights violations in other countries, by entertaining civil suits against foreign officials for torture, killings, disappearances, and other violations of human rights.[43] The cases are comparatively few and monetary judgments ordinarily remain unpaid, but such proceedings serve to increase awareness, to judge, to record, and, perhaps, in some measure even to deter, if only by denying gross violators and their assets a haven in the United States.

The Cold War and Its End

The cold war, which had begun even before the Universal Declaration was proclaimed,[44] fractured the unanimous commitment by the victorious Allies to promote human rights. In time, however, each side saw in the human rights idea an important focus of policy and a powerful ideological weapon. During the decades of their confrontations with communism, the United States and the other Western powers proclaimed their commitment to authentic democracy, to freedom, and to human rights as the hallmark of their ideology, what they stood for, and what distinguished them from their cold war adversaries. They used respect for human rights as a touchstone for friendly relations and alliances, for trade, and for financial assistance. For its part, the Soviet bloc insisted, to its own people and to the unaligned world, that it alone had authentic democracy and that only the socialist ideology represented a sincere commitment to authentic human rights, especially to economic and social rights, and to the right of peoples to self-determination and economic self-determination.

Then, in 1975, at Helsinki, the Soviet bloc, which had abstained when the General Assembly proclaimed the Universal Declaration, made a clear commitment to human rights. It did so as the price of détente and in exchange for commitments by the West not to seek to push back the postwar frontiers in Eastern and Central Europe (including the division of Germany). It explicitly committed itself to the principles of the Universal Declaration; it agreed to abide by international human rights treaties, including the covenants and conventions that it had ratified but ignored; and it acknowledged the right of all "to know and to act upon their rights." As a result, Helsinki monitoring groups grew up and provided the foundations and the legitimacy for an ever-spreading network of nongovernmental human rights monitoring organizations.[45]

The end of the cold war had particular resonance for human rights in the Soviet Union and in its former empire. The Helsinki Accords were incorporated into wider commitments among the parties, set forth in documents emerging from conferences in Paris, Vienna, Bonn, and especially Copenhagen and Moscow.[46] These documents elaborated a shared commitment to human rights in important detail and specified democracy as an important human right and a foundation for other human rights. Thus, the human rights ideology spread to countries in Eastern and Central Europe. Later, political and economic developments in Western Europe, as part of progress toward European Union, attracted "applications" from countries in Central and Eastern Europe and from other neighbors that required of them commitment to and acceptance into the European human rights system. In 1997–1998, an enlarged and restructured European human rights system that included Eastern and Central European states strengthened the commitment to human rights in that region and lengthened the reach of its influence beyond its borders.[47]

Acceptance of the ideology of international human rights throughout the international political-economic system expanded with the end of the cold war. The end of apartheid soon followed, along with the revival of the UN Security Council, enabling it to act against gross violations of human rights that threatened international peace and security, as in the former Yugoslavia and in Rwanda, and the establishment of ad hoc international tribunals to try war crimes and crimes against humanity.[48] Sharp divisions within the Human Rights Committee softened, allowing it to put some teeth into its monitoring process. A parallel Committee on Economic and Social Rights, which had been established in 1985 by the UN General Assembly, also began to wield influence. Ratifications of the Covenants increased steadily, as did ratifications of the Genocide Convention, the Convention on the Elimination of All Forms of Racial Discrimination, the Convention on the Elimination of All Forms of Discrimination against Women, the Convention against Torture, a new Convention on the Rights of the Child.

The Third World

The end of colonialism, the proliferation of new states, and the emergence of the Third World and its transformation after the cold war into the "developing world" may have complicated the politics of human rights, but they also contributed strength to the human rights movement. The multiplication of states as a result of rapid decolonization had slowed the conversion of the Universal Declaration into covenants and conventions, but the Third World— although sometimes resenting Western self-righteousness—made its own commitment to the human rights ideology, and sometimes its members were able to exploit the cold war for particular human rights interests they favored. They added a right to self-determination and a right to "economic self-determination" to both Covenants and pursued a particular interest in supporting economic and social rights, both as a contribution to their own development and as a basis for seeking international financial assistance.

Through the Third World's commitment to particular rights and its insistence on equality and nondiscrimination, its general commitment to international human rights helped these to emerge as principal norms in covenants and conventions. Because the countries of the Third World considered apartheid in South Africa a major affront, they joined—and led—the fight against it, and moved to create and strengthen international human rights institutions as a weapon against it. What began as a step aimed at apartheid resulted in the establishment of a subcommission of the UN Commission on Human Rights to consider evidence of consistent patterns of gross violations of human rights generally.[49] The successful pressure for sanctions against apartheid became a precedent for sanctions against other gross violations.[50] At Vienna in 1993, when a few countries sought to dilute the human rights idea by appealing to "cultural relativism" and "Asian values," others, including some Asian governments and Asian nongovernmental organizations (NGOs), insisted on the universality of human rights and supported the affirmation of the human rights idea.[51] During and after the 1993 conference, Third World countries were generally less defensive of their "sovereignty" than were the bigger powers, such as China, Russia, and even the United States.

Regional Human Rights

The international human rights movement also was richly enhanced by the growth of regional human rights norms and institutions. The European human rights system was born during the early days of the Universal Declaration, from common sources and out of some shared ancestry. The European Human Rights Convention developed in stages, adding protocols as member states gained confidence in each other, in their common enterprise, and in the institutions they had created. The European system developed an effective European Commission of Human Rights and a prestigious Court of Human Rights, which in time produced a rich, eclectic jurisprudence. Major member states, even those with their own rich rights tradition, such as the United Kingdom, submitted to judgment and mended their ways. For example, in a series of cases, the United Kingdom was ordered to respect the freedom of the press of *The Sunday Times;* to halt degrading treatment in a mental hospital; to discontinue and forbid corporal punishment of schoolchildren. The European Court held invalid British laws in Northern Ireland prohibiting sodomy; it prohibited extradition of a person from Great Britain to the state of Virginia for trial because if convicted he might spend long periods on death row, which, in the circumstances, would violate the provision against torture or cruel, inhuman, or degrading treatment or punishment. In these and other cases, the United Kingdom agreed to change its behavior and to reform its practices. The success of the European system has led to its conversion, on the eve of the new century, into an expanded full-time court. The European countries also produced a European Social Charter, which has contributed to economic and social rights.[52]

Political and economic developments in Europe, including Eastern and Central Europe after the cold war, brought additional states into the European human rights system and expanded its institutions. At the same time, the European Economic Community, moving steadily toward European Union, developed particular economic and social human rights, notably in respect of the right to work and free movement of persons among states. The European Court of Justice in Luxembourg added its own independent jurisprudence of human rights.[53]

The states of the Americas, with their own human rights convention and their own institutions, paralleled the experience of Europe, slowly and steadily— although no doubt the inter-American system of human rights has been hindered in its growth because the participation of the United States has been only marginal.[54] The inter-American system—the American Convention on Human Rights, implemented by the Inter-American Commission on Human Rights, and the Inter-American Court, under the authority of the Organization of American States—also has contributed to human rights. The Inter-American Court held Honduras responsible for the abduction and disappearance of a citizen and ordered compensation to survivors.[55] It advised that the extension of the death penalty by Guatemala to additional crimes violated the American Convention. Both governments have listened and obeyed.[56]

The African Commission also has been making some moves toward implementation of human rights. The African states are in the process of establishing an African Court of Human and Peoples' Rights.[57]

Mobilizing Shame

The various influences that induce compliance with human rights norms are cumulative, and some of them add up to an underappreciated means of enforcing human rights, which has been characterized as "mobilizing shame." Intergovernmental as well as governmental policies and actions combine with those of NGOs and the public media, and in many countries also public opinion, to mobilize and maximize public shame.

The effectiveness of such inducements to comply is subtle but demonstrable. Why did China go to such lengths in the 1990s, and again in the year 2000, and expend so much diplomatic capital, to avoid having the UN Human Rights Commission designate a rapporteur to investigate the condition of human rights in China? Why do more than 100 governments become parties to covenants and conventions, obligate themselves to report on human rights conditions, resist and respond to criticism by international bodies and other governments and by NGOs and the media, rather than suffer criticism for failure to participate in international human rights arrangements? Indeed, why do countries such as the United States refrain from assuming human rights obligations, or do so with embarrassing reservations, rather than court criticism and obloquy for violating obligations they have assumed?

HAS IT MADE A DIFFERENCE?

When front pages and television news continue to report grave human rights violations, including genocide and other crimes against humanity; when there are daily reports of torture, prolonged arbitrary detention, racism, abuse of women, exploitation of children—one cannot escape asking: What has changed? Are the human rights of human beings respected better than they were a half century ago, before the advent of the age of rights?

At the end of the twentieth century, human rights, essentially as defined in the Universal Declaration, is a universal ideology. Under international influence, the ideology of human rights has been "constitutionalized" in almost all countries. And virtually all countries are now committed internationally to respect and ensure the human rights of their citizens. International institutions monitor and criticize, often supported by governments with blandishments, carrots, and occasional sticks. Intergovernmental and governmental activities combine with those of NGOs and the media to mobilize and maximize "shame," in efforts to deter, terminate, and remedy human rights violations.

The human rights ideology has helped shape world events. International human rights ended apartheid. International human rights helped end colonialism and achieve the present world system of nearly 200 states. International human rights had an important role in ending the cold war and in bringing human rights and the seeds of democracy to the former Soviet empire and beyond. "Dirty war," disappearances, and extrajudicial killings in Latin America ended in substantial measure through the influence of international human rights. An international tribunal in the former Yugoslavia has indicted a head of state, and there and in Rwanda tribunals have convicted people of genocide and related crimes. A former head of state, Augusto Pinochet, was arrested for extradition to stand trial for the torture and murder of many citizens during his "reign" in Chile (although he was not brought to trial due to poor health). International human rights bodies, notably the European human rights system, have addressed and remedied violations by powerful member states. The domain of international and regional human rights bodies continues to expand.

Undeniably, there have been terrible human rights failures—in Cambodia, Bosnia, Rwanda. There, and elsewhere, national constitutions and international norms failed to deter; international institutions and powerful governments failed to respond promptly and adequately. (The expectation that they would fail to respond no doubt contributed to their failure to deter.) But international human rights may be credited with whatever responses there have been, however inadequate, however delayed; and international human rights inspired all subsequent and continuing efforts to address the terrible violations. The major powers have sometimes declared gross violations of human rights to be "threats to international peace and security" and made them the responsibility of the UN Security Council, leading to international sanctions (and even to military intervention, as in Kosovo in 1999). International tribunals are sitting to bring gross violators to trial; a permanent international criminal tribunal to adjudicate crimes of genocide, war crimes, and crimes against humanity is being created. Various governments have moved to support international human rights and made their bilateral and multilateral influence an established force in international relations.

Some human rights failures reflect the character of the international system and its deficiencies. The human rights ideology and human rights institutions can address only violations for which established societies and governments can be held responsible. They do not—cannot—address terrible violations of human life and welfare that occur as a result of wars (including civil wars) or massive violations of human rights by mobs or terrorists. But even in situations such as those in the former Yugoslavia, in troubled parts of Africa, in East Timor, the international community cannot escape responsibility.

In some countries the culture of human rights has met resistance from an older societal culture, a culture of gender inequalities and mistreatment of "others." For some governments international human rights has met resistance from a culture of "sovereignty" that dies hard. But the fruits of international human rights are to be judged by transformations in domestic society and their consequences in the lives of human beings. In sum, by the end of the twentieth century many more societies than before 1948 are societies with human rights systems; there are fewer patterns of gross violation, and institutions exist that help deter, prevent, and remedy abuses. Societies where these systems are absent or deficient are now considered "abnormal," in "emergency," and are under continuing pressures to change and to remedy deficiencies.

Every human being in every country now has claim to the freedoms, protections, and benefits of the human rights ideology. Each has claim to those rights against his or her own society. Every human being's rights now have claim on international responsibility and protection. No country can now say that the human rights of any human being subject to its jurisdiction is no one else's business. The world and its institutions may or may not respond, but responsibility persists. If there are periods of international neglect or indifference, governments remain ever subject to challenge and to change.

Many hundreds of millions—even billions—of human beings who enjoyed no human rights half a century ago now live under human rights regimes. Increasing numbers of countries provide constitutional protection for individual rights; increasing numbers of countries have accepted international obligations and are subject to some international monitoring and scrutiny. But much depends—will depend—on vigilance, by national bodies, by other governments that care, by international institutions, by nongovernmental organizations and by the press.

AN AGENDA FOR THE NEXT CENTURY

International human rights are here to stay, but its agenda needs serious attention for the new century. Norms and institutions have to be reappraised. There is a need to address the full responsibility of states toward the human rights of their inhabitants; the responsibility of other states, especially of other parties to human rights agreements; the responsibility of international institutions and of their state members (including especially members of the UN Security Council); and the responsibility of other nonstate actors.

Some urgent items for that agenda include: reviewing the international norms and strengthening international human rights institutions; attending to the weaknesses of norms and institutions in safeguarding the rights of women and of minorities; considering the rights of neglected people and categories of people, such as refugees; addressing concerns arising from new economic and social developments; building bridges between the human rights movement and the religious realm; and addressing issues of religious freedom arising out of differing religious identities.

Political developments in the latter years of the twentieth century have thrown up new human rights issues and others not previously addressed or recognized. These include human rights and "transitional justice," and the claims of justice, of truth, and of history, such as have been pursued in South Africa, the former Soviet empire, Cambodia, Argentina, Chile, El Salvador,

Guatemala, and Haiti. They also include human rights issues of collective humanitarian intervention, as in Kosovo in 1999, and human rights in times and places of United Nations peacekeeping, as in East Timor.

Women

Prominent on the human rights agenda for the future must be the achievement of the equality of women promised in many instruments and essential to human dignity and to development. The Convention on the Elimination of All Forms of Discrimination Against Women (CEDAW), modeled after the Convention on the Elimination of All Forms of Racial Discrimination (CERD), has attracted numerous reservations, reflecting deeply ingrained historical, cultural, and religious attitudes. The treaty body monitoring compliance with CEDAW has weaker powers than the committee monitoring CERD, differences that must be eliminated.

Obstacles to be overcome in the pursuit of equal rights for women are reflected in some of the unusual provisions in CEDAW. Article 5(a) requires state parties to "modify the social and cultural patterns of conduct of men and women, with a view to achieving the elimination of prejudices and customary and all other practices which are based on the idea of the inferiority or the superiority of either of the sexes or on stereotyped roles of men and women." But such unusual provisions are frequently subjected to reservations. The Convention is silent on the serious problems of violence against women and of unequal relations in the home. Equal rights for women will require concerted efforts by all elements in the international human rights movement to eliminate reservations and to have the provisions of CEDAW carried out in good faith and largeness of spirit.

Minorities

Post–World War II inattention to the problem of minorities must be repaired.[58] In 1945 the UN Charter, and in 1948 the Universal Declaration, apparently assumed that the special protection of minorities, once perceived to be essential for maintaining peace in Europe, was no longer necessary: Peace would be maintained by the UN Charter and the Security Council, while minority groups would be protected by protecting the human rights of their members, the human rights of all.

Later, the international Covenants established the rights of peoples to political and economic self-determination. But the rights of minority groups, of their members as members of the group, even of individual members in relation to the group, have remained inconclusive. The plight of minorities and its relation to internal and international peace, remains a source of grievous concern for human rights as well as for international peace and security.

The tragedy of the former Yugoslavia, in Bosnia and in Kosovo, suggests the need for earlier, planned, coordinated, collective intervention under UN and regional auspices to prevent conflict and crimes against humanity, and to do so by any necessary means, both to maintain peace and to promote amicable relations among ethnic and religious communities. All of the facilities of the United Nations, regional bodies, and more developed nations must be coordinated to that end. Of particular urgency is the long-neglected plight of the Roma (Gypsies).

Human Rights and Religion

Article 18 of the Universal Declaration of Human Rights and the comparable Article 18 in the ICCPR recognize rights to freedom of thought, conscience, and religion. But some religions have resisted some freedoms for other religions, including, for example, the right to change one's religion or the right to proselytize.

The world of religion and the world of human rights have not always coexisted comfortably. Religion, and some particular religions, have not been comfortable with human rights as an autonomous ideology that is not necessarily rooted in religion. The human rights ideology, on the other hand, has resisted the claims of some religions to disregard the claims of other religions. Some religions have invoked religious dogma to justify distinctions based on religion, gender, or sexual orientation, distinctions that may be contrary to the human rights idea. The rise of "fundamentalism," sometimes brigaded with political authority, has weakened adherence by some governments to the human rights ideology and to international covenants and conventions, notably, the ICCPR and CEDAW.[59] Representatives of human rights and of religion, and of particular religions, must enter into dialogue, to develop understanding and cooperation in the new century.

Refugees

The international system failed refugees before World War II, and it has not done enough for them since. Even the Universal Declaration of Human Rights has failed refugees: It seems to recognize an individual's right to seek political asylum and to enjoy it, but it does not clearly recognize a right to receive asylum so it can be enjoyed, and it does not address the rights of refugees or of persons displaced within their home territories who are not fleeing political repression. Nor did the 1951 Convention Relating to the Status of Refugees give to any refugee a right to asylum. An incidental provision committing states to *non-refoulement*—not to send a refugee to a country where their life or freedom would be threatened—falls short of giving a refugee a right to be admitted somewhere for haven.[60] The Refugee Convention, like the Universal Declaration, draws understandable lines between political and other refugees, between refugees outside their country and internally displaced persons; but having drawn such lines, it does not attend adequately to people on either side of those lines.

The refugee remains the stepchild of the human rights movement. Refugees are left to the heroic efforts of the UN High Commissioner for Refugees and to the mercies of governments. At the end of the twentieth century, many millions of refugees and displaced persons are victims of "compassion fatigue." There is no sign that the international system is mobilizing itself to address their tragedies by developing programs for discouraging refugee flow, for example, by monitoring and improving human rights conditions in countries from which they might flee; by providing foreign assistance to discourage an exodus of economic refugees; by developing a legal right of asylum for at least some refugees and imposing obligations on states to share the burdens of asylum; and by encouraging states to see that they have a human, even a national interest, in recognizing and respecting the human rights of refugees. Asylum apart, the human rights movement must consider the human rights of refugees and displaced persons wherever they find themselves.

Realizing Compliance with Human Rights

It is time for the international community to review the norms and institutions of international human rights, to help improve national institutions on which individual rights depend, and to strengthen international institutions and enable them to monitor and improve human rights conditions wherever they are troubled.

There is much to be done to make compliance with international human rights norms *real*: to move states beyond nominal commitment to authentic commitment; to make the reporting system required by covenants and conventions more meaningful; to enhance the authority of the treaty committees; and to move beyond voluntary reporting by states parties to include international monitoring, investigation, and judicial protection, as some regional human rights systems have done.

It is time for the human rights treaty system to address and sharply reduce reservations to human rights covenants and conventions. In the past, in order to encourage ratification, the international community was prepared to accept reservations liberally and with hardly a question. The community saw virtue in promoting adherence to treaties even if it was only nominal and even essentially hypocritical. The international community must begin to insist on bona fide compliance with covenants and conventions, with their spirit and purpose.

It is time to remind all states, again and again, that the condition of human rights everywhere is their business, that gross violations anywhere are detrimental to the national interests of all. It is time for all to recognize the relation of human rights violations to domestic peace and security and to international peace and security. It is necessary to achieve commitment by the big powers—the United States, Europe, Japan—and by others in Asia, Africa, and the Americas, to take steps against gross violations. It is time to recognize the responsibility implied in any multilateral convention, that every state party should hold other parties to their commitments, if necessary by pressing complaints before committees, commissions, courts, and tribunals; by various carrots, if necessary by various sticks.

Human Rights and Globalization

Today's world is not that of 1948; human rights were a radical advance in, and for, the world of fifty years ago. Now the human rights idea and ideology call for adaptation to a changed new century. Half a century ago the human rights movement, seeking acceptance of the rights ideology in a political system constituted by states, persuaded them that "sovereignty" and other "state values" are not the ultimate values, that state values have to serve human values, the values of billions of human beings. Now the human rights movement must adapt to the age of globalization, "the market," and cyberspace. International human rights eroded the "sovereignty" of states by subjecting human rights conditions at home to international scrutiny and by imposing responsibility on states regarding violations by other states. But where is sovereignty and where is responsibility for human rights in the coming age? In particular, who is responsible for violations of human rights by global companies?

Even in the age of globalization, legal responsibility in a state system remains in the states. But states, singly or jointly, can impose obligations on private entities, including multinationals, to respect human rights, and the international system should monitor and enforce such obligations. States can impose obligations on companies to respect and ensure the human rights of human beings on whom their global activities impinge. They have, perhaps, already begun to do so: The International Covenant on Civil and Political Rights commits states parties "to respect and ensure" the rights recognized in the Covenant. There would seem to be an obligation on states parties to ensure that companies subject to their control and jurisdiction, wherever they operate, refrain from using slave labor or child labor; avoid complicity in torture, mistreatment, and other repressive measures; and support economic and social rights for the people among whom they operate. The responsibility of states and of companies has still to be clearly recognized and vigorously implemented.[61]

PROSPECTS:
THE FUTURE OF THE HUMAN RIGHTS IDEOLOGY

Changes in the international political system suggest that the coming century will be even more receptive to the human rights ideology than was the past half century. After World War II, the human rights ideology strove to achieve universality and acceptability to both sides in the cold war and to all economic systems, to socialism as well as to capitalism and to all their variants. The end of communism and of the Soviet empire eliminated an ideology inconsistent with the human rights ideology, and no new alternative secular ideology is on the horizon. In the twenty-first century, I am persuaded, the human condition will be judged, at home and abroad, by the human rights ideology. I do not expect any essential dissolution of the marriage of the Liberal State and the Welfare State, which the Universal Declaration consecrated; the commitment to both civil-political rights and economic-social rights will remain the human rights legacy for the new century.

The degrees of individual enterprise and of public enterprise, of economic freedom and of governmental regulation, will continue to differ in place and in time. Countries will continue to differ in what limitations on rights are required in the public interest and in how much derogation from rights is permitted during public emergency. There will be advances in human rights, and some retreats. One cannot expect an end to terrorism and disorder and internal wars, nor a guarantee against massive refugee flows and more genocide. But the ideology of human rights, and the related ideology of constitutionalism, I am persuaded, will remain the universal ideology, while the world continues its struggle with poverty and underdevelopment.

In the new century, every human being in every country of the world now has a claim against his or her society to the freedoms, protections, and benefits of the human rights ideology. Every human being's rights now have a claim to international responsibility and protection. But the human rights that are enjoyed by individual human beings will depend on maintaining a human rights culture, which depends in turn on the commitment and responsibility of governments and institutions, nongovernmental organizations, and each of us.

NOTES

1. The reader may find exposition and explanation of unfamiliar terms in a growing number of books and articles including some devoted specifically to human rights, among them: Louis Henkin, Gerald Neuron, Diane Orentlicher, and David Leebron, *Human Rights* (New York: Foundation Press, 1999); and Henry Steiner and Philip Alston, eds., *International Human Rights in Context* (Oxford: Clarendon Press, 1996). There are also periodicals devoted entirely to human rights—for example, *Human Rights Quarterly*—and human rights law reviews associated with law schools; the *American Journal of International Law* regularly addresses human rights issues and developments.

2. 87 *Congressional Record* 44, 46-47 (1941).

3. *The Public Papers and Addresses of Franklin D. Roosevelt: 1940*, ed. Samuel I. Rosenman (New York: Random House, 1941), p. 672.

4. The Atlantic Charter was issued on August 14, 1941, in a joint statement by President Roosevelt and Prime Minister Churchill. After the United States entered the war, the Allies, on January 1, 1942, signed the United Nations Declaration in which they pledged their adherence to the principles of the Atlantic Charter. For the text of the Atlantic Charter, see United States Department of State Executive Agreement Series No. 236, *Cooperative War Effort* (Washington, DC: U.S. Government Printing Office, 1942).

5. The dictum, often quoted, appears in President Franklin Roosevelt's Message on the State of the Union, January 11, 1944, 90 *Congressional Record* 55, 57 (1944). An earlier version, "for necessitous men are not, truly speaking, free men," appears in an opinion by Lord Henley, Lord Chancellor of England, in *Vernon v. Bethell*, 28 English Reports 838 (1762).

6. For a more detailed story, see Henkin et al., *Human Rights*, part I.

7. Lord Acton, quoted in Hersch Lauterpacht, *International Law and Human Rights* (New York: Praeger, 1950), p. 126.

8. Writing after the rebirth of the ideology of rights in the mid-twentieth century, an American philosopher observed: "Certainly there was, just a relatively few years ago, fairly general agreement that the doctrine of natural rights had been thoroughly and irretrievably discredited." Richard Wasserstrom, "Rights, Human Rights and Racial Discrimination," *Journal of Philosophy*, Vol. 61, No. 20, October 29, 1964, pp. 628-41.

9. This commitment to the ideology of rights also appeared in the bill of rights of Virginia and in other early state constitutions. See generally Henkin et al., *Human Rights*, part II.

10. The United States also early established "judicial review" of the actions of the legislative and executive branches, which was to become the hallmark and bulwark of constitutional human rights.

11. *Wesberry v. Sanders*, 376 U.S. 1 (1964); *Reynolds v. Sims*, 377 U.S. 533 (1964).

12. President Woodrow Wilson declared that to be an aim of U.S. entry into World War I. See Woodrow Wilson, "An Address to a Joint Session of Congress (Fourteen Points Address)," (1918), in Arthur S. Link, ed., *The Papers of Woodrow Wilson*, Vol. 45 (Princeton, NJ: Princeton University Press, 1984), p. 534.

13. For the origins and growth of "international human rights" generally, see Henkin et al., *Human Rights*, part III.

14. Examples of such undertakings include early bilateral treaties for reciprocal religious or ethnic toleration, minorities treaties before and after World War I, or the conventions promoted by the International Labour Office affiliated with the League of Nations after World War I.

15. The "International Bill of Rights" is not a formal designation but is now commonly used to refer to the Universal Declaration together with the International Covenant on Civil and Political Rights (ICCPR) and the International Covenant on Economic, Social and Cultural Rights (IESCR), described more fully below.

16. See Louis Henkin, "Human Rights from Dumbarton Oaks," in Ernest R. May and Angeliki Laiou, eds., *The Dumbarton Oaks Conversations and the United Nations 1944–1994* (Cambridge, MA: Harvard University Press, 1998).

17. The principal organs of the United Nations, as set out in Article 7(1) of its Charter, include the Security Council, the General Assembly, the Economic and Social Council (ECOSOC), the Trusteeship Council, the International Court of Justice, and the Secretariat. Article 68 of the Charter directed the Economic and Social Council to set up commissions in economic and social fields "and for the promotion of human rights." The UN Commission on Human Rights was the first commission set up by ECOSOC and the Universal Declaration of Human Rights was the first product of that Commission. The UN organization, its organs and suborgans, have lives and agendas of their own. The UN General Assembly, a principal organ, has promoted human rights resolutions, declarations, treaties, and other norms, has considered particular human rights problems, and has sometimes recommended actions to alleviate them. The UN Human Rights Commission, in addition to drafting the Universal Declaration and a number of human rights treaties, has helped to develop subsidiary bodies and procedures for monitoring the condition of human rights and responding to human rights violations. See generally, Henkin et al., *Human Rights,* p. 689.

18. "Charter of the International Military Tribunal (IMT)," in Agreement for the Prosecution and Punishment of the Major War Criminals of the European Axis (London Agreement), August 8, 1945, 58 Stat. 1544, E.A.S. No. 472, 82 U.N.T.S. 280.

19. The principles of the Nuremberg Charter were unanimously approved by the United Nations General Assembly; see G.A. Res. 95, U.N. doc. A/236 (1946). Their status as international law is not in doubt.

20. See Vratislav Pechota, "The Development of the Covenant on Civil and Political Rights," in Louis Henkin, ed., *The International Bill of Rights: The Covenant on Civil and Political Rights* (New York: Columbia University Press, 1981). International human rights agreements are generally drafted by committees acting under the auspices of the UN General Assembly, then submitted for comment to all the members of the United Nations. The final drafts are adopted by the General Assembly and submitted to member states of the United Nations, inviting them to become parties. The United Nations Organization is not a party to such agreements but provides administrative and financial services for the preparation, conclusion, and implementation of the agreements. Covenants, conventions, and protocols are all international agreements, binding on the states that become parties to them by procedures indicated in the particular treaty, usually by signature subject to subsequent ratification. Between signature and ratification, a state is not legally bound by the terms of the treaty but is deemed to have an obligation to proceed to ratification within a reasonable time and not to act contrary to the spirit of the agreement in the interim. See the Vienna Convention on the Law of Treaties, U.N. Doc A/CONF. 39/27 (1969), Article 18. Usually a state also may become a party to the treaty by depositing an "instrument of accession" instead of signing and ratifying.

21. The Human Rights Committee charged with monitoring the ICCPR, in a "general comment" interpreting the Covenant, has declared that states parties to the Covenant do not have a right to withdraw. See General Comment No. 26, U.N. Doc. CCPR/C/21/Rev.1/Add.9 (1997).

22. The Human Rights Committee established pursuant to ICCPR, Part IV, is not to be confused with the UN Commission on Human Rights, the body that drafted the Universal Declaration and the Covenants and is a suborgan of the UN Economic and Social Council. The Human Rights Committee is a "treaty body" established by the states-parties to the

ICCPR. The members of the Committee are elected by, and responsible to, the states parties to that Covenant, performing the tasks assigned to it by the Covenant. But the United Nations provides financial and administrative support for the Committee. Comparable "treaty bodies" have been created by conventions adopted by the UN General Assembly on particular human rights. The ICESCR did not establish a "treaty body," but, following the successful development of the Human Rights Committee under the ICCPR, the Economic and Social Council, pursuant to a 1985 resolution, established the Committee on Economic, Social and Cultural Rights to provide supervision in respect of the ICESCR. See ECOSOC Res. 1985/17. The Committee on Economic, Social and Cultural Rights has advised the creation of an Optional Protocol to the ICESCR, modeled after the Optional Protocol to the ICCPR, by which states parties would agree to have the Committee consider communications by individuals concerning compliance with the Covenant.

23. See Optional Protocol to the International Covenant on Civil and Political Rights, adopted and opened for signature, ratification, and accession by UN General Assembly resolution 2200 A (XXI), December 16, 1966.

24. The Committee's General Comments have sometimes been controversial. See, for example, General Comment No. 24 on Reservations. See Henkin et al., *Human Rights,* pp. 789, 791-93. For a collection of general comments by human rights treaty bodies, see UN, *Compilation of General Comments and General Recommendations Adopted by Human Rights Treaty Bodies* (Geneva: UN, 1997). Document Symbol: HRI/GEN/1/Rev.3.

25. See generally Dominick McGoldrick, *The Human Rights Committee* (Oxford: Clarendon Press, 1991); and Manfred Nowak, *U.N. Covenant on Civil and Political Rights: CCPR Commentary* (Arlington, VA: N. P. Engel, 1993).

26. Ratifications and accessions of various human rights treaties as of November 1, 1999: Convention on the Prevention and Punishment of the Crime of Genocide, 78 *United Nations Treaty Series* [UNTS] 277 (December 9, 1948), 130 parties; International Convention on the Elimination of All Forms of Racial Discrimination, 660 U.N.T.S. 195 (December 21, 1965), 156 parties; Convention on the Elimination of All Forms of Discrimination Against Women, G.A. Res. 34/180 (December 18, 1979), 165 parties; Convention Against Torture and Other Cruel, Inhuman, or Degrading Punishment, G.A. Res. 39/46 (December 10, 1984), 119 parties; Convention on the Rights of the Child, G.A. Res. 44/25 (November 20, 1989), 191 parties. Not unrelated are the Geneva Conventions (not developed under UN auspices) establishing humanitarian law. At one time "human rights law" was distinguished and separated from "humanitarian law" dealing with the laws of war. Increasingly, the line between these two fields has blurred. At Nuremberg, the Nuremberg Charter dealt both with violations of the laws of war and with crimes against humanity. With the extension of humanitarian law to include crimes not during war, but also in internal wars and nonwar situations, the international norms have ceased to observe a sharp distinction between the two fields. In the case of the former Yugoslavia and the forthcoming International Criminal Court, norms and institutions have dealt with subjects from both fields. For example, the International Criminal Court will have jurisdiction over war crimes as well as crimes against humanity. The "Landmine Convention" also has been seen as a human rights agreement, especially as it affects civilian populations before, during, and apart from war. This Convention was not prepared under the auspices of the United Nations, but the Secretary-General of the United Nations is the Depositary and state parties must inform the Security Council of their intent to withdraw from the treaty. See The Convention on the Prohibition of the Use, Stockpiling, Production, and Transfer of Anti–Personnel Mines and on Their Destruction (also known as the Ottawa Convention), 36 *International Legal Materials* [ILM] 1507 (September 8, 1997), signed by 135 countries and ratified by 76.

27. For example, the Committee Against Torture was given some authority to receive complaints and to initiate "confidential inquiry," which may even lead to a visit to the

territory of a state suspected of treaty violation. See Convention Against Torture, art. 20. There is no "treaty body" to implement the Genocide Convention, which was adopted before the Covenant and its method of implementation were adopted.

28. European Convention for the Protection of Human Rights and Fundamental Freedoms, Nov. 4, 1950, 213 U.N.T.S. 22; American Convention on Human Rights, Nov. 22, 1969, 9 I.L.M. 673, 683. The European states also have adopted the European Social Charter. The European system was established under the authority of the Council of Europe, which continues to exercise governing authority over the system. On the European system, see chapter 5 in this volume; on the inter-American system, see chapter 6 .

29. See chapter 7 in this volume. The African Charter on Human and Peoples' Rights (also known as the "Banjul Charter"), OAU Doc. CAB/LEG/67/3 rev. 5 (1981), 21 I.L.M. 58, entered into force October 21, 1986. Fifty-three countries had ratified the African Charter as of March 1, 1999. See also Evelyn Ankumah, The African Commission on Human and Peoples' Rights: Practice and Procedures (Boston: M. Nijhoff, 1996); Dr. Phillip K. A. Amoah, "The African Charter on Human and Peoples' Rights: A Decade of Achievement in Securing Human Rights for Africans?" Africa Legal Aid Quarterly (July-September 1996); and see generally Henkin et al., Human Rights, pp. 344 et seq., 600 et seq.

30. Draft Additional Protocol to the African Charter on Human and Peoples' Rights, OAU Doc. OAU/LEG/MIN/AFCHPR/PROT.1 rev. 2 (1997).

31. In 1948 the Republic of South Africa established apartheid, a comprehensive system of racial separation and discrimination with an exclusively white government. Apartheid became a target of international condemnation led by Third World states, joined by virtually all other states; a system of sanctions against South Africa grew in scope and intensity. The United Nations also adopted the International Convention on the Suppression and Punishment of the Crime of Apartheid, by General Assembly Resolution 3068 (XXVIII) of November 30, 1973. Apartheid was abolished in 1989, and a democratic government was established in 1994. See chapters 9 and 13 in this volume.

32. See, for example, the U.S. Reservations, Understandings and Declarations to the ICCPR, 138 Congressional Record S4781-01 (1992), quoted in Henkin et al., Human Rights, p. 784.

33. The International Covenant on Economic, Social and Cultural Rights (ICESCR) was signed for the United States by President Jimmy Carter on October 5, 1977, with proposed reservations, understandings, and declarations. In 1994 the Foreign Relations Committee of the U.S. Senate recommended that the Senate consent to U.S. ratification of the Convention on Discrimination Against Women, but as of May 2000 the Senate had not acted on the recommendation.

34. See the American Journal of International Law (AJIL), Vol. 93 (January 1999) for a series of articles on the International Criminal Court. For the U.S. position on the court see David J. Scheffer, "Developments in International Law: The United States and the International Criminal Court," 93 AJIL 12 (1999).

35. The United States has been called a "world leader in executing juveniles." Report of Human Rights Watch Children's Rights Project (March 1995). Executions for crimes committed by a person under the age of 18 are inconsistent with Article 6(5) of the ICCPR, but the United States has entered a reservation to that Article.

36. "The participants were content with the non-binding character of the [Helsinki] accord; for the United States it also obviated the need to seek consent of the U.S. Senate." See Louis Henkin, International Law: Politics and Values (Boston: M. Nijhoff, 1995), p. 181. Although not legally binding, the accord was an important human rights instrument during the cold war and laid the groundwork for the growth of constitutionalism in the former Soviet Union and in Eastern and Central Europe. Henkin et al., Human Rights, p. 355.

37. See Henkin et al., Human Rights, pp. 816 et seq.

38. See the Comprehensive Anti-Apartheid Act of 1986, 1986 P.L. 99-440.

39. Trade Act of 1974, 19 U.S.C. Section 2432, Freedom of Emigration in East-West Trade (Jackson-Vanik Amendment). See Henkin et al., Human Rights, p. 825.

40. See Henkin et al., *Human Rights*, p. 841 et seq.

41. See chapter 12 in this volume.

42. The International Religious Freedom Act, 105 P.L. 292, 112 Stat. 2787., Oct. 27, 1998.

43. U.S. courts exercise this influence pursuant to the Alien Tort Act, 18 U.S.C. § 1350. The leading case is *Filartiga v. Pena-Irala*, 630 F.2d 876 (2d Cir., 1980). Congress extended the jurisdiction of the courts to include citizen victims of torture and killing; see the Torture Victims Protection Act of 1991, March 12, 1992, P.L. 102-256, 106 Stat. 73.

44. The onset of the cold war is commonly associated with the communist takeover of Czechoslovakia in early 1948. The Universal Declaration was completed during 1948 and was proclaimed by the UN General Assembly in December 1948.

45. See Henkin et al., *Human Rights*, pp. 355-740.

46. See Ibid., p. 91.

47. Protocol No. 11 to the European Convention replaced the original system of implementation consisting of a commission and a court working part-time, with a single, enlarged, full-time court. See Nicolas Bratza Q.C. and Michael O'Boyle, "The Legacy of the Commission to the New Court Under the Eleventh Protocol," in Michele de Salvia and Mark E. Villiger, *The Birth of European Human Rights Law* (Baden-Baden: Nomos, 1998), p. 377, quoted in Henkin et al., *Human Rights*, p. 554. Also see chapter 5 in this volume.

48. The tribunals were established by resolutions of the UN Security Council under its authority to address threats to international peace and security. See UN Security Council Resolution 827 (1993) establishing the International Criminal Tribunal for the former Yugoslavia, and UN Security Council Resolution 955 (1994) establishing the International Tribunal for Rwanda. See also Henkin et al., *Human Rights*, pp. 618-629; and chapter 9 by Richard Goldstone in this volume.

49. See Philip Alston, "The Commission on Human Rights" in Philip Alston, ed., *The United Nations and Human Rights: A Critical Appraisal* (New York: Oxford University Press, 1992), quoted in Henkin et al., *Human Rights*, p. 688.

50. Economic sanctions under the authority of the Security Council were also imposed against Libya, the former Yugoslavia, Somalia, and others. See Henkin et al., *Human Rights*, p. 695. On the degree to which economic sanctions contributed to the end of apartheid, see Ibid., p. 704, and chapter 13 in this volume.

51. See Henkin et al., *Human Rights*, pp. 112-16.

52. See generally A. H. Robertson, Human Rights in Europe: A Study of the European Convention on Human Rights (Manchester: Manchester University Press, 1993); Mark Janis and Richard S. Kay, European Human Rights Law (Hartford, CT: University of Connecticut Law School Foundation Press, 1990); D. J. Harris, M. O'Boyle, and C. Warbrick, Law of the European Convention on Human Rights (London: Reed Elsevier, 1995). See also Henkin et al., Human Rights, p. 551; and chapter 5 in this volume.

53. The European Court of Justice, sitting in Luxembourg as the Court of the European Community, now the European Union, is to be distinguished from the European Court of Human Rights, which sits in Strasbourg, and which was established under the authority of the Council of Europe. See chapter 5 in this volume; and Henkin et al., Human Rights, p. 599.

54. The United States is a member of the Organization of American States and thereby committed to the American Declaration of the Rights and Duties of Man, adopted in May 1948. The United States signed the American Convention of Human Rights in 1978, subject to reservations, understandings, and declarations but, as of early 2000, the United States has not ratified the Convention. See chapter 6 in this volume. For further information on the American Convention generally, see Scott Davidson, *Inter-American Human Rights System* (Brookfield, VT: Dartmouth Publishing, 1997); Henkin et al., *Human Rights*, pp. 342 et seq., 523 et seq., 784 et seq.

55. In the *Velasquez Rodriguez Case*, 4 Inter-Am. Ct. H.R. (1998, ser. C), the American Court found the Honduran government responsible for the abduction and disappearance of

Velasquez Rodriguez and that the legal process of Honduras was ineffective to provide a remedy. Several witnesses had been either harassed or assassinated. The Court ordered the Honduran government to pay compensation to the abduction victim's next of kin. See Henkin et al., *Human Rights*, p. 525.

56.   Henkin et al., *Human Rights*. The Court stated that, despite Guatemala's reservation at the time of ratification, it violated the American Convention when it extended the death penalty to crimes not covered by its law at the time it became party to the Convention. See *Restrictions to the Death Penalty* (Arts. 4[2] and 4[4] of the American Convention on Human Rights), Advisory Opinion OC–3/83 of September 8, 1983, Inter–Am. Ct. H.R. (Ser. A), No. 3 (1983).

57.   See chapter 7 in this volume.

58.   See Henkin et al., *Human Rights*, part III, Chapter 2, § H.

59.   The example of Pakistan is described in chapter 8 in this volume.

60.   The U.S. Supreme Court has declared that the obligation of *non-refoulement* applies only to refugees already in a state's territory and does not prohibit reaching outside its territory, for example to the high seas, to return a refugee even to oppression or death. *Sale v. Haitian Ctrs. Council, Inc.*, 509 U.S. 155 (1993).

61.   There is also, and in particular, an agenda for the United States. History and national interest call for a leading role for the United States in shaping the international human rights agenda and in ensuring "constitutionalism." International human rights often have been declared a keystone of U.S. foreign policy. In a letter to Benjamin Galloway, in 1812, Thomas Jefferson wrote: "I hope and firmly believe that the whole world will sooner or later feel benefit from the issue of our assertion of the rights of man." *The Writings of Thomas Jefferson*, Memorial Edition, eds. Andrew Lipscomb and Albert Bergh, (Washington, DC: Thomas Jefferson Memorial Association, 1903) Vol. 13, p. 130. But unless the United States moves to the forefront of international human rights—by adhering to the principal covenants and conventions (avoiding or abandoning reservations), by submitting to scrutiny and judgment by international institutions, by assuming responsibility through international institutions to ensure respect for human rights where it is grossly jeopardized, the United States will not earn leadership in international human rights over the twenty-first century.

Human Rights:
Not Merely an Internal Affair

WEI JINGSHENG [*]

Wei Jingsheng was one of the leaders of China's democracy wall movement and the author of an article entitled "The Fifth Modernization" on the indispensability of democracy to Deng Xiaoping's proposed "Four Modernizations." In October 1979 he was convicted for fomenting "counterrevolution" and served fourteen years in prison. Released in 1993, Wei was rearrested in March 1994 and held prisoner until September 1997, when he was removed from his cell and forced to board a plane bound for the United States. He currently serves as a visiting scholar at Columbia University's Center for the Study of Human Rights. While he was in prison he was awarded the Olaf Palme Memorial Prize in 1994, the Robert F. Kennedy Memorial Human Rights Award in 1996, and the National Endowment for Democracy Award for 1997. He was also nominated several times for the Nobel Peace Prize. His prison letters were published in the West in the spring of 1997 as *The Courage to Stand Alone* (trans. Kristina M. Torgeson).

Many of my ideas about society's obligation to protect the basic human rights of its citizens crystallized in 1966, when I came face to face with unspeakable poverty during a trip to northwestern China.[2] I had joined the Red Guard in early 1966, the first year of the Cultural Revolution. Following Mao's orders, the Red Guard traveled about the countryside, "exchanging revolutionary experiences" with Communist Party cadres and "lighting revolutionary fires." But once our initial enthusiasm had worn off a bit, we began to have doubts: If the people who held the power and were the objects of these rebellions were all bad, then, we reasoned, the entire nation and party must have gone bad! None of this was easy for a sixteen-year-old like myself to figure out. I felt that the only way to interpret this complex and contradictory situation accurately was to gain more practical information, so my friends and I boarded a train heading for the Northwest.

At every stop west of Xi'an, crowds of beggars surrounded the train, and as was my habit, I began to hand some of my food to them. But the fellow opposite me said, "Don't give them any more food; they're probably bad class elements, former landlords or rich peasants. . . . We should let them starve." Near the city of Lanzhou, our train stopped at a very small station. In a crowd of children begging at my window, I noticed a girl of seventeen or so whose face and body were smeared with soot and dirt, and whose hair was long and tangled. I thought that even if this girl was from the family of a landlord or a rich peasant, she herself certainly was not rich or a landlord, and so, I rationalized, even if I gave her a bit of food I could not be accused of having an "unclear class sense." As I leaned out the window with some cakes in my hands, I had a shock: I suddenly realized that this girl had no clothes, nothing with which to cover her body but her disheveled and filthy hair.

The train journey lasted two more days, and I was haunted by this scene. Was this situation the "fruit" of socialism? If it was due to a few bad local leaders' evil deeds, death would not be punishment enough for them. I concluded that, in order to discern a society's true respect for human rights, indeed, the true face of society, it was not enough to know conditions in the cities and among the upper echelons; one had to investigate conditions at the lowest levels as well. I did not imagine then that this investigation would continue for so many years.

My journey would lead me to the Democracy Wall, where, in the winter of 1978, my friends and I published our views on human rights, democracy, and the rule of law. For this, many of us spent our youths and even middle years in prison. I discovered, after I left prison in 1997 and arrived in the United States, that some of these friends had been lost forever. However, the price they paid has brought incalculable gains. In the China of twenty years ago, few people understood what human rights were about; due to the deceptive propaganda of the Chinese Communist Party, people had a twisted idea about human rights and the rule of law. They hoped that the emergence of a few good men from inside the party would better their lot and regarded human rights as a favor bestowed on them by their rulers. It was this ignorance that was used by the dictators to control, oppress, and exploit the majority of the people.

My friends and I sought to make people aware of their own rights and interests and free them from the deception by their oppressors, and although it took twenty years, our efforts have yielded dramatic results. Today the majority of Chinese not only understand what human rights mean but are also striving mightily to achieve the rights that belong to them in the first place. I have found that when many people around the world today talk about human rights, they often have very different concepts of what human rights mean. Thus I feel that it is necessary to spell out what human rights mean. One of the ideas about human rights still prevalent in academic and political circles comes from the Marxist concept that "man's nature is the sum of his social relations." Some people take this to mean that, as different societies have different social relations and the sums of such relations are different, there are also different human natures. Thus, different views on and practices of human rights are appropriate for different types of human natures, and the rationality of all of these should be fully recognized. It would be unnatural to have uniform requirements.

People are not, however, merely products of social relations, nor indeed of any relations. We are not robots, nor are we created by other people based on a pattern for man. Rather, we are products of nature, and our essential qualities are likewise a product of nature. These are instinctive and very basic, and they constitute a shared human legacy that is inborn, possessed by all, and on which all other human natures and social relations are based. Human rights and basic freedoms refer to the satisfying or realizing of this part of human nature. They are the sum of hopes and aspirations that emerge naturally and do not need to be taught.

Human rights are themselves a type of social relation, in the sense that respect and protection of human rights and basic freedoms require social institutions, a social system, and a mechanism to ensure their effectiveness. These primary-level social relations emerge from man's basic nature or, put another way, are the foundation of all social relations.

In contrast are those social relations that are derived from and stipulated or manufactured by man. For example, wherever a great amount of social injustice is enshrined in law—that is to say, where the cornerstone of a legal system is social injustice maintained through violence—the social models are societies of enslavement, such as slavery and fascism. But we cannot say that within these societies the basic freedoms and rights of some of the people actually have been extinguished by law. Law derives from people's social nature; it is not the sole or most basic standard for social relations. Human rights are a more fundamental standard, and no law can change this.

Another school of thought suggests that, because of differences in cultural traditions and social systems, different human rights standards should be applied to different countries. The most typical representative of this school of thought is the so-called Asian values theory, which holds that people should be content with the human rights standards stipulated in the laws of their country.

If such a theory were valid, however, then all human rights conditions would be reasonable and there would be no such thing as "human rights problems." What, then, would be the use of talking about "international cooperation on human rights," "condemning so-and-so for gross human rights violations," "resolutely imposing sanctions against so-and-so's apartheid," and so forth? China, for example, is a sovereign state, but so are other states. China's leaders may say that its human rights standards are "stipulated by law and represent the will of the government," but is this not also true of other countries? Human rights conditions in China are, say its leaders, the consequences of "cultural traditions, the social system, and historical changes." But do they think that in other countries human rights conditions just fell out of the sky? The Chinese leadership says China's "internal affairs" will bear no interference, but does it think other countries welcome China's interference in their "internal affairs"? All this goes to show that the "theory of different standards" does not hold water, because China's leaders cannot prove that their laws and policies are of a reasonable standard while those of others are not. In order to prove that theirs are reasonable, they must cite more objective standards, and they cannot do so.

Thus it is clear that, although the safeguarding of human rights and basic freedoms depends on legislation and policy enforcement on the part of sovereign states, human rights themselves are based on objective standards that cannot be modified by legislation and cannot be changed by the will of the government. "Human rights issues" pertain to how a government protects and respects the rights of its individual citizens, not how reasonable the government is in its actions. These issues have to do with how to protect the relatively weak rights of individuals under the relatively strong organs of power. They are objective standards that apply equally to all governments and all individuals, and no one is entitled to special standards. Like objective existence and objective laws, they are objective truths. That was why Rousseau called them "natural rights."

These natural rights are rights with which every person is born. They are things that we fight for as a matter of course. No one needs to be taught by "hostile countries and hostile forces" to do so. They are the natural laws and natural rights of life. Just like eating or having sex, they are instinctive, and that is why they are called "natural." It is obscene sophistry to try to argue that people can do without food because there are some people who have nothing to eat, or that people can do without sex because there are widows and bachelors around. It is similarly insupportable to argue that people do not need human rights because they are able to adapt to an animal-like existence, or because there are people who consciously act in a servile manner; or to argue that there are no such things as objective human rights standards simply because dictatorial slave societies still exist.

It is precisely because human rights are independent of the will of the government, and even independent of the will of all mankind, that people fight for the realization and expansion of human rights as a natural matter of course, without outside provocation. They gradually come to the realization that the more widespread and reliable the protection of human rights is, the more their own human rights are protected.

However, just as a person's understanding of objective truths and objective laws is a gradual and progressive process, a person's understanding and comprehension of human rights is a gradual and progressive process. Thus, one may say that China's theories and practices in this regard are simply less advanced and that human rights conditions differ in different countries and nations under different cultural conditions and social systems. However, the existence of different conditions and views cannot be taken as an excuse to violate and disregard human rights; nor does it demonstrate that laws enacted by individuals can override objective truths or prove that laws that violate human rights are justified. Any doctrine that preaches the supremacy of law or holds that the law is not the servant of the people's will or the embodiment of objective truths is just another form of fascism. Where the people and the truth become the servant of absolute law and its enforcers, and where the people and the truth become subordinate to the ruler's will as expressed in the name of the law and the state, this is fascism.

Chinese people as a whole find the fascist roots of this "doctrine of the supremacy of law" quite unacceptable. Most Chinese people judge whether a person is right or wrong based on whether he or she abides by the law, but they also judge whether or not the law is right by looking at whether it protects and serves the people. They take particular care in judging those who enforce the law. There is no acceptance or approval of a doctrine of "the supremacy of the law": When there is a conflict between the people and the law, most Chinese people favor putting the people first.

Although this may sound like the human rights theory handed down since the time of Rousseau, it is also the essence of the humanistic and democratic tradition found in traditional Chinese culture. This tradition has been deeply rooted in Chinese people's hearts for over two thousand years. It cannot be pushed aside for a feudal or prefeudal ideology that says that the "law" is supreme over the rights of human beings.

China's rulers and their allies in Western academia try to respond to such arguments by taking a step back. They agree that it is, perhaps, permissible to discuss the issue of human rights and to carry out international cooperation on human rights, but they still argue that it is "unnatural" to preach specific values, ideologies, and models.

This argument is no stronger than the others. The difference between a democratic system that respects and protects human rights and basic freedoms and a totalitarian system that does not lies in the differences in their social models, in a difference in ideologies—the theories on the basis of which social models are established and exist—and in a difference in values, the basis for these ideologies.

Whether a system respects and protects human rights is what basically distinguishes the values of democracy and freedom from those of totalitarianism and enslavement. The values of Hitler or any totalitarian ruler can only produce fascism or Nazism, an ideology that takes away or suppresses individual rights and freedoms in the name of the state or the society. A social system established on the basis of such an ideology can only be a Nazi or totalitarian social model.

If people are allowed to discuss the issue of human rights and carry out international cooperation on human rights, they will naturally try to interfere with, stop, and change those systems or institutions that do not respect and protect human rights. For example, opposition to, and sanctions against, South African apartheid illustrated the potential power of large-scale international cooperation on human rights. If, in such an exercise, people are not allowed to promote values based on the basic human right of equality for all, or to rely on the ideology of "democracy based on individuals" in trying to promote a social model of democracy and freedom, but instead are allowed to speak only within certain limits prescribed by law, such cooperation on human rights cannot be effective. Instead it is nothing more than a fig leaf covering the ugly features of the anti–human rights social model of enslavement; it is merely a clever trick to oppose social progress. Discussion of the issue of human rights and international cooperation on human rights is not merely an academic exercise, but is essential to the protection of human rights. If we are not able to exert pressure from within and without regarding various human rights issues, then we will have little means to safeguard human rights. Therefore, dictators and their Western allies have advanced yet another rule: It is permissible to discuss and even protect human rights, but no international pressure will be tolerated. The logical extension of this argument is that emancipation of human rights can come about only through the dictatorship's own choice.

Any social model, without exception, that is based on dictatorship and enslavement, and that does not respect human rights, is held together by force and in defiance of reason. However, if it is reasonable and can accept reasonable exchanges of views, it can evolve toward a democratic social model that respects human rights. This prerequisite is essential if inadequate protection of human rights is to be rectified and remedied through discussion and cooperation. Even then, the governments of these countries may not take the initiative to make major moves to improve their human rights conditions unless they are subjected to pressures from within and without. The civil rights movement that took place in the United States not long ago is an obvious case in point.

A social model that must be held together by deception and violence can give rise only to a society of enslavement where human rights are not respected. Such regimes recognize authority based on violence and strength, or the threat of violence, but they do not recognize rights that should be respected and protected. Their maxim is that political power grows out of the barrel of a gun; in other words, if you win a country on horseback, you must rule it on horseback. Brute force rather than the people's will constitutes the cornerstone of these regimes. Such is the essence of dictatorship.

In such circumstances, there are only two ways for the people to bring about changes: either by using violence to counter violence and toppling the government through revolution, or by forcing it to change gradually, that is, to reform, through the exertion of pressure from within and without. Reform is better because it is less destructive. Although it entails greater difficulty and complexity, it ensures a more stable and predictable situation. It will be socially, politically, economically, and culturally less damaging to the country itself and to countries with related interests. Thus one way to minimize losses and setbacks for all sides is for countries with related interests to exert pressure and help bring about internal progress and reform.

If, however, other countries are not allowed to exert pressure, and the forces of reform are left to fight the bloody and powerful apparatus of violence alone, they will have only one choice: violent revolution with its numerous setbacks, huge losses, and uncertain future.

The Chinese Communist Party has said that the fascist regimes of Hitler and Mussolini owed their expansion to the fact that the international community "did not exert any pressure or intervene in their internal affairs." In various official documents, the party called this a "policy of appeasement" and said that "the stupid imperialist governments and profit-seeking bourgeoisie" were thus partly to blame for the outbreak of World War II. I think that is a correct historical conclusion, and it is a principle that applies today as well. The lesson should be heeded by China's friends.

The majority of Chinese people today seek to realize their fundamental human rights. Their goals are not complicated. Workers demand the rights to work, to receive reasonable pay, and to organize to protect their interests; peasants demand the rights to own their own land and to be free of excessive taxes and levies; couples demand the rights to bear children, to protect their children against mistreatment, and to be free of hunger and cold; and so forth. Ordinary citizens of China are relying on themselves to fight for their rights. With this huge internal pressure bearing down on it, the Chinese Communist Party is fast losing its grip on Chinese society.

China's friends should recognize that they now face a serious choice. The present time offers a great opportunity to exert outside pressure on the Chinese Communist Party to abandon its outdated human rights policy and convert to a democratic political system. Or, through appeasement, China's friends can instead help the Chinese Communist Party ride out a difficult period so that this oppressive, exploitative regime can be prolonged. But the latter leads inevitably to a third and most likely scenario following the pattern of recent events in Zaire, the Philippines, and Indonesia. When the West, placing its commercial interests first, chooses a policy of appeasement, dictatorships may be prolonged for a certain period of time. But it is impossible to maintain a regime that is spurned by the entire society, and if the people are forced to use violence to end the rule of the dictatorship, the process will inevitably bring significant shocks and destruction to the international community as well as to the country concerned. As China accounts for one-quarter of the world's population, its impact would be enormous.

More important, if Western support delays the downfall of a dictatorship, the damage to China's economic, cultural, and sociopsychological lives will be even more severe, and there will be more difficulties to surmount once a new social system is established. Any Western power that lends its help and support to a dictatorship spurned by the people should be held responsible for the consequences from such a scenario.

In reality, it is the citizens—those who wage heroic struggles against the totalitarian regime—who will bear the brunt of the consequences. Such an unfair outcome would undoubtedly cast a dark shadow on the society's psyche for a long time. One of the first signs of this shadow would be resentment toward pro-Western politicians. This shadow in the minds of the people would have a long-term destructive effect on the relationship with the West.

Human rights are never merely luxuries or hobbies. They concern the destiny and future of humankind, and no national borders or customs check-points can stop their impact. The positions and policies we adopt on the issue of human rights today will influence the lives and political relations of humankind for hundreds of years. We should not leave these decisions in the hands of a few business-people who have no sense of political responsibility. Only when every responsible political leader adheres to the "rights" position and policies will the world have a better tomorrow.

NOTES

* Wei Jingsheng drew portions of this chapter from his autobiography, *The Courage to Stand Alone: Letters from Prison and Other Writings,* translated by Kristina M. Torgeson, ©1997 by Wei Jingsheng. Used by permission of Viking Penguin, a division of Penguin Putnam Inc.

1. See also Wei Jingsheng, "From Maoist Fanatic to Political Dissident: An Autobiographical Essay (1979)" in Wei, *The Courage to Stand Alone,* Appendix III, pp.229-48.

The American Road
to a Human Rights Policy

JIMMY CARTER*

Jimmy Carter was the thirty-ninth President of the United States (1977–
1981). He now is chairman of the nonprofit Carter Center, affiliated with
Emory University in Atlanta, Georgia. The Carter Center "wages peace" by
bringing warring parties to the negotiating table, monitoring elections, and
urging states to safeguard human rights and build strong democracies through
economic development. The Center also works to fight disease, increase crop
production, and promote preventive health care in the United States and
abroad. President Carter's fourteen books include *Keeping Faith: Memoirs of a
President, Turning Point: A Candidate, a State, and a Nation Come of Age*, and
Talking Peace: A Vision for the Next Generation.

In 1981, as I left the U.S. presidency, I said, "America did not invent human
rights. In a very real sense . . . human rights invented America."[1] The United
States is founded—indeed, predicated—on the principles enshrined in the
Declaration of Independence and our Bill of Rights. The pursuit of liberty and
of human freedom that united this nation in revolution continues to bind us
together and to create a special role for America in the world. We invent a new,
more responsible America every time we take the lead in attempting to secure
and expand basic human rights at home and abroad. This does not mean we

should appoint ourselves the world policeman. It means we must use our awesome resources to function both as a responsible and participatory world citizen and as a world leader.

We Americans have never been perfect in our observance of human rights. Constitutionally protected slavery marred the first century of our existence. Women acquired the right to vote in national elections only in 1920, after a seventy-five-year struggle. Even today, the United States does not always fulfill all its promises to its citizens.[2] But we are progressing as we consistently expand our understanding of what human rights mean.

SOURCES OF INCREASING HUMAN RIGHTS AWARENESS

Today no nation can avoid discussing human rights. Media attention, the activities of international and regional organizations, the huge increase in the numbers of nongovernmental organizations (NGOs) devoted to human rights concerns, and the foreign policies of many governments force every nation at least to defend its policies and often to correct them.

The new prominence of human rights can be traced to several circumstances that emerged out of the upheavals of World War II. One was the momentum caused by the process of decolonization in Asia and Africa and the subsequent process of economic and political development. A second reason for the salience of human rights is the technological revolution, including information technology and biotechnology. Fax machines, television, and e-mail give individuals the power to learn about or communicate with others around the world, without dependence on a government's permission or vulnerability to its control. Meanwhile a revolution in biotechnology has the potential to provide significantly increased access to food and economic prosperity. A third reason is American leadership, both from the leaders of the grass-roots civil rights movement and from individuals in government committed to human rights.

Decolonization and Development

Colonial rule reached its peak between the two world wars. All of sub-Saharan Africa, except for Ethiopia and Liberia, was under European control, and so were large parts of Asia. After World War II, it became increasingly clear that colonialism was antithetical to principles in the United Nations Charter and the Universal Declaration of Human Rights. Revolutionary struggles for independence swept through Asia first, bringing independence to Indonesia in 1945, the Philippines in 1946, India in 1947, Burma in 1948, Laos in 1949, Cambodia in 1953, and North and South Vietnam in 1954. The same struggle swept over Africa, starting with the creation of Ghana in 1957, and during the 1960s resulted in the independence of the former French, British, and Belgian territories on that continent. The Portuguese territories were freed in the 1970s. Many of the revolutionaries used language taken from the U.S. Declaration of Independence and the Bill of Rights, although the words of Marx and Lenin often were influential as well. The transition of governments in Zimbabwe in 1980, in Namibia in 1990, and finally in South Africa in 1994 was based on majority rule.

As new nations claimed the right of self-determination, membership in the UN grew from the 51 original member states in 1945 to 185 nations today. This process helped spread the human rights message. The representatives of new states often articulated their struggles in human rights terms, and they transformed the UN General Assembly into a much more pluralistic body, unafraid to speak out against abuses committed by the Western world and eager to hold developed nations to the universal standards they formally endorsed.

The spotlight that exposed the gap between theory and practice in the foreign policy of various democracies also fixed itself upon domestic shortcomings in the United States. As Martin Luther King, Jr., wrote, "The nations of Asia and Africa are moving with jet-like speed toward the goal of political independence, and we still creep at horse and buggy pace toward the gaining of a cup of coffee at a lunch counter."[3] The American civil rights leaders admired the success of revolutionary movements fighting for freedom abroad. Mohandas K. Gandhi's nonviolent independence movement in India served as a model of peaceful resistance and a major inspiration to other leaders, including Dr. King. In turn, Dr. King's writings, speeches, and living example inspired leaders abroad, from South Africa's Nelson Mandela to Tibet's Dalai Lama. Many have spoken of how his example of nonviolence inspired them in leading their own advocacy campaigns.

In 1960 black students and others desiring change began to create nonviolent grass-roots groups and to organize sit-ins, challenging segregation laws in the southeastern United States and encouraging black voter registration. Within two years, 70,000 people became involved in the movement; 3,600 were arrested and many died in the struggle. The task they set for themselves was daunting, yet even in the face of entrenched tradition and opposition, they managed to bring about change.

The civil rights period was a turning point in my own life as well as in the course of our nation.[4] In 1962, as I campaigned for the State Senate in Georgia, I faced strong opposition from those who supported the entrenched segregationist laws and traditions in the South. This election opened my eyes to the tasks ahead.

Later, in my inauguration address as governor to succeed the archconservative Lester Maddox, I said, "The time for racial discrimination is over. Our people have already made this major and difficult decision, but we cannot underestimate the challenge of hundreds of minor decisions yet to be made. . . . No poor, rural, weak, or black person should ever have to bear the additional burden of being deprived of the opportunity of an education, a job, or simple justice."[5]

The civil rights movement brought an end to legal segregation in the American South and immediate benefits came to all citizens. However, the results of decolonization within the less developed world have been mixed. Tragically, the euphoria of the early days of independence, when it seemed as if self-government would bring prosperity and human rights to the nations of Africa and Asia, has in too many cases turned into despair. Poverty, war, and despotism have limited the victories that were achieved. The state of human rights is distressing in many new nations.

To address these and other challenge to human rights, my wife Rosalynn and I founded the Carter Center in 1982. This nonprofit NGO gives special attention to the poorest nations. At the Center, we eradicate disease, teach farmers how to increase crop yields, monitor elections, and help people devise strategies for their own development. Because I believe that war is the greatest violation of basic human rights that one people can inflict upon another, I have been eager to help when invited by adversaries to engage in conflict prevention and conflict resolution efforts.

Technology

Another force for change is technology. Modern communications have helped bring human rights to the forefront of policy and public consciousness. Anyone in possession of a fax machine with a telephone link or a computer and an e-mail account now can perform human rights advocacy work anywhere in the world.[6] Anyone who can log on to the Web site of an NGO such as Human Rights Watch or Amnesty International can learn instantly of human rights violations. At the Carter Center, we use a Web site to explain our mission, recruit interns, display information about our ongoing projects and conferences, and solicit support for our work.[7] The free flow of information available through these new media should give hope to those who would otherwise find themselves silenced by government repression or inadequate resources.

Biotechnology also plays a role in human rights because of its potential to make it easier for people to achieve food self-sufficiency.[8] At the dawn of the twenty-first century, starvation and malnutrition remain serious threats. Recent statistics from the Food and Agriculture Organization show that almost

800 million people in developing countries are undernourished.[9] Nowhere is this problem more critical than in sub-Saharan Africa, where the population is likely to double over the next twenty-five years. Wars and bad government policies should receive much of the blame for food shortages. This is a problem that can be overcome.

Responsible agricultural biotechnology can play a pivotal role in improving health and nutrition. Existing technologies can increase farmland productivity, but efforts must be made to share these relatively simple techniques with small-scale farmers. For over a decade, the Carter Center and the Sasakawa-Africa Association have been involved in a grass-roots agricultural effort in twelve African countries called Sasakawa–Global 2000 (SG 2000), led by the American agricultural scientist and Nobel laureate Norman Borlaug. Working with heads of state, ministries of agriculture, international development agencies, and more than 600,000 family-run small-scale farms, SG 2000 has proven that it is possible to double, triple, and even quadruple crop yields applying existing technology and simple techniques such as contour planting, use of improved seed and modest amounts of fertilizer, and timely weed control.

Important new discoveries in biotechnology can improve the economic outlook for millions. For instance, a remarkable opportunity exists to use biotechnological advances in maize, or corn, the primary food grain consumed by people throughout the world who are most in danger of starvation. Until recently all maize was deficient in lycine and tryptophan, two amino acids that are necessary for the nourishment of people and animals. Scientists at CIMMYT, the international agricultural research center in Mexico, developed seed that produce what we call quality-protein maize, which includes these amino acids and is, in effect, a complete food. We have helped to introduce this crop in Ghana, South Africa, Brazil, and China and are now proposing to plant it in North Korea.

My concern is that many people in developing countries around the world, as well as residents of low-income communities in the United States, may not have access to these new technologies. Here and elsewhere the gap is increasing between resources available to the wealthy and those accessible to the poor. Nevertheless, information technology already has made a profound difference by decreasing the isolation and powerlessness of human rights advocates and victims of human rights abuses, and biotechnology has great potential to prevent starvation and increase prosperity.

American Leadership

A third source of the new emphasis on human rights arises from American leadership after World War II. When my administration announced its intention to give human rights a higher priority in American policy, we were following the lead of former presidents, including Harry Truman and Lyndon Johnson. President Truman forcefully and effectively advocated human rights on an international scale with support for the formation of the United Nations, recognition of the State of Israel, and efforts to establish democracies in Japan and Germany after World War II and to reintegrate these vanquished nations into the global community. As I started my career in public service in the early 1960s, I was also deeply impressed by President Johnson's reforms on behalf of civil and social rights at home. His administration secured the passage of important civil rights legislation, including the Voting Rights Act of 1965 and the Civil Rights Act of 1964, the most comprehensive and far-reaching civil rights legislation since the Civil War. Johnson also introduced social programs such as Medicare and created the Department of Housing and Urban Development (HUD) to address the decline of America's inner cities.

In the early 1970s, the American people had been deeply embarrassed by the conduct of the Vietnam War, the revelations of the Watergate scandal, and the illegal activities of the Central Intelligence Agency (CIA). I believed I was elected president in 1976 to attempt to restore justice and morality to government. My administration deliberately set out to put human rights high on the United States foreign policy agenda. In my inaugural address I said: "Because we are free we can never be indifferent to the fate of freedom elsewhere. Our moral sense dictates a clear-cut preference for those societies which share with us an abiding respect for individual human rights. We do not seek to intimidate, but it is clear that a world which others can dominate with impunity would be inhospitable to decency and a threat to the well-being of all people."[10]

I wanted to spread throughout the executive branch the understanding that a concern for human rights should be our guiding spirit. Before the presidential election in 1976, a Democratic Congress had enacted a law requiring the State Department to evaluate and report on the state of human rights in nations designated to receive military-related aid. We aimed to follow through in implementing this legislation.

Less than five weeks after I assumed office, we announced our intention to reduce U.S. aid to Argentina, Ethiopia, and Uruguay because of gross human rights violations committed by their ruling regimes. I declared my intention to regard every American ambassador as my personal human rights rapporteur: I asked them to take personal responsibility for writing and submitting their *Country Reports* on human rights.[11] The State Department's new Bureau of Human Rights and Humanitarian Affairs began to play a key role in U.S. human rights goals. Patricia Derian, whom I asked to head the Bureau as its coordinator, helped develop the position to one that deserved the status of assistant secretary.

Derian had entered the international human rights arena with an extensive background in civil rights in Mississippi, and her passion helped fuel our progress. She was not shy about using unequivocal words like "torture" when remonstrating with leaders of foreign countries that had poor records on human rights. Her candor forced many a government to realize that the United States truly meant to bring human rights into serious discussion.

Our goal was to infuse the subject of human rights with new meaning, to show that we saw human rights not as a flowery phrase but as a universal responsibility. The fate of human rights activists and political prisoners in the Soviet Union and Eastern Europe was one of my earliest concerns and remained important to me throughout my term. But it was essential that human rights not be used merely as a weapon of the cold war. We had to hold anticommunist regimes to an equally strict standard.

We decided that one of our major roles would be to try to effect change in Latin America, where numerous military governments had taken power. In the 1960s and 1970s, human rights abuses were widespread in many countries there, among them Argentina, Brazil, Chile, Uruguay, Bolivia, El Salvador, Guatemala, Haiti, Nicaragua, Paraguay, and Cuba. We sought to emphasize the human rights violations that we thought we could best affect, namely, the problems of summary executions and the torture of political prisoners. We signed the American Convention on Human Rights in June 1977. This Convention, which the U.S. Congress has not yet ratified, created a new Inter-American Court of Human Rights and gave to the Inter-American Commission on Human Rights (which had been established in 1959 by the Organization of American States) the authority to supervise the observance of the civil and political rights and freedoms listed in the Convention.[12] Within a year, the number of ratifying countries went from two to fourteen, committing their regimes to respect and protect the twenty-six rights and freedoms enumerated in the Convention and allowing the Court to investigate alleged abuses, which included the disappearance of civilians in several repressive countries. In addition, we quadrupled the budget of the Inter-American Commission on Human Rights; worked to cut off foreign economic or security aid when necessary; and used bilateral diplomacy in support of human rights. My wife, Rosalynn, went as my representative to Brazil, Peru, Ecuador, Venezuela, Costa Rica, Jamaica, and Colombia to seek a better understanding of how the United States could encourage the transition to democracy. Our successes proved the influence that the United States can bring to bear in garnering international support for human rights covenants; we should never forget that we have such power.

The Bill of Rights in the U.S. Constitution has guided our way at home, but it is the International Bill of Human Rights that provides a guide for the entire world. In 1977, my first year as president, I signed the two international covenants (the International Covenant on Civil and Political Rights and the International Covenant on Economic, Social and Cultural Rights) on human rights that, together with the Universal Declaration of Human Rights, constitute this International Bill of Human Rights.[13] These covenants do not reflect the world as it is. Yet they incorporate the same inspiration and impetus for change that our early American legislators included in our founding documents.

RECOMMENDATIONS

Implementing effective human rights policy has never been easy, even in a country that boasts a legacy that includes the Declaration of Independence and the Bill of Rights. However, my recommendations to advance human rights in the twenty-first century are directed at the American policymaker and the American public, because the United States, with all its resources, is in a unique leadership position to explore and develop "what works" in human rights policy. A few immediate steps by the United States would serve to advance human rights in the near future. First, the United States should promote, not oppose, the institutionalization of an International Criminal Court, addressing the basic human right to safety and justice.[14] Second, we should ratify the international Convention on the Rights of the Child.[15] Third, we must join other nations in outlawing land mines.[16] Fourth, we must ratify the International Covenant on Economic, Social and Cultural Rights. And fifth, whatever our legal commitments, we must work harder to close the growing division between rich and poor, addressing human rights on an economic and social level. I urge these steps because the United States has the resources to implement change in these areas if it can muster sufficient political will.

It is unfortunate that the U.S. government has sought to block efforts to create an International Criminal Court. The Geneva Conventions and the Genocide Convention as well as our current mechanisms to secure state compliance to end genocide and crimes against humanity have failed. The atrocities perpetrated in the former Yugoslavia and Rwanda are the sad evidence of this. We owe it to the world to do all we can to ensure that efficient mechanisms are in place to prosecute those who commit such crimes. Were our government to support the International Criminal Court, it is likely that the Court would be established quickly. We could then reap the benefits of having a permanent court for prosecuting suspected perpetrators of crimes against humanity, without having to wait years for the procedures and structures of special tribunals to be institutionalized. The permanent Court would have a legitimacy that the tribunals set up by the UN Security Council to prosecute crimes against humanity in the former Yugoslavia and Rwanda have lacked, owing both to their ad hoc status and to their institutional growing pains. As the major financial supporter of these courts, the United States is familiar with their virtues and their vices, and it should be aware that the International Criminal Court would be a more effective and efficient option. By ending our obstructionist policies toward the Court, we would be acting upon our long-standing national conviction that judicial processes must not be vulnerable to politics or personal preferences. A Court with U.S. support could act as a strong deterrent to crimes against humanity. The International Criminal Court represents a long-term investment in the future safety of humankind.

Only two nations have failed to guarantee international protection for the rights of children: Somalia and the United States. Somalia can explain its refusal by pointing to the fact that it lacks a working government, but the United States has a much more difficult task explaining its stance. Some American critics of the Convention on the Rights of the Child misinterpret the document, worrying, for instance, that it undermines parental rights, when, in fact, it repeatedly emphasizes the primacy of the role and authority of parents. One of the primary impediments cited for our refusal to ratify is that the treaty prohibits the death penalty for children. Some key members of the U.S. Senate insist that a global commitment would constitute an unacceptable infringement on states' rights in the United States. Although U.S. laws do secure most basic rights for American children, we need to support this agreement for the sake of children everywhere. The United States should be a world leader, not a laggard, in global efforts to protect the world's children.

The United States has led opposition to the global effort to outlaw the use of land mines. These terrible weapons ensnare victims who are primarily helpless and innocent citizens rather than soldiers engaged in active warfare. The United States claims it must employ land mines in order to protect American forces who are helping to defend the demilitarized zone between North and South Korea. This is a hollow excuse.

I was pleased when the U.S. Senate finally ratified the International Covenant on Civil and Political Rights in 1992, though disappointed that it was encumbered with reservations, understandings, and declarations. I am still hopeful that the United States eventually will ratify the International Covenant on Economic, Social and Cultural Rights. Human rights are not only a matter of political and civil rights, such as reducing the incidence of summary executions or torture of political prisoners, protecting the right to emigrate freely, and defending against discrimination; they also comprise basic rights to a peaceful existence, a job, food, shelter, medical care, and education. Making a pledge of the scope and breadth embodied in these Covenants, even if not fully realizable all at once, would publicly commit our nation to strive toward securing basic standards of material existence, social justice, and cultural opportunities for our citizens. We underestimate the tremendous global influence of the United States. When we fail to ratify these Covenants, it sends a message of despair to those who suffer human rights abuses and encourages the persecutors to be more intransigent.

The growing division between the rich and the poor is a topic on which I have written extensively, and there have been few reasons for my concerns to diminish. According to the United Nations Development Programme, in thirty-five years the gap between the richest and poorest has nearly tripled.[17] This is unconscionable in a world that has the resources we amassed in the twentieth century. If we do not succeed in reducing the disparity, it threatens to upset the human rights gains that we have achieved since World War II. We know that disparity breeds discontent and violence. The United States should reexamine its legislative priorities and its aid to foreign countries in this light.

We also should aim to achieve a more equitable international effort to reduce global poverty: Foreign aid deserves a much greater percentage of the U.S. budget, and polls show that U.S. citizens would support such an increase. Although for years the United States has been one of the largest foreign aid donors in absolute terms, it provides less foreign aid, as a percentage of its gross national product, than any other major industrialized nation. Few Americans, however, seem to know that we are one of the stingiest countries on earth when it comes to foreign aid. Each American contributes just twelve and a half cents in foreign assistance for every dollar given by a Norwegian, for example.[18] In a public opinion poll commissioned by the U.S. Agency for International Development (USAID), Americans estimated the foreign aid share of the U.S. budget at 15 percent, far higher than the actual figure, which is barely 1 percent of total federal spending. Once informed of the actual amount, Americans said they would raise the amount of aid we provide. The median target cited was close to 5 percent of the federal budget. In other words, U.S. citizens are willing to support a level of foreign aid many times over what the United States now makes available.[19] In another poll, Americans were asked to estimate the U.S. share of all development aid, given by all countries in the world. The median respondent estimated that the United States was responsible for 60 percent of all the world's aid and said it should be 40 percent. In fact, the U.S. share is just 13 percent.[20] While these polls tell us that Americans overestimate how supportive we are to the rest of the world, they also tell us that our citizens are prepared to be much more generous than we actually are. Increased foreign aid, thoughtfully applied, could lead to major improvements in human rights around the world. Foreign assistance constitutes one of the best ways to ensure democratic institution building and freedom. It also works to reduce the likelihood of political instability and its potential for violence and atrocities.

Even if U.S. foreign aid increases, however, governments cannot shoulder the entire burden of coordinating training programs, supplying agricultural equipment, and providing other economic assistance. Corporations, universities, and NGOs also have a role to play in expanding opportunities for education, adequate health care, and food supply. For example, many NGOs have the skills and resources to work in collaboration with governments and governmental organizations. The Oslo Peace Accords superbly illustrated this. A group of social science professors from Norway with no governmental experience went into Gaza to analyze the plight of Palestinian refugees, and there they began to talk to some low-ranking Israelis. Through personal connections, this group was able to secure the help of Norway's foreign ministry to develop the secret negotiations that eventually resulted in the Oslo agreement.

Both the United Nations and the U.S. government (through USAID) have programs that work in partnership with NGOs to support grass-roots development activities. The U.S. government should work to strengthen these partnerships and increase the numbers of local NGOs involved. Hundreds of NGOs around the world are eager to be called upon by government officials and to supply information and coordination from the ground. Other nations should follow the example set by Norway and tap this enormous potential.

CONCLUSION

The United States is now unchallenged as the world's only superpower. A superpower should be known as the dedicated champion of peace, freedom and democracy, human rights, and the alleviation of suffering. It should exert its maximum effort to secure these goals wherever and whenever possible and should coordinate its efforts with the United Nations and nongovernmental organizations. Now, more than ever, human rights advocates must continue to help the United States choose policy paths that will serve as an example and lead to responsible, moral, and just governance worldwide. We must do this without arrogance. We should be proud of our progress but humble in light of the long struggle behind us and the hurdles ahead.

As we enter the next century, bloody civil conflicts envelop parts of Africa and southeastern Europe, health crises strike the developing world, and inequalities persist in our own society. The United States must never forget the human responsibilities that go hand in hand with the human rights we are fortunate to hold and protect. As Article 29 of the Universal Declaration of Human Rights states: "Everyone has duties to the community in which alone the free and full development of his personality is possible." We should view these duties as a blessing that allows us to learn more about the world in which we live and to connect more fully with our fellow citizens of the world. The maxim "think globally, act locally" cannot be repeated often enough, but our leaders must also "act globally." Our teachers, our business community leaders, our scientists, our human rights advocates, and, above all, our elected officials can help map paths for responsible public action and human rights policy. Likewise, activists such as Wei Jingsheng and Leonid Romankov can inspire peaceful resistance to oppression around the world.[21] Let us keep the faith in human action.

NOTES

*   I wish to thank Ingrid Tamm Grudin at the Carr Center for Human Rights Policy for her contributions to this chapter.
1.   "Farewell Address to the Nation," January 14, 1981, in *Public Papers of the Presidents of the United States: Jimmy Carter, 1980–81* (Washington, DC: U.S. Government Printing Office, 1982), Book III, p. 2892.
2.   See, for example, the report of Amnesty International's campaign on the USA, *United States of America: Rights for All* (London: Amnesty International Publications, 1998).
3.   "Letter from the Birmingham Jail," Martin Luther King, Jr., *I Have a Dream: Writings and Speeches that Changed the World,* ed. James Melvin Washington (San Francisco: HarperSanFrancisco, 1992), p. 88.
4.   Jimmy Carter, *Turning Point: A Candidate, a State, and a Nation Come of Age* (New York: Times Books, 1992).
5.   January 12, 1971, in Jimmy Carter, *A Government as Good as Its People,* new ed. (Fayetteville: University of Arkansas Press, 1996), p. 4.
6.   On the eve of the tenth anniversary of the Tiananmen Square killings, it was reported by Reuters that, "in a sign of jitters, authorities pulled the plug on cyberspace chat rooms and U.S. television network CNN at major hotels and apartment buildings in Beijing. Other international satellite channels have also been suspended 'for maintenance.'" Beijing, Thursday, June 3, 1999, 3:40 PM ET, "China Calm on Tiananmen Eve, Scores Detained."
7.   The Carter Center's Web site is <http://www.CarterCenter.org/>.
8.   The right to food is called for by the International Convention on Economic, Cultural and Social Rights. In May 1997 the Director-General of the UN Food and Agriculture Organization and the UN High Commissioner for Human Rights signed a Memorandum of Understanding for cooperation in defining the rights related to food and in proposing ways to implement and realize these rights. As of June 1999, twenty countries had incorporated the right to adequate food into their constitutions.
9.   In addition, 34 million people in industrialized countries and countries in transition also suffer from chronic food insecurity. See the Food and Agricultural Organization's report, "The State of Food Insecurity in the World 1999" on their Web site: <http://www.fao.org/FOCUS/E/SOFI/home-e.htm>.

10. "Inaugural Address," January 20, 1977, in *Public Papers of the Presidents of the United States: Jimmy Carter, 1977* (Washington, DC: U.S. Government Printing Office, 1977), Book I, p. 3.

11. The *Country Reports* on human rights were initiated by Congress in 1974, as John Shattuck describes in his contribution to this volume.

12. See Juan Mendez's contribution in this volume.

13. The International Covenant on Civil and Political Rights (ICCPR) and the International Covenant on Economic, Social and Cultural Rights (ICESCR) were adopted by the UN General Assembly in 1966. See Paul Williams, ed. *The International Bill of Human Rights* (Glen Ellen, CA: Entwhistle Books, 1981).

14. The International Criminal Court (ICC) will be formally established after sixty countries have ratified the Rome Statute of the ICC. As of April 12, 2000, the ICC Rome Statute has ninety-six signatories and eight ratifications. The United States has not signed.

15. The United Nations Convention on the Rights of the Child was adopted by the United Nations General Assembly in 1989. It is the most widely and rapidly ratified human rights treaty in history: as of April 2000, 191 of 193 countries had ratified it. The Convention establishes goals for every nation to achieve on behalf of its children. It calls for freedom from violence, abuse, hazardous employment, exploitation, abduction or sale; freedom from hunger and protection from diseases; free compulsory primary education; adequate health care; equal treatment regardless of gender, race or cultural background; freedom of thought and the right to express opinions; and safe exposure and access to leisure, play, culture and art.

16. In March 1999, the 1997 Mine Ban Treaty became binding international law, signed by 135 nations and ratified by 65. Kenneth Roth in this volume discusses the role of nongovernmental organizations in bringing this treaty into force.

17. The ratio of the income of the world's richest 20 percent to that of the poorest 20 percent increased between 1965 and 1990, from 30:1 to 82:1. United Nations Development Programme (UNDP), *Human Development Report 1998* (New York: UNDP, 1998), p. 29.

18. *World Development Indicators 1999* (Washington, DC: World Bank, 1999), p. 350.

19. See USAID's "Polls and Public Opinion" fact sheet for the results of the poll, "Americans and Foreign Aid," Program on International Policy Attitudes for the United States Agency on International Development, January 23, 1995.

20. Steven Kull and I. M. Destler, *Misreading the Public: The Myth of a New Isolationism* (Washington, DC: Brookings Institution Press, 1999), pp. 127-28.

21. See chapters two and four in this volume.

FOUR

Opening Totalitarian Societies
to the Outside World:
A View from Russia

LEONID ROMANKOV

Leonid Romankov is a member of the St. Petersburg Legislative Assembly and chairman of the parliament's Commission on Education, Culture and Science. A 1961 graduate of the Leningrad Polytechnical Institute (now the State Technical University of St. Petersburg) with a Ph.D., he worked for more than twenty-five years as an electrical engineer. In the Soviet era, he was a member of Leningrad's dissident movement, and is the author of a book of poetry called *Fragmenty.*

Despite advances in human civilization, some countries continue to exist under totalitarian governments that trample on basic human freedoms and rights. Moreover, some of these countries present a threat to the rest of humanity, as they possess stockpiles of dangerous weapons, and their relations with the rest of the world are not checked or constrained, either by their own citizens or by international organizations. Until recently Russia was such a country, and Iraq, Libya, North Korea, China, and others remain so.

It is significant, however, that even such countries often make official declarations that acknowledge a generally accepted set of democratic values, at least in the field of human rights. For example, the Soviet Union signed the Helsinki Final Act of 1975. It did so mainly in exchange for Western acceptance of postwar territorial arrangements in Eastern Europe, and Soviet leaders had no real intention of living up to the Act's human rights provisions. Nevertheless, this official commitment gave encouragement to dissidents inside the Soviet Union, and it provided a lever for pressure from outside. Once countries have formally declared their support for human rights values, it becomes more difficult for the state to deem the struggle for recognition of these rights a crime.

I believe the decision by totalitarian states to formally (if not practically) recognize these shared values results in part from the international program of support for human rights movements around the world. These legal commitments serve both as the encouraging fruit of efforts to force observance of human rights and as a useful tool by which to transform totalitarian governments into more democratic ones.

In this chapter I explore how international contacts effected domestic circumstances in the Soviet Union. I leave aside economic pressures from without, such as the arms race, economic sanctions, and the like. These do play a role, since difficult economic conditions for those living in totalitarian countries can make individuals more receptive to criticisms of the regime. However, if one does not recognize that one lives in lower conditions than citizens of other countries, then economic difficulties have a much weaker political impact. Only when one realizes that life could be better, and that indeed elsewhere living conditions are better, is one moved to act, to criticize, and to demand improvements. Thus knowledge of the outside world as a basis for comparison is essential to the creation of pressure from within for change.

The effectiveness of these outside influences is illustrated by my own experience of transformation, from a student in a communist youth group who religiously believed in the rightness and justice of communist ideas, to a member of the dissident movement in Soviet times, and ultimately to my current position as a political representative, democratically elected three times to the legislative body of St. Petersburg.

THE EDUCATION OF A DEMOCRAT

I was born in 1937, and thus I grew up in Stalin's time. As a young adult entering the Leningrad Polytechnical Institute to study electronics, I remained in complete ignorance of the prison camps, the assassinations and executions, and other forms of Stalinist repression. This was true even though members of my very own family were among those who suffered. My uncle was arrested in 1937 and disappeared.

In 1938 my mother's cousin, Nicolai Davidenkoff, was imprisoned for a year and a half for "membership in an anti-Stalinist organization" when he was a student of Leningrad University. After serving during World War II as a reporter, he was again arrested and this time spent six years in a Siberian labor camp. He was shot in 1951. I learned of these events only later. Acute awareness of the mortal danger of any and all political "heresy" led my parents to a complete refusal to criticize the system in the presence of their children.

My awakening, like that of many other Soviet citizens, did not really begin until Khrushchev's 1956 report to the Twentieth Party Congress, in which he denounced Stalin's excesses. My friends and I became curious to know more.

My friend Yuri Gendler was one of my sources; he introduced me to books that analyzed Stalin's path to power, such as *The New Class* by the Yugoslav Milovan Djilas and *The Technology of Power* and *The Origins of the Partocracy* by the emigrant Russian writer Abdurakhman Avtorkhanov.[1]

At this time, the first reprints of previously inaccessible poets appeared. We discovered the poetry of Marina Tsvetayeva, Anna Akhmatova, Osip Mandelshtam, and Nicolai Gumilev. These were the poets of the "silver age of Russian poetry."

They made their greatest impression on us not just because of what they wrote. To be sure, their lines were beautiful and honest, especially when we compared them with the falsity of the rest of the writing around us that sang the praises of Soviet power and of the genius leader Stalin. But their greatest impact on us came when we learned their fates. Gumilev was shot by Bolsheviks in August 1921 for "membership in an anti-Soviet conspiracy." Osip Mandelshtam, a brilliant poet and author of a poem that openly accused Stalin of violent repression, died in a Far East labor camp. Marina Tsvetayeva, returning after she had emigrated from the Soviet Union, committed suicide in 1941. Anna Akhmatova, the fourth representative of the silver age of Russian poetry, was unable to publish her work, and her life was constantly threatened in the Stalin era. In the cultural "thaw" following Stalin's death, Akhmatova was gradually rehabilitated, or officially reaccepted in the literary scene.

The realization that Soviet power had essentially killed or marginalized these splendid poets and then banned their works forced me to revise my previous illusions. The same was true for many of my friends. We all were inheritors of the Russian tradition that gave great significance to poetry. The dissident movement in Moscow began with poetry readings in front of the Pushkin monument on the main street, and from the poetry magazine *Syntaxis,* passed from hand to hand in laboriously typewritten *samizdat* copies.

During the early 1960s more new literature began to appear. We shared samizdat manuscripts of the prison-camp memoirs of such writers as Alexander

Solzhenitsyn and especially his first eye-opening novel, *One Day in the Life of Ivan Denisovich*. The evidence contained in these books mounted; with horror I began to understand the bloodiness of our prized "Great October Revolution."

In Russia, reading was one of the most popular pastimes. Perhaps because personal initiative in various fields was impossible, people had free time to read. Thus the dissemination of "forbidden" literature played an enormous role. Many people read books by former political prisoners who described life in prisons and camps. We read Alexander Solzhenitsyn's *The First Circle* and *The Cancer Ward;* Varlam Shalamov's *Kolyma Notebooks;* and Eugeniia Ginzburg's book, *The Steep Way* (published in English as *Into the Whirlwind),* which described conditions in the women's prisons and camps. Vladimir Bukovsky's book *And the Wind Returns . . .* and works by Vadim Delone and Anatolii Marchenko described the regime's use of prisons and psychiatric hospitals to "reeducate" dissidents. People read non-Marxist philosophical texts, such as Nicolai Berdyaev's *The Origin and the Meaning of Russian Communism* and *The Fate of Russia;* and reflections on the revolution written by emigrants such as Ivan Bunin's, *Cursed Days,* which described the cruelty and brutishness of Red Army soldiers, and Nina Berberova's *Italics Mine,* dedicated to the memories of her meetings with the poets of the silver age in the first days of the revolution.

Newspapers and journals, such as *Russkaya Mysl'* (Russian thought), *Posev* (Sowing), and *Grani* (Edges), together with the underground publication *Khronika Tekushchikh Sobytii* (A chronicle of current events), the women's journal *Mariya,* and others, greatly broadened the strength of protest against the communist monolith.

For those people who were remote from access to forbidden literature, broadcasts from outside, such as Radio Free Europe, the Voice of America, and *Deutsche Welle,* were crucial. Satellite television, radio, and computers, which in later years would play a large role in bringing in outside information, were then accessible only to a very limited number of people.

So-called *magnitizdat* also circulated: These were recordings of songs by much-loved "bards" such as Bulat Okudzhava, Alexander Galich, Vladimir Vysotsky, and Yuly Kim. Some contained denunciations of the regime and thus contributed to our awareness that Russia's actual economic and political circumstances contradicted official pronouncements.

The rare opportunities for travel abroad (tourism for members of the trade unions, performance tours for artists, delegations for bureaucrats) were beginning to multiply the accounts of what lay "over the hill." They, too, had a significant effect on our view of the world. It was becoming clear that Soviet newspapers' cries of "rotting capitalism" were simply propaganda. Some cynics even argue that perestroika itself was the idea of those very party bureaucrats who were beginning to see that all they could gain from theft and bribes and privileges was nothing compared to the opportunities available to an average bureaucrat in a developed country; they invented perestroika, it was sometimes said, just because they wanted similar opportunities for themselves.

Contacts with foreign tourists, although dangerous and rare, also gave us information about life in the West. Any opportunity for exchange between people furthered the opening of a closed society and helped rid our minds of all that had been pounded in by communist propaganda.

In my own case, I had grown up with the view that Western society was extremely unjust and that it oppressed "simple people," but my confidence in that view was shaken by an English specialist in Russian poetry who came to Leningrad to study. In 1962 my friendship with Sheelagh Duffin opened my eyes to a new view of the West. In addition to all her other gifts to me, I was particularly grateful for copies of *Animal Farm* and *1984* by George Orwell.

This friendship also precipitated my first run-ins with the KGB. Technically, I was forbidden to meet with any foreigners, as I was then working in an official institute that did defense work. On this pretext, the authorities tried to recruit me as an agent to gather information, through Sheelagh, whose father was a military man. They invited me many times, sometimes proposing to help my career, other times threatening me. It was not easy, but I refused as politely as I could. This was a strange time—it became known as "the thaw"—and the authorities finally left me alone, warning me that in an earlier day I would have been "stood up against the wall."

Working as an engineer in Leningrad's All-Union Television Institute, I became a member of the Institute's quasi-professional volleyball team. With the team I visited many different parts of the Soviet Union for sports competitions, including Ukraine, the Baltic Republics, Georgia, and many other places. I also traveled on summer vacations with various expeditions, mostly archaeological. This hobby took me to Kyrgizia, Siberia, Moldavia, Turkmenistan, Tadjikistan, Altai, Karelia, Crimea, Rostov on Don, and other places all over the Soviet Union.

As I traveled, I saw that living conditions in the country were incredibly poor. I saw people who were deprived of all rights before their local party committees. Over and over, I saw the same thing: As a rule, upon visiting a new city, we would first see the very rich and well-designed local party committee building. Its inhabitants would ride around in black Volga automobiles, patronize exclusive "closed" dining rooms and shops, and enjoy state-provided *dachas* (vacation homes) and other privileges. But for everyone else, we would find familiar patterns: the housing was poor and in bad condition; there was nothing in the food shops; and in conversation people would tell us—if they were not afraid to speak—how poorly they lived. Once on the Issyk-Kul Lake in the Tian Shan Mountains, I asked a man why everyone drank so much alcohol. He replied, "If we didn't drink, what would we eat?"

I understood that something had to be changed.

The human rights movement in Russia began in various parts of the Soviet Union but was especially active in Moscow and Leningrad. In 1956–1957 in Leningrad, the group led by Revolt Pimenov was arrested for distributing leaflets and samizdat. In 1964 the KGB caught the people who circulated the samizdat magazine *Kolokol* (Bell) and members of Igor Ogurtsov's Leningrad dissident group. In Moscow an open demonstration took place December 5, 1964, with nearly 200 people shouting the slogan "Respect Your Own Constitution!" This event is often identified as the beginning of the human rights movement in the Soviet Union. From this time, the movement began to spread, especially in the Baltic Republics, Armenia, and Georgia.

My friends and I made small contributions. We copied and circulated both samizdat (underground manuscripts from within the Soviet Union) and *tamizdat* books (those from foreign sources), first by typewriter and photographic prints, later with computers and photocopiers. We shared newspapers and magazines. We listened to Western radio. We began to write and sign letters of protest against repressive conditions.

Bold writings moved through our society as if they were transfusions of new blood into our country's circulatory system. These included works like the open letters of Lydia Chukovskaya concerning repressions against writers, Andrei Sakharov's article "Ideas about Progress, Co-existence and Intellectual Freedom," and the novels of Solzhenitsyn. The protest songs of Alexander Galich and of Vladimir Vysotsky captured our everyday life with angry and humorous lyrics; the whole country was singing their songs.

The human rights movement chose as its form of protest the demand that the government observe its own laws. As a result, unjust punishments such as arrest, imprisonment in camps, and placement in psychiatric hospitals become widely publicized, thanks to Western correspondents and local samizdat. Each story elicited a new wave of letters in defense of those persecuted.

International public opinion created certain guaranties of protection, at least for the most famous dissidents, such as Andrei Sakharov, Alexander Solzhenitsyn, Vladimir Bukovsky, and General Grigorenko. International social organizations such as PEN, Helsinki Watch, Amnesty International, and Charter 77 defended writers such as Yuly Daniel, Andrei Sinyavsky, and Efim Etkind. Officials of other countries addressed themselves directly to Russia's communist leaders to petition for an end to the persecution of particular victims of the regime.

Court proceedings, protest letters, and the like cited international documents on human rights that were beginning to be known to us, such as the

Universal Declaration of Human Rights, the International Covenant on Civil and Political Rights, and the Convention against Torture and other Cruel, Inhuman or Degrading Treatment or Punishment.

When my friends and I came across the International Covenant on Civil and Political Rights, we memorized paragraph 2 of Article 19: "Everyone has the right to freedom of opinion and expression; this right includes freedom to hold opinions without interference and to seek, receive and impart information and ideas through any media and regardless of frontiers." We learned these words by heart so we could repeat them when the KGB questioned us. We argued that we were absolutely within our rights to circulate samizdat; this article assured us that there was no crime in our actions, and our own government must recognize this because it had ratified the Covenant.[2]

In this period the authorities tried in varying degrees to suppress the democratic movement. Khrushchev used his psychiatric hospitals; Brezhnev employed his camps; and, in 1982, Andropov began an especially cruel and merciless smothering of freedoms. But because of pressure from within and without, the state was no longer able to act without restraint. Thus the government began to punish dissidents in a new way, by exiling them to other countries, revoking their citizenship rather than murdering them (though this, too, remained an instrument of the regime until as late as 1985). Solzhenitsyn was one who was exiled to the West in 1974.

Any country in the civilized world cares about its reputation and prestige because they affect a country's access to loans and new technologies and its opportunities to trade and to sell its products. Thus, when reports by international human rights organizations in the world press seriously affect a country's reputation, a country must view this seriously. In response, the government may make cosmetic changes to its appearance, for example, by pardoning a few dissidents, releasing them abroad, or fabricating criminal charges, rather than charging them with political crimes, as a basis for their arrest. When dissident Yuli Rybakov wrote the slogan "Freedom to political prisoners!" on the wall of the Peter and Paul fortress in 1976, for instance, he was accused of stealing a typewriter and sentenced to six years of labor camp. Released in 1982, he is now a deputy in Russia's State Duma.

In 1982 I too experienced a milder version of this repression. When the KGB searched my apartment, they found nearly fifty "forbidden" books. The next day I was fired from the institute where I had worked for twenty years, and where I had advanced to the position of senior scientific specialist. I was interrogated repeatedly by the KGB, a frightening and demoralizing experience. I feared I would be imprisoned. In the end, I received an official warning from the public prosecutor: If I continued such "anti-Soviet activity," I would be arrested.

For a month and a half, I was without a job, but then a friend of mine was brave enough to propose me for a new job in the Russian Academy of Science Analytical Instruments Institute. One advantage was that this institute was not engaged in defense work, and thus the KGB could exert less influence than they could in my previous place of employment. But still, they sometimes visited me in my job and asked me to work for them as an informer, arguing that I knew many dissidents and could be extremely useful to them. I received a variety of "If not . . ." threats. It was not a good time for me then. I continued to circulate samizdat, trying to be more careful, but I believed then that I would end my days, like so many of my friends and colleagues, in "sunny Siberia."

The first glimmer of light was when Gorbachev took over and began to speak about glasnost (openness) and perestroika (restructuring). And the first visible sign of change came when Andrei Sakharov was released from exile on December 23, 1986. My own first experience of the new freedom came in 1989, when I was allowed to travel to France to visit the dancer Rudolf Nureyev, an old friend of my family. I was fifty-two years old, and it was my first visit abroad.

In 1990 the first democratic elections to the Lensoviet—Leningrad's Council of People's Deputies (now the Legislative Assembly of St. Petersburg)—were held. It was the first time voters could choose between candidates rather than selecting the lone person on the ballot. People were inspired: Finally they had an opportunity to elect an honest candidate instead of a communist apparatchik. Friends said to me: "You began by fighting against communism; now you should run for a seat in the Lensoviet in order to continue the fight."

I raised campaign funds by selling 100 copies of my biography at $2 each and pasting campaign posters on walls throughout my district, and I took up all opportunities to participate in public debates. It was fantastic to watch the inhabitants of Leningrad overwhelmingly support us, a formerly small group of dissidents, against the formerly dominant power of communism. Our shared idea was to transform the closed, totalitarian country with its administratively ruled economy into an open society with a free market economy. Many scientists and other educated people decided to join in; we thought we had sufficient knowledge and will to make a success of this task.[3]

Unfortunately, the realities were much more complicated than we had thought. Though I won my race against thirteen opponents, the obstacles I faced in government included the ingrained fears of seventy years of repression; the fact that only military industries had been developed; heavy industry's destruction of Russia's villages and its agriculture; the lack of a tradition of private initiative; the disappearance of the moral forces of culture and religion; and adamant resistance from former party and KGB people. But step by step, we have gained experience with democracy.

In the Lensoviet, I served on the Commission on Human Rights and the Commission on Culture. One of our first actions was to return to the religious communities the buildings that had belonged to them before the revolution. Because these buildings had been occupied by many different institutions—from factories to museums—it was challenging to settle the competing claims. We also offered help—in the form of tax breaks, finding office space, and rent reductions—to the unions of former political prisoners (e.g., the group called Memorial) and to artists, writers, and other creative people who had been forced "underground" in Soviet times.[4]

As time went on, the buildings and offices that had been occupied by Communist Party committees were made available to cultural centers, the courts, and the new democratic parties. We organized a referendum that resulted in the restoration of the name Saint Petersburg to our city.

Between 1990 and 1993 the communist faction in the legislative assembly, consisting of communist functionaries and KGB people, tried to resist the reforms, but they were in the minority. People often said that the Lensoviet (now called the "Petrosoviet") was the most democratic legislative body in Russia. It was a very romantic time.

The human rights and civil liberties situation in Russia has changed from the time before perestroika. Arrest for political reasons is very rare, although from time to time the FSB (former KGB) tries to show its teeth; for example, Alexander Nikitin and Grigory Pasko were accused of giving out state secrets when they released information on the military's pollution of the environment. But a major difference is that today democratic forces within Russia and public opinion outside can often protect them. The press is free, but those with money dominate the airwaves. Some journalists end up owing their souls to the government in exchange for its funding or other support.

And human rights problems persist, especially police torture during interrogations; the violent and sometimes fatal "hazing" of young soldiers in the army known as *dedovshchina;* and poor prison conditions. Also of concern are relations with people of the Caucasus nationality and the human rights of the Russians who now live in the former Soviet republics, especially the Central Asian regions. In my town, city officials increasingly place pressure on the free press and against those who oppose St. Petersburg's executive power. The city's governor sometimes uses the tax police against those firms that offer financial support to the newspapers and television organizations that have dared to criticize the governor's policies; the same mechanism is used against opposition parties and the firms and banks that support them. These issues require our continued attention.

CONCLUSION

It is odd to reflect upon my new life as a professional politician. I could say that it all began with the Russian poetry of the silver age. I am deeply convinced that the reading of the right books—or more broadly, the intelligentsia's efforts to process factual information about the state of Soviet society—paved the way for the end of communist dictatorship in Russia.

My experience and that of my country suggest the powerful influence of information. It is a tool that should be applied in other countries where repression is still strong and human rights are still in need of protection. The international community should:

- Distribute democratically oriented information through all channels—books, foreign newspapers, radio, satellite television, and now the Internet
- Arrange international visits, exchanges, and scientific and cultural personal contacts for ordinary citizens as well as for those in power
- Provide international support for human rights activists and their organizations, by promoting awareness of their persecution and applying pressure for their defense both on a governmental level and through nongovernmental organizations and influential individuals such as well-known authors and social and religious leaders
- Monitor the repressive country's human rights conditions, and report the results to the citizens of that country as well as to the rest of the world.

Protection of human rights in totalitarian countries requires that the international community make the most of all opportunities to use information tools, which can help transform totalitarian governments into more democratic ones that are more responsible and reliable members of the international community. The goal is to save human lives, secure better living conditions for all the world's citizens, and reduce the risk to the rest of humanity.

NOTES

1. In 1968 Yuri Gendler was arrested and sentenced to four years in the labor camps. After that, he emigrated; he now lives in Prague, where he is the director of the Russian department of Radio Liberty.
2. The Soviet Union ratified the ICCPR on October 16, 1973.
3. "All of the deputies on the city council elected in 1990 were 'democratic-romantics,' but in addition to their declarations and appeals, they did enact much legislation that was useful in establishing new standards." Valentina Rumiantseva and Marina Makarewith, *Dwadzat perwyi* (Twenty-first) (St. Petersburg: 1994). Other books that describe this time include Alexander Sungurov, *Etudy politicheskoi dzizny Peterburga* (Studies of political life in Saint Petersburg) (St. Petersburg: 1996); and Alexander Vinnikov, *Tsena svobody* (The price of freedom) (St. Petersburg: 1998).
4. One such group of former underground artists is the "Free Culture Foundation," to which we gave one of the most prominent buildings in the city center, called "Pushkinskaja 10."

PART II

Human Rights Enforcement: State and Individual Accountability

Human Rights in Europe

SHIRLEY WILLIAMS[*]

Shirley Williams is Public Service Professor of Elective Politics at the John F. Kennedy School of Government, Harvard University. She has been a Member of the European Commission's Comité des Sages "For a Europe of Civic and Social Rights," 1995–1996; and of the Goldstone Committee on Human Responsibilities and Duties leading to the Valencia Declaration, April 1999. In the United Kingdom, she has been a Member of Parliament, 1964–1979 and 1981–1983; Privy Councilor since 1974; in the Cabinet as Secretary of State, Prices and Consumer Protection, 1974–1976; and Secretary of State for Education and Science as well as Paymaster-General, 1976–1979. She has been a Member of the House of Lords since 1992; spokesperson on Foreign, Commonwealth and European Affairs for the Liberal Democrats since 1998 and their Deputy Leader since June 1999.

In the last half century, the continent of Europe—the very continent that scorned and traduced human rights before and during World War II—has developed the most robust institutional machinery in the world for protecting the human rights of its citizens.

This chapter offers an institutional and historical overview of Europe's mechanisms for human rights promotion and protection. It describes the work of the Council of Europe in maintaining and protecting human rights, as defined by the 1950 European Convention for the Protection of Human Rights and Fundamental Freedoms. It explores the evolution of human rights, from the 1957 Treaty of Rome which established the European Economic Community, through to their further development in the 1997 European Union Treaty of Amsterdam. The complementarity of these two sets of institutions—the Council of Europe and the European Union—contributes to the protection of the human rights of Europeans, both by offering individuals a courtroom remedy when their rights are violated and by establishing standards that must be met by applicants for membership in either body. Because acceptance of certain norms of civilized conduct and respect for human rights and fundamental freedoms are prerequisites for accession to the European Union, the economic and geopolitical attractions of joining offer an incentive to borderline states to improve their internal behavior and their human rights climate.

Europe has developed two separate and independent legal structures that deal with human rights. The first, constructed around the European Court of Human Rights in Strasbourg, is attached to the Council of Europe, and the other, comprising the European Court of Justice in Luxembourg, is associated with the European Union. Each institution is independent of, but not without influence on, the other.[1]

The Council of Europe is an international body currently composed of forty-one member states defined as European, which concerns itself with all matters except defense. One of the criteria for membership requires a state to commit itself to uphold the European Convention on Human Rights. The Council exerts its judicial influence on human rights through the European Court of Human Rights (ECHR) based at Strasbourg in France. Each member state is entitled to appoint one judge to the court, and each pledges to accept the Court's judgments. The European Court of Human Rights and the Inter-American Court of Human Rights are the only two international courts in the world that recognize the right of individuals to petition against violations of human rights by the governments of its member states. (Individuals are required first to exhaust all available domestic remedies.)[2] A Committee of Ministers composed of the foreign ministers of member states, or their representatives, is responsible for monitoring compliance with the judgments of the Court, and the Court's record since it was established in 1959 has generally been good.

The other legal structure dealing with human rights in Europe has the European Court of Justice (ECJ) at its core. The European Court of Justice is the highest judicial body in the European Community (EC); it settles disputes between member states, or between member states and European institutions.

Its main responsibility is the interpretation of the treaties that establish the EC and the European Union (EU). The Court is part of the EU, which consists of three "pillars" in the terminology of the 1992 Maastricht Treaty. The first of these pillars is the European Community itself.[3] Its laws, known as the *acquis communautaire,* or "Community patrimony," are binding on member states.[4]

The other two pillars of the European Union are intergovernmental rather than supranational. The second pillar concerns foreign and security policy (sometimes referred to as CFSP, for "common foreign and security policy"), and the third is that of justice and home affairs (JHA). Intergovernmental decisions concerning second-pillar and third-pillar issues usually are reached by consensus and do not have direct effect. The European Court of Justice has had no jurisdiction over these issues, which are reserved to member states. However, during the negotiations on the Amsterdam Treaty, the question of extending the ECJ's jurisdiction to some parts of the third pillar was raised.

Responsibilities falling to national governments under the third pillar can be transferred to the first (Community) pillar by a procedure known as the *passerelle,* or "bridge."[5] The procedure was adopted during the negotiations on the Treaty of Amsterdam, signed on June 18, 1997, when visas, refugee, and asylum policy, which had been "third-pillar" issues of justice and home affairs, were brought within the purview of the first (Community) pillar under the Schengen Agreement,[6] and thereby within the jurisdiction of the Court of Justice.[7] As the scope of the EC has widened, so has the jurisdiction of the ECJ.

Individuals do not have the right to petition the European Court of Justice against the acts of member states or of European institutions, except for cases where those acts directly violate EU treaty law, such as Article 119, dealing with sex discrimination, in the 1957 Treaty of Rome that established the European Economic Community.[8] Generally, therefore, an individual seeking redress from acts or omissions of a European government must look to the European Court of Human Rights in Strasbourg rather than to the European Court of Justice in Luxembourg for a remedy.

The European Parliament has campaigned for over a decade to rectify this position and to bring the protection of fundamental human rights with the *acquis communautaire,* and therefore within the jurisdiction of the European Court of Justice. On April 12, 1989, the Parliament called for a Declaration on Fundamental Rights and Freedoms to be made by member states. A year later, on December 12, 1990, Parliament called for these rights to become the basis for a new European Constitution.

Owing to resistance from member state governments, not least that of a United Kingdom adamantly opposed to further transfers of sovereignty to the

European Union, these sentiments remained unrealized. Only during the second summit meeting of the German presidency under a newly elected chancellor, Gerhard Schroeder, did matters move forward. The Cologne European Council of heads of state and government concluded on June 3 and 4, 1999, that there should be a charter of fundamental rights "in order to make their overriding importance and relevance more visible to the Union's citizens." They further agreed that this charter should be "elaborated" by a body consisting of representatives of the European Parliament and the national parliaments as well as representatives of member state governments.

At the European Council meeting held under the Finnish presidency, at Tampere, Finland on October 15 and 16, 1999, the composition of this body was laid out in detail, as were its working methods: There were to be fifteen representatives of the EU governments, one representative of the Commission's president, sixteen members of the European Parliament chosen by the European Parliament, and thirty members of national parliaments, two designated by each. This body was instructed to be as transparent as possible, inviting outsiders to contribute to its deliberations, making documents public, and holding its hearings in public.[9] It was instructed to present a draft Charter of Fundamental Rights to the final summit of the French presidency, at Nice in December 2000.

However, while EU national governments are willing to entertain the idea of a charter, they are not united on whether such a charter should be integrated into the treaties and thereby have the force of law and, in effect, become the European Bill of Rights, or be limited to a declaration. The European Parliament does not share these doubts. Most recently, on March 16, 2000, in a resolution calling for a Charter of Fundamental Rights to be drawn up, the Parliament made clear that its final assent "will depend to a large extent on whether the Charter has fully binding legal status by being incorporated into the Treaty on European Union."[10]

THE ORIGINS OF
EUROPEAN HUMAN RIGHTS LAW INSTITUTIONS

The climate of Europe immediately after World War II was highly favorable to the nurturing of human rights. The atrocities of the war were part of the legacy bequeathed to Europe's postwar leaders. Those leaders were appalled at the willingness of the Nazi and fascist governments to disregard human rights and indeed humanity itself in pursuit of their political enemies, which culminated in the systematic horror of the "final solution." Even those countries that had been defeated and then occupied uneasily recognized that within their own states collaborators and sympathizers with fascism were numerous, ranging from the

Petainists of France to the supporters of Quisling in Norway. There was a widespread desire to erect political structures that would protect fundamental human rights. There was also huge respect among Europeans for the United States and a growing appreciation of its rights-based constitutional structure.

The Charter of the Nuremberg International Military Tribunal of August 8, 1945, and the subsequent trials that began in February 1946 established that even sovereign states could be held responsible for acts condemned as criminal by international law. The principle of international law had thereby taken a step forward to the essential corollary of enforcement. Nuremberg was, of course, victors' justice, but at least that justice was reached through a recognizably legitimate process.

There were also political factors that made the protection of human rights in postwar Europe urgent as well as desirable. By April 1947 relations between the Soviet Union and its wartime allies were deteriorating rapidly, culminating in the breakdown of the Four Power Council of Foreign Ministers over the issue of German reparations.[11] A quarter century before, reparations owed to the victors of World War I had contributed to the economic instability of the 1920s that in its turn fed German fascism. In the immediate postwar years, 1945 to 1948, aware that the desperate economic plight of Western Europe made the continent vulnerable to communism, the United States concluded that a much more ambitious plan for economic recovery was necessary and that Germany would inevitably have to be at the heart of any such plan. European recovery without Germany was impossible. That meant a strong Germany, not the agricultural desert of the Morgenthau plan, nor the pre-Bismarckian Germany of regions and principalities of which the French government dreamed.[12]

To Germany's fearful neighbors, the quid pro quo for its rebirth was continuing American involvement in Europe, achieved through the Marshall Plan and, later, the North Atlantic Treaty of 1949. Both the United States and Germany's neighbors wanted a political framework as well, one that would encourage Germany to develop democratic institutions and the rule of law within a more closely integrated Europe.

The Federal Republic of Germany evolved rapidly into a rights-based democracy, much influenced by the American model. In June 1948 the three Western allies met in London and agreed, despite profound French disquiet, to convene a German constitutional assembly. Less than a year later the constitutional assembly produced a basic constitution, the *Grundgesetz*. Drafted in part by Carl Joachim Friedrich, a German academic who had emigrated to the United States and become a distinguished professor at Harvard University, the constitution spelled out in detail the fundamental rights of German citizens. Judges who sat on the Constitutional Court were conscious of their awesome responsibility for establishing democracy in a country at once so powerful and yet so haunted by the demons of its recent past.

Germany's Constitutional Court has become as fierce a guardian of these rights as the U.S. Supreme Court has been of the Bill of Rights and has critically influenced the evolution of human rights law in Europe. In particular, in its insistence that powers cannot be transferred from the Federal Republic to the European Community unless fundamental human rights are protected and democratic institutions fully developed, the German Constitutional Court has acted as both guardian and goad to European institutions. Its judgments in the *Solange* cases of the early 1970s (discussed below) encouraged the European Parliament to demand more powers and the ECJ to take more initiative in expanding its purview of human rights.

A democratic Federal Republic of Germany was a crucial element in the establishment of a stable democratic Western Europe, but it was not the only one. A framework was needed capable of embracing all the countries of Western Europe within a structure of respect for human rights. That framework was the Council of Europe and, at its center, the European Court of Human Rights.

THE COUNCIL OF EUROPE
AND THE EUROPEAN COURT OF HUMAN RIGHTS

In March 1948 the governments of Belgium, the Netherlands, Luxembourg, Britain, and France signed the Brussels Treaty setting up a Consultative Council of their foreign ministers. Two months later at the Hague Congress of the European Movement, chaired by Winston Churchill in his most visionary style, over 700 delegates from sixteen countries agreed to take matters further. Presided over by Churchill and led by Léon Blum for France, Alcide de Gasperi for Italy, and Paul-Henri Spaak for Belgium, the International Committee of the European Movement drew up plans for a new Council of Europe, intended to protect human rights, encourage democracy, and stimulate closer political and cultural relations among the countries of Europe. The Treaty establishing the Council was signed by ten countries in London on May 5, 1949, one month after the North Atlantic Treaty. The following year the members of the Council of Europe approved the draft Convention for the Protection of Human Rights and Fundamental Freedoms. On September 3, 1953, the tenth signatory ratified the Convention, thereby bringing it into effect.[13] The group of countries represented initially has grown to forty-one, extending across the continent to include Russia and Ukraine. Only Bosnia, Serbia, and some former Soviet republics do not yet belong.

The European Convention on Human Rights (ECHR) constituted, and still constitutes, the core the Council of Europe. It is a simple document, drafted mainly by British civil servants. Although the Convention was deeply influenced by the United Nations' 1948 Universal Declaration of Human Rights (UDHR), and indeed makes direct reference to the UDHR in its preamble, the European Convention is distinct from—and more binding than—the UDHR in two ways. First, the ECHR, unlike the UDHR, is enforceable in a court: the European Court of Human Rights in Strasbourg. Second, a state cannot be admitted to the Council of Europe unless it commits itself to upholding the principles outlined in the Convention.

Most European states have gone beyond simple ratification of the ECHR, by incorporating the Convention into their domestic law (although this is optional). Indeed, in some Council of Europe member states, once the state ratifies an international treaty, its provisions automatically become part of domestic law. In common law countries and in some civil law countries, incorporation into domestic law must be approved separately by the legislature, since it affects the rights of citizens. In the case of the United Kingdom, with its historic doctrine—or perhaps dogma—of parliamentary sovereignty, according to which no Parliament can bind its successors, incorporation has proved very controversial. Since the Court's inception, the United Kingdom, the first signatory of the European Convention, accepted the jurisdiction of the Court to hear complaints by other states, but it had been unwilling to incorporate Court judgments or the Convention itself directly into domestic law. This produced anomalies that only cumbrous and expensive legal processes could resolve. The dilemma was bypassed ingeniously in the recent Human Rights Act (1998) of the British Parliament, which combines parliamentary sovereignty with effective remedies for violations of the Convention.[14]

Both state signatories and European citizens have standing to make a complaint in court under the Convention. As is fairly typical of international treaties, any member state may bring a case before the ECHR against another state signatory on the grounds that it has acted in breach of the Convention. The Convention's more radical innovation is contained in Article 25, which allows an individual or group of individuals or a nongovernmental organization (NGO) to petition the Court of Human Rights directly, alleging a violation of human rights by a Council of Europe member state.

Of the thousands of cases, most of them individual petitions, filed since the Court was established in 1959, few ever reach the Court. Until November 1, 1998, and for most of the Court's history, the European Commission of Human Rights, a part-time body whose members were chosen by the Council of Europe governing bodies,[15] scrutinized all cases in order to ascertain whether all domestic remedies had been exhausted and whether a case was otherwise admissible. Aside from exhaustion of domestic remedies, the criteria of inadmissibility has included factors such as whether the subject matter of the case is substantially similar to a case recently considered by the Court or another international body (and should therefore be governed by that decision rather than separately adjudicated); whether the claim is incompatible with the Convention; and whether the case is manifestly ill-founded or an abuse of the right of application. The petitioner could take no further action until the Commission had resolved the question of admissibility, but at any time during the pretrial process the Commission could refer a case to the Court of Human Rights, as could a respondent.

Once the Commission decided a case was admissible, it would report to the Committee of Ministers appointed by the governments of the member states giving its opinion on the case. The final decision on whether the case should proceed would be taken by the Committee unless it had already been referred to the Court. Cases that survived these tests would then become subjects of mediation by the Commission, which sought to achieve a negotiated settlement between the parties out of court. Only if this failed would the case proceed to the ECHR.

By the beginning of the 1990s, as the former states of the Soviet bloc sought to join the Council of Europe, the number of cases submitted to the European Commission of Human Rights multiplied. By 1996 new cases exceeded 4,000, ten times as many as in the 1970s.[16] It became clear that the Court's work would have to be reorganized. The Council of Europe took drastic action. The Commission was abolished and the Court became a full-time body in permanent session, composed of one judge nominated by each member state, sitting in four chambers.

The European Court of Human Rights now has jurisdiction over approximately 800 million citizens, all of whom, as of November 1, 1998, automatically enjoy this right of petition directly to the Court. The Court, instead of the Commission, now undertakes the screening process to see whether all domestic remedies have been exhausted and other criteria of admissibility have been met. There is no reference to the Committee of Ministers. If the judge in charge of this pretrial review (the *juge-rapporteur*) doubts the admissibility of a case, he or she will refer the matter for decision by a committee of three judges. Any verdict of inadmissibility must be unanimous. There is no appeal against its verdict.

Historically, the great majority of cases have fallen at the first fence of admissibility, having been deemed to lack the necessary merit to warrant further consideration. Approximately 22 percent of cases held to have merit have been resolved in mediated settlements. Between July 1954 and December 1997, of the 4,161 applications declared admissible by the Commission, 903 were eventually referred to the Court, which had by the end of 1997 handed down 867 judgments.

Judgments are now made by a chamber of seven judges and, in exceptional cases, are revised by a Grand Chamber of seventeen judges. The judgments are final and binding under European law, and the moral standing of the Court is such that its judgments are usually respected. The Council of Europe's Committee of Ministers supervises the execution of such judgments. It is left up to each member state to decide on the best method for compliance with the Court's judgments. In some cases a state may need to pass legislation to implement the judgment, while in others it may need only to take administrative action. A recent example of national legislation passed to ensure compatibility with ECHR judgements included lifting the ban on openly homosexual men and women as recruits in the UK armed forces.

Despite criticism of certain judicial appointments, the Council of Europe's institutions have profoundly influenced human rights awareness and protections and the promotion of democracy throughout Europe. The rights protected by the Convention draw on the same universal enlightenment values as do those in the U.S. Constitution and the constitutions of other democracies.[17] Officials of the Council have explained the Convention's provisions to the general European public and, significantly, through a series of educational programs, to the countries of Central and Eastern Europe that are making the transition to plural democracy. The programs cover an extensive field of activities, such as institution building and training of legal professionals, in twenty-one countries of Central and Eastern Europe. Sixteen of these countries have already advanced to full Council of Europe membership.

The Court itself has issued several landmark judgments that have been accepted by, though hardly welcome in, its member states. Among the most influential have been those concerning the rights of prisoners, mental patients, and others detained against their will. The Commission's position on the rights of prisoners, for instance, evolved from accepting restrictions on prisoners' correspondence as inherent in imprisonment itself, to a much more careful examination of whether such restrictions could be justified, given Article 8 of the Convention.[18] In the *Golder* case, the Court concluded that there was no justification for restricting the plaintiff's right to communicate with a lawyer in seeking advice on civil proceedings.[19] Subsequent cases have demonstrated that the Court will not support control over prisoners' correspondence if it exceeds "what is required by the legitimate aim pursued."[20] In consequence, prison rules have had to be changed in several countries.

In a case concerning the detention of a person no longer suffering from mental illness, the court awarded a sum in respect of nonpecuniary damages, as well as costs and expenses, for his detention in breach of Article 5(1) of the Convention.[21]

Membership of the Council of Europe has become, over the years, the talisman of a nation's democratic bona fides. In recent years it has become expected that a nation wishing to join the Council of Europe will ratify the Convention on Human Rights as well and improve its performance within a set period. The new member thereby comes under pressure to respect human rights in its own country. Membership is much more than a moral obligation, for it entails the implementation, by law, administrative regulation, or in other ways, of the verdicts of the ECHR. Furthermore, membership is now the gateway to joining other organizations, not least the EU itself. Indeed, Turkey, now an officially recognized candidate for EU membership, deferred the execution of the Kurdish rebel leader Abdullah Ocalan until the ECHR had heard his appeal. Turkish national law permits the death penalty. The EU has made the abolition of the death penalty a condition of membership.

The status of the Council of Europe was undoubtedly enhanced by the end of the cold war and the disintegration of the Soviet bloc after 1989. It was an organization with considerable experience in constructing democratic institutions and establishing an independent judicial system in cooperation with new members, some of them former dictatorships. It did not have to be invented. Its structure was also well adapted to dealing with new members, since it had been predicated from its foundation on doing so. It offered the immediate respectability of entry to the community of established Western European democracies in association with the United States. Because all member states are equally bound by the verdicts of the Court of Human Rights, and every member state is entitled to appoint a judge to the Court, there are no status distinctions between old and new members. So the political benefits of membership were almost entirely positive for a new member state: a high credit rating in the democracy stakes. Virtually every country that can claim to be European, from Turkey to Russia, has now signed and ratified the Convention.

Whether a similar benefit obtains in the case of the Council of Europe itself is a more controversial issue. Fears of dilution of the Court's high standards have been voiced by lawyers from some of the older member states.[22] Judges coming from nations where the judiciary has been an instrument of the state may take a very different view of the rights of the individual vis-à-vis the state than those brought up in the tradition of an independent judiciary. However, the assembly of the Council of Europe retains the right to reelect judges. Their initial term is normally six years, but after the first election for the reorganized Court in 1998, when the Eleventh Protocol came into force, half the judges were appointed for a term of only three years. This right to reelect judges will give considerable influence to the Assembly of the Council of Europe, whose choice of judges is often influenced by political considerations. It should, however, be possible to assess the individual record of the new judges. Much will depend on the criteria for reelection that are taken into account by the Assembly. It will be open to members to insist on demanding standards for the upholding of human rights.

THE EUROPEAN ECONOMIC COMMUNITY, THE EC, AND THE EUROPEAN COURT OF JUSTICE

The second pan-European postwar institution to establish its own framework of law was the European Economic Community (EEC), which subsequently became the European Union. Its founding charter, the 1957 Treaty of Rome, makes little reference to human rights or to democracy, beyond referring to the principles of the UN Charter in its preamble. While its authors declare that one of the primary objectives of the EU is to "preserve and strengthen liberty," curiously they appear to view that liberty as a by-product of the Common Market. The preamble to the Treaty of Rome declares that the founders:

DETERMINED to lay the foundations of an ever closer union among the peoples of Europe,

RESOLVED to ensure the economic and social progress of their countries by common action to eliminate the barriers which divide Europe,

AFFIRMING as the essential objective of their efforts the constant improvements of the living and working conditions of their peoples,

RECOGNIZING that the removal of existing obstacles calls for concerted action in order to guarantee steady expansion, balanced trade and fair competition,

ANXIOUS to strengthen the unity of their economies and to ensure their harmonious development by reducing the differences existing between the various regions and the backwardness of the less favored regions,

DESIRING to contribute, by means of a common commercial policy, to the progressive abolition of restrictions on international trade,

INTENDING to confirm the solidarity which binds Europe and the overseas countries and desiring to ensure the development of their prosperity, in accordance with the principles of the Charter of the United Nations,

RESOLVED by thus pooling their resources to preserve and strengthen peace and liberty, and calling upon the other peoples of Europe who share their ideal to join in their efforts . . . HAVE DECIDED to create a European Community. . . .

Apart from this oblique reference to human rights principles, incorporated only by reference to the UN Charter, the preamble reads like a formal obeisance to received values rather than a commitment to make the protection of human rights the cornerstone of European Community efforts. This apparent neglect can be accounted for in several ways. Most obviously, what became the European Union began as the European *Economic* Community. Its stated emphases were market liberalization and the freeing of trade. More to the point, when the Treaty of Rome was signed on March 25, 1957, the UN Declaration of Human Rights had been adopted less than a decade earlier, while the European Convention on Human Rights had been signed by all the countries who were then Council of Europe members as recently as November 4, 1950. The framers may simply have assumed that, given this recent history, human rights would be respected. Beyond two articles that bear on human rights principles, the framers felt no need to spell out the rights again in the Treaty of Rome.[23]

The ECJ began its work in Luxembourg in 1952 by quietly interpreting the letter of the Treaty of Paris (1952), which had established the European Coal and Steel Community, and later of the Treaty of Rome (1957). Yet even within these fairly narrow, principally economic bounds, issues of human rights could not be excluded. The Court established two principles early on that have proven essential to the survival of the supranational Community. The first of these was the principle of direct effect, namely that Community law binds member states directly and not through their own national governments.[24] The second was the principle of the supremacy of Community law over national law, indeed even over national constitutional law, but only within the narrow areas in which the European Community had established jurisdiction. These principles provided the European Court of Justice with mighty weapons, and over the years, the Court has used them to widen the scope of its authority. The founding members of the European Economic Community could not have predicted the remarkable extent to which this fundamentally economic charter—and the economic integration that it helped generate—would help citizens realize the rights spelled out in other documents.

Key Articles of the Treaty of Rome

Although the body of the Treaty of Rome contains few provisions that bear any direct relation to human rights, the two that come the closest have given legal ground to judges serving on the European Court of Justice to interpret the Treaty expansively. The two articles in the Treaty of Rome that offered some opportunity to create a beachhead for human rights are Article 48 on freedom of movement and Article 119 on sex discrimination. Article 48 decreed freedom of movement for workers in the European Community, and then added flesh to the bare legal bones in a second subhead: "Such freedom of movement shall entail the *abolition of any discrimination based on nationality* between workers of the Member states as regards employment, remuneration and other conditions of work and employment" (emphasis added).

This constituted an open invitation to lawyers, nongovernmental organizations, and others to define and test what "discrimination" meant under this Article. Freedom of movement has become a significant arena for development of the Treaty's coverage. Article 48, providing for the freedom of movement of workers, Article 52, on the right of establishment (of businesses), and Article 5, on the right to provide services anywhere within the Community, have resulted in the extension of social rights, such as pensions and employment benefits, to workers wherever they are employed within the Community on the same basis as for national citizens.

The right of freedom of movement also has come to encompass other fundamental human rights, except in situations entirely internal to member states such as criminal law. In his Opinion on the *Konstantinidis* case, the Advocate General declared that a person who exercises freedom of movement under the articles is "entitled to assume that, wherever he goes to earn his living in the European Community, he will be treated in accordance with a common code of fundamental values, in particular those laid down in the European Convention on Human Rights."[25]

The *Rutili* case established the limits within which freedom of movement could be restricted. Rutili was an Italian working in France and much engaged in trade union activities. He was ordered to leave the *département* (administrative district) in which he was conducting those activities. Ruling in favor of Rutili, the Court interpreted Article 48(3) of the Treaty of Rome in the light of Articles 8 to 11 of the European Convention on Human Rights and the second article of Protocol 4 to the Convention, which provides that restrictions can be imposed only on the grounds of national security or public safety "where they are necessary for the protection of those interests in a democratic society."[26] The Court has continued to interpret the freedom of movement provisions of the treaties on the basis of the European Convention's definition of fundamental rights and freedoms.[27]

The European Community's founders, somewhat ahead of their time, did not stop at discrimination on grounds of nationality. In Article 119 they produced an equally sweeping prohibition of discrimination in the remuneration of male and female workers. The article states flatly: "Each member state shall during the first stage ensure, *and subsequently maintain,* the application of the principle that men and women should receive equal pay for equal work."[28] The Equal Pay Directive passed by the Council of the EC on February 10, 1975, clearly stated that "the principle of equal pay for men and women outlined in Article 119 of the Treaty . . . means for the same work, or for work to which equal value is attributed, the elimination of all discrimination on grounds of sex with regard to all aspects and conditions of remuneration." The European Commission brought proceedings against the United Kingdom in April 1979 because its Equal Pay Act failed to comply fully with the terms of the Directive. The Commission was upheld by the ECJ in July 1982, and the British government was obliged to amend the Equal Pay regulations to include a third basis for claiming equal pay, namely work of equal value.[29]

The ECJ has insisted, in its verdicts, on strict interpretation of the Directive. One of many examples was a case concerning pensions brought before the Court in 1987, in which the pension scheme excluded part-time workers unless they had worked full time for a minimum of fifteen years out of twenty. The employer argued that he wanted to encourage full-time work for the benefit of his company. The ECJ held that the requirement to work full-time for a minimum period disproportionately affected women. It would be contrary to Article 119 unless it could be explained by factors that did not involve discrimination on the grounds of sex.[30]

Apart from equal pay and other remuneration, the EC in 1976 adopted the Equal Treatment Directive (76/207), which requires that in such matters as promotion, training, working conditions, and dismissal procedures, the sexes must be "treated on a non-discriminatory basis."

The Activist Court: Building on Case Law

In the development of the European Community, the ECJ has, as much as the political leaders, expanded the conception of the Court's human rights responsibilities. In 1969, deciding the case of *Stauder v. City of Ulm,* the ECJ made its first reference to human rights. The case concerned the way in which citizens were required to identify themselves as welfare beneficiaries for the purpose of buying subsidized butter. (The plaintiff objected to having to provide his name.)[31] The *Stauder* Court took the occasion to declare that fundamental rights "were enshrined in the general principles of Community law and protected by the Court."[32]

A much bigger challenge to the Court's understanding of its duties occurred only a year later, in the *Internationale Handelsgesellschaft* case, where the issue arose of which laws would take precedence when EC regulations and national protections (in this case established by the German Constitution) came into conflict.[33] The Community had introduced a regulation (a form of Community law) setting up a system whereby exporters were required to put down a deposit as a guarantee against a customer's failure to pay. A German company challenged the regulation on the grounds that it was not compatible with the fundamental rights of German citizens that were enshrined in the German Constitution (a constitution notable for the protection it affords to individual rights). A lower German court had upheld the right of the company to resist payment of the deposit, but the European Court of Justice in a preliminary ruling held that "the protection of such rights, whilst inspired by the constitutional traditions common to the Member states, must be ensured within the framework of the structures and objectives of the Community." Thus the German company was required to comply with EC rules, even if those rules appeared to be at odds with those of the German state. The reference to respect for fundamental rights as part of the general principles of law reinforced the ECJ's *Stauder* decision, but the European Community protections fell far short of the guarantees embodied in the German Constitution.

The company appealed to Germany's Federal Constitutional Court (the FCC or *Bundesverfassungsgericht*) arguing that the regulation was in conflict with the fundamental rights of German citizens guaranteed by their constitution. The FCC disregarded the preliminary ruling of the ECJ. The court recognized that under Article 24 of its constitution, the Federal Republic of Germany could transfer sovereign powers to an international body, in this case the European Community. But the transfer had to be compatible with the constitutional order of the Federal Republic. Community law did not offer the same protection for human rights as did German law: There was no catalogue of human rights in the European treaties; the European Parliament was not directly elected and was therefore not accountable to the people. As long as (*solange* in German) Community law did not adequately protect the human rights of German citizens, German courts had to retain their ability to refer questions on the constitutionality of Community law to the FCC. The case became known as "Solange 1."

The *Internationale Handelsgesellsschaft* verdict thereby challenged the supremacy of EC law, though the FCC argued that it had provided an opportunity for the two legal orders, domestic and Community, to be reconciled.[34]

By 1970, the time of the *Handelsgesellschaft* case, the economy of the German Federal Republic was already more powerful than those of each of the other five original members of the European Economic Community: Italy, France, Belgium, The Netherlands, and Luxembourg. This challenge to the decision of the Community's Court was therefore of the utmost seriousness. Over the next decade, not only the Commission and the Court, but even the politicians in the Community's Council of Ministers and in its highest body, the heads of government assembled in the European Council, worked urgently to correct the democratic deficit Germany's Constitutional Court had so forcefully identified.

In a series of decisions in the 1970s, the European Court of Justice began to articulate a set of fundamental rights at the core of the European Community. Each judgment built incrementally on its predecessor, and eventually the Court read "an unwritten Bill of Rights" into Community law, as one of its own judges, G. Frederico Mancini, called it.[35] The Court was the most creative and active of the Community's institutions during these years of "Eurosclerosis." The ECJ occasionally even overstepped the bounds of what the member states held to be its proper role, as the *Handelsgesellschaft* case illustrated. It was aided and abetted in this by the European Commission, the guardian of the Treaty of Rome, whose members encouraged the judges to issue rulings that furthered European integration and increased the strength of the Community.

In *Nold v. Commission,* a plaintiff again argued that a Commission decision violated the individual rights protected by the German Constitution. In this 1973 case, the Court drew not only on the general principles of law but also on common constitutional traditions and human rights treaties "on which the Member States have collaborated or of which they are signatories,"[36] a reference that was clearly meant to include the European Convention on Human Rights. In the following year in the *Rutili* case,[37] the Court specifically invoked Articles 8 to 11 of the European Convention in support of its decision.[38]

One of the most remarkable illustrations of the Court's new determination to uphold individual human rights can be found in *Van Duyn v. Home Office,* which was decided only a few months after *Nold.*[39] In its judgment, the ECJ held that the principle of "direct effect" extended to directives as well as to regulations, even though directives required member states to take steps to implement them. Furthermore, the Court ruled, this would apply even if the directive in question had not yet been transposed into national law. Not only did this judgment constitute a very broad interpretation of the Community's powers, it also served as a weapon against the widespread evasion of Community law practiced by member states that simply failed to implement EC laws at the national level. The judgment was strongly criticized by some national judges, but their concerns evoked few echoes among politicians at the time, who thus appeared to support the judges' interpretation of European integration.

A significant 1979 case, *Wünsche Handelsgesellschaft*,[40] also known as "Solange 2," enabled Germany's Federal Constitutional Court to revisit the issue of the protection of human rights raised in the Solange 1 case in the light of these developments. By this time, the FCC accepted that Community safeguards of fundamental rights were adequate and comparable to those of Germany's *Grundgesetz*. The decision of the European Council that, starting in 1979, the European Parliament should be directly elected, went some way to meet the FCC's earlier objections.

The FCC also decided that the ECJ was "a lawful judge" within the terms of Article 101 of the German Constitution and that therefore applications from German courts to the FCC to review the constitutionality of EC law in respect of human rights would no longer be admissible.[41] The Constitutional Court, however, in this new decision (which went some way to reverse the decision in the Solange 1 case), relied heavily on the presumption that any transfer of powers to the EC would remain within the terms of Germany's ratification of the treaties.

To bolster the democratic legitimacy of the substantial new transfers of powers required by the Maastricht Treaty (1992), the *Grundgesetz* itself was amended by a new Article 23. This Article required the Bundestag and the Bundesrat (the upper House representing the German *Länder*, or states) each to ratify the Treaty, and any further changes that affected the content of the *Grundgesetz*, by a two-thirds majority, thereby protecting not only the constitution but also the interests of the *Länder*.[42]

The European Court of Justice spent the 1970s developing a more precise and detailed catalogue of human rights, steadily extending the Community's jurisdiction and therefore its own. Judge Mancini commented that "reading an unwritten Bill of Rights into Community law is indeed the most striking contribution the Court has made to the development of a constitution for Europe."[43] The ECJ did not need to wait for cases to come before it in order to hand down opinions; under Article 177 of the Treaty of Rome, the ECJ could, at the request of a court or tribunal of a member state, offer a preliminary ruling on the interpretation of the Treaty or on the validity or interpretation of the acts of the EEC institutions. Indeed, in instances in which national law could not offer a judicial remedy, the national court was obliged to seek such preliminary rulings.

Article 177 enabled the ECJ to win the trust and cooperation of member states' judges and thereby to extend its influence over national as well as Community law. Preliminary rulings have been of great significance in developing the corpus of EC law. Their use has been mutually beneficial to national courts and the European Court, as they enable ECJ judges to familiarize themselves with the traditions of others, namely, the *code civile*, the common law, and the modern constitutions of member states.

Hidden away in Luxembourg, a country far from the continent's major transport and information highways, the Court attracted little attention. For years it was undisturbed in its quiet task of building and strengthening the Community. The dominant concern of the EEC's political leaders during this period of relative stagnation in the 1970s revolved around the expansion of the Community to include the United Kingdom, Denmark, and Ireland; they were engaged in "widening rather than deepening" the Community.

THE TINDEMANS REPORT
AND ITS SEQUELAE: INTEGRATION AND
THE EXTENSION OF HUMAN RIGHTS IN EUROPE

The expansion of the Community to include three nations that remained skeptical about closer European integration, the United Kingdom, Denmark, and Ireland was not, however, the only preoccupation of Europe's political leaders in the 1970s. The 1973 oil shock, and the recession that followed it, brought them close to despair. In an effort to shape a vision for the future, Leo Tindemans, the Belgian prime minister and one of Europe's elder statesmen, was invited in 1975 by his fellow heads of state in the European Council to define the term "European Union." In the letter accompanying his report, Tindemans wrote: "The crisis in Europe is so serious that we must, in the immediate future, save what has already been achieved and, working on this basis, take drastic measures to take a significant leap forward." This theme of advance by way of crisis would be repeated many times as the Community staggered forward.[44]

Prime Minister Tindemans's report was years in advance of the political will of the member states, calling as it did for a single decision-making center, a common foreign policy, economic and monetary union, and a transfer of many powers to the Community. For the first time, the report used the term "A Citizen's Europe." Tindemans saw the recognition and protection of fundamental individual rights as the necessary complement of the greater powers he believed the European institutions should exercise. "The European Council should instruct the institutions to propose how best to set about this recognition and protection. The latter must at all events mean that individuals will have the right of direct appeal to the Court of Justice against an act of an institution in violation of these fundamental rights."[45] Twenty years later, Tindemans's proposal for the right of direct appeal to the ECJ had yet to be realized.

Parliament's Declaration

The European Parliament was enthusiastic about Tindemans's message and would soon be rejoicing in the democratic legitimacy to be conferred upon it by direct election of its members in the 1979 elections, pursuant to a 1977 European Council decision. On April 5, 1977, the Parliament, together with the European Council of the EEC and the Commission on Fundamental Rights of the Council of Europe, issued a common declaration that put the European Convention for the Protection of Human Rights and Fundamental Freedoms at the center of the principles of law intended to guide all European institutions. "The European Parliament, the Council and the Commission stress the prime importance they attach to the principle of fundamental rights, as derived in particular from the constitutions of the member states and the European Convention for the Protection of Human Rights and Fundamental Freedoms," the declaration reads. "In the exercise of their powers and in pursuance of the aims of the European Communities they respect and will continue to respect these rights."[46]

The motivations for the declaration were not wholly abstract ones. The first enlargement of the Community in 1972 may have included countries with deep internal differences of opinion about European integration, but at least all three—Denmark, the United Kingdom, and Ireland—were well-established democracies. The next enlargements were likely to be more problematic, for the three countries applying in the later 1970s for full membership—Greece, Portugal, and Spain—had been dictatorships less than a decade before.[47] Several of the existing members therefore felt that a strong framework of respect for human rights within the Community's institutions was an essential precondition for enlargement. When Greece joined the EEC in January 1981, work by the European Parliament on a draft treaty for European Union was already beginning, based on the report by Altiero Spinelli, an Italian member of the European Parliament with strong federalist aspirations. Published in February 1984, the Draft Treaty was adopted by the European Parliament by an overwhelming majority (237 to 31, with 43 members of the European Parliament abstaining).[48]

The member states, with one or two exceptions, were far from ready to move as rapidly in the direction of a federal Europe as the European Parliament proposed. Those with the real political power, the governments of member states, still easily dismissed the European Parliament. The Dooge Committee on institutional change, set up at the June 1984 Fontainebleau Summit of European heads of government, simply buried the Draft Treaty of European Union in favor of a French government draft that fell far short of Spinelli's radical ideas.

However, governments did catch something of the mood of the times. The ice was beginning to break in Central Europe, with the round table talks between the Polish government and Solidarity. Associating the Community with building democracy and protecting human rights was no longer suspect; it was part of its raison d'être. Even the redoubtable prime minister of the United Kingdom, Margaret Thatcher, began to show enthusiasm for such objectives.

The Solemn Declaration of Stuttgart

At their 1983 Stuttgart summit meeting under the German presidency, precipitated by the accession negotiations with Spain and Portugal, the EEC's European Council announced "a relaunch of the European Community."[49] The main subjects it addressed were reform of the common agricultural policy and reform of the Community's financial structure. However, the ten heads of state and government also signed a Solemn Declaration on European Union, based on a draft European Act prepared by the Italian and German governments. The preamble of the Solemn Declaration invoked the promotion of democracy on the basis of fundamental rights and referred again to the constitutions and laws of member states and to the European Convention on Human Rights. In the same context, it also mentioned the European Social Charter, the first such reference by the European Council to social rights.[50] The Declaration, for the first time, imposed as a condition of membership in the Community "respect for and maintenance of representative democracy and human rights in each Member State." European member states had never before felt it necessary to spell out these requirements so explicitly.

A declaration, however solemn, is not of course a legal act. The member states' commitment to these principles was formally enshrined in the next treaty, the Single European Act of 1986, which was largely directed at completion of the common European market, and which turned the European Economic Community into the European Union. The preamble of the Single European Act used words identical to those of the Stuttgart Declaration about promoting democracy on the basis of fundamental rights and referred again to the European Convention on Human Rights and to the European Social Charter. The Act went so far that it is hard now to believe that the British government's representatives gave serious thought to what they had signed, for during the later negotiations on the Maastricht Treaty, British representatives were at pains to limit the powers of European institutions to protect the rights of citizens.

By the end of the 1980s, the development of what was now the European Union had begun to be driven by outside events. The fall of the Berlin Wall and the unstoppable momentum toward a unified Germany concentrated the minds of Germany's partners. After initial hesitation, most European finance ministers concluded on the basis of the 1988 Delors Committee Report that economic and monetary union was the best way to harness the economic might of the new unified Germany within the European framework.[51] Plans for the second preparatory stage of monetary union moved on apace. By February 7, 1992, the same year in which the single market was to be completed, the new treaty was ready for signing at Maastricht.

The Maastricht Treaty, 1992

Maastricht was in many ways an unsatisfactory treaty, cobbling together the very disparate views of member states in a series of awkward compromises, as the protection of fundamental human rights illustrates. For the first time in a European treaty, reference was made to the individual citizen. Indeed, the Treaty established a number of rights—a very limited number—pertaining to citizens of the European Union, such as the right to vote, to run for office in European parliamentary and local elections in member states other than one's own, and to hold a common European passport.

Despite the many declarations and preambles of the previous fifteen years, however, the Maastricht Treaty did little to enforce the fundamental rights of individual European citizens that were now enshrined at the European Union's core. The European Court of Justice continued to be restricted. In the eyes of at least some member states, the unnoticed activism of the 1970s Court of Justice had, by the 1990s, developed into a threat to national sovereignty.

In a third major German case, Germany's accession to the Maastricht Treaty was challenged by Manfred Brunner, a former senior commission official.[52] Brunner argued that the right of German citizens to elect a government under Article 38 of the *Grundgesetz* would be infringed by the continuing transfer of powers from the Bundestag to the European Union. The FCC found that the transfer of powers was legitimate so long as it did not diminish the powers of the German government to the point of being meaningless. The scope of any transferred powers must therefore be clear and limited. Their legitimation remained a matter for the Bundestag, at least until such time as the EU was fully democratic. Nor could the Bundestag confer on the Union the power to create its own powers (the so-called Kompetenz-Kompetenz question). The national member states remained masters of the treaties and had to go through a democratic process before any powers could be transferred.

The European Union's evolution toward guaranteeing democracy and human rights was, however, not to the taste of all member states. France and the United Kingdom were far from enthusiastic. The United Kingdom had long opposed any strengthening of the powers of the European Parliament. Its Conservative government, which was in power from June 1979 until May 1997, was also profoundly suspicious of the ECJ, which it regarded as an instrument to bring about closer integration.

Largely because of the British government's opposition, the jurisdiction of the Court was extended very little if at all by the Maastricht Treaty. Article L of the Treaty limited the scope of the Court's jurisdiction to the existing treaties, as amended by the Maastricht Treaty, and to the interpretation of any conventions made under the intergovernmental third pillar concerning the fields of justice and home affairs. Even this latter function, together with the resolution of any disputes about the application of such conventions, depended on an invitation from a member state party to the convention asking the Court of Justice to provide an interpretation or resolve a dispute.

Although the Maastricht Treaty did little to advance formal protection of human rights, events again took over. In the post–cold war world, neutrality in disputes between East and West was no longer an objection to membership in the European Union, and all three of Western Europe's traditionally neutral countries—Austria, Sweden, and Finland, which had all been members of the European Free Trade Association—applied for membership.[53] The European Council, meeting in Copenhagen in June 1993, confirmed that all three would be invited to accede and that negotiations would be completed by January 1, 1995. The Council also noted that several of the countries of Central and Eastern Europe that were emerging from the disintegrating Soviet bloc wanted to become full members of the European Union, and set explicit conditions that applicant states would be required to meet before membership would be granted. "Membership requires that the candidate country has achieved stability of institutions guaranteeing democracy, the rule of law, human rights and respect for and protection of minorities."[54] The Council also laid down in some detail the process for European Union enlargement, which still applies today, and which requires new members to accept in toto the *acquis communautaire*.

The Amsterdam Treaty, 1996

The Maastricht Treaty had left unresolved many of the European Union's shortcomings regarding expansion. Institutions that had been framed for six or nine members were inadequate to serve twenty or more. The Union's decision-making procedures, even with fifteen members, were extremely complex, far beyond the understanding of even the most active citizens. Its second and third pillars (on foreign and security policy and internal security), constructed at Maastricht to accommodate the British determination to defend national sovereignty, were clearly shaky. Aspirations to a common foreign and defense policy had been made ridiculous by the European Union's inability to mount any common position on Bosnia, which was rescued from complete disaster only by the United States. Internal security was running up against the difficulty of maintaining separate immigration, visa, and asylum policies while trying to coordinate the strengthening of the EU's external borders. These thorny problems were bequeathed to the new Inter-Governmental Conference (IGC), which began in 1996 and concluded in October 1997 with the Treaty of Amsterdam.[55]

The IGC, like its predecessor, which drew up the Treaty of Maastricht, was bedeviled by differences too wide to bridge on many of the problems it addressed. Little progress was made on institutional reform. Great Britain's Conservative government, still in power during most of the long negotiations, adamantly opposed the inclusion of any part of the two intergovernmental pillars in the European Community's integrated structure. In the end, London was simply bypassed on asylum and immigration policy, which were brought within the Community structure. On the creation of a zone of "freedom, security and justice," where European citizens would enjoy freedom of movement without internal frontiers, the British government firmly maintained its opt-out: Frontier controls between the United Kingdom and Ireland on one hand, and the rest of the European Community on the other, still continue.

On social rights, most governments were reluctant to go beyond the terms already included in the Social Policy Protocol of the Maastricht Treaty,[56] despite a radical report from the Commission's Comité des Sages calling for a basic list of fundamental civic and social rights such as equality before the law, the right of association, and the right of collective bargaining to be written into the new treaty.[57] Nor did the Comité's proposal for a continuing dialogue between the EU's institutions and nongovernmental organizations (NGOs), to scrutinize and update such rights, commend itself to the Council of Ministers, despite support from the European Parliament's Social Affairs Committee. At least, however, following Labour's victory in the British general election, the United Kingdom signed the Social Policy Protocol in May 1997, thereby ending the exemption it had obtained at Maastricht.

In human rights terms, the Amsterdam Treaty had several substantial achievements to its credit. The most significant was the new Article F1, and the corresponding amendment to Article 236 of the Treaty establishing the European Community. For the first time, the heads of government assembled as the European Council would have the power to suspend certain rights under the Treaty, including voting rights, of a member state found to be in serious and persistent breach of the founding principles of the Union, as set out in Title 1: "the principles of liberty, democracy, respect for human rights and fundamental freedoms and the rule of law."[58]

In determining the existence of such a breach, the Council must be unanimous (apart from the accused member state), and the European Parliament also must assent by a two-thirds majority, which must represent an absolute majority of all the Parliament's members. Once a breach has been determined, it requires only a "qualified majority"—based on weighted votes—to suspend a member state's rights or subsequently to vary or revoke that suspension.

Thus thirteen years after the European Parliament agreed in its Draft Treaty that the rights of a member state could be suspended for a serious and persistent breach of human rights, the European Council agreed to provide, by treaty, a mechanism for enforcement. In doing so, however, the Council maintained control of the procedure. According to the Treaty of Amsterdam, a determination could be initiated only by the Commission or by one-third of the member states; the European Parliament cannot do so. The determination itself would be made by a unanimous vote of the Council, not by the European Court of Justice as the European Parliament had proposed in 1984. Once again the governments would be judges in their own cause and therefore reluctant to create precedents that might one day affect themselves.

The Amsterdam Treaty reiterates (by amended Article O) the necessity for any European state seeking membership in the European Union to adhere to the same human rights principles. It has the potential to bring about human rights advances in two additional ways. The new Article 6a extends the grounds on which the Council may take action against discrimination, so that they now include sex, racial and ethnic origin, religion and belief, disability, age and sexual orientation, a veritable litany of political correctness. Unfortunately, this broad provision is largely vitiated by the constraints of the required procedure. The final decision on "appropriate action," whatever that may be, rests with the European Council and requires a unanimous vote before any action can be undertaken. What saves the Article from futility, however, is that it amends the original founding Treaty of Rome and therefore falls within the jurisdiction of the European Court of Justice. Powerful NGOs are already mobilizing to test the Court's resolve to combat discrimination on these new grounds. The ECJ's record with regard to cases concerning discrimination on grounds of nationality (Article 6) or sex in the context of pay and working conditions (Article 119) has been positive and liberal. In the latter area, the Court's interpretations of Article 119 and of the Directives based on it have been consistently broad, inclusive, and sensitive to family responsibilities: It has extended equal treatment to part-time workers, required equal treatment from occupational pension schemes, and offered extensive protection for the rights of pregnant workers.

It will be up to the ECJ to realize the potential of the third human rights achievement of the Amsterdam Treaty. The IGC brought a substantial part of the third pillar on internal security—that concerned with visa, immigration, and asylum policy—into the first pillar, making it a European Community affair, and thereby within the jurisdiction of the ECJ. Member state governments were not motivated mainly by human rights considerations but by their determination to protect and strengthen the external borders of the Community while allowing free movement within it. The Schengen Agreement of 1985, by which border and customs controls among the (now thirteen) state parties were eliminated, was reached outside the EC's legal structure by five original member states eager to establish a European zone without frontiers.[59] Though it has operated unevenly and not very successfully, this Agreement is now being brought within the Community, with the Council overseeing implementation of its provisions. However, member states procedures may continue to differ for up to five years, and Britain and Ireland, as islands, may remain outside the operation of the Agreement with their own separate border controls.

The negotiations at the IGC on the new Title IIIA, bringing visas, asylum, immigration, and policies on free movement of people within the European Community, were, as usual, not unaffected by external events. Among these events was the growing threat from organized crime, in particular the drug trade and the sex trade, including trade in young children. Organized crime has been exacerbated by the collapse of the Soviet bloc and the consequent loss of authority and corruption of its legal order. Police forces in Western Europe have been compelled by the "wild east" to work closely with Central European nations in an effort to contain these and other criminal activities.

Also influencing the Amsterdam negotiating process were the huge flows of refugees and displaced people from Bosnia and other parts of the former Federal Republic of Yugoslavia, many of whom had sought refuge in Germany. Internal unrest and dire poverty also had driven thousands of Albanians to Italy. Faced with such huge pressures from their chaotic and impoverished neighbors to the south and east, the European Union's negotiators sought to shore up their external borders and to tighten immigration and asylum policy. They moved from trying to establish common policies to setting minimum standards on asylum and refugees. They proposed a common visa regime to be operative within five years and established an agreed list of third countries whose nationals would be required to obtain visas (limited to three months) in order to enter the European Union.

Bringing immigration, visa, and refugee policy within the first pillar, the Community pillar, of the European Union meant bringing such policies within the purview of the European Court of Justice. But the Treaty's negotiators, foreseeing a flood of cases, took steps to limit the Court's jurisdiction on these issues.[60] The ECJ can offer preliminary rulings at the request of a national court only if no other remedy is available in national law. The Court is excluded from jurisdiction over any measure relating to domestic law and order or internal security, areas that are of great concern to defenders of human rights. This exclusion also applies to what remains of the third (justice and home affairs) pillar, now limited to police and judicial cooperation on criminal matters, so neither individual citizens nor the European Parliament can file petitions related to these areas. Access to the ECJ by individual citizens or by the European Parliament would trespass on the principle of national sovereignty, under which law and order and police matters remain with member states. What is within the Court's powers is to rule on the legality of the so-called framework decisions, on broad strategy, and on disputes between member states, within this residuary intergovernmental third pillar.

FEDERATION AND CONFEDERATION:
AN UNEASY BALANCE

The Amsterdam compromise, in which part of the third pillar on internal security was moved into the first (Community) pillar, while part remained outside, exemplifies the uneasy balance between federalism and confederalism that characterizes the European Union itself. The role of the European Court of Justice as defender of human rights is now well established within the Community sphere. Outside it, there is no redress for the citizen through the European Court of Justice. In that sense, it is not a Supreme Court for the European Union.

For redress of human rights grievances outside the European Community sphere, citizens must look instead to the European Convention and its ultimate interpreter and guardian, the European Court of Human Rights at Strasbourg, which operates within the structure of the Council of Europe. Among its forty-one members, however, several of the newcomers lack a democratic tradition or a tradition of an independent judiciary, and it remains to be seen whether the Court will therefore become more cautious in the defense of individual rights, or whether instead the new members will be influenced by the Council's culture of liberty.

Within the European Union, the European Council of heads of state and government remains very much in the driver's seat. Time and again, it is the

European Council and the Council of Ministers—not the Court or the Parliament—that have played the key role. As the inevitable spillover from the single market seeps into the remaining areas under national control, member states exert themselves to retain influence within the European Union's institutions. They invoke the principle of subsidiarity, under which actions should be taken at the lowest administrative level consonant with efficacy. The principle is embodied in Article 3b(2) of the Treaty of Union, which reads, "In areas which do not fall within its exclusive competence, the Community shall take action, in accordance with the principle of subsidiarity, only if and in so far as the objectives of the proposed action cannot be sufficiently achieved by the member states and can therefore, by reason of the scale or effects of the proposed action, be better achieved by the Community." Yet the growing authority of the Court of Justice cannot be gainsaid. At the very least, the member states of the European Union are now fully and explicitly committed to respect for the fundamental human rights of their own citizens.

Yet an anomaly lies at the heart of the European approach to human rights. The Universal Declaration of Human Rights of 1948, which in turn inspired the European Convention for the Protection of Human Rights and Fundamental Freedoms, was intended to be exactly what it said: universal. Fundamental rights were not derived from the law of nations but were inherent in being human itself. Many conventions and international treaties in the past fifty years have reiterated that principle. It underlies the concept of crimes against humanity, where the jurisdiction is often said to be universal.[61]

In practice, however, there are double standards, and the European Union is no exception, having one standard for its own people and another for nationals of other countries. The limitations on the role of the European Court of Justice with respect to immigration, asylum, and refugees will make it difficult to establish universal norms embodying respect for human rights. The insistence of national governments that the measures they take to maintain law and order and internal security are outside the Court's jurisdiction (even though Title IIIA now puts immigration, asylum, and refugees within the Community structure) leaves third-country nationals vulnerable. Though the European Court of Human Rights may provide some protection for asylum-seekers and refugees, it remains to be seen what balance will be struck between the imperatives of civil liberty and those of internal security. Much will depend in practice on the economic and political prospects of the European Union's neighbors and on the willingness of the EU to help them achieve stability.

International human rights norms have now, however, clearly entered into the European conscience and onto the policy agenda. Indeed, awareness of human rights is growing rapidly beyond the EU as well. In the words of Mary

Robinson, the UN High Commissioner for Human Rights, "a culture of human rights is growing throughout the world."[62] Learning from the grim experiences in Bosnia, Rwanda, and now Kosovo, the European Union is assuming a global role as an advocate of human rights and a significant source of financial aid for countries building democratic institutions. EU external development policy was linked in the Maastricht Treaty of 1992 to "the general objective of developing and consolidating democracy and the rule of law, and to that of respecting human rights and fundamental freedoms." A region of obvious interest given such an objective is Central and Eastern Europe, many of whose nations are candidates for European Union membership. The EU, working closely with the Organization for Security and Cooperation in Europe (OSCE) and the Council of Europe, has supported educational programs dealing with human rights and the rights of minorities. The objective, however, embraces countries well beyond the bounds of Europe.

EU institutions have other instruments to promote human rights. The European Parliament lobbies other governments about respect for human rights and sends delegations to them that sometimes include senior officials. Since 1995 all EU external agreements with other countries, in such areas as association, economic cooperation, or development cooperation agreements, include legally binding provisions on human rights that apply to the EU and the other party alike. If either party fails to respect these provisions, the agreement can be restricted or even suspended.[63]

In 1994 all human rights initiatives within the EU were brought together in a single chapter of the European budget, which in 1998 had EU 75.8 million available. The European Parliament, which takes a lively interest in human rights matters, would like a much larger budget for the purpose. Several member states as well as the European Parliament itself have been concerned about the lack of a legal basis for this sum, and from time to time it has been challenged.

On July 24, 1997, the Commission presented a proposal for a Council Regulation on the Development and Consolidation of Democracy and the Rule of Law and Respect for Human Rights and Freedoms, setting out operational objectives and criteria for Community funding. The proposed regulation would also set out decision-making procedures, provision for regular evaluation of activities undertaken, and a requirement for an Annual Report to the Council and the European Parliament on operations funded. Mindful of the complaints about long delays in the financing of Community aid projects, the regulation also provided for immediate help in the case of emergencies. The regulation was approved in April 1999, and is therefore now part of Community Law.[64]

In 1997 the European Parliament voted 3 million euros for the proposed International Criminal Court and the ad hoc UN war crimes tribunals in Rwanda and the former Yugoslavia. The EU's fifteen member states have been strong advocates of the International Criminal Court. EU member states were also prominent in the attempt to arrest Senator Augusto Pinochet, the former president and dictator of Chile, so that he might stand trial for crimes against humanity.[65] Spain sought to extradite him from Britain. He was arrested and detained while the case for his extradition and for the lifting of his immunity as head of state was considered by the House of Lords, Britain's highest court. Another four member governments were believed to be considering similar prosecutions of Pinochet.

In the words of Lord Nicholls, speaking for the majority in the first House of Lords decision on the Pinochet case, "international law has made plain that certain types of conduct, including torture and hostage-taking, are not acceptable conduct on the part of anyone. This applies as much to heads of state or even more so, as it does to everyone else; the contrary conclusion would make a mockery of international law."[66]

That opinion was reiterated even more strongly in the second judgment on March 24, 1999, regarding Senator Pinochet's immunity as a head of state. Dismissing the claim of immunity for a former head of state from prosecution for crimes against humanity, Lord Phillips of Worth Matravers, one of the seven law lords who heard the case, concluded:

> Since the Second World War states have recognized that not all criminal conduct can be left to be dealt with as a domestic matter by the laws and the courts of the territories in which such conduct occurs. There are some categories of crime of such gravity that they shock the consciousness of mankind and cannot be tolerated by the international community. Any individual who commits such a crime offends against international law. The nature of these crimes is such that they are likely to involve the concerted conduct of many and liable to involve the complicity of the officials of the state in which they occur, if not of the state itself. In these circumstances it is desirable that jurisdiction should exist to prosecute individuals for such conduct outside the territory in which such conduct occurs.[67]

With grinding slowness, the international rule of law is thus being constructed. The European contribution is the postwar evolution of the doctrine of fundamental human rights, an evolution tht progresses gradually toward a European Union Charter or Bill of Rights, within a region of the world notorious in this century for its contempt for human rights. It is a notable, if half-hidden, achievement.

NOTES

*   Special thanks are due to Lord Lester of Herne Hill, Q.C. and to Andrew Duff of The Federal Trust for their generous help and advice.

1. The human rights of third-country nationals are protected under the 1950 European Convention for the Protection of Human Rights and Fundamental Freedoms, sometimes referred to as the European Convention, Rome, November 4, 1950, Council of Europe, *European Treaty Series,* No 5. They are not similarly protected under European Union law.

2. Individual petitions, known as "communications," also can be brought before the United Nations Human Rights Committee, established under the International Covenant on Civil and Political Rights (ICCPR), by citizens of countries that have signed the First Optional Protocol to the ICCPR, as all European Union members except the United Kingdom have now done.

3. The three pillars of the Treaty on European Union are: the Community dimension corresponding to the provisions set out in the Treaty establishing the European Community such as Union citizenship, Community policies, and Economic and Monetary Union (first pillar); common foreign and security policy, which is covered by Title V of the Treaty on European Union (second pillar); and cooperation in the fields of justice and home affairs, which is covered by Title VI of the Treaty on European Union (third pillar)."

4. *Acquis communautaire:* The acquis communautaire or community patrimony is the body of common rights and obligations that binds all the member states together within the European Union. The Union has committed itself to maintaining the acquis communautaire in its entirety and developing it further.

5. The Treaty of Amsterdam, which entered into force May 1, 1999, provides for some of the fields covered by the third pillar to be transferred to the first pillar. Following such transfers, only provisions on police and judicial cooperation remain in Title VI, within the intergovernmental area.

6. The Schengen Agreement is now accepted by thirteen of the fifteen EU member states, outside the framework of the European Community because it proved impossible to reach a unanimous decision. Britain and Ireland remain outside Schengen at present, and there are special arrangements for Denmark. See Andrew Duff, ed., *The Treaty of Amsterdam: Text and Commentary* (London: Sweet and Maxwell for the Federal Trust, 1997).

7. The United Kingdom and Ireland did not transfer responsibility for visas, asylum, and refugee policy to the Community in June 1997, nor have they removed internal border controls as the other member states have done. On March 12, 1999, however, the British government indicated its willingness to cooperate on law enforcement and judicial cooperation, including the Schengen information system, providing there was no conflict with its national border and immigration controls. The pressure of large flows of refugees and asylum seekers into the European Union is forcing common policies even on reluctant member states like the United Kingdom.

8. The right to challenge the acts, or failures to act, of the member states and of European institutions is reserved to "privileged litigants," namely other member states or corporate entities directly and individually affected.

9. These steps to increase transparency by the European Council were motivated by a deep concern among the EU's leaders about the hostility and lack of trust in European bureaucracy and in European politicians, demonstrated by opinion polls and exacerbated by the resignation of the entire Executive Commission of the European Union on March 16, 1999. This resignation followed an independent report which criticized the Commission for failure to control mismanagement, fraud, and cronyism.

10. European Parliament resolution on the Charter of Fundamental Rights (adopted on 16 March 2000), available on the Web site of the European Parliament, <http://www.europarl.eu.int/charter/docs/en/text3.htm>.

11. Francois Duchêne, *Jean Monnet: The First Statesman of Interdependence* (New York: W.W. Norton, 1994), p. 166.

12. Ibid., p. 186.

13. The ten initial signatories were Belgium, Denmark, France, Ireland, Italy, Luxembourg, The Netherlands, Norway, Sweden, and the United Kingdom.

14. The United Kingdom's Human Rights Act of 1998 obliges a minister to state in writing that in his or her view the provisions of any given bill are compatible with the rights protected by the European Convention. Alternatively, the minister can declare that the government wishes Parliament to proceed with the bill notwithstanding the minister's inability to make a statement of compatibility. In practice, however, it would be very difficult to pass a bill on this basis. Furthermore, it is unlawful for any public authority in the United Kingdom to act in a way that is incompatible with a right specified by the Convention, and if it does so, proceedings can be brought in the U.K. courts by anyone who is, or would be, a victim of the unlawful act. The U.K. courts, under the Act, have to interpret statutes so as to be compatible with Convention rights "as far as possible," but if necessary may declare legislation incompatible. If a provision of legislation is declared to be incompatible with a Convention right, or if it conflicts with a finding of the European Court of Human Rights in proceedings against the United Kingdom, the minister "may" by order amend the legislation to remove the incompatibility. The use of the word "may" protects the sovereignty of Parliament.

    In practice, ministers would know that a failure to act when a declaration had been made, or when a judgment of incompatibility had been made by a U.K. court, would almost certainly lead to successful legal proceedings against the government in a national court or in the ECHR.

15. Members of the Human Rights Commission were nominated by the Council of Europe's Consultative Assembly, which is made up of members of Parliament who have themselves been appointed by their respective governments; from those nominated, members of the Commission were selected by the Committee of Ministers representing member states.

16. In the 1970s the number of applications averaged 429 a year. In 1996 there were 4,758 applications and in 1997, 4,750. Between 1955 and 1997, 39,047 applications were registered, and 33,123 decisions were taken. Most applications were declared inadmissible; 4,161, just over one in ten of the registered applications, were held to be admissible. Council of Europe, *Yearbook of the European Convention on Human Rights* (Boston: M. Nijhoff, 1997).

17. Europe's wartime experiences gave particular meaning to the right to life and to prohibitions on torture and cruel or inhuman punishment. The Convention protects the rights of privacy and family life but also recognizes the authority of the state. For example, Article 10, the right to free expression, Article 11, the right of peaceful assembly, and Article 1 of Protocol 1, the right to the peaceful enjoyment of one's possessions, are all qualified by the demands of national security or public safety "for the prevention of disorder or crime, for the protection of health or morals, or for the protection of the . . . rights of others." The "general interest" also can be invoked to justify controls on the use of property, according to Protocol 1; it was signed in March 1952, against considerable resistance, at a time when many European governments were engaged in planning the economy and operating publicly owned companies.

18. Article 8 concerns the right to respect for private and family life.

19. *Golder v. UK,* February 21, 1975, series A, No. 18 (1979–80), 1 EHRR.

20. *Pfeifer and Planck v. Austria,* February 25, 1992, Series A, No. 227 (1992), 18 EHRR 692.

21. *Johnson v. UK,* October 24, 1997 (1999), 27 EHRR 296.

22. Lord Lester of Herne Hill, Q.C., "Getting Off Lightly," *The Guardian,* May 31, 1999.

23. Article 48 on freedom of movement and Article 119 on sex discrimination.

24. Lammy Betten and Nicholas Grief, *European Law and Human Rights* (London: Longman, 1998), pp. 56-58.

25. Case C 168/91, (1992) ECR1-1191, quoted in Betten and Grief, *European Law and Human Rights*. The Advocate General is an officer of the European Court of Justice whose job is to assist the Court by delivering impartial opinions on cases brought before the Court. See ECJ Web site, "Composition and organization: The Members of the Court" at <http://www.europa.eu.int/cj/en/pres/co.htm>.

26. Article 8 of the European Convention deals with right to respect for private and family life; Article 9 with freedom of thought, conscience, and religion; Article 10 with freedom of expression; and Article 11 with freedom of assembly and association.

27. Case 36/75, *Rutili v. Minister for the Interior* (1975), European Court Reports (ECR) 1219, quoted in Betten and Grief, *European Law and Human Rights*.

28. Article 119 of the European Convention on Human Rights (emphasis added).

29. *Commission of the European Communities v. the United Kingdom of Great Britain and Northern Ireland* (1982), ICR 578.

30. *Bilka Kaufhaus Gmbh v. Mrs K. Weber von Hartz* (1987), ICR 110.

31. Case 29/69 *Stauder v. City of Ulm Sozialamt* (1969), ECR 419.

32. Ibid.

33. Judgment of 17/12/1970, *Internationale Handelsgesellschaft mbH v. Einfuhr- und Vorratsstelle für Getreide und Futtermittel* (Rep. [1970], p. 1125) (DK70-235), Case 11/70 ECR.

34. Juliane Kokott, "German Constitutional Jurisprudence and European Integration: Part One," *European Public Law*, Vol. 2, No. 2 (Dordrecht: Kluwer Law International, 1996).

35. G. Frederico Mancini, "The Making of a Constitution for Europe," in Robert Keohane and Stanley Hoffmann, eds., *The New European Community: Decisionmaking and Institutional Change* (Boulder, CO: Westview Press, 1991), p. 188.

36. Case 4/73, *J. Nold v. Commission* (1974), ECR 491, reprinted in 2 *Common Market Law Reports* (CMLR), 338 (1974).

37. Case 36/75, *Rutili v. Minister for the Interior*.

38. Betten and Grief, *European Law and Human Rights*, p. 59.

39. Case 41/74, *Van Duyn v. Home Office*, 1974 ECR 1337 [1975], 1 CMLR 1.

40. BverfGE 73 (1987), 3 CMLR 225.

41. Nigel G. Foster, "The German Constitution and EC Membership," *Public Law*, Autumn 1994, p. 393.

42. Foster, "The German Constitution and EC Membership," p. 399.

43. Ibid.

44. Leo Tindemans, *Report on European Union*, presented to the Council on December 29, 1975. "European Union: Report by Mr. Leo Tindemans to the European Council," *EC Bulletin*, Supplement 1/1976.

45. Ibid., Section A: Protection of Rights.

46. *Common Declaration by the Parliament and Council and the Commission on Fundamental Rights*, April 5, 1977.

47. Greece joined in 1981; Portugal and Spain in 1986.

48. *Draft Treaty establishing the European Union*, European Parliament, February 1984.

49. *The Declaration of the European Council, Stuttgart*, June 19, 1983.

50. The European Social Charter opened for signature at Turin in October 1961 and was adopted in 1989. It set forth nineteen fundamental social and economic rights. It was subsequently amended, and a revised Charter was adopted in 1996.

51. European Commission, *Report on Economic and Monetary Union in the European Community* (1989).

52. 2 BvR 2134/92 and 2 BvR 2159/92, *Brunner v. European Union Treaty* (1994), 1 CMLR 57, 95-96 (BGH 1994) (Ger.).

53. The European Free Trade Association, established in 1960, now comprises Norway, Liechtenstein, Iceland, and Switzerland.

54. The Conclusions of the Copenhagen European Council, June 21 and 22, 1993.

55. *The Treaty amending the Treaty on European Union and the Treaty establishing the European Communities,* Amsterdam 1997.

56. "The Social Policy Protocol was adopted by the European Council in December 1991 at Maastricht. It is annexed to the Treaty establishing the European Community and marks further progress on the European Social Charter. It was signed by eleven member states (since the United Kingdom did not share the social policy objectives of the other member states) who wished to make major advances on the basis of the Social Policy Agreement annexed to the Protocol. Following enlargement of the Union to include Austria, Finland and Sweden, the Protocol now reflects the views of fourteen member states. Following the election of a new Government in May 1997, the United Kingdom decided to join the Social Policy Agreement. Once the Treaty of Amsterdam enters into force, the Social Policy Protocol will therefore cease to apply." EU Web site glossary, <http://www.europa.eu.int/scadplus/leg/en/cig/g4000s.htm#s7>.

57. *Report of the Comité des Sages,* under the Chairmanship of Maria Lourdes de Pintasilgo, European Commission, February 1996. (The author was a member of this Comité.)

58. Title 1, Amsterdam Treaty. The Amsterdam Treaty was adopted by the Amsterdam European Council on June 16 and 17, 1997, and signed on October 2, 1997; it entered into force on May 1, 1999.

59. Duff, *Treaty of Amsterdam.*

60. Ibid., p. 21.

61. "The Pinochet Case: Bringing the General to Justice," *The Economist,* November 28, 1998.

62. Mary Robinson, Message of the High Commissioner for Human Rights on the Fiftieth Anniversary of the Universal Declaration of Human Rights, December 10, 1998, at United Nations Headquarters in New York.

63. The European Union suspended its economic cooperation with Togo, a member of the Lomé Convention associated countries, following postpresidential election disputes in June 1998. Cooperation under the Convention with Nigeria, on the other hand, has been resumed following Nigeria's return to democratic civilian rule.

64. Com (97), 357 final 97/0191(SYN), as amended by COM (99), 13 final 97/0191/A (SYN)/.

65. *Parliamentary Debates (Hansard), House of Commons Official Report,* December 9, 1998, cols. 214-17 (London: HMSO, The Stationery Office Ltd.).

66. Opinions of the Lords of Appeal for Judgment in the Cause *Regina v. Bartle and the Commissioner of Police of the Metropolis and Others (Appellants) ex parte Pinochet (Respondent) (On Appeal from a Divisional court of the Queen's Bench Division);* and *Regina v. Evans et al.* (unamended), November 25, 1998, House of Lords, London. This judgment was set aside because one of the judges, Lord Hoffmann, was subsequently held to have had an interest in the case, as an unpaid advisor to Amnesty International. A new panel of seven Law Lords was convened to determine the case. On March 24, 1999, the House of Lords confirmed the earlier judgment.

67. Lord Phillips of Worth Matravers, March 24, 1999. Opinions of the Lords of Appeal for Judgment in the Cause *Regina v. Bartle and the Commissioner of Police of the Metropolis and Others (Appellants) ex parte Pinochet (Respondent) (On Appeal from a Divisional court of the Queen's Bench Division);* and *Regina v. Evans et al.,* March 24, 1999, House of Lords, London. On March 2, 2000 British Home Secretary Jack Straw ruled that Pinochet should not be extradited due to failing health. He returned to Chile that day and may yet stand trial at home. The new government of President Ricardo Lagos holds that General Pinochet must be found either mentally unfit to stand trial, and will then have to leave public office, or he can continue as a Senator and risk the possibility of trial.

The Inter-American System
of Protection:
Its Contributions to the
International Law of Human Rights

JUAN E. MÉNDEZ[*]

Juan E. Méndez is Director, Center for Civil and Human Rights, Notre Dame Law School; Executive Director, Inter-American Institute on Human Rights (IIHR), San José, Costa Rica (1996–1999); and Member-Elect, Inter-American Commission on Human Rights, Organization of American States.

Over a period of fifty years, the nations of the Western Hemisphere have developed a relatively sophisticated and progressive system of international human rights protection for their citizens. Though the region is often thought of as Latin America, the system also comprises the independent nations of the Caribbean, which include Spanish-speaking Cuba and the Dominican Republic, French-speaking Haiti, and about a dozen English-speaking island nations, plus English-speaking United States and Canada. Also included is Suriname, whose official language is Dutch; and Brazil, where Portuguese is spoken. The cultural diversity of the region is, however, even greater than these officially recognized languages suggest, given the many different indigenous peoples (in some countries comprising the majority of the population) and the vast contingents from Europe, Africa, and Asia whose ancestors came as immigrants or slaves.

Needless to say, the inter-American region is diverse also in the degree of economic and political development of the thirty-five nations. While some have been stable democracies for a long time, many have lived even recently under military dictatorships or through the ravages of armed conflict. For those reasons, the existence of a regional system of protection is in many ways a remarkable achievement. Moreover, the system already has yielded some important contributions to the development of international law. Nevertheless, it still has many flaws and weaknesses, and there is no assurance that in the future the system will be stronger and more effective than it is now.

In this chapter, therefore, after reviewing the origins of the inter-American system for the protection and promotion of human rights and democracy and the contributions of that system to international law, I outline the challenges that it faces in the future and the issues where change is most urgently needed. I conclude that a concerted effort is required to adapt to rapidly changing realities and to maintain the relevance of this system to the progressive development of human rights and democracy.[1]

ORIGINS: HUMAN RIGHTS AND DEMOCRACY

The development of mechanisms of supranational protection has been made possible because, since 1948, a regional political and diplomatic body, the Organization of American States (OAS), has favored dialogue concerning hemispheric affairs and has promoted cooperation and joint ventures among its member nations in a wide array of common interests. In some ways, the umbrella of the OAS can be a burden and a straitjacket for the human rights protection system because at times it provides the channels for undue political pressure on the system. But there is no doubt that also it has often afforded an appropriate forum to condemn violations and seek their redress.

The human rights protection scheme was born at the same time as the OAS was born as a political organization. The Charter of the OAS and the first human rights instrument for the Americas, the American Declaration on the Rights and Duties of Man, were signed in the same conference in Bogota in 1948. In 1959 a resolution of the General Assembly of the OAS created the Inter-American Commission on Human Rights, basically as an organ of promotion rather than of protection. The Commission had enough flexibility, however, to interpret its mandate from the start as allowing it to monitor a country's compliance with the norms of the American Declaration. A General Assembly Resolution in 1965 formalized the Commission's competence to handle individual communications. In 1967 the OAS Charter was amended, and the Commission became a "principal organ" of the OAS.

A multilateral human rights treaty, the American Convention on Human Rights (ACHR), also known as the Pact of San José, Costa Rica, was signed in 1969; it entered into effect in 1979 when the requisite number of states ratified it. The Convention reinforced the treaty underpinnings of the Commission; it also created an Inter-American Court of Human Rights, based in San José. (The Commission's headquarters are in Washington, D.C., site of the OAS's General Secretariat.) Together these treaty bodies form the mechanisms of protection: They are entitled to issue advisory opinions as well as decisions in case complaints. The Commission also pursues a variety of advocacy functions.

A significant feature of this system is that it also has jurisdiction—albeit limited—over Canada and the United States. Because these countries are members of the OAS, complaints can be brought before the Inter-American Commission alleging violations by their authorities of rights enumerated in the American Declaration. Both countries have signed but not ratified the American Convention, so complaints against them cannot be brought before the Inter-American Court. The prospects of ratification in both countries are slim at this point, for reasons that would exceed the scope of this chapter. Suffice to say that, although both Canada and the United States have given strong political support for the integrity of the system, especially in the face of the challenges to be described, their ability to influence the behavior of other states under the system is hampered by their very limited participation in it.

The 1948 conference also issued an American Charter on Social Guarantees that signaled the region's belief that both social justice and civil and political rights were necessary to ensure the benefits of democracy to all. Taken together, the three original instruments—the Declaration, the Convention, and the Charter—leave no doubt about the interdependence among civil, political, economic, social, and cultural rights, and of these rights with the sustainability of democracy as a form of government.[2] In fact, a distinguishing feature of the inter-American human rights system is its specific reference to representative democracy as the region's preferred, some would say exclusive, form of government. In contrast, for example, the Charter of the United Nations (UN) does not establish democracy as a requirement of membership, since at its inception the need was to preserve peace, even between nations with widely differing systems of government. Consequently, nations that were invited to join the UN were required only to be "peace-loving" and to express a commitment to respecting fundamental rights.[3]

In recent years, however, some influential commentators have found a "right to democracy" emerging in international law.[4] The original intent in the creation of an inter-American system of protection surely can be counted as an early precedent of such a principle. Of course, the world's most advanced regional system of protection, in force in Europe, also makes specific reference to democracy in the European Convention on the Protection of Human Rights and Fundamental Freedoms.[5] The similarities between Europe and America, however, are deceiving. In Europe, signing and ratifying the European Convention on Human Rights and all its Protocols is a specific condition of membership in the European Community, whereas the OAS member states can decide whether they wish to become a party to the American Convention and, even if they are, whether they will be bound by the Court's jurisdiction to hear case complaints. More to the point, when confronted with a situation of lack of democracy, in the case of Greece after the so-called colonels' coup in 1967, the European organs (in this case the Council of Ministers) acted to preserve democracy and threatened Greece with suspension. As is painfully obvious, in contrast, countless military dictatorships and authoritarian regimes in Latin America have remained for years as members in good standing of the OAS.

The history of implementation of this "democracy clause" in the Americas is checkered at best. Not only has it not been regarded as an obstacle to harmonious relations with right-wing regimes, but even where it has been applied in specific cases, it has been applied with a strong ideological bent. For example, it was invoked against Cuba in 1962, when the General Assembly meeting in Punta del Este, Uruguay, suspended that country's rights of membership in the OAS. Arguing that the suspension affects the Castro government and not the state of Cuba (since the OAS has no power to expel any of its members), the Inter-American Commission has for years held that it retains the power to monitor events in Cuba and to condemn the government for human rights violations, under the dubious theory that the suspension affects Cuba's rights of membership but not its obligations.[6] Indeed, such an interpretation does tend to protect human rights better than if the Commission simply ignored what happened in Cuba until that state is back in the OAS fold. But it has proven an ingenious yet ultimately fruitless legal theory because Cuba steadfastly refuses to deal with the Commission on any level, arguing conveniently that it is not bound by obligations if it is not allowed also to exercise rights. More than three decades later, Cubans do not enjoy freedom of expression or association, and prosecution of political dissidents is conducted without any semblance of due process. For this and for many other reasons, the suspension of Cuba's membership has proven to be an ineffective approach to the promotion of democracy and to the protection of human rights.

In the 1960s, governments that included dictators like the Somozas, Trujillos, and Stroessners of the hemisphere voted the application of the democracy clause to Cuba, but a lack of "representative democracy" was not deemed important enough to apply a similar treatment to the Brazilian military dictatorship instituted in 1964, or to the governments of Generals Pinochet, Videla, and others. To its credit, however, in the 1970s the Inter-American Commission did report on human rights violations in those countries, and occasionally the General Assembly lent its voice to the Commission's condemnation, although it studiously avoided any question of suspension of rights of membership. Even with this limitation, the late 1970s and early 1980s were years of the Commission's most productive and commendable work, especially through site visits and comprehensive *Country Reports* that contributed enormously to the justified isolation of those regimes.

The question of multilateral defense of democracy came up again in the 1990s when most countries recovered elected governments and embarked on transitions to democracy. In 1991 the General Assembly adopted the "Declaration of Santiago," in which the member states pledged to respond collectively to threats to constitutional order in any sister nation.[7] The Declaration (also referred to as the "Commitment") of Santiago, spelled out in OAS General Assembly Resolution No. 1080, was ratified in successive statements in the following years. Although it was less vague than the Rodríguez Larreta doctrine of half a century earlier (see footnote 7), it did suffer from a similar limitation regarding the lack of a clear mechanism of implementation. That limitation became readily apparent very soon, as the OAS was confronted with the "self-coup" of President Alberto Fujimori of April 5, 1992, when he dissolved Peru's Congress and replaced most of the judiciary. The Santiago commitment was invoked to deny the hemisphere's support for Fujimori's authoritarianism, but as a practical mechanism it failed quite miserably. Ironically, it fell to Professor Gros Espiell, then Minister of Foreign Relations of Uruguay and Chair of the Council of Ministers of the OAS, to apply the Santiago rule and negotiate a return to democracy in Peru. As a result of these efforts, in late 1992 Fujimori held elections for a "Democratic Constituent Congress" (called the CCD for its initials in Spanish) and won them handily. The OAS declared the job done, although most of the opposition had boycotted the elections. The CCD eventually enacted a constitution that concentrates power in the executive, and Peru has not yet recovered an independent judiciary.

The Santiago norm and the OAS fared somewhat better in the next two challenges to democracy in the hemisphere, at least one of which was clearly inspired by Fujimori's success. The OAS had occasion to act collectively in Guatemala and in Haiti. In Guatemala, international pressure turned back the 1993 attempt by President Jorge Serrano to dissolve Congress and rule by executive fiat. In Haiti, it took more than two years for the 1991 military coup against Jean-Bertrand Aristide to be rolled back, and the OAS's efforts were helped considerably by the involvement of the United Nations.[8]

On balance, the results of this reaffirmation of democracy in the 1990s are at best mixed. It appears, on the positive side, that Latin American democracies emerging from years of military tyranny have responded in good faith to threats to constitutional order in their neighboring countries. Debates about these events at the General Assembly or at specially convened meetings of the Council of Ministers help to delegitimize undemocratic adventures. But there is a tendency to be satisfied with a nominal return to elections, as in Peru, as long as they are more or less defensible as expressions of majority opinion, and even if they are not free and fair by rigorous standards. There is also no political will to allow independent organs such as the Inter-American Commission to play a role in determining how well objective standards of respect for human rights and democracy are being met in the course of such crises. Although the Commission continues to do its job in those circumstances, the political organs, in applying the Santiago Commitment, have not relied on the Commission's findings or asked its advice.

More broadly, the new interest in democracy has not gone significantly beyond the matter of periodic elections. Of course, the region's commitment to elected government is a very welcome improvement over the situation in the 1970s. But the new constitutional governments are not necessarily democratic when it comes to deeper aspects of democracy, such as commitment to the rule of law, to promotion of participation, to respect for the autonomy and independence of institutions of control such as the judiciary, or to the role of organizations of civil society. The work of the organs of protection (the Commission and the Court) continues to be largely misunderstood, and as a result both organs face periodic attempts to undermine their authority from governments and occasionally also from political organs of the OAS. A pervasive attitude, though one that rarely is articulated, is that the system of protection is for dictatorships, not for democracies, or, in other words, that democratic governments should be given a much larger benefit of the doubt or margin of appreciation than dictatorships were given in the past when analyzing a complaint of human rights violations. Of course, no such distinction can be found in the relevant instruments.

It must be noted that the Charter of the OAS and the other instruments from 1948 and later refer consistently to "representative democracy," not simply to "democracy." Perhaps no profound philosophical distinction was meant at the time, but in the closing years of the century the term "representative democracy" sometimes has been understood (at the OAS General Assembly among other places) to be distinct from "participatory democracy." It seems that, in the minds of some of the present-day elected leaders of Latin America, "representative democracy" is meant to convey an emphasis on the legitimacy of the representation by those who have been elected to government posts and who for that reason are supposed to know what is best for all concerned. There is genuine interest in Latin America, with the problems of legitimacy and governance involved in the patterns of participation by different segments of society in the affairs of the community. The promotion of participation in politics, however, is not generally meant to deny the legitimacy of representative democracy or to replace it with some form of "mass democracy." "Representation," therefore, if used in distinction to participation, is an undemocratic concept.

In addition, those who in these times insist on the adjective rather than on the noun in "representative democracy" frequently do so as part of their objection to modern theories of the role of civil society in a democracy. These debates are still quite amorphous, but it appears that many Latin American rulers are highly suspicious of nongovernmental organizations (NGOs) and of the role assigned to them in international relations, in development assistance, and in community affairs. This is odd at a time when the state is being stripped down to a minimum of functions, leaving to independent organizations a variety of tasks that in the past were handled by the state. This forced delegation of duties generally is not accompanied by a serious and respectful attitude toward the separate but complementary roles of the state and of the organizations of civil society. Instead, independent organizations are dismissed as "nonrepresentative" or are accused of hidden political agendas.

At this stage, the relationship between democracy and human rights in the inter-American system is a well-established concept but it is in a state of unsatisfactory development, in part because the organs of the system have not had occasion to deal with these issues in any more than a tangential fashion. If the emerging "right to democracy" evolves toward objective and nonideological standards, the Commission and the Court may contribute significantly in the future. As for now, however, the checkered history of democracy in the hemisphere seems to be acting as an inhibiting factor.

HIGHLIGHTS OF THE SYSTEM'S CONTRIBUTIONS TO HUMAN RIGHTS LAW

The inter-American system has made some valuable contributions to the development of international human rights law. In the following paragraphs I mention only some of them, particularly in the areas where those contributions are unique in comparison to the universal or other regional systems.

Promoting Freedom of Expression

The American Convention on Human Rights has the most advanced protection of free expression of any of the international instruments.[9] Article 13 specifically prohibits prior censorship (except of public exhibitions, and then it is allowed only to prevent access by children and adolescents). In contrast, both the International Covenant on Civil and Political Rights (ICCPR) and the European Convention on Human Rights (ECHR) allow some forms of prior restraints on expression, albeit in narrow circumstances.[10] The ACHR is also more protective of free speech than other instruments on the controversial matter of "hate speech." The ICCPR mandates that domestic law must prohibit speech that is "propaganda for war" as well as "any advocacy of national, racial or religious hatred that constitutes incitement to discrimination, hostility or violence."[11] The ACHR has a similar norm, but the restriction is narrower: "Any propaganda for war and any advocacy of national, racial, or religious hatred *that constitute incitements to lawless violence* . . . shall be considered as offenses punishable by law."[12] The provisions on freedom of expression in the Americas are closer to those found in the domestic law and Constitution of the United States, which are more protective of this fundamental right than the present state of international human rights law generally.

There have not been too many opportunities for the organs to expand on the meaning of these clauses, but some decisions and opinions have tended to confirm the special place that free expression has in a democratic society, as it promotes informed debate on the issues of common concern. For example, the Inter-American Court of Human Rights has said that laws that prescribe mandatory affiliation of journalists with a professional association as a licensing requirement are inconsistent with the ACHR.[13] The matter originated in a complaint against Costa Rica by a journalist who refused to join the Colegio de Periodistas and thus risked prosecution for practicing his profession without a license. Although the advisory opinion is not binding on Costa Rica, in 1995 the country's Constitutional Court ruled that Costa Rica should amend its law to bring it into compliance with the authoritative construction of the ACHR issued by its main organ of implementation.

The Inter-American Commission also was asked to act on a case in which Horacio Verbitsky, an Argentine journalist, was given a suspended sentence under a statute that punished *desacato* (contempt) of certain public figures. In proceedings before the Commission, the Argentine government and Verbitsky reached a settlement by which Argentina promised to repeal the desacato statute. At the request of both parties, the Commission issued a report on the incompatibility of such statutes with the ACHR and on a state's obligation to alter any such law to bring it into compliance with the ACHR.[14] In another case, the Commission found that judicially imposed restrictions on the circulation of a book, ordered at the request of people who felt that its contents damaged their reputations, are also prohibited by the ACHR's clear prohibition on prior restraints.[15]

Despite these highly progressive standards, freedom of expression in real terms in the region faces a paradoxical situation. On one hand, since the advent of democracy there is a very vibrant debate of all public policy issues, investigative journalism is at an all-time high, and the press enjoys credibility and prestige in most countries as never before in Latin American history. On the other hand, exercise of journalism continues to be very hazardous. The Inter-American Press Association, the industry's most prominent group in the region, has given great priority to its campaign against murders of journalists, and it issued the "Declaration of Chapultepec" on this issue.[16] In addition, the legal framework in domestic law continues to be, at best, precarious and stacked against journalists. Despite the Court's advisory opinion, at least thirteen states still have desacato laws on their books, while laws on defamation, libel, or slander are hopelessly outdated in most countries. Proof of falsehood can result in criminal punishment regardless of the author's intent and regardless also of the position of the offended. So far only the Supreme Court of Argentina has required that "actual malice" on the part of the author be shown, which is the modern trend in protection of freedom of expression. This doctrine, originating in the U.S. Supreme Court's decision in *New York Times v. Sullivan,* has acquired the status of international law at least in Europe, via the European Court's ruling in *Lingens v. Austria.*[17] Neither the Inter-American Commission nor the Court have yet had to rule on a matter challenging domestic standards on defamation, libel, or slander.

The ACHR also incorporates a norm that is highly controversial among journalists and communications media, known as the "right of reply." Article 14 grants this right to "anyone injured by inaccurate or offensive statements or ideas disseminated to the public." On this issue there are also no precedents by the system's organs, but domestic courts in many countries regularly provide remedies to people who prove such an injury.

The system has made an important contribution in a related matter: the right to information. Article 13 of the ACHR specifies that freedom of thought and expression "includes freedom to *seek, receive and impart information and ideas*" (emphasis added). In this regard, many recently amended constitutions have established the mechanism of *habeas data* to allow individuals to obtain information about themselves that exists in government files. Although in most places this mechanism has yet to be codified, some courts have stated that it is available and enforceable even without specific law or regulation.[18] This right is proving of great importance to the victims of past human rights violations and their families, as they attempt to establish a "right to truth" regarding the fate and whereabouts of the *desaparecidos* (disappeared). The Inter-American Commission and the Court both have made important contributions to the development of the rights of families and society to demand investigation and disclosure from the state regarding such atrocities.[19]

With regard to freedom of expression, the standards in force in the Americas are very progressive, but they should be used and applied much more. This area is one of too many where domestic implementation of international obligations continues to lag. Nevertheless, as matters are brought before the system, it is very likely that domestic courts will continue the process of incorporating international standards into national law.[20]

Confronting "Disappearances"

In the 1970s and early 1980s, the Commission was besieged with urgent complaints about arrests conducted in secret, where the authorities denied any responsibility or knowledge of the fate and whereabouts of the victims. This tragic phenomenon came to be known as forced disappearance of persons, and the Commission had to find a way to deal effectively with the problem, as more and more military dictatorships resorted to it.[21] If inquiries before domestic agencies and even *habeas corpus* writs proved ineffective, there was little hope that a person so abducted could be found via the long and cumbersome procedures for case complaints outlined in the American Convention. Thus the Commission realized that there had to be a quick response, because it was in those early hours following a "deniable" detention that the authorities decided the fate of the detainee. The person could be released, sent into "legalized" detention, killed and the body disposed of secretly, or held in clandestine detention centers where he or she could be tortured and interrogated. If the Commission could let the government know that the international community was aware of the disappearance of a person, then the pressure on that government could influence the decision. The Commission devised a method by which it would act promptly when it received a complaint of a disappearance: It immediately sent a telegram or an urgent message to the government, or telephoned the country's mission to the OAS in Washington, seeking information on the whereabouts of the person and reasons for the arrest. Many of these inquiries were ignored, but in a number of cases they succeeded in forcing the release of a *desaparecido* or official acknowledgment of the detention.

In time, as the Commission learned more about this practice, it campaigned strongly against it in international fora, particularly before the OAS General Assembly. At the Commission's behest, the General Assembly passed at least two resolutions condemning the practice as a "crime against humanity" and urging governments to act in concert against it. The Commission then drafted first a Declaration and then a Convention on the topic and the General Assembly eventually approved both.[22]

The first adversarial cases to reach the Inter-American Court were about disappearances. The Commission had decided to bring these cases, against Honduras, as a way of highlighting the seriousness of the violation and obtaining support from the Court in the struggle to eradicate the practice. In the *Velásquez* and *Godínez* decisions, the Court confirmed that such disappearances constitute crimes against humanity under international law and that, as a result, governments have an affirmative duty to investigate them and to prosecute and punish whoever may be responsible.[23] The Court also found that, because the purpose of a disappearance is to eliminate traces of the government's role in a serious crime, the standard of proof and burden of persuasion must, after an initial presentation by the Commission, shift to the government to demonstrate that it has done all in its power to redress the wrong. The Court based this reasoning on its *dictum* that states have an obligation to organize their whole apparatus so that human rights are adequately protected. This obligation "to guarantee" the enjoyment of rights gives rise to a standard of "due diligence" that can apply to other situations as well. In that sense, the *Velásquez* decision has been quoted repeatedly for the proposition that governments have duties even if the action that violates a person's right is committed by a private person. Applied, for example, to issues of domestic violence against women, this due diligence standard effectively blurs the distinction between the public and the private sphere when it comes to human rights.

Opposing Impunity for Serious Violations

The prevalence of disappearances carried with it another distinct Latin American problem: the impunity enjoyed by those who abused their power to commit egregious violations of human rights. In many cases it was—and is—simply de facto impunity: Courts and prosecutors just look the other way, or security forces apply enough pressure to discourage any serious investigation of these crimes. But some dictatorships also enacted "self-amnesty" laws, effectively barring future investigations and prosecutions. Impunity eventually came to dominate the political agenda of the transitions to democratic governance, as newly elected governments issued amnesty laws as a way to placate still-powerful military establishments.

Early on, the Commission pointed out the serious problem of impunity for massive and systematic violations. In the course of on-site visits and in comprehensive country reports, it called on military regimes to investigate disappearances and massacres and to punish those responsible. It also issued early pronouncements against self-amnesty laws and called attention to their glaring inconsistency with the state's obligations under the American Convention. During the transitions, the Commission continued to advocate its pioneering view that blanket amnesties, even if passed by democratically elected governments, were a violation of a state's obligation to provide a remedy to the victims. In its two 1992 reports, the Commission found that such laws and decrees passed in democratic times by Argentina and Uruguay violated the ACHR.[24]

In *Velásquez,* the Inter-American Court established an affirmative obligation on the part of states to investigate, prosecute, and punish human rights violations that rise to the level of crimes against humanity. These pronouncements have gone a long way toward establishing a widely recognized emerging principle in international law that a state has an obligation to punish certain crimes.[25] In that sense, the inter-American organs have contributed doctrinally to the international community's willingness to institute forms of universal jurisdiction, such as the ad hoc war crimes tribunals for the former Yugoslavia and Rwanda and the establishment of a permanent International Criminal Court via the Rome Statute.[26] In a sense, they likewise contribute to the newly aggressive stance of European courts opening prosecutions for genocide and crimes against humanity committed in other lands, as in the dramatic arrest of General Augusto Pinochet in London at the request of a Spanish judge.[27]

Establishing a Right to Truth

The Commission and the Court repeatedly have stated that governments—even successor democratic governments—have an obligation to the families of victims to disclose all that is known about the fate and whereabouts of their loved ones. In *Velásquez,* the Court even said that this obligation remains in force for as long as there is any uncertainty about the victim's fate.

Based on similar arguments, some newly emerging democracies in Latin America have experimented with "Truth Commissions," attempting to gather all pertinent information and present it to the victims and society. Such efforts in Argentina, Chile, El Salvador, Haiti, and currently in Guatemala have been followed closely, not only within those countries but also abroad. Although their results leave ample ground for interpretation, they undoubtedly have become a major tool against impunity for the perpetrators and oblivion for the victims.[28]

In all of these cases, the Truth Commissions availed themselves of information gathered locally but also by the Inter-American Commission when conducting on-site visits or hearing cases about the country.

In the reports on Argentina and Uruguay, the Commission insisted on the victims' right to know, in addition to their right to see justice done. These opinions, as well as those by the Court in *Velásquez*, have become central to a "right to truth" that is developing in the opinions of domestic courts in Latin America. This principle states that courts are obliged to find the means to give effect to the victims' right to know the truth about severe human rights violations.[29] This obligation is not limited to disclosing documents in secret files; it entails active investigation designed to discover hidden truth. Amnesty or pseudoamnesty laws may not be invoked against this right.

Incorporating International Standards in Domestic Law

Most Latin American countries take the position that the international treaties to which they subscribe are self-executing, in the sense that they automatically become part of domestic law without any need for implementing legislation. In recent years many countries have amended their constitutions to incorporate the terms of human rights treaties either directly into the constitution or explicitly state that such terms take precedence over laws passed by congress. It is a measure of the prestige enjoyed by the inter-American system that the American Convention is one of those treaties that is being given heightened status in domestic laws throughout Latin America. Of course, what constituent assemblies enact does not always translate so easily into similar attitudes by judges and prosecutors; nevertheless, in many Latin American countries, domestic courts are becoming more and more aware of the need to apply international standards. The highest courts of Argentina and Costa Rica even have gone as far as to say not only that ratified treaties are the law of the land, but also that lower courts are bound by the interpretation given to treaty norms by their authoritative organs. In Argentina, the Supreme Court thus gave binding status to an opinion of the Commission regarding limits on the length of preventive detention. In Costa Rica, the Constitutional Court did the same with an advisory opinion by the Inter-American Court on freedom of expression.[30]

Protecting Minorities and the Underprivileged

In regard to minorities and the underprivileged, the organs have lagged behind. The Commission has been working hard on a Declaration on the Rights of Indigenous Peoples that has yet to be approved by the General Assembly. It did conduct a partially successful process of "friendly settlement" between the Nicaraguan government and the Miskito indigenous minority in the context of the contra war.[31] The Inter-American Court had an early occasion to deal with serious violations committed against an ethnic minority in *Aloeboetoe v. Suriname,* a case where the Court dealt only with reparations, because at an earlier (merits) stage of the proceeding, Suriname had acknowledged its international liability. In the damages decision, the Court acknowledged, but did not fully accept, the argument for recognizing cultural traditions regarding compensation.[32] Given the importance of the rights of ethnic minorities to the full realization of human rights in the Americas, the system certainly has not yet yielded all it can offer.

The same is true, at least in part, with regard to women's rights. The region has the world's first international treaty concerning violence against women, which can be an effective tool as an international response to domestic violence. But neither the Commission nor the Court played a role in drafting it or getting it approved; the initiative belonged to another organ of the OAS, the Inter-American Commission on Women. Although the Convention—sometimes known as the Convention of Belem do Pará—was approved in 1994, it has yet to be implemented in any way through the inter-American system.[33] Some NGOs have presented cases invoking Belem Do Para before the Inter-American Commission, but none had yet been resolved as of early 2000.[34] The Commission appointed one of its members as Special Rapporteur on the rights of women, and a comprehensive report on the status of women in the Americas has recently been issued.[35] The rights of women, of indigenous peoples, and of children are the unfinished business of the system.

THE FUTURE OF THE INTER-AMERICAN SYSTEM

Although it has many strengths, the future of the inter-American system of human rights will depend on an honest evaluation of its weaknesses and a determined effort to reform them, with urgent attention to its most immediate needs, as I outline them next. That honest evaluation is made difficult, however, by the persistent attempts of some governments to undermine the organs by attacking the strengths of the system, not its weaknesses.

The System's Weaknesses

The system's greatest current challenges concern the execution of judgments, the processes for appointing judges and commissioners, and the wide diversity of forms of state membership. In addition, there are renewed attacks on both organs and a dangerous tendency in some governments to ignore their decisions. Recent announcements by Trinidad and Tobago and by Peru of their decisions to withdraw partially from the system also may become a serious setback, especially if the political and diplomatic price to pay for such decisions is ultimately not very high.

Execution of Judgments   One of the system's most evident weaknesses lies in the execution of judgments. Should a state decide to ignore a judgment of one of the organs, the system's ability to force compliance is not great. Some countries have publicly taken the position that the "recommendations" of the Commission are not binding. This position had, for a while, some support in an opinion issued by the Court. In the *Loayza Tamayo* case, the Court declared that states must "heed" the recommendations contained in the Commission's reports and do their best to implement them, pursuant to the principle of good faith; it thus reversed its previous jurisprudence. [36] With regard to state compliance with the recommendations included in the reports adopted between 1983 and 1993, the Commission has acknowledged the "unfortunate" fact that "the IACHR has not received feedback from the authorities on any of its recommendations or follow-up to the requests they contain."[37]

The effectiveness of a protection system clearly depends not only on the existence of jurisdictional organs whose decisions have been declared legally final and binding, but also on the existence of mechanisms to ensure that, once the victim's rights have been recognized, he or she can obtain execution of judgment in the domestic sphere or demand compulsory compliance.

Article 68.2 of the Convention establishes that "that part of the judgment that stipulates compensatory damages *may* be executed in the country concerned in accordance with domestic procedure governing the execution of judgments against the state" (emphasis added). This rule, which produced some optimism, was not the result of a harmonious interpretation. The rule can be said to leave any dispositive parts of a judgment that are not of a compensatory nature outside its sphere of application. Even in cases of execution of compensation, this procedure "may" be executed. In other words, the procedure is discretionary, not obligatory, for the state party.

Although there are weighty legal arguments to support the compulsory nature of the execution of judgments—both its compensatory and its noncompensatory parts—they do not make up for the absence of an effective system to enforce application of the Court's rulings. In cases of noncompliance by the state, the only enforcement mechanism that the American Convention envisages is a mention in the annual reports that the Court and Commission transmit to the General Assembly, in which the Court "shall specify, in particular, the cases in which a State has not complied with its judgments, making any pertinent recommendations" (Article 65). However, this complaint mechanism does not make any provision for sanctions that the Assembly could adopt or coercive measures that could be applied. There is a moral sanction, at least, or a political one, but it is never more than symbolic.

It has been stated that "the Assembly may adopt countermeasures within the framework of the Charter of the Organization, but may not execute the judgments of the Inter-American Court of Human Rights."[38] Even the system of countermeasures (diplomatic pressure or sanctions, for example) is of doubtful effectiveness due to the political nature of the Assembly. A state that refuses to comply can use its entire diplomatic arsenal to avoid even symbolic sanction.

This concern is not unfounded. As violations of human rights committed by unpopular dictatorships were growing increasingly severe in Latin America, at the tenth session of the General Assembly (November 1980), some governments, led by Argentina, successfully impeded the approval of General Assembly resolutions based on Commission reports that accused them of serious human rights violations. Only one—very vitiated—resolution was adopted, which did not mention any one state but only made broad hortatory statements directed, presumably, to all states.[39]

More recently, in the well-known *Velásquez* and *Aloboetoe* cases, the procedure set forth in the Convention was shown to be ineffective even though the states that initially resisted the judgments did not have much political power.[40] In *Velásquez*, Honduras paid the compensation only after the legally established time limit and when the Honduras currency had been devalued. This situation gave rise to a complaint by the Commission that the Court accepted; it ordered the state to compensate for the delay and adjust the compensation to maintain its value. Again the state did not comply, either in the manner or within the time limit that had been established. At the prospect of a General Assembly condemnation, Honduras declared its intention to comply, but only years later, after a change of government, did it pay in full. In the same way, in the *Aloboetoe* case, Suriname for a long time paid only 1 percent of a compensation award of about U.S. $400,000, and it did not carry out any of the other measures called for by the judgment, such as reopening a school and equipping a medical clinic.

The absence of a coercive mechanism debilitates both the position of the victim and the effectiveness of the protection system. As Oscar Fappiano, delegate to the IACHR, has argued, the cycle of "initiating another denunciation before the IACHR based on a further non-compliance and the eventual submission of the case to the Inter-American Court of Human Rights and so on, converts the system into ineffectual ritualism."[41]

Quite the opposite occurs in the European system where, in addition to committing themselves to accept the tribunal's decisions in any lawsuits in which they are involved, the high contracting parties agree that the Committee of Ministers, to whom judgments are transmitted, shall supervise their execution.[42] It is rare that states that are found guilty do not comply with judgments because acceptance of the European Convention on Human Rights and the obligatory jurisdiction of its organs is an express condition of membership in the European Community. Thus states have a strong incentive to comply. The decisions of both the Commission and the Court appear on the agenda of the Committee of Ministers until the state provides a response, and noncompliance entails the very real possibility of suspension from the European Community. Compliance with judgments is also simplified owing to the type of matters that the Court generally hears. As these are developed democracies, the cases before the Court are generally of a relatively technical or juridical nature, and not the kinds of extremely serious and traumatic violations that leave open wounds for generations. Last, and probably as a consequence of the foregoing, the European states do not consider that the Court's decisions affect national honor or dignity, and therefore, they adapt their laws and practices to its resolutions; although doing so this can sometimes be complex, it does not imply any particular stigma.

The Appointment of Judges and Commissioners   Another weakness of the inter-American system lies in the procedure for the election of judges and commissioners and the conditions that would guarantee the impartiality and independence of both the organs and their members. One problem area is the mechanism for selection of judges and commissioners and the rules on conflicts of interest. Another is the Court's composition for specific cases—ad hoc judges— and the authorization granted by the Convention for judges to continue in office.

Judges and commissioners currently are appointed by means of a laborious diplomatic effort, carried out almost exclusively and in an exclusionist manner, by the respective ministries of foreign affairs. Interest in proposing competent, independent candidates is tainted by issues that are clearly political and by exchanges of favors between states. Thus states do not always propose the most qualified individuals.[43] The American Convention is clear, however, in establishing that judges and commissioners shall be people of the highest moral authority and of recognized competence in the field of human rights.[44] In practice, commissioners recuse themselves in cases where their state of nationality is a party, but at the Court, a judge has discretion to decide whether the fact that his or her state of nationality is a party will affect his or her ability to make a fair decision.[45]

A further cause for concern arises because secondary regulations have not been completely adapted to the Convention's rules on conflict of interest for judges and commissioners. It might be appropriate to extend the rules on conflict of interest to a large range of situations that have not been included to date. For example, members of the Foreign Service and officials of the executive and legislative branches should not be selected. With respect to people who are judges and magistrates in domestic courts, their appointment to the Inter-American Court is highly controversial as well, especially if they belong to the highest courts in their countries. However, it is not a good idea for the Inter-American Court to be deprived altogether of trained judicial minds. These measures would strengthen the system, while providing a very clear signal of scrupulousness to states and petitioners.

Since its very first case, another issue, which has no legal basis, has arisen with respect to a practice of the Court. If none of the judges called upon to hear a case is a national of the defendant state, or if a judge recuses him- or herself on such grounds, the state has the right to appoint an ad hoc judge to represent it. This has been the practice up to the present, although the Convention expressly grants states this power only in state-versus-state cases, a situation that has never occurred in the inter-American system.[46] It has been said that the justification for the ad hoc judges in individual cases lies in the need to have someone who knows the legal system and the law of the defendant state. However, there are at least two forceful arguments against this; first, the applicable law is international human rights law rather than domestic law; second, it would be sufficient to have a Court assistant, without judicial functions, fulfill the role of expert on domestic law.[47]

The power to appoint ad hoc judges is an unacceptable procedural advantage for defendant states that invalidates the old rule of "equality of arms" during the proceedings.[48] It is also unjustified in the eyes of the victims of the violation, who must be surprised to see that the state they hold responsible for their grievance has the power to appoint a person of its confidence not only to have a vote on the outcome of the case but also, basically, to be a lobbyist in a very effective position.[49]

Another controversial practice of the Court concerns the question of the continuation of the judges' mandate provided for in the Convention after the expiration of their term of office. The Court sometimes allows such judges to remain as members of the Court while cases they began are still pending. Thus in practice, the Court sits with different members depending on which case it is hearing.

Extremely awkward situations could arise; for example, the same person might simultaneously be a judge with an extended mandate in one case and a lawyer in another matter being heard by the Court. Even without reaching this extreme, at present it is possible that a judge whose mandate has concluded may continue to hear the merits of a case because he or she took part in the preliminary review stage, or may be involved in the execution of judgment stage because he or she drafted the judgment on indemnification or compensation. In both cases the spirit and the letter of the law would be distorted above and beyond the fact that the coexistence of two or three Courts is inadvisable.[50] However these situations are solved, the current system gives rise to well-founded misgivings. The rule needs to be interpreted definitively, as there are substantial differences according to the language in which is it is written.[51] A restrictive, clear, and reasonable criterion that avoids any inconsistent interpretations in the future should be established.

Both the Court and the Commission should ensure that they are models of impartiality and independence, because their authority is based on ethics. Only in this way will they be able to put pressure on the states to comply and will their decisions have a legitimacy that is beyond all doubt.

State Membership in the Inter-American System   In the Americas, in contrast to the situation in Europe, several aspects of state membership in the system of promotion and protection of human rights are problematic. First, of the thirty-five member states, twenty-four have ratified the Convention. Curiously enough, among the states that have not done so are both some of the smallest English-speaking countries of the Caribbean and major hemispheric powers such as the United States and Canada. Furthermore, although all of the countries of Latin America have ratified the Convention, some are not yet among the twenty OAS member states that have recognized the obligatory jurisdiction of the Court.[52] Thus, in effect, the Court does not protect a large number of inhabitants of the Americas.

Moreover, some states have tried to leave the system. In May 1998 Trinidad and Tobago unexpectedly denounced the American Convention in order to impose the death penalty without possibility of appeal to the system's organs. In August 1998 the state simply refused to appear before the Court at a hearing on provisional measures. In Guatemala, a lawsuit seeking a declaration that the acceptance of the Inter-American Court's jurisdiction was unconstitutional and null, owing to alleged defects in its internal procedure, is still pending before the Constitutional Court. The press has published the Peruvian government's declaration of intention, never implemented, to denounce the Convention in order to be able to apply the death penalty without any constraints.[53]

It is at least an anomaly that a region consisting of thirty-five states has six different regimes in regard to international protection. First, there are countries that have signed and ratified the ACHR and have agreed to be bound by the decisions of the Court. Second, there are countries that are parties to the ACHR but have not agreed to the jurisdiction of the Court. Third, there are countries (i.e., the United States) that have signed but not ratified the ACHR. According to the law of treaties, such countries have some limited obligations toward the ACHR. Fourth, there are countries that have neither signed nor ratified the ACHR; they are subject to the Commission's treatment of cases under the Declaration. Fifth, countries that have reduced their commitment to the process, such as Peru and Trinidad and Tobago, still have lingering obligations with regard to pending cases or to cases that happen in the one-year interregnum between when they declare their intention and when it goes into effect.[54] (Peru purports to extricate itself from the Court's jurisdiction "with immediate effect," a proposition the dubious legality of which will soon be tested.) Finally, there is Cuba, whose special case we mentioned earlier.

Recently, during discussions on the reform of the system, many voices were heard in favor of increasing and streamlining membership, by making the basic principles and rules of the American Convention more flexible. For instance, with regard to the death penalty, some favor allowing states not only to retain it without limits but also to expand it to new criminal offenses. It would be a serious setback for the defense of human rights in the hemisphere if such a strategy or proposal is accepted to attract more members. Moreover, doing so would constitute a negation of the nature of a human rights treaty; if it is modified, it should be to offer greater protection to those to whom it is addressed, not just to suit governments.[55]

The Discussion on Reform

The inter-American system's contributions to human rights augurs a promising future, provided that the states continue and strengthen their commitment to the cause of human rights and do not try to undermine its bases. Over the last few years, however, the system has suffered some not very subtle attacks by several states within the OAS. It has been said, for example, that the American system was conceived to deal with military dictatorships and that, in today's democracies, numerous and severe violations of human rights no longer occur; therefore, the system should accentuate its work of advocacy and cut back on its work on protection.

This argument is weak, and it is plagued with historical and conceptual errors. In the first place, the inter-American system is based on democracy. We should not forget that the American Declaration was proclaimed in the aftermath of the victory of democracy against Nazism and fascism. The Commission was created in 1959 when democracies were springing up in the hemisphere following the fall of several dictators, and the American Convention itself is clearly inspired by the European Convention, conceived for the free democracies of Europe.[56]

Second, serious human rights violations continue to occur in the young American democracies as well as elsewhere. The media and the most recent reports of Amnesty International and Human Rights Watch confirm that there are still serious problems with military and security forces and cases of torture and disappearance; the press is subject to assaults even by democratic governments; the courts are often neither independent nor impartial. One could draw up a very long list of violations of the rights of women, indigenous people, children, and prisoners.[57]

Third, the argument invoked to urge the reform of the system reveals the attitude that some of these supposedly democratic states have toward human rights. They seem to believe that the protection system is conceived *against* the states rather than *for* the people. This line of argument is similar to that of the military governments in the past. In fact, however, to paraphrase Pedro Nikken, president of the Inter-American Institute of Human Rights, it is government mentality that needs to be reformed, not the American Convention.[58]

Although the rationale offered for the proposals is the need to "strengthen" or "modernize" the inter-American system, it is clear that, in reality, the purpose is to increase political control of its organs. Thus the proposed reforms have not been directed at establishing new rights but at altering the system's structure and its modus operandi. One of the most frequently heard proposals is to increase the number of commissioners. Doing this has two objectives: The declared aim is to reduce the Commission's considerable burden of work, while the unstated aim is to control its independence. However, an increase in the number of members would only increase costs, prolong discussions in order to reach decisions, and so on. The real solution requires the OAS to provide the Commission with resources so that, at the very least, its president can work full time, the commissioners can meet more frequently, and it can hire necessary professional personnel.

There has been some insistence on the proposal to reduce the Commission and the Court to a single organ, following the European decision to abolish the European Commission of Human Rights and make the European Court of Human Rights a full-time body in permanent session, allowing the right of petition directly to the Court. The new European system has been in place less than one year at this writing, and it is patently too soon to evaluate it.

Significantly, however, there are already some concerns that the Commission's fact-finding powers have been lost, without any other body acquiring them, since the single Court has no such attributes. This situation is particularly problematic with the states newly incorporated into the system, because their judiciaries are not as functional and efficient as those of the older European member states, and thus have no capacity to build a record on which an international organ can base a fair decision. This problem is, of course, particularly acute in most Latin American and Caribbean countries today. For that reason, to propose a single organ for our region is an intellectual conceit that could have unintended but serious adverse consequences. The Commission's fact-finding powers, as well as its country reports, on-site visits, and promotional activities, are still very necessary.

In addition to making the rules more "flexible," it also has been proposed that the confidentiality of the proceedings should be "increased" as, according to the state that proposed it, this was a basic principle of the inter-American system.[59] This state proposed that, before opening an investigation, the Commission should be obliged to consult with the state being denounced so that it would have the opportunity to make some type of prior declaration or send information on the validity of the complaint. Essentially, however, doing so would grant an accused state the right to dictate under what conditions or in what circumstances the Commission could open an investigation.[60]

Fortunately, the resolve shown by the Commission, by NGOs, and by users of the system seems to have won the day, at least for the time being. After conferences in late 1996 and in 1997, the push for "reform" of the system has abated. We should be pleased that the system was able to overcome the harsh and systematic attack of powerful states in the region. However, recent experience counsels us to be alert and not to rule out the possibility that, at any moment, some states may return to the attack. Although they have declared themselves committed to and concerned about human rights, their international actions are directed at weakening the protection system. Furthermore, the General Assembly's almost complete lack of political response to attempts to undermine the system is a cause for concern.

Specific Needs

Many issues have to be considered in order to strengthen our system in the proper sense of the word. Included here are only the most urgent, and the simplest and safest to carry out (because, for example, they do not require amendments to the Convention). If adopted, these measures would unquestionably make a significant impact on the system and help modernize it, with the consequent improvement in the level of human rights protection in the hemisphere. The most urgent issues are the victim's participation in Court hearings, the progressive judicialization of the system, and the effective execution of judgments.

Expanding victim participation before the Court

One of the most important failings of the system is the very limited participation of the victim in proceedings before the Court, although experience under domestic law has demonstrated that the victim's participation is of fundamental importance for the comprehensiveness of the investigation and for the transparency of any system of adjudication.

No rules in either the inter-American or the European system suggest that intervention by the victim is prohibited. However, under both systems it has been the Commission's practice to allow the interested party a role in proceedings before the judicial organs by extending judicial standing to petitioners and allowing them access to the Court alongside its own delegation in an advisory capacity. In 1983 Europe changed its rules to allow the victim full and autonomous standing once the case was submitted to the Court.

In the inter-American system, victims' representatives have only a restricted participation before the Court, much as in Europe before 1983. The Inter-American Court established this form of victim participation, via precedent, starting with its very first case. Even that restricted participation was in itself a small victory: What had taken years in Europe was obtained instantaneously in the inter-American system, establishing a precedent that was applied to all subsequent contentious cases.

Likewise, the Court's jurisprudence rapidly granted the victim the role of autonomous party in the compensatory stage of the proceedings, so that those who were prejudiced could address themselves directly to the Court with full procedural rights.[61] The Court introduced several amendments in order to establish by regulation the rights that its practices had granted victims.[62]

The fact that the victim has been granted a procedural role only in the compensatory stage, at least up to now, reflects a phase in the evolution of international human rights law in which the victim's only right was compensation. A start was made to changing this paradigm years ago, with recognition of the emerging principle of the right to justice and truth, which, in turn, corresponds to the obligation of the state to investigate the facts, reveal them to society, and punish those responsible.

To date, the practice adopted by the Commission—of inviting victim representatives to join its delegation before the Court—has benefited it as well as the victims because this participation increases the Commission's investigative capacity and enhances preparations for the hearings and access to evidence. As for the victims, they thus have a means of intervening in the proceedings to determine international responsibility.[63]

We believe that it is not advisable to continue this system because, although the Commission and the victim might have a shared interest before the Court, they might have very different interests or points of view, and not just with regard to compensation.[64]

At the present phase in the development of international human rights law, the victim should have the right to speak about all formal and substantial aspects of the case, because it is essentially the victim's own case. Not only is this right an issue of justice; recognition of this right would improve the operation of the system.

Judicialization of the system   A second matter of some concern is the politicization of the inter-American system. It is present not only in the selection of judges and commissioners but also in the processing of cases. The Commission, rather than the Court, is the organ most frequently under pressure from the states and the users of the system; the rage expressed by Fujimori and his partisans at the Court in mid-1999, due to the decision in the Castillo Petruzzi case, is a significant exception.[65]

The Convention grants the Commission political and diplomatic as well as quasi-judicial powers, and, on occasion, the Commission has blurred the distinction between one and the other. For example, in the case complaint mechanism, where all proceedings should be as rigorously judicial as possible both in content and in form, states and petitioners have had recourse to extrajuridical arguments. They also have made those arguments *ex parte* or even outside the hearing room. Fortunately, these practices are less common now, but they should be banned altogether because they affect the Commission's credibility and make it vulnerable. In contrast, deciding individual cases by strictly applying the rules of the Convention strengthens the Commission. With the same aim of avoiding any criticism of politicization, it would be beneficial for the Commission to establish and use objective, widely recognized criteria for procedural issues that have not been regulated and for the interpretation of rules. There is no doubt of the benefits in terms of legal certainty that determining and making transparent the criteria used to open one case and not another, to transmit one case to the Court and not another, and so on, would imply for petitioners and states. Doing this would put an end to suspicions of arbitrariness in the processing of cases.

Making the execution of judgments effective   As noted earlier, there is much work to be done to make the execution of judgments effective, and the states have a cardinal obligation in this task. Some of them have enacted laws establishing domestic procedures that oblige them to implement decisions of international organs. Although a powerful argument can be made that even without such legislation those judgments are automatically enforceable in domestic courts, such legislation is useful in eliminating any doubt about it.[66] For example, in Colombia, Law 288 of 1996 establishes "the instruments for compensating victims of human rights violations in accordance with the provisions of certain international organs," specifically, the Committee for Human Rights and the Inter-American Commission. The Court's decisions are not, however, included in these provisions. In Argentina, also, there is draft legislation that regulates only matters relating to compliance with the recommendations of the Inter-American Commission, presumably because there is no doubt that the Inter-American Court's decisions are directly enforceable in Argentine courts.[67]

Peru has adopted the same procedure as Colombia in its Law No. 23,506 on habeas corpus and *Amparo*,[68] and mentions the same organs as the Colombian Law 288; however, it establishes a *numero apertus* procedure that implicitly includes the Inter-American Court in San José.[69] Thus, it is a better model to follow.

Still a better model is the case of Costa Rica, where the Headquarters Agreement between the government and the Court establishes that the decisions of the Court and, when applicable, those of its president, chief justice, will have the same executory force as those pronounced by the Costa Rican courts. Consequently, Law 3667, which regulates matters concerning the enforcement of judicial decisions, is applicable to the execution of judgments. This implementation mechanism is probably one of the best and most extensive conceived to date.

NEW HORIZONS

Seventy percent of the cases handled by the organs of the inter-American system of human rights protection have involved significant violations of essential rights, such as deaths, disappearances, torture, that are inderogable, that is, they may not be suspended even during states of emergency. In dealing with this type of case, the system was responding to the demands and needs imposed by reigning social and political conditions in Latin America. This capacity to respond was one of the main sources of prestige of the Court and the Commission. In keeping with the changing political environment, the system now has begun to process cases relating to other basic human rights, such as the right to a fair trial, the independence of the judiciary, and freedom of expression. At the same time, it has created new instruments to enhance its operations, such as the office of a Special Rapporteur *(relatoría)* on a variety of issues. Recently, for example, the Commission appointed a Special Rapporteur on freedom of expression.

On the threshold of the twenty-first century, the situation of human rights in the Americas and the position adopted by major states in the region do not give much cause for optimism; they oblige us to remain alert. Nevertheless, the inter-American system for the promotion and protection of human rights has saved lives, influenced the return to democracy in several countries, and condemned dictatorial regimes; it has, so far, overcome even the strongest and most systematic attempts to weaken it.

This situation indicates an admirable strength and suggests that the system will continue to respond to new social demands. The issues are as crucial as the independence of national judiciaries; the development of freedom of expression; the respect and promotion of the cultural diversity of indigenous communities; the abolition of discrimination against women; the protection of minorities; and the implementation of economic, social, and cultural rights. The system must continue to adapt to a very dynamic reality, and it must continue to resist attempts to weaken it. Distinct but complementary responsibilities exist among the organs of the system, the governments, other OAS bodies, and civil society organizations. Chief among the latter are those that represent victims of human rights violations and specialize in litigation before these organs. If every actor fulfills his or her obligation, the system can be a formidable help to the region as it meets the diverse new challenges of the new century.

NOTES

*   The author gratefully acknowledges the contribution to this article of Javier Mariezcurrena.

1.   The system has improved its performance over the years largely because of the dedication and courage of Latin American human rights activists who make it work through using it creatively and often courageously. One of the pioneers in using the system was Emilio F. Mignone of Argentina, whose death in December 1998 was a great loss to the worldwide human rights movement. It is worth mentioning at least some of the nongovernmental organizations that have continued his legacy in this regard: his own Centro de Estudios Legales y Sociales (CELS), of Buenos Aires; the Comisión Colombiana de Juristas (CCJ) of Bogotá; Programa Venezolano de Educación-Acción en Derechos Humanos (PROVEA) of Caracas; Asociación Pro-Derechos Humanos (APRODEH) of Lima; and the Oficina de Derechos Humanos del Arzobispado (ODHA) of Guatemala. Among the international NGOs are: Human Rights Watch (New York and Washington) and the Center for Justice and International Law (CEJIL), of Washington and San José. The author is proud to acknowledge past affiliations with the latter two organizations and long-term friendships in all the former.

2.   Just as at the universal level, however, the rhetorical importance given to economic, social, and cultural rights has not been matched by substantial standard-setting or development

of effective protection machinery. The 1948 Charter on Social Justice is virtually forgotten nowadays. The only multilateral treaty designed to address economic, social, and cultural rights is the Protocol of San Salvador, approved November 17, 1988, as an addition to the American Convention on Human Rights, but as of November 1999 it has been signed only by fifteen states, with eleven instruments of ratification having been deposited (eleven were required for it to come into force). In one important way, the Protocol of San Salvador is a step in the wrong direction, because it creates a deliberately weak and ineffective mechanism of protection, thereby widening the gap between one set of rights and another in terms of their justiciability.

3. UN Charter, Preamble and arts. 1, 2 and 4.

4. Thomas Franck, "The Emerging Right to Democratic Governance," *American Journal of International Law*, No. 86 (1988), pp. 46-91.

5. Preamble and Articles 8 to 11 of the European Convention on the Protection of Human Rights and Fundamental Freedoms, reprinted in *Twenty-Five Human Rights Documents* (New York: Center for the Study of Human Rights, Columbia University, 1994), p. 147 et seq. The Preamble states: "[The governments] reaffirming their profound belief in those Fundamental Freedoms which are the foundation of justice and peace in the world and are best maintained on the one hand by an effective political democracy." In Articles 8 to 11, the restrictions that are allowed to the rights to privacy, freedom of conscience and religion, freedom of expression and freedom of association and assembly, are only those "necessary in a democratic society" to preserve public safety and other collective needs.

6. For a comprehensive analysis of Cuba's legal situation vis-à-vis the inter-American system of protection, see Thomas Buergenthal, Robert Norris, and Dinah Shelton, *La Protección de los Derechos Humanos en las Américas* (San José: Civitas-IIHR, 1983), pp. 120-35.

7. It took forty-six years for the OAS to adopt this doctrine, first proposed in 1945 by Uruguayan minister Rodríguez Larreta. At the time, the so-called Rodríguez Larreta doctrine was apparently considered dangerously vague and interventionist in character, especially because no treaty or protection procedure to implement it was offered. Héctor Gros Espiell, "La democracia en el sistema interamericano de promocion y proteccion de los derechos humanos," in *Estudios sobre Derechos Humanos II* (Madrid: Civitas-IIHR, 1988), p. 129. See also Antonio A. Cançado Trindade, "Democracia y Derechos Humanos: El regimen emergente de la promocion internacional de la democracia y el estado de derecho," in Rafael Nieto, ed., *La Corte y el Sistema Interamericano de Derechos Humanos* (San José: IACourtHR, 1994).

8. See Douglass Cassel, "Lecciones en las Américas: Lineamientos para una respuesta internacional ante la amnistía de las atrocidades" in *Revista IIDH*, No. 24 (San José: IIHR), 1996, p. 318; Héctor Gros Espiell, "La democracia en el sistema interamericano," in *Lecciones y Ensayos* (Buenos Aires: School of Law and Social Sciences of the University of Buenos Aires, 1999), p. 621.

9. The American Convention on Human Rights (ACHR) was signed in 1969 and came into force in 1979. See, for example, F.V. Garcia-Amador, ed., *The Inter-American System: Treaties, Conventions and Other Documents* (New York: Oceana Publications, 1983); Organization of American States (OAS), *The Organization of American States: Advancing Democracy, Human Rights and the Rule of Law in the Americas* (Washington, DC: Inter-American Dialogue, 1994); Alfred Glenn Mower, *Regional Human Rights: A Comparative Study of the West European and Inter-American Systems,* Studies in Human Rights, No. 12 (New York: Greenwood Press, 1991); Cecilia Medina Quiroga, *The Battle of Human Rights: Gross, Systematic Violations and the Inter-American System* (Dordrecht: M. Nijhoff, 1988); and Lawrence J. LeBlanc, *The OAS and the Promotion and Protection of Human Rights* (The Hague: Nijhoff, 1977).

10. Article 19, ICCPR, allows restrictions, "but these shall only be such as are provided by law and necessary: (a) For respect of the rights or reputations of others; (b) For the protection of national security or of public order (*ordre public),* or of public health or morals." In the

ECHR, restrictions may be even broader: Article 10.2: "The exercise of these freedoms, since it carries with it duties and responsibilities, may be subject to such formalities, conditions, restrictions or penalties as are prescribed by law and are necessary in a democratic society, in the interests of national security, territorial integrity or public safety, for the prevention of disorder or crime, for the protection of health and morals, for the protection of the reputation or rights of others, for preventing the disclosure of information received in confidence, or for maintaining the authority and impartiality of the judiciary." Note that, unlike the ACHR and the First Amendment of the United States Constitution, neither article prohibits those restrictions from being imposed as a prior restraint.

11. ICCPR, art. 20.
12. ACHR, Article 13, para. 5, emphasis added.
13. Inter-American Court of Human Rights, Advisory Opinion O.C. 5/85, *Compulsory membership in an association prescribed by law for the practice of journalism,* November 13, 1985.
14. Inter-American Commission of Human Rights, *Report on the compatibility of desacato laws with the American Convention on Human Rights,* in *IACHR Annual Report, 1994* (Washington, DC: General Secretariat of the Organization of American States, 1995).
15. Inter-American Commission of Human Rights, *Martorell v. Chile,* Report No. 11/96, case 11.230, May 3, 1996, in *IACHR Annual Report, 1996* (Washington, DC: General Secretariat of the Organization of American States, 1997).
16. The Declaration of Chapultepec is reprinted on the Robert R. McCormick Tribune Foundation home page, <http://www.rrmtf.org/journalism/jchap.htm>; it is also available on the Inter-American Press Association (IAPA) home page, at <http://www.sipiapa.org/eng/chapul/decla.html>, as of June 8, 1999. See also Libertad de Prensa en las Américas, *Informe Anual 1999 de la Sociedad Interamerica de Prensa* (Miami: IAPA, 1999), p. 88.
17. *New York Times Company v. Sullivan,* 376 U.S. 254, 1964; *Lingens v. Austria European Court of Human Rights,* judgment of July 8, 1986; see also *Castells v. Spain,* European Court of Human Rights, judgment of April 23, 1992; Supreme Court of Argentina, *Morales Solá J. M. sobre injurias,* judgment of November 12, 1996. Unfortunately, the Argentine Supreme Court has protected the freedom of expression only inconsistently; see for example, *Menem, Eduardo s/querella por calumnias e injurias,* judgment of October 20, 1998.
18. Supreme Court of Argentina, *Urteaga Facundo Raúl c/Estado Nacional, Estado Mayor Conjunto de las FFAA, s/ amparo ley 16.986,* known as the *Urteaga* case.
19. Inter-American Court of Human Rights, *Velásquez Rodríguez* case, judgment of July 29, 1988; Inter-American Commission of Human Rights, Report No. 28/92, Argentina, October 2, 1992; Report No. 29/92 Uruguay, October 2, 1992; and Report No. 36/96 Chile, October 15, 1996.
20. See Viviana Krsticevic, Juan E. Méndez, Drew Porter, and José Miguel Vivanco, "Freedom of Expression and National Security in the Inter-American System of Human Rights Protection," in Sandra Coliver, Joan Fitzpatrick, and Paul Hoffman, eds., *Secrecy and Liberty: National Security, Freedom of Expression and Access to Information* (Boston: M. Nijhoff, 1999). (Article XIX is a London-based international NGO dedicated to freedom of expression.)
21. Among the countries in which people "disappeared" at the hands of their governments during the 1970s and early 1980s were Argentina, Bolivia, Brazil, Chile, Colombia, El Salvador, Guatemala, Haiti, Honduras, Paraguay, Peru, and Uruguay.
22. The General Assembly of the OAS, at its thirteenth Regular Session in November 1983, declared in Resolution No. 666: "The practice of the forced disappearance of persons in the Americas is an affront to the conscience of the hemisphere and constitutes a crime against humanity." The Inter-American Convention on the Forced Disappearance of Persons of 1994 (AG/Res. 1256 (XXIV-O/94) entered into force March 28, 1996, and is available from: <http://www.oas.org/juridico/english/Treaties/a-60.html> as of June 9,

1999. Other OAS declarations on disappearances were approved by the General Assembly as: AG/RES. 890 (XVII-O/87, AG/RES. 950 (XVIII-O/88), AG/RES. 1014 (XIX-O/89, AG/RES. 1033 (XX-O/90), and AG/RES. 1172 (XXII-O/92). The United Nations has a similar instrument: Declaration on the Protection of all Persons from Enforced Disappearance, UN General Assembly Resolution 47/133, December 18, 1992.

23.   Inter-American Court of Human Rights, *Velásquez Rodríguez* case, and *Godínez Cruz* case, judgment of January 20, 1989. The two cases were processed together although decided separately. A companion case, called *Fairen Garbi and Solis Corrales,* judgment of March 15, 1989, ended in a decision finding no violation on the part of Honduras for lack of evidence.

24.   Inter-American Commission of Human Rights, Reports No. 28/92 and 29/92. In Argentina, the government of Raúl Alfonsín had passed the laws of *Punto Final* and *Obediencia Debida;* in 1989 and 1990 his successor, Carlos Menem, issued pardons to all the remaining military either convicted or under prosecution for human rights violations. In Uruguay, the government of Julio Sanguinetti had issued the *Ley de Caducidad de la Pretensión Punitiva del Estado* in 1986. Although they were not called amnesties, these laws, too, effectively prevented investigation and prosecution of past human rights violations.

25.   See Aryeh Neier, "What Should be Done About the Guilty?" *The New York Review of Books,* February 1, 1999, p. 32; Diane F. Orentlicher, "Addressing Gross Human Rights Abuses: Punishment and Victim Compensation," in Louis Henkin and John L. Hargrove, eds., *Human Rights: An Agenda for the Next Century* (Washington, DC: American Society of International Law, 1994); Naomi Roth-Arriaza, ed., *Impunity and Human Rights in International Law and Practice* (New York: Oxford University Press, 1995); Theo Van Boven, UN Special Rapporteur, *Study Concerning the Right to Restitution, Compensation and Reparations for Gross and Consistent Violations of Human Rights,* UN ESCOR, Commission on Human Rights, 45th Session, UN Doc. E/CN.4/Sub.2/1993/8 (1993); Louis Joinet, UN Special Rapporteur, *Final Report on Question of Impunity of Perpetrators of Violations of Human Rights (Civil and Political Rights),* UN ESCOR, Commission on Human Rights, 48th Session, UN Doc.E/CN.4/Sub.2/1996/18 (1996).

26.   UN Doc. A/Conf.183/9, 1998, in M. Cherif Bassiouni, comp., *The Statute of the International Criminal Court: A Documentary History* (Ardsley, NY: Transnational Publishers, 1998).

27.   Diane Orentlicher, "Putting Limits on Lawlessness: From Nuremberg to Pinochet," *Washington Post,* October 25, 1998; Warren Hodhe, "Britain Decides to Let the Pinochet Extradition Case Proceed," *New York Times,* April 16, 1999; Davis Graves, "Pinochet Extradition 'Non Unjust,'" *Daily Telegraph* (London), April 16, 1999; Christina Lamb, "Pinochet Vows to Fight Extradition Plea to the Death," *Sunday Telegraph* (London), April 18, 1999; and Human Rights Watch Web site: <http://www.hrw.org>.

28.   See Priscilla Hayner, "Fifteen Truth Commissions, 1974 to 1994: A Comparative Study," *Human Rights Quarterly,* Vol. 16, No. 4 (November 1994). Truth Commissions have indeed become and important tool in the struggle for human rights, although at times some proponents have been misguided in thinking they should be a substitute for justice. In 1998 the South African Truth and Reconciliation Commission ended its work and released its report. See chapter 9 in this volume.

29.   Federal Criminal Court of Appeal of Buenos Aires, Cause No. 450, Suarez Mason, Carlos Guillermo s/homicidio, privación de la libertad, etc., known as the Lapaco case, and Supreme Court of Argentina, Urteaga case cit. See also Juan E. Méndez, "The Right to Truth" in Christopher Joyner, ed., *Reining in Impunity for International Crimes and Serious Violations of Fundamental Human Rights* (Siracusa, Italy: Association Internationale de Droit Pénal, Eres, 1998).

30.   In Argentina, Supreme Court, *Giroldi H.D. s/recurso de casación,* judgment of April 7, 1995, known as the *Giroldi* case; in Costa Rica, Sala IV (Constitutional) of the Supreme Court, judgment No. 2313-95.

31. See Juan E. Méndez, "La Participación de la Comisión Interamericana de Derechos Humanos en los Conflictos entre los Miskitos y el Gobierno de Nicaragua," in Vargas Carreño, ed., *Human Rights in the Americas: Homage to the Memory of Carlos A. Dunshee de Abranches* (Washington, DC: OAS, 1984).

32. Inter-American Court of Human Rights, *Aloeboetoe et al.* case, Reparations, judgment of September 10, 1993.

33. The Inter-American Convention on the Prevention, Punishment and Eradication of Violence Against Women has been ratified by twenty-nine member states of the OAS as of early 2000. This Convention contemplates a somewhat unusual mechanism of implementation: The Inter-American Commission on Women is entrusted with monitoring compliance, which is supposed to take place via periodic reports to it by governments; this commission cannot entertain individual complaints, although these presumably could be presented to the Inter-American Commission on Human Rights.

34. There are historically few cases that deal with issues related to the discrimination of women in the inter-American System. See the following Inter-American Commission of Human Rights cases: *Raquel Tirado Mejia v. Peru,* 1996, *X and Y v. Argentina,* 1996, and Inter-American Court of Human Rights, Advisory Opinion OC-4/84, of January 1984.

35. See "Report of the Inter-American Commission on Human Rights on the Status of Women in the Americas," adopted by the Inter-American Commission on Human Rights on March 6, 1998, <http://www.cidh.org>.

36. Inter-American Court, *Caballero Delgado* and *Santana* case, judgment of December 8, 1995; *Genie Lacayo* case, judgment of January 29, 1997; *Loayza Tamayo,* judgment of September 17, 1997.

37. See Viviana Krsticevic, "Líneas de trabajo para mejorar la eficacia del sistema," in Juan E. Méndez and Francisco Cox, eds., *El Futuro del Sistema Interamericano de Protección de los Derechos Humanos* (San José: IIHR, 1998), p. 426.

38. Oscar Fappiano, "La ejecución de las decisiones de tribunales internacionales por parte de los órganos locales," in Martín Abregú and Christian Courtis, eds., *La aplicación de los tratados de derechos humanos por los tribunales locales* (Buenos Aires: CELS-Del Puerto, 1997), p. 149.

39. Thomas Buergenthal, *El sistema interamericano para la protección de los derechos humanos in Anuario Jurídico Interamericano* (Washington, DC: General Secretariat of the Organization of American States, 1981), p. 161.

40. For an overview of these and other cases, Víctor Manuel Rodríguez Rescia, "Eficacia de la Jurisprudencia de la Corte Interamericana de Derechos Humanos," in Nieto, *La Corte y el Sistema Interamericano de Derechos Humanos,* p. 469.

41. Fappiano, "La ejecución de las decisiones de tribunales internacionales por parte de los órganos locales," p. 149.

42. Articles 53 and 54 of the ECHR.

43. The obvious opposition of the states, which currently maintain ironclad control of candidacies, should not make us cease considering proposals to improve the selection system. Faúndez Ledesma has mentioned the possibility of entrusting the nomination and screening of candidates to NGOs, universities, etc.; such nominations should be discussed in the respective Congresses, with governments remaining responsible for ratifying the nominations and, of course, being free to vote for any of the candidates. See Héctor Faúndez Ledesma, "La independencia e imparcialidad de los miembros de la Comisión y de la Corte: paradojas y desafíos," in Méndez and Cox, *El futuro del sistema interamericano de protección de los derechos humanos.*

44. Articles 34 and 52.1 of the American Convention.

45. See, for example, Judge Nieto in *Caballero Delgado and Santana* case.

46. This is evident from art. 55 of the Convention, especially paragraphs 2 and 3.

47. Faúndez Ledesma, "La independencia e imparcialidad," p. 197.

48. It could be argued that this procedural inequality could be solved by granting the Commission (which acts as a sort of prosecutor once the case has arrived at the Court) a right to appoint an ad hoc judge. In my view, this would not only be cumbersome and impractical: it would also miss the point. It is the victim, not the Commission, that must have procedural rights equal to those of the government. This point is linked to another important defect in the present system: the limited participation of the victim in the proceedings, a matter to which I refer below.

49. States should see that this advantage is merely relative, as experienced by Honduras, Suriname and Peru, where the ad hoc judges—Espinal Irías, Cançado Trindade, and Vidal respectively—voted with the majorities to condemn the state that appointed them. Certainly, however, there have been cases where judges have forgotten their function and showed extreme partiality in favor of the state that appointed them. In one case (*Neira Alegría v. Peru)*, the ad hoc judge, Mr. Orihuela, tried by all possible means to impede the Court's judgment.

50. Faúndez Ledesma, "La independencia e imparcialidad."

51. In Portuguese and Spanish, the rule establishes that judges who conclude their mandates will continue to serve with regard to cases that are in the *judgment stage,* while the English and French versions empower them to serve *with regard to cases that they have begun to hear and that are still pending.* See Ibid., p. 192.

52. Figures in this paragraph are based on those presented by the then-Chairman of the Inter-American Commission on Human Rights, Dr. Carlos Ayala Corao, at the Third Annual Congress of the Federation of Inter-American Ombudsmen, Lima, September 1998. In December 1998 Mexico and Brazil accepted the Court's jurisdiction. Haiti and the Dominican Republic did the same in early 1999. As discussed above, however, Trinidad and Tobago denounced the whole Convention in May 1998, effective May 1999. And, in July 1999, Peru announced that it withdrew its recognition of the Court's jurisdiction in adversarial cases.

53. Jamaica has withdrawn its consent to the Optional Protocol granting the UN Human Rights Committee jurisdiction to hear complaints.

54. ACHR, art. 78, in *Twenty-Five Human Rights Documents,* pp. 144-45.

55. Pedro Nikken, "Perfeccionar el Sistema Interamericano de derechos humanos sin reformar el pacto de San José," in Méndez and Cox, *El Futuro del Sistema Interamericano de Protección de los Derechos Humanos,* p. 29.

56. Nikken, "Perfeccionar el Sistema," p. 31.

57. Amnesty International campaigns, including the report on the United States, *Rights for All,* can be found at <http://www.amnesty.org/campaign/index.html>. Amnesty International annual reports from 1993 give detailed information on human rights violations across the world, and can be found at: <http://www.amnesty.org/ailib/aireport/index.html>. Human Rights Watch (HRW) campaigns can be found at <http://www.hrw.org/hrw/campaigns/campaigns.html>. HRW reports, including country reports and a catalogue of its books, can be found at <http://www.hrw.org/research/nations.html>.

58. Nikken, "Perfeccionar el Sistema."

59. The Convention makes no reference to confidentiality, except for the obligation temporarily not to publish the report mentioned in art. 50.2.

60. See José Miguel Vivanco, "El Sistema Interamericano de Protección de Derechos Humanos: su reforma," paper presented at the Sixteenth Interdisciplinary Course in Human Rights organized by Inter-American Institute on Human Rights (IIHR), June 1998, San José, Costa Rica.

61. Later on, the Court permitted NGOs to participate as *amicus curiae* and to present briefs at advisory opinion proceedings, and their representatives to take part in oral hearings about those briefs on a procedural footing equal to the Commission and the states.

62. Another way that representatives of the victims may participate is when a voluntary discontinuance of a case or a friendly settlement ending the proceedings is submitted for

the Court's consideration; in both cases the Court must hear their opinion. This is set out in the regulations.

63. However, this practice is unsatisfactory because it is wholly discretionary. Should the Commission decide not to include any representative of the victims in its delegation for a case, they would have no recourse to demand compliance with previous practice.

64. In the *Cayara* case, for example, the petitioners' lawyers (including the author) had to defend before the Court the legality of acts of the Commission that we had strongly opposed in the previous stage. *Cayara* involved a massacre of peasants by the Peruvian army, in retaliation for an ambush by *Sendero Luminoso* guerrillas. It also involved subsequent murders, disappearances, and threats against witnesses and investigators as well as other interference with the investigation and prosecution of the case. The Commission ended its inquiry and sent the case to the Court but immediately received a harsh challenge to this decision from the Peruvian government. In a futile and irregular attempt to placate the government, the Commission withdrew the case from the Court and reopened it, a procedure not contemplated in the Convention. When the Court finally heard the case, the Peruvian government invoked preliminary objections based on this irregular action by the Commission. The Court agreed, and the *Cayara* case, through no fault of the petitioners, was never heard on the merits. *Cayara* case, Inter-American Court of Human Rights, Preliminary Objections, judgment of February 3, 1993.

65. *Castillo Petruzzi* case, Inter-American Court, judgment of May 30, 1999; see also, for example, "Fujimori afirma que Gobierno no acatará fallo de Corte Interamericana de Derechos Humanos," *Gestión*, June 4, 1999; "El Perú no acatará fallo de la CIDH," *Expreso*, June 4, 1999.

66. For more information, see Rodriguez Rescia, "Eficacia de la Jurisprudencia," pp. 468ff. He also looks at the situation in other countries.

67. Fappiano, "La ejecución de las decisiones," p. 153.

68. *Amparo* is a creation of Latin American law that operates as a swift remedy to actions that violate constitutional rights other than the right to physical integrity and personal freedom because the latter are covered by habeas corpus. *Amparo* is grounded on constitutional protections.

69. *Numero apertus* means that the statute provides for payment of compensation ordered by a variety of international tribunals without specifying any one in particular.

SEVEN

The Construction of the African Human Rights System: Prospects and Pitfalls

MAKAU MUTUA[*]

Makau Mutua is Professor of Law, State University of New York at Buffalo Law School; Director, Human Rights Center, SUNY Buffalo; and Chair, Kenya Human Rights Commission.

The regional African human rights system is based on the African Charter on Human and Peoples' Rights (the African or Banjul Charter),[1] which entered into force on October 21, 1986, upon ratification by a simple majority of member states of the Organization of African Unity (OAU).[2] In June 1998 the OAU adopted the Protocol to the African Charter on Human and Peoples' Rights on the Establishment of an African Court on Human and Peoples' Rights.[3] The African Human Rights Court is intended to complement[4] the African Commission on Human and Peoples' Rights, the body that has exercised continental oversight over human rights since 1987.[5] The Protocol suggests that the African Human Rights Court will make the promotion and the protection of human rights within the regional system more effective.[6] But the mere addition of a court, although a significant development, is unlikely by itself to address sufficiently the normative and structural weaknesses that have plagued the African human rights system since its inception.

The modern African state is in many respects the colonial state in a different guise. The African state has been such an egregious human rights violator that skepticism about its ability to create an effective regional human rights system is appropriate.[7] Although the Banjul Charter makes a significant contribution to the human rights corpus, it creates an ineffectual enforcement system. Its most notable contributions are the codification of the three "generations" of rights[8]: civil and political rights; economic, social, and cultural rights; and group or people's rights. It also imposes duties on individuals.[9] But many commentators have focused on the weaknesses in the African system. These include the "clawback" clauses or express limitations on certain rights in the African Charter, the potential abuse of the language of duties, and the absence of an effective protection mandate for the African Commission.[10]

Recent changes in the African state, particularly those related to demands for more open political societies, may augur well for the protection of civil and political rights.[11] Emergent democracies such as Namibia, Malawi, Benin, South Africa, Tanzania, and Mali are more inclined than their predecessors to respect human rights at home and to agree to a more viable regional system. In this context, the African Human Rights Court is likely to operate in a less hostile or cynical environment than the climate that determined and sharply limited the powers and effectiveness of the African Commission. In addition, the 1994 Rwandese genocide and the recent atrocities in Nigeria, Liberia, Somalia, Ethiopia, Sudan, Sierra Leone, Burundi, the Republic of the Congo, and the Democratic Republic of the Congo have further illuminated the need for stronger domestic and regional guarantees for human rights. In fact, at no time in recent African history have the conditions for the creation of an effective regional human rights system been more favorable.

This chapter critically evaluates the African human rights system and assesses its potential impact on human rights conditions on the continent. It examines the normative aspects and institutional arrangements created under the African Charter and the Protocol for the African Human Rights Court. It asks whether a clear and mutually reinforcing division of labor between the African Commission and the African Human Rights Court could be developed to promote and protect human rights on the continent more effectively. Should, for example, the mandate of the African Commission be limited primarily to promotional activities and the African Human Rights Court exclusively given the protective function? What relationship should the Court have to the African Commission?

The chapter explores the effect of the African human rights system in four principal areas. First, it examines the normative, conceptual, and historical aspects of the African Charter and its contribution to the human rights corpus. Second, it looks at the work of the African Commission in the development of the law of the African Charter, including the problems that it has faced. Third, it addresses the norms and structure governing the African Human Rights Court and its potential to fill the lacunae left by the African Commission and to alleviate some of its weaknesses. Finally, it discusses ways in which the African human rights system can penetrate the legal and political cultures of African states to inspire, encourage, and ensure the internalization of human rights.

THE AFRICAN CHARTER: A DIAGNOSIS

The African Charter is not an accident of history. Its creation by the Organization of African Unity came at a time of increased scrutiny of states for their human rights practices and the ascendancy of human rights as a legitimate subject of international discourse. For African states, the rhetoric of human rights had a special resonance for several reasons. First, postcolonial African states were born out of the anticolonial human rights struggle, a fight for political and economic self-determination. Second, black-ruled African states deployed human rights arguments to demonize and delegitimize the colonial and minority white-ruled states of Angola, Mozambique, Namibia, Rhodesia (now Zimbabwe), and apartheid South Africa. Finally, the atrocities of some of the most brutal dictatorships the African continent has ever known heightened the urgency for a regional human rights system. The abominations of Idi Amin of Uganda, Jean-Bedel Bokassa of the Central African Empire, and Macias Nguema of Equatorial Guinea came to be viewed internationally as paradigmatic of African leadership. As this author has pointed out elsewhere, in 1981 African leaders adopted the African Charter to salvage their international image, even though none of them was democratically elected. It is ironic that this club of dictators would give birth to the African human rights system.[12]

Normatively, the African Charter is an innovative human rights document. It substantially departs from the narrow formulations of other regional and universal human rights instruments. It creates an expansive catalog of rights and imposes duties on individuals, features that are absent from other human rights instruments. The Charter's sixty-eight articles are divided into four chapters: Human and Peoples' Rights, Duties, Procedure of the Commission, and Applicable Principles.[13] It prescribes the aforementioned three "generations" of rights. Its most controversial provisions impose duties on individual members of African societies. The Charter links the concepts of human rights, people's rights, and individual and state duties.

The problems of the African human rights system, which thus far has been anchored in the African Commission, are well documented.[14] They include the normative weaknesses in the African Charter and the general impotence of its implementing body, the African Commission. But the distinctive contributions of the African Charter to the human rights corpus, which include the concept of duty and the inclusion of the "three generations" of rights in one instrument, have also been articulated and applauded by some scholars.[15]

Perhaps the most serious flaw in the African Charter concerns its "clawback" clauses, which permeate the African Charter and permit African states to restrict basic human rights to the maximum extent allowed by domestic law.[16] These clauses are especially significant because most domestic laws in Africa date from the colonial period and are therefore highly repressive and draconian. The postcolonial state, like its predecessor, impermissibly and contrary to international human rights standards, restricts most civil and political rights, particularly those pertaining to political participation, free expression, association and assembly, movement, and conscience. Ironically, these same rights are further eroded by the African Charter.

Clawback clauses—that is, qualifications or limitations—permeate the provisions of the African Charter dealing with such fundamental freedoms as civil and political rights. Clauses like "except for reasons and conditions previously laid down by law," "subject to law and order," "within the law," "abides by the law," "in accordance with the provisions of the law," and other restrictions justified for the "protection of national security" severely limit fundamental freedoms.[17]

The African Charter does not have a general derogation clause, a provision that would permit states to suspend certain rights during national emergencies. This omission is all the more serious because the Charter in effect permits states through the clawback clauses to suspend, de facto, many fundamental rights in their municipal laws.[18] In any event, nothing in the Charter prevents African states from denying certain rights during national "emergencies."[19] A revision of the Charter should excise the offending clawback clauses and insert a provision on nonderogable rights and another specifying which rights states can derogate from, when, and under what conditions. Regrettably, there have been no serious efforts to revisit the African Charter.

Another controversial question in the Charter concerns its language of duties. The African Charter takes the view that individual rights cannot make sense in a social and political vacuum, unless they are coupled with duties on individuals. In other words, the Charter argues that the individual egoist is not the center of the moral universe. Thus it seeks to balance the rights of the individual with those of the community and political society through the imposition of duties on the individual. The Charter contemplates two types of duties: duties that individuals owe to other individuals, to the community, and the state, on one hand, and duties that the state bears to its subjects, on the other.

Individuals owe duties to the "family and society, the State and other legally recognized communities."[20] Furthermore, each individual has a "duty to respect and consider his fellow beings without discrimination."[21] Significantly, every individual has a duty to "preserve the harmonious development of the family and to work for the cohesion and respect of the family; to respect his parents at all times, to maintain them in case of need."[22] Among other matters, these provisions raise questions about the commitment of the African Charter to women's rights. Some legal scholars fear that either the African Charter does not adequately protect or could be used to abuse women's rights.[23] Advocates of women's rights believe the family provisions to condone and support repressive and retrogressive structures and practices of social and political ordering.[24] Women's rights advocates interpret this language, which places duties on the state and individuals to the family, as entrenching oppressive family structures that marginalize and exclude women from participation in most spheres outside the home. Some advocates argue that the Charter supports the discriminatory treatment of women on the basis of gender in marriage, in property ownership, and in inheritance, and imposes on them unconscionable labor and reproductive burdens.

In my view, these fears are exaggerated because a progressive and liberal construction of the Charter seems to leave no room for the discriminatory treatment of women. I believe the Charter could be read differently. It can be argued that these are not the practices that the Charter condones when it requires states to assist families as the "custodians of morals and traditional values." Such an interpretation would be a cynical misreading of the Charter. These words can be read as reference to those traditional values that enhance the dignity of the individual and emphasize the dignity of motherhood and the importance of the female as the central link in the reproductive chain. In many societies across precolonial Africa, women were highly valued as equals in the process of regeneration of life.[25]

The Charter's veneration of African culture also has been construed as reinforcing gender oppression. The charge here is that the Charter sees itself as the savior of an African culture that is permanent, static, and unchanging. Viewed this way, the Charter would freeze in time and protect from reform, radical change, or repudiation those cultural norms, practices, and institutions that are harmful to women. Again, taken in its totality as a human rights document, the Charter does not support such a backward reading. The Charter seems to guarantee, unambiguously and without equivocation, the equal rights of women in its gender and equality provision by requiring states to "eliminate every discrimination"[26] against women and to protect women's rights in international human rights instruments.

Read in conjunction with other provisions, the Charter seems to leave no room for discriminatory treatment against women. To allay these fears, however, and to prevent a conservative human rights court from ever giving the Charter a discriminatory interpretation in gender matters, the African Charter should be supplemented by an optional protocol to fully address women's rights issues in all their complexity and multiple dimensions.[27] A protocol on women's rights is being discussed by nongovernmental organizations (NGOs) and governments in Africa.

The more general critique sees the language of duties as "little more than the formulation, entrenchment, and legitimation of state rights and privileges against individuals and peoples."[28] These critics of the language of duties, however, only point to a theoretical danger that states might capitalize on the "duty" concept to violate fundamental rights.[29] The fear is frequently expressed that emphasis on duties may lead to the "trumping" of individual rights, if the two come into conflict.[30] In my view, these criticisms, while understandable, are mistaken. African states have not notoriously violated human rights because of their adherence to the concept of duty. The disastrous human rights performance of many African states has been triggered by insecure regimes whose narrow political classes have no sense of national interest and will stop at nothing, including murder, to retain power. Thus, it is not plausible to argue that individuals should not owe any duties to the state. In fact, they do, in tax, criminal, and other laws. A valid criticism of the language of duties rather should focus on the precise meaning, content, conditions of compliance, and application of those duties. More work should be done to clarify the status of the duties in the Charter and to define their moral and legal dimensions and implications for enforcement. Unfortunately, no such efforts have been made by the African Commission.

THE AFRICAN COMMISSION: AMBIGUITY AND ANEMIA

The African human rights system is anchored by the African Charter and implemented by the African Commission. The Commission is vested largely with promotional functions and an ambiguous protective function. Thus far the system lacks a credible enforcement mechanism. This situation is hardly surprising because virtually no African state, other than The Gambia, Senegal, and Botswana, could boast of even a nominal democracy in 1981, the year that the OAU adopted the African Charter.[31] Hopes by observers of the African Commission that it would robustly construe the Charter to alleviate its weaknesses have gone largely unrealized. In its specific functions and its performance in general, the African Commission has been a disappointment.

The African Commission was established in 1987, the year after the African Charter entered into force. The eleven members of the African Commission, the commissioners, are elected by secret ballot by the OAU Assembly of Heads of State and Government from a list nominated by states parties to the African Charter. The commissioners, who serve in their personal capacity, are elected for a six-year term and are eligible for reelection. Only by the unanimous agreement of all other commissioners can a member of the Commission be removed from office for failure of performance.[32]

The basic functions of the African Commission are both promotional and protective.[33] The promotional function, which the Charter emphasizes, includes research and dissemination of information through workshops and symposia, the encouragement of national and local human rights institutions, the formulation of principles to address legal problems in human rights, and cooperation with African and international human rights institutions. The Commission is empowered to interpret the Charter at the request of a state party, the OAU, or any organization recognized by the OAU.[34] This role is one of the areas that the commissioners could seize upon to interpret and clarify the Charter. In contrast, the provision relating to the protective function is quite terse. It provides, without elaborating, only that the Commission shall "ensure the protection of human and people's rights" in the Charter.[35]

More concretely, the African Charter charges the Commission with three principal functions: examining state reports,[36] considering communications alleging violations,[37] and expounding or elaborating the African Charter.[38] These functions follow the general script of other regional and universal human rights bodies.[39] In particular, the Commission seems to have drawn substantially from the procedures and experiences of the United Nations Human Rights Committee (UNHCR).[40] Its Rules of Procedure, which provide for process before the Commission, and the Reporting Guidelines, which specify the form and content of state reports, mirror the lessons of other human rights bodies.[41] The Guidelines were supplemented by General Directives, an unpublished document that was sent to foreign ministers of states parties in 1990 and are just a précis of the Guidelines.[42]

The Commission's primary protective function, that of considering complaints filed by individual victims as well as NGOs,[43] has a large potential that thus far has not been realized. First, the Charter places no restriction on who may file a communication, an opening that allows any individual, group, or

NGO, whether they are the direct victims of the violation complained of or not, to lodge a petition.[44] However, communications can be considered by the Commission only if they: indicate their authors, even if the authors wish to remain anonymous to the public; are not written in language that is insulting or disparaging to the state or the OAU; are not incompatible with the OAU Charter and the African Charter; are not based exclusively on media reports; are sent after the petitioner exhausts local remedies, unless these are obviously unduly prolonged; are submitted within a reasonable time after local remedies are exhausted; and do not deal with a matter that has been settled by the states concerned in accordance with international instruments.[45]

Communications are considered in private or closed sessions although the Charter does not explicitly require it.[46] If the Commission determines that one or more communications "relate to special cases which reveal the existence of a series of serious or massive violations" of human rights, it must draw the attention of the OAU to such a situation and, presumably, conduct an onsite investigation.[47] In the case of an emergency, the Commission must inform the chair of the OAU and request an in-depth study, which would generally calls for on-site fact-finding.[48] This provision was a dead letter until 1995 when the Commission, with the assistance of the OAU Secretary-General, secured the agreement of Senegal and Togo for field investigations.[49] The Commission's power to conduct such investigations is clearly authorized by the Charter, which empowers it to "resort to any appropriate method of investigation."[50] Until recently, however, the commissioners had been reluctant to claim these powers.

The Commission's formula for considering individual communications closely mirrors that of the UN Human Rights Committee. In a format similar to that of the UNHRC, the Commission arranges its decisions into sections dealing with facts, argument, admissibility, merits of the case, and the finding. Each of these sections is, however, invariably thin in both substance and reasoning. Two examples will suffice. In *Constitutional Rights Project v. Nigeria,*[51] a petition challenging a death penalty case that was imposed in violation of due process protections, the Commission adopted a blandly scripted presentation, "declared" a violation of the Charter provisions, and "recommended" that Nigeria free the petitioners.[52] Nigeria did not. In another case, *Civil Liberties Organization v. Nigeria,*[53] the Commission found that the government enacted laws, in violation of the African Charter, that abridged due process rights and undermined the independence of the judiciary. These examples point to anemia and lack of imagination on the part of the Commission. Although they show some movement toward the development of a human rights jurisprudence, they are too tentative and insubstantial.

It is fair to say, however, that the communications, or individual petitions, procedure has come a long way since the early days. A predictable tradition of considering petitions is slowly evolving. There is an established format for these petitions, and an analysis of the last ten years shows a steady, if cautious, development of this procedure.

It is also clear, however, that the decisions referred to here, and others before them, are formulaic and do not reference jurisprudence from national and international tribunals or fire the imagination. They are nonbinding and attract little, if any, attention from governments and the human rights community. The decisions cannot be published without permission from the OAU Assembly of Heads of State and Government.[54] As explained by two human rights advocates, the African Commission has revised its initial strict interpretation that Article 59 prohibited the publication of communications:

> This [the strict interpretation] changed with the Seventh Activity Report of the Commission, adopted by the Assembly in June 1994. For the first time, this report made available information on the first fifty-two communications decided by the Commission. The information disclosed includes a summary of the parties to the communication, the factual background, and the Commission's summary decision. With the adoption of the Commission's Eighth [1995] and Ninth [1996] Annual Activity Reports, the Commission went a step further and issued full texts of its final decisions.[55]

The publication of the Commission's decisions takes place only after they have been submitted to the OAU Assembly.[56] Although the procedure appears quasi-judicial, the Commission sees its principal objective as creating a dialogue between the parties, leading to the amicable settlement of the dispute.[57] In any case, neither the Charter nor the Commission provides for enforceable remedies or a mechanism for encouraging and tracking state compliance with decisions. To many victims, the Commission's findings are remote if not virtually meaningless.[58]

This overall gloomy picture is by no means universally shared. Some see in the communications procedure the gradual evolution of an effective mechanism. A comparison of the decisions over the years shows that the quality of the Commission's reasoning and decision making has continued to evolve positively. Since 1996, the decisions of the Commission have been more substantive and elaborate on the issues of law and fact that are raised in and considered in communications.[59]

State reporting, which is required by the Charter, follows the pattern of other human rights bodies.[60] The Charter tersely provides that a state shall submit, every two years, a "report on the legislative or other measures taken with a view to giving effect to the rights and freedoms" enumerated within it.[61] The Charter does not say to what body the reports are to be submitted; whether, how, and with what goal the reports should be evaluated; nor what action should be taken after such evaluation. The Commission, not surprisingly, has filled in these gaps by borrowing heavily from other treaty bodies.[62] Unfortunately, it has mimicked both the good and the bad in those bodies.

The Reporting Guidelines, which are detailed, are supposed to guide states in the preparation of their reports. In particular, the Guidelines specify both the form and content of reports. Thus reports must describe in detail the legislative regime as well as the actual application and protection of specific human rights. In reality, however, many of the reports submitted thus far have been woefully inadequate on both counts.[63] The initial report of Ghana, for example, was only a scant five pages while that of Egypt, although ten times as long, only described abstractly some legislation without commentary on the state of human rights conditions on the ground.[64]

Reports are examined in public, and state representatives and the commissioners engage in "constructive dialogue" to assist and encourage states implement the Charter. After considering a report, the Commission communicates its comments and general observations to the state in question.[65] Although the Charter came into force in 1987, the majority of states parties have never submitted their reports, and the Commission has been powerless to force compliance.[66] The reporting process seems to have yielded very little so far as many of the state representatives have appeared either incompetent or ill-prepared.[67] States do not seem to take the reporting seriously, and so far the Commission's comments and observations on state reports have not had any discernible effect.

But the African Commission has taken some steps that have the potential to increase its impact on states. In 1996 the Commission appointed one of its members as a Special Rapporteur on Summary and Extra-judicial Executions. This office is potentially significant if it is used to investigate, report, and open dialogue with states.[68] Additionally, the Commission's country-specific and thematic resolutions raise its visibility and engage states directly. Such resolutions, for example, have called on Sudan to allow detainees access to lawyers and doctors and have asked the government to support negotiations for the settlement of the conflict with the South.[69] Another resolution urges African states to respect the rights of prisoners and to ratify the Convention Against Torture and Other Cruel, Inhuman or Degrading Treatment.[70] These Resolutions have received little publicity, and there are no indications that states take them seriously. Yet however small and tentative, the resolutions are steps in the right direction.

THE AFRICAN HUMAN RIGHTS COURT:
FEARS AND HOPES

Both the European and the inter-American human rights systems give the impression that a human rights court is an indispensable component of an effective regime for the protection of human rights. Norms prescribing state conduct are not meaningful unless they are anchored in functioning and effective institutions. In the case of the African regional system, this truism merits special attention because the norms in both the African Charter and the African Commission itself have been regarded as weak and ineffectual. Hence the push for a human rights court, an institution that is intended to correct some of the more glaring failures of the African system.

There have been two polar views on the creation of an African human rights court. One view holds that such a court must be established as soon as possible to salvage the entire system from its near-total irrelevance and obscurity.[71] According to this view, the deficiencies of the African system, both normative and institutional, are so crippling that only an effective human rights court can jump-start the process of its redemption. The court is here seen as a way to put some teeth in the system. The state is the target that must be restrained.

The other view is gradualist and sees the work of the African system as primarily promotional, not adjudicative. According to it, the major problem in Africa is the lack of awareness by the general populace of its rights and the processes for vindicating those rights. Proponents argue that the regional system must therefore first educate the public by promoting human rights. The task of protection, which would include a human rights court, is seen as less urgent.[72] Proponents of this view argue that a court might be paralyzed by the same problems that have beset the African Commission. They urge that the African Commission be strengthened, instead of dissipating scarce resources to create another, possibly impotent, institution.[73]

From the mid to late 1990s, the gradualist view gave way to the proponents of a human rights court largely due to the lobbying efforts of African NGOs and human rights academics. It had become clear by the mid-1990s, even to pro-establishment figures, that the African system was a disappointment, even an embarrassment, for the continent. In 1994 the conservative OAU Assembly of Heads of State and Government asked its Secretary-General to call a meeting of government experts to "ponder in conjunction with the African Commission on Human and Peoples' Rights over the means to enhance the efficiency of the Commission in considering particularly the establishment of an African Court on Human and Peoples' Rights."[74]

Events moved speedily over the next several years. In September 1995 a draft document on an African human rights court was produced by a meeting of experts organized in Cape Town, South Africa, by the OAU Secretariat in collaboration with the African Commission and the International Commission of Jurists.[75] Later that month an OAU meeting of governmental legal experts produced the Cape Town Draft, a protocol for a human rights court. After several rounds of meetings and more drafts, the Draft Protocol was adopted by the conference of OAU Ministers of Justice and Attorneys General in December 1997. The OAU Council of Ministers adopted the Draft Protocol in February 1998, and the OAU Assembly gave its final blessing in June 1998, opening the Protocol for signature by OAU member states.[76]

The consensus among government officials, NGOs, and academics on the need for a human rights court in the African regional system has steadily gained momentum. This realization is indicative of the shortcomings that currently plague the African system. While the push for the court is not a repudiation of the African Commission, it is an acknowledgment of its general ineffectiveness. The hope appears to be that a court will strengthen the regional system and help to realize its promise. But that will not happen unless the court avoids the pitfalls that have trapped the African Commission.

The existence of other regional human rights courts in the Americas and Europe has given impetus to the African initiative and advanced the idea within the modern African state that its conduct toward its own citizens is no longer exclusively an internal, domestic matter. Even in Asia, where states have been more resistant to the application and internalization of the human rights corpus—and where as of yet there is no regional human rights system—that resistance is bound to come under increasing attack by NGOs due to the establishment of a human rights court in Africa. The regional supervision of a state's internal conduct toward its nationals is becoming a reality.

There is little doubt that both the European Court of Human Rights and the Inter-American Court of Human Rights have given the idea of international enforcement concreteness in a way that did not seem plausible a mere fifty years ago. Africa, a continent that has been plagued by serious human rights violations since colonial rule, is now poised to erode further the power of the sovereign state with the establishment of the African Court on Human and Peoples' Rights.[77] At the adoption of the Draft Protocol in December 1997, Salim Ahmed Salim, the OAU Secretary-General, stated that human rights "is a basic requirement in any society and a pre-requisite for human progress and development."

The African Human Rights Court is an attempt to address some of the weaknesses of the African system. Its basic function is protective, and it seeks to complement the work of the African Commission, whose work is basically promotional.[78] Although the African Commission's mandate includes state reporting[79] and the consideration of individual petitions,[80] a function that is protective, it is the promotional activities that have been the centerpiece of its operations.[81] But commentators agree that both the state reporting and the communications procedures have been disappointing, partly due to the lack of powers and the absence of textual clarity.

The Court would be composed of eleven judges elected in their individual capacity by the OAU Assembly of Heads of States and Government from among "jurists of high moral character and of recognized practical, judicial or academic competence and experience in the field of human and people's rights."[82] Judges would serve for a six-year term and be eligible for reelection only once. It is a shortcoming that all judges, except the President of the Court, serve on a part-time basis. Although their independence is formally guaranteed and they are protected by the immunities of diplomats under international law, part-time service undermines the integrity and independence of the Court. A judge can be removed only by the unanimous decision of all the other judges of the Court. A judge who is a national of a state party to a case must recuse him or herself to avoid bias. The Court appoints its own registrar and registry staff.[83]

The Court's jurisdiction is not circumscribed or limited to cases or disputes that arise out of the African Charter. The Protocol provides that actions could be brought before it on the basis of any instrument, including international human rights treaties, which are ratified by the state party in question. Furthermore, the Court can apply as sources of law any relevant human rights instrument ratified by the state, in addition to the African Charter. The Court is empowered to decide if it has jurisdiction in the event of a dispute.[84] It can exercise both contentious and conciliatory jurisdiction,[85] and may issue advisory opinions on "any legal matter relating to the Charter or any other relevant human rights instruments." Such an opinion can be requested by a wide variety of entities, including a member state of the OAU, the OAU or any of its organs, or even an African NGO, provided it is recognized by the OAU.[86]

One serious shortcoming of the African Human Rights Court relates to the Protocol's limitation of access on individuals and NGOs. The Court has two types of access, one automatic, the other optional. The African Commission, states party, and African intergovernmental organizations enjoy unfettered or "automatic" access to the court once a state ratifies the Protocol.[87] In contrast, however, individuals and NGOs cannot bring a suit against a state unless two conditions are met. First, the Court has discretion to grant or deny such access.[88] Second, at the time of ratification of the Draft Protocol or thereafter, the state must have made a declaration accepting the jurisdiction of the Court to hear such cases.[89] While this limitation may have been necessary to get states on board,[90] it is nevertheless disappointing and a terrible blow to the standing and reputation of the Court in the eyes of most Africans. After all, it is individuals and NGOs, and not the African Commission, regional intergovernmental organizations, or states party, that would be the primary beneficiaries and users of the Court. The Court is not an institution for the protection of the rights of states or OAU organs but primarily for the protection of citizens from the state and other governmental agencies. This limitation will render the Court virtually meaningless unless it is interpreted broadly and liberally.

The Court is technically independent of the African Commission, although it may request the Commission's opinion with respect to the admissibility of a case brought by an individual or an NGO.[91] In ruling on admissibility of a case, the Court also must take into account the requirements that individual petitions must meet under the African Charter.[92] Presumably, the Court should not hear cases that do not meet these criteria. The Court also may consider cases or transfer them to the African Commission if it feels that the matter requires an amicable settlement, not adversarial adjudication.[93]

It is vital that the Court determine its own rules of procedure, which should enhance its independence.[94] Proceedings before the Court generally would be conducted in public, and parties would be entitled to legal representation of their own choice.[95] Witnesses or parties to a case "shall enjoy all protection and facilities, in accordance with international law" in connection with their appearance before the Court.[96] This rule would shield witnesses from various pressures and intimidation and facilitate their ability to participate in proceedings more fully and freely.

The Court is given wide powers in conducting proceedings. It seems to have discretionary jurisdiction and need not take all the cases that come before it. This should allow the Court to avoid overload and to hear only those cases that have the potential to advance human rights protection. The Court may hear submissions from all parties, including oral, written, and expert testimony. States are required to assist the Court and provide facilities for the efficient handling of cases. Once the Court finds a violation, it may order remedies, including "fair compensation or reparation." In cases of "extreme gravity and urgency," the Court may order provisional remedies, such as an injunction, to avoid irreparable harm to victims, actual or potential.[97]

The Court's judgments, which are final and without appeal,[98] are binding on states.[99] In its annual report to the OAU, the Court specifically lists states that have not complied with its judgments.[100] This is a "shaming" tactic that marks the violator. The OAU Council of Ministers is required to monitor the execution of the judgment on behalf of the OAU Assembly. Presumably the OAU Assembly can take additional measures to force compliance, such as passing resolutions urging states to respect the Court's judgments. Alternatively, the OAU Chairman could be empowered to write to delinquent states asking that they honor the Court's judgments.

Critics and supporters alike have argued that it makes little sense to create an institution that duplicates the weaknesses of the African Commission. In the context of the OAU, an organization with scarce financial resources and limited moral clarity and vision, the establishment of a new body should be approached with caution. A human rights court will be useful only if it genuinely seeks to correct the shortcomings of the African system and provides victims of human rights violations with a real and accessible forum to vindicate their basic rights. What the OAU and the African regional system do not need is yet another remote and opaque bureaucracy, one that promises little and delivers nothing. If that were the case, then it would make more sense to expend additional resources and energy to address the problems of the African Commission and defer the establishment of a court for another day. Several important questions will have to be addressed if the Human Rights Court is to become a significant player in human rights in Africa.

The Human Rights Court also faces institutional problems. These concerns are external to the Court and are compounded by matters internal to it, such as the tenure of judges and its effect on the independence of the Court and the limitation of access to the Court to individuals and NGOs. It is absolutely critical that the Court is, and be perceived as, separate and independent from the African Commission to avoid burdening it with the severe image problems and the anemia associated with its older sibling. This dissociation would be possible if there was a clear-cut division of labor between the African Human Rights Court and the African Commission, but that is not currently the case. The drafters of the African Charter did not contemplate a court, and as a result the African Commission was vested with both promotional and protective functions. One clear protective function is the individual complaint procedure, which makes the Commission "courtlike" because of its quasi-judicial character.

The African Charter should be revised to remove protective functions from the African Commission and to vest them exclusively with the African Human Rights Court. The African Commission should be charged only with promotional functions, the most basic of which should be state reporting and dialogue with NGOs and government institutions in member states to encourage promotion, advocacy, and the incorporation of human rights norms into state policies and domestic legislation.[101] This unambiguous demarcation of areas of competence should alleviate the problem of hierarchy or "competition" between the two institutions, and may enhance cooperation and mutual reinforcement. Importantly, it should avoid tainting one body with the shortcomings of the other. Thus the African Commission would clearly be the "political" body while the Court alone would be the judicial or "legal" organ of the African human rights system.

The Court has broad powers and may, presumably at its discretion, exercise contentious, conciliatory, or advisory jurisdiction. The Protocol does not seem to impose a mandatory jurisdiction on the Court—that is, require it to hear every admissible case. While certain entities are entitled to submit cases to it, the Court has discretion under the admissibility clause to consider or transfer cases to the African Commission.[102] This discretion is essential if one considers the purposes of adjudication that the Court ought to carve out for itself to become effective, relevant, and visible in the struggle against the culture of impunity and human rights violations.

Three basic purposes are associated with national and international adjudicatory bodies; these are: vindicating the rule of law by providing justice in an individual case; protecting rights through deterrence and behavior modification; and expounding legal instruments and making law through elucidation and interpretation.[103] To fulfill its promise, the African Human Rights Court will have to reflect carefully on these roles and decide where it has the potential to make a meaningful contribution.

The African Human Rights Court should not be viewed as a forum for offering individual justice to victims of human rights violations. While such a goal is certainly noble, it is impossible. The Court can act neither as a forum of first instance nor as the mandatory court of appeal for all cases. Cast in this role, the Court would be paralyzed by a torrential caseload. Examples from other fora tell why: The most poignant case is that of the UN Human Rights Committee, the body that oversees the implementation of the International Covenant on Civil and Political Rights (ICCPR).[104] Under the Optional Protocol to the ICCPR, individuals can petition the HRC for the vindication of their rights.[105] The HRC's mandatory jurisdiction to consider all admissible cases has created a backlog of at least three years.[106] The possible ratification of the Optional Protocol by states with large populations, such as China, India, the United States, and Indonesia—together with the victims' growing familiarity with the procedure—can only add to the inability of the HRC to respond to all individual cases.

The African Human Rights Court need not make this mistake. It will not survive if it adopts a mandatory jurisdiction because the volume of cases is bound to be enormous. Instead, the Court should hear only those cases that have the potential to expound on the African Charter and make law that would guide African states in developing legal and political cultures that respect human rights. In other words, the Court should not be concerned with individual cases where it looks "backward" to attempt to correct or punish a past wrong to an individual.

Rather, the Court should look forward and create a body of law with precedential value and an interpretation of the substantive law of the African Charter and other key universal human rights documents to direct states. Here the Court would protect rights by judgments that by their nature deter states from future misconduct by modifying their behavior. Individual justice would be a coincidence in the few cases the Court would hear. Moreover, individual courts in OAU member states should look to the African Human Rights Court for direction in the development and application of human rights law.

Finally, the African Human Rights Court should benefit from the experiences of the European Court of Human Rights (ECHR) and the Inter-American Court of Human Rights, as well as national fora such as the Constitutional Court of South Africa, which have taken the lead in developing human rights jurisprudence. The Court should closely examine the factors that have made these institutions effective. Legal scholars Laurence Helfer and Anne-Marie Slaughter have created a checklist of such factors that the African Human Rights Court ought to contemplate.[107] Helfer and Slaughter have organized them into three clusters: factors controlled by states party to the treaty that created the Court (e.g., the tribunal's composition, its investigative powers, and the legal status of its decisions); factors that the tribunal itself controls (e.g., quality of legal reasoning and degrees of autonomy from political interests); and factors beyond the control of the tribunal and the states party (e.g., the cultural identities of states and the nature of abuses monitored by the tribunals).[108]

This checklist can be particularly useful if judges are independent and motivated by the drive to make the African Human Rights Court the central institution in the development of a legal culture based on the rule of law. Over the past decade, there has been a general movement in Africa toward more accountable and open governments. The Court comes in an environment of increased awareness about the proper limits of governmental conduct. For the first time since decolonization, states seem to be more willing to foster or at least to allow the creation of institutions of public accountability. Ultimately, effective supranational adjudication will not be possible in Africa unless the OAU system and individual member states treat, and expect, the African Human Rights Court to lead them in transforming the continent's dismal legacy of state despotism.

CONCLUSION

Africa has been traumatized by human rights violations of historic proportions over the last five centuries. The recent chapter in that long history of abuses is still being authored under the direction of the postcolonial state. But the people of Africa, like people elsewhere, have never stopped struggling for better conditions of life and especially for more enlightened and accountable political societies. The popular repudiation of one-party and undemocratic states over the past decade has once again given hope that the predatory impulses of the postcolonial state might be arrested. Within states, nongovernmental organizations have multiplied during that period and governments are being forced to revise policies and laws that are offensive to basic human rights. At the continental level, NGOs and human rights advocates have demanded that the African Commission become part of this movement toward change.

This is the lens through which Africans now view the African human rights system. While many Africans feel that the idea of the African Commission was a step in the right direction, they believe that it has been largely ineffectual. Further, a regional human rights system worth its name needs strong institutions to anchor its norms. The African Human Rights Court is an attempt to fulfill that promise. However, the Court will be a disappointment unless states party to it revisit the African Charter and strengthen many of its substantive provisions. Moreover, the Court will not meet the expectations of Africans if the OAU does not provide it with material and moral support to allow it to function as the independent and significant institution it ought to be. Finally, of course, the initial integrity and vitality of the Court will rest with those who will be privileged to serve as its first bench. Unless these conditions are met, the African Human Rights Court is condemned to remain a two-legged stool, a lame institution unable to fulfill its promise as a seat from which human rights can be advanced. In that case, the Court will have failed to redeem the troubled African regional system.

NOTES

*   This chapter draws heavily upon my article "The African Human Rights Court: a Two-Legged Stool?" *Human Rights Quarterly* Vol. 21, No.2 (1999), pp. 342-63, ©The Johns Hopkins University Press. Used by permission of The Johns Hopkins University Press.

1. Organization of African Unity, *The African Charter on Human and Peoples' Rights* (1981), Doc. CAB/LEG/67/3/Rev.5, reprinted in 21 *International Legal Materials* (ILM) 59 (1982).

2. The African Charter was adopted in 1981 by the eighteenth Assembly of Heads of State and Government of the OAU, the official body of African states. It is also known as the Banjul Charter because a final draft of it was produced in Banjul, the capital of The Gambia.

3. Assembly of Heads of State and Government of the Organization of African Unity, *Protocol to the African Charter on Human and Peoples' Rights on the Establishment of an African Court on Human and Peoples' Rights* (Ougadougou, Burkina Faso, June 1998), OAU/LEG/MIN/ AFCHPR/PROT.(1) Rev.2 (hereafter Protocol). See also "African Foreign Ministers Discuss Human Rights," *Africa News,* April 15, 1999.

4. The Protocol enters into force thirty days after ratification by fifteen OAU member states. See the Protocol, article 34. Although by November 1999 the Protocol had been signed by thirty-five states, only three, Burkina Faso, Senegal, and The Gambia, had ratified it. The Protocol states in the preamble that the African Human Rights Court shall "complement and reinforce the functions of the African Commission on Human and Peoples' Rights." See Protocol, preamble. Elsewhere, the Protocol clarifies and emphasizes that the African Human Rights Court shall "complement the protective mandate of the African Commission on Human and Peoples' Rights." Ibid., art. 2. See also Gino J. Naldi and Konstantinos Magliveras, "Reinforcing the African System of Human Rights: The Protocol for the Establishment of an African Court of Human and Peoples' Rights," *Netherlands Quarterly of Human Rights,* Vol. 16 (1998), p. 431; U. Oji Umozurike, *The African Charter on Human and Peoples' Rights* (Boston: M. Nijhoff, 1997), pp. 92-93.

5. Until the Protocol comes into force and a Human Rights Court is established, the African Commission on Human and Peoples' Rights (hereafter African Commission) will remain the sole supervisory organ for the implementation of the African Charter on Human and Peoples' Rights.

6. See generally Protocol, preamble.

7. For discussions and analyses of the colonial imprint on the African postcolonial state, see Mahmood Mamdani, *Citizen and Subject: Contemporary Africa and the Legacy of Late Colonialism* (Princeton, NJ: Princeton University Press, 1996); Crawford Young, "The Heritage of Colonialism," in John W. Harbeson and Donald Rothschild, eds., *Africa in World Politics* (Boulder, CO: Westview Press, 1991), p. 19; Robert H. Jackson, "Juridical Statehood in Sub-Saharan Africa," *Journal of International Affairs,* Vol. 1 (1992), p. 46; Ali A. Mazrui, "The African State as a Political Refugee: Institutional Collapse and Human Displacement," *International Journal of Refugee Law,* Special Issue (1995), p. 21; Makau wa Mutua, "Why Redraw the Map of Africa: a Moral and Legal Inquiry," *Michigan Journal of International Law,* Vol. 16 (1995), p. 1113. Discussing Africa's colonial legacy, one author notes that the "most obvious and powerful expressions of the continued African conceptual reliance on European political forms are the African states themselves. The states are direct and uncritical successors of the colonies." See Art Hansen, "African Refugees: Defining and Defending Human Rights," in Ronald Cohen, Goran Hyden, and Winston Nagan, eds., *Human Rights and Governance in Africa* (Gainesville, FL: University Press of Florida, 1993), pp. 139, 161.

8. "Generations" of rights refers to the sequence in time in which the different categories of rights were codified and accepted internationally. But the "dating" of rights language is problematic because all categories of rights are interrelated, indivisible, and interdependent of one another, irrespective of the time of their recognition.

9. On duties of the individual, see African Charter, arts. 27-29. For a discussion of the concept of duties in human rights discourse and the African Charter, see Makau wa Mutua, "The Banjul Charter and the African Cultural Fingerprint: An Evaluation of the Language of Duties," *Virginia Journal of International Law,* Vol. 25 (1995), p. 339.

10. For discussions of these problems, see Richard Gittleman, "The African Charter on Human and Peoples' Rights: A Legal Analysis," *Virginia Journal of International Law,* Vol. 22 (1982), p. 667; Richard Gittleman, "The African Commission on Human and Peoples' Rights: Prospects and Procedures," in Hurst Hannum, ed., *Guide to International Human Rights Practice* (Philadelphia: University of Pennsylvania Press, 1984), p. 153; Cees Flinterman and Evelyn Ankumah, "The African Charter on Human and Peoples' Rights" in Hurst Hannum, ed., *Guide to International Human Rights Practice* (Philadelphia: University of Pennsylvania Press, 1992), p. 159.

11. See Makau wa Mutua, "African Renaissance," *New York Times,* May 11, 1991 (describing the demands by Africans for political democracy); Human Rights Watch, *Human Rights Watch World Report 1993* (New York: Human Rights Watch, 1992), pp. 6-9 (reporting

Africa's political upheavals, including those related to demands for political reforms and democracy).

12. See Makau wa Mutua, "The African Human Rights System in a Comparative Perspective," *Review of the African Commission on Human and Peoples' Rights,* Vol. 3 (1993), pp. 5, 7.

13. See generally African Charter.

14. For analyses of some normative and structural problems of the African human rights system, see Richard Gittleman, "The African Charter on Human and Peoples' Rights: A Legal Analysis," *Virginia Journal of International Law,* Vol. 22 (1982), p. 667; Cees Flinterman and Evelyn Ankumah, "The African Charter on Human and Peoples' Rights," *Guide to International Human Rights,* p. 159; Olosula Ojo and Amadu Sessay, "The OAU and Human Rights: Prospects for the 1980s and Beyond," *Human Rights Quarterly,* Vol. 16 (1994), p. 8; Evelyn Ankumah, *The African Commission on Human and Peoples' Rights: Practice and Procedures* (Boston: M. Nijhoff, 1996) (hereafter *Practice and Procedures of African Commission*).

15. B. Obinna Okere, "The Protection of Human Rights in Africa and the African Charter on Human and Peoples' Rights: A Comparative Analysis with the European and American Systems," *Human Rights Quarterly,* Vol. 6 (1984), p. 141; Josiah Cobbah, "African Values and the Human Rights Debate: An African Perspective," *Human Rights Quarterly,* Vol. 9 (1987), p. 309; Makau wa Mutua, "The African Cultural Fingerprint," p. 339.

16. See Mutua, "The African System in a Comparative Perspective," p. 7.

17. Ibid., p. 7.

18. Arthur E. Anthony, "Beyond the Paper Tiger: the Challenge of a Human Rights Court in Africa," *Texas International Law Journal,* Vol. 32 (1997), pp. 511, 518.

19. See Thomas Buergenthal, *International Human Rights in a Nutshell* (St. Paul, MN: West Publishing, 1995), pp. 233-34.

20. African Charter, art. 27(1).

21. Ibid., art. 28.

22. Ibid., art. 29(1).

23. For discussions of the Charter's view on women, see Claude E. Welch, Jr., "Human Rights and African Women: A Comparison of Protection under Two Major Treaties," *Human Rights Quarterly,* Vol. 15 (1993), p. 548; Florence Butegwa, "Using the African Charter on Human and Peoples' Rights to Secure Women's Access to Land in Africa," in Rebecca Cook, ed., *Human Rights of Women: National and International Perspectives* (Philadelphia: University of Pennsylvania Press, 1994), p. 495; Chaloka Beyani, "Towards a More Effective Guarantee of Women's Rights in the African Human Rights System," in Cook, ed., *Human Rights of Women,* p. 285; Joe Oloka-Onyango, "The Plight of the Larger Half: Human Rights, Gender Violence and the Legal Status of Refugee and Internally Displaced Women in Africa," *Denver Journal of International Law and Policy,* Vol. 24 (1996), pp. 349, 371-74.

24. African Charter, Article 18 refers to the family as the "natural unit and basis of society" and requires the state to "assist the family which is the custodian of morals and traditional values recognized by the community." Elsewhere, the Charter provides that the individual owes "duties towards his family and society." Ibid., art. 27(1). Further, that every individual has the duty to "preserve the harmonious development of the family and to work for the cohesion and respect of the family; to respect his parents at all times, to maintain them in case of need." Ibid., art. 29(1).

25. See Mutua, "The African Cultural Fingerprint," pp. 371-72.

26. Ibid., p. 372. The Charter states that the "state shall ensure the elimination of every discrimination against women and also ensure the protection of the rights of the woman and the child as stipulated in international declarations and conventions." African Charter, art. 18(3). Among the international conventions applicable here would include the Convention on the Elimination of All Forms of Discrimination against Women, opened for signature Mar. 1, 1980, 1249 *United Nations Treaty Series* 14 (CEDAW). Normatively,

CEDAW is perceived as a very progressive and forward-looking document and many African states are parties to it.

27. There already have been calls for a protocol on women's rights. See Rachel Murray, "Report of the 1996 Sessions of the African Commission on Human and Peoples' Rights," *Human Rights Law Journal,* Vol. 18 (1997), pp. 16, 19.

28. H. W. O. Okoth-Ogendo, "Human and Peoples' Rights: What Point Is Africa Trying to Make?" in Cohen, Hyden, and Nagan, eds., *Human Rights and Governance,* pp. 74, 78-79.

29. Ibid., p. 79.

30. Ronald Cohen, "Endless Teardrops: Prolegomena to the Study of Human Rights in Africa," in Cohen, Hyden, and Nagan, eds., p. 15.

31. Mutua, "The African Human Rights System in a Comparative Perspective," p. 7.

32. African Charter, arts. 30, 31(2), 33, 36, 39.

33. Ibid., art. 45, sets out the functions of the African Commission.

34. Ibid., art. 45(3).

35. Ibid., art. 45(2).

36. States which are parties must submit, every two years, a report on the legislative and other measures taken to give effect to rights in the African Charter. Ibid., art. 62.

37. Ibid., arts. 47 and 55. The Charter permits two types of communications: from individuals, nongovernmental organizations, and groups, on one hand, and interstate communications, on the other. The latter has never been invoked and are not discussed in this chapter.

38. Ibid., art. 45(3).

39. See Philip Alston, "Appraising the Human Rights Regime," in Philip Alston, ed., *The United Nations and Human Rights: a Critical Appraisal* (New York: Oxford University Press, 1992), p. 1; Buergenthal, *International Human Rights in a Nutshell,* pp. 21-247, describes UN Charter-based and treaty-based human rights instruments and bodies as well the African Inter-American and European human rights systems.

40. The UN Human Rights Committee is the treaty body that oversees the implementation of the International Covenant on Civil and Political Rights (ICCPR). International Covenant on Civil and Political Rights, G.A. Res. 2200 A(XXI), U.N. GAOR, 21st Sess., Supp. No. 16, p. 52, U.N. Doc. A/6316 (1966).

41. The Rules of Procedure of the African Commission on Human and Peoples' Rights, adopted on October 6, 1995, are reproduced in *Human Rights Law Journal,* Vol. 18 (1997), pp. 154-63 (hereafter *Rules of Procedure*). "Guidelines for National Periodic Reports," Second Annual Activity Report of the African Commission on Human and Peoples' Rights, Annex III, June 1989, AFR/COM/HPR.5(VI).

42. Astrid Danielsen, *The State Reporting Procedure Under the African Commission* (Copenhagen: Danish Centre for Human Rights, 1994), pp. 51-52; Ankumah, *The African Commission on Human and Peoples' Rights: Practice and Procedures,* pp. 82-83.

43. The African Charter requires that the Commission "cooperate" with African and international NGOs in its work. African Charter, art. 45(1)(a) and (c). Thus the Commission grants human rights NGOs observer status which allows their representatives to participate in the public sessions of the Commission. Rules of Procedure, Rule 75.

44. African Charter, art. 55.

45. Ibid., art. 56.

46. Rules of Procedure, Rule 106. The Commission, which makes its own rules of procedure, may justify closed sessions for communications under article 59 of the Charter, which provides, in part, that "all measures taken within the provisions of the present Charter shall remain confidential" until the OAU decides otherwise. But this provision is overbroad and vague. A literal interpretation of "all measures" would be absurd. Perhaps the Commission could open at least part, if not all, of the communications processes to the public.

47. African Charter, art. 58(1).

48. Ibid., art. 58(3).

49. "Final Communiqué of the 17th Ordinary Session of the African Commission on Human and Peoples' Rights," March 12-22, 1995, Lome, Togo, available at <http://www1.umn.edu/humanrts/africa/achpr17f.html>; see also Ankumah, *Practice and Procedures of the African Commission,* p. 47.

50. African Charter, art. 46.

51. Communication 60/91, "Decisions and Reports: African Commission on Human and Peoples' Rights," *Human Rights Law Journal,* Vol. 18 (1997), p. 28.

52. Ibid.

53. Communication 129/94, Ibid., pp. 35, 36.

54. The Charter provides that all "measures taken within the provisions of the present Charter shall remain confidential until such a time as the Assembly of Heads of State and Government shall decide otherwise." See African Charter, art. 59(1).

55. Chidi Anselm Odinkalu and Camilla Christensen, "The African Commission on Human and Peoples' Rights: The Development of its Non-state Communications Procedures," *Human Rights Quarterly,* Vol. 20 (1998), pp. 235, 277.

56. Ibid.

57. Communications 16/88, 17/88, 18/88, *Comite Culturel pour la Democratie au Benin, Hilaire Badjogoume, El Hadj Boubacare Diawara v. Benin.* (The decision notes that "it is the primary objective of the Commission in the communications procedure to initiate a dialogue between the parties which will result in an amicable settlement to the satisfaction of both and which remedies the prejudice complained of." Odinkalu and Christensen, "The Development of Non-state Communications," n. 51, p. 244.

58. See African Commission on Human and Peoples' Rights, *Report of the 16th Session of the African Commission on Human and Peoples' Rights* (London: African Society of International and Comparative Law, 1996), pp. 62-83 for more communications by the Commission. For a very thoughtful analysis of the communications procedure before the African Commission, see Odinkalu and Christensen, "The Development of Non-state Communications."

59. Odinkalu and Christensen, "The Development of Non-state Communications."

60. African Charter, art. 62.

61. Ibid.

62. See Felice D. Gaer, "First Fruits: Reporting by States Under the African Charter on Human and Peoples' Rights," *Netherlands Human Rights Quarterly,* Vol. 10 (1992), p. 29, for an evaluation of the initial state reporting under the African Charter.

63. See generally, Ankumah, *Practice and Procedures of African Commission,* pp. 79-110.

64. Ibid., pp. 91-92.

65. Rules of Procedure, Rule 106.

66. Mohamed Komeja, "The African System of Human and Peoples' Rights: An Annotated Bibliography," *East African Journal of Peace and Human Rights,* Vol. 3 (1996), pp. 271, 284-85.

67. Ankumah, *Practice and Procedures of the African Commission,* p. 99.

68. Rachel Murray, "Report of the 1996 Sessions of the African Commission on Human and Peoples' Rights," *Human Rights Law Journal,* Vol. 18 (1997), p. 16.

69. See *Report of the 16th Session of the African Commission on Human and Peoples' Rights,* pp. 89-90.

70. Ibid., p. 95.

71. See Mutua, "The African System in a Comparative Perspective," p. 10; Komeja, "The African System of Human and Peoples' Rights," p. 287.

72. See Ankumah, *Practice and Procedures of the African Commission,* pp. 194-95.

73. Ibid., p. 195.

74. See Report of Government Experts Meeting, AHG/Res 230(xxx), 30th Ordinary Session of the Assembly of Heads of State and Government, Tunis, Tunisia, June 1994, cited in Ibrahim Ali Badawi El-Sheikh, "Draft Protocol to the African Charter on Human and

Peoples' Rights on the Establishment of an African Court on Human and Peoples' Rights: Introductory Note," *African Journal of International and Comparative Law,* Vol. 9 (1997), pp. 943, 944 (hereafter "Draft Protocol to the African Charter").

75.   Ibid., p. 944.

76.   See "Report of Government Experts Meeting on the Establishment of an African Court of Human and Peoples' Rights," September 6-12, 1995, Cape Town, South Africa, OAU/ LEG/EXP/AFCHPR/RPT(1)Rev.1; "International Conference on Human Rights Commission Opens in Addis," Xinhua News Agency, May 18, 1998; "Pursuit for Peace Remains Major Task for Africa: Salim," Xinhua News Agency, June 18, 1998.

77.   Ibid.

78.   The Protocol acknowledges this contrast—in essence the weaknesses and the incompleteness of the African Commission—when its states in its preamble that the African Human Rights Court will "complement and reinforce the functions of the African Commission on Human and Peoples' Rights." Protocol, preamble. It adds, further, that the African Human Rights Court shall "complement the protective mandate of the African Commission." Ibid., art. 2.

79.   African Charter, art. 62.

80.   These include state-to-state and "other" communications, which could come from individuals, groups, and organizations. Ibid., arts. 55, 56.

81.   The principal activities of the African Charter, which are promotional, are to collect documents, undertake studies, organize seminars, disseminate information, encourage national and local institutions concerned with human rights, formulate principles to resolve human rights problems, and interpret the African Charter. Ibid., art 45.

82.   Protocol, art. 11(1).

83.   Ibid., arts. 15(1), 15(4), 17, 19, 22, 24.

84.   Ibid., arts. 3(1), 3(2), 7.

85.   Ibid., art. 9, which allows the court to attempt the "amicable settlement" of disputes.

86.   Ibid., art. 4(1).

87.   Ibid., art. 5(1), 5(2).

88.   Ibid., art. 5(3) provides that the "*court may entitle* relevant Non Governmental Organizations (NGOs) with observer status before the [African] Commission, and individuals to institute cases directly before it . . . " (emphasis added).

89.   Ibid., art. 5(3), 34(6).

90.   Ambassador Badawi, a member of the African Commission and its former chair, alludes to this when he notes that the "question of allowing NGOs and individuals to submit cases to the court was one of the most complicated issues during the consideration of the Draft Protocol." See Badawi El-Sheikh, "Draft Protocol of the African Charter."

91.   Protocol, art. 6(1).

92.   Ibid., art. 6(2). See African Charter, art. 56, for a list of the requirements that communications before the African Commission must meet.

93.   Protocol, art. 6(3).

94.   Ibid., art. 33.

95.   Ibid., art. 10(1), (2). Free legal representation may also be provided where the "interests of justice so require." Ibid., art. 10(2).

96.   Ibid., art. 10(3).

97.   Ibid., arts. 26, 26(1), 27(1), 27(2).

98.   Ibid., art. 28.

99.   Ibid., art. 30 provides, in part, that states "*undertake to comply with the judgement* in any case in which they are parties within the time stipulated by the Court and *to guarantee its execution*" (emphasis added).

100. Ibid., art. 31.

101. At a recent meeting, NGOs and members of the African Commission started a dialogue on possible amendments and revisions to the African Charter. These included women's rights, clawback clauses, and derogation of rights. Ibid., p. 19.

102. Protocol, art. 6(3).
103. See Henry J. Steiner, "Individual Claims in a World of Massive Violations: What Role for the Human Rights Committee?" in Philip Alston and J. Crawford, eds., *The Future of UN Human Rights Treaty Monitoring* (Cambridge: Cambridge University Press, forthcoming 2000).
104. See International Covenant on Civil and Political Rights, G.A. Res. 2200 A(XXI), U.N. GAOR, 21st Sess., Supp. No. 16, p. 52, U.N. Doc. A/6316 (1996).
105. See Optional Protocol to the ICCPR, G.A. Res. 2200 A(XXI), 21 U.N. GAOR Supp. No. 16, p. 59, U.N. Doc. A/6316 (1966).
106. For statistics on the twenty years since the HRC communications procedure became effective under the Optional Protocol, see *1997 Report of the Human Rights Committee,* GAOR Supp. No. 40 (A/52/40), Section VII(A).
107. See generally Laurence R. Helfer and Anne-Marie Slaughter, "Towards a Theory of Effective Supranational Adjudication," *Yale Law Journal,* Vol. 107 (1997), p. 273.
108. Ibid., pp. 298-337.

EIGHT

Human Rights in Pakistan:
A System in the Making

ASMA JAHANGIR

Asma Jahangir is an Advocate in the Supreme Court of Pakistan. She is a
founder and former Chair of the Human Rights Commission of Pakistan and
is presently UN Special Rapporteur on extrajudicial, summary, and arbitrary
executions.

In its fifty-three years of existence, Pakistan has been governed more by military
dictatorships than by elected governments. Today is no exception, as the
country's fourth military coup took place on October 12, 1999, ending the
deeply corrupt and autocratic reign of Prime Minister Nawaz Sharif. Sharif had
been groomed by the army to lead Pakistan, but his former military patrons fell
out with him and stepped in to purge Pakistan of its ills, many of which are in
fact the legacy of past military rule. While previous coup leaders bypassed any
reference to human rights and openly undermined the value of democracy, this
group of generals characterized their "reluctant" intervention as one intended to
save democracy and human rights. Their rhetoric reveals the power of international and national constraints and pressures to uphold the rights of the people,
although recent events, described in the conclusion, reveal troubling gaps
between rhetoric and reality. Only in the last decade or so has the language of
human rights entered the parlance of political debate in Pakistan. The fight for

democracy in Pakistan has, however, consistently centered around human rights issues: the right to freedom of speech and expression; the right to freedom from fear, arbitrary arrests, and police excesses; and the right to housing, education, health, and employment.

Many Pakistanis welcomed the 1999 coup because, in the eleven years since the demise of the country's last military dictator in 1988 and the restoration of the electoral process, their hopes had been dashed. Their high expectations about upholding human rights had not been—and indeed could not be—met in a fragile democracy headed by an elite with vested interests. The underlying core of this problem, which this chapter addresses, is the Pakistani legal system and the ways in which the judicial system has enshrined, perpetuated, and advanced notions of inequality instead of protecting and respecting the rights of its citizens. The judicial institutionalization of Islam has taken a particularly heavy toll on the rights of women and religious minorities, and critics of discriminatory laws are branded un-Islamic or traitorous. When states in the European or inter-American system violate international human rights standards, citizens can appeal to regional umbrella organizations in order to influence state practice or to make state law conform with international norms. In Pakistan, by contrast, critics of abuses must work very much within the state system to document human rights abuses, to provide legal aid to the unjustly detained, and to lobby for systemic judicial reform. While organizations like the Human Rights Commission of Pakistan have registered some gains, only when the judiciary gains true independence will the state stand any chance of meeting the aspirations of citizens. In the absence of regional human rights instruments, Pakistani human rights advocates have to some extent used regional and international public opinion in an effort to develop respect for basic human rights at home.

The ordinary people in Pakistan aspire to live a dignified life. They continue to demand security of life, justice, economic and social rights, and political freedoms. In every general election (whenever these are fairly held), the electorate has supported the call for improving the rights of the people. However, Pakistan's political leadership has never been able to deliver its promises of promoting these rights. The partnership of the feudal and affluent classes of Pakistan with religious orthodoxy and the armed forces has made any progress toward human rights almost impossible. Together they control all state institutions. Those in power and their allies have mastered the art of maintaining the status quo, deviation from which is extremely threatening to their economic and social interests. Toward this end, they have studiously avoided resolving the differences between the country's various communities; in fact, in some cases they have consciously contributed to sharpening these differences and increasing the tensions between ethnic and religious groups. The hostility between Pakistan and its eastern neighbor, India, which has been continuous since independence in 1947, also has been skillfully used to subvert demands for political freedom in the name of national security. The creed of "national Islamization" has been used as a stick to beat all emancipatory and human rights movements and at the same time has empowered the ruling classes, including the religious right.[1]

Pakistan is a country of extreme diversity and polarization. Regional variations mark its political and cultural landscape. In theory there is a common bond of religion among the 95 percent of the population that is Muslim. But they are divided into different Islamic sects, dominated by their differences in sectarian beliefs. Stark economic disparities characterize a state in which abject poverty and nuclear capability exist side by side. The country has one of the lowest literacy rates in the world. Its women are among the worst affected; they are disempowered at all levels of society.[2] Yet it was in Pakistan that a woman was first elected as prime minister of a Muslim state. Decades of authoritarian rule have severely corroded the institutions of the state and seriously limited the scope of public debate within civil society. While today the press in Pakistan is relatively free, the electronic media are still strictly controlled by the government and invariably assume a conservative policy toward all human rights issues.[3] Despite mass illiteracy, the average citizen is by no means politically ignorant. It is a society of relatively few strong individuals and numerous ineffectual and corrupt institutions.

Still in search of its national identity, Pakistan continues to grapple with its ideological claims as a homeland for India's Muslims on one hand and the imperatives of a modern nation-state on the other. Its founder, Muhammad Ali Jinnah, had envisaged a country in which "You are free to go to your mosques [or] belong to any religion or caste or creed—that has nothing to do with the business of the state." Alas, his vision remains unrealized and is, if anything, more distant than ever. Claiming Islam to be the raison d'être of Pakistan, successive rulers have, despite the debacle of Bangladesh, outdone one another in manipulating religion. Even a democratically elected leader such as Zulfikar Ali Bhutto had no qualms about politicizing Islam to bolster his insecure regime. The aspirations of the people of Pakistan, especially those inspired by what in 1988 appeared to be the end of military rule, thus have been dramatically at odds with the political and ideological postures of the state.

The political uses made of Islam continue to undermine and obscure the vital issue of elementary social and economic justice for all. Islam also has been deployed to deny or ignore the aspirations of a multicultural population. The religion itself is hardly a monolith: Beyond some basic elements of creed and ritual, its practices are enormously diverse, encompassing a broad spectrum of cultural contexts and ideological beliefs. The state's insistence on imposing a selective and narrowly defined Islam has served to polarize an already fragmented society.

Islamist movements in Pakistan have arisen in reaction to a variety of forces, domestic as well as international. They have gained strength from increasing frustration with the rampant corruption of the ruling elite and the corresponding denial of social justice. The blatant uses made of Islam by the state also have provided impetus to the mushrooming of purportedly "Islamic" organizations that seek brute power through increasingly violent means. The syndrome of being holier-than-thou, or being more "Islamic" than the state, has allowed small groups of extremists to hold the majority ransom to their versions of Islam. Especially since the end of the cold war, Islamist movements have gained momentum as countervailing cultural and political forces to a perceived Western hegemony. Despite numerous theological variations among the Islamists, they overwhelmingly share repressive views on women and human rights issues as justified by extremely literal, narrow, and lopsided interpretations of Islam.

INDEPENDENCE AND ITS IMPACT
ON CULTURAL AND ETHNIC RIGHTS

Even before independence, a sizable number of Pakistanis were involved in some way or another in movements of emancipation. The Balochis and the Pakhtoons struggled hard to keep British colonial influence away from their regions. The Bengalis were in the forefront of the India and Pakistan movement and took great pride in their culture and identity. Sindhi nationalists similarly struggled to preserve their ethnic identity. The only ethnic group that kept away from all such movements were the Punjabis. As the power brokers, their elites felt comfortable in any situation. Pakistan's theocratic policies find great support in Punjab; the Punjabi leadership sees any reference to ethnic rights as a threat to the unity of the country.

Independence posed a challenge to all such movements. The new state was uncertain of its viability, formed as it was of two parts separated by a thousand miles. Dissent was discouraged on the rationale of forging unity in a geographically disparate and otherwise diverse society. Any struggle for political rights was seen as unpatriotic and had to be suppressed. The Bengalis, for example, were snubbed by the founders of the nation for raising the issue of giving their language an official status, and Balochi and Pakhtoon nationalists were dubbed "traitors." Political rights were denied, and a multiparty system was seen as a threat to national unity. This denial was justified under the guise of building a Pakistani identity based on a strong sense of Muslimhood.

To the extent that Islam was a justification for the creation of Pakistan, the founders could not avoid mentioning it in the Constitution, but they did so only as a matter of form.[4] Protection was provided for religious minorities, fundamental rights were guaranteed, and an independent judiciary was promised. The president had to be a Muslim, but beyond this there was no major impetus to "Islamize" the society or the state.

Islamization set into the system gradually, initially creeping in as politicians made expedient use of it, and later Zia ul Haq institutionalized it.[5] The rights of religious minorities and women suffered as a result. An atmosphere was created where no room was left for any discussion of national identity except on the basis of religion, and the rights of ethnic minorities were indirectly impinged upon. This deterioration of human rights was initiated by the political leadership—both civil and military—and supported by the judiciary of the country.

It is against this complex backdrop of historical, political, and cultural dimensions that the current situation of human rights in Pakistan has to be understood. Therefore, this chapter examines the historic processes through which Islam was institutionalized into the Pakistani state structure and undermined human rights. The withdrawal of support for human rights by state institutions is seen through the deterioration in the judicial system, which gave its blessing to autocratic rule and subsequently to the suppression of women and religious minorities. The genesis of the religious right wing and its ascent to power through the military dictator Zia ul Haq, and how this changed the status of women and religious minorities in the country, is described. The chapter then details two of the most frequently abused laws based on religion, namely, the Hadood law and the laws pertaining to blasphemy.

The concluding section is a consideration of the post–Zia era, the transition to democracy since 1988, the coup of 1999, and the prospects for human rights in Pakistan. It examines the prospects for a revival of some old secular values and a strengthening of human rights. For this transition to take place, however, a culture of respect for human rights must go beyond rhetoric, to be fostered and developed. The prerequisites for this transition must include regional peace, strengthening of state institutions, and an end to the legal anomalies that mar any progress to a free society. Central to it are the rights of women and of religious and ethnic minorities. Their empowerment will by itself reduce the power wielded by the orthodoxy and extreme conservatives.

JUDICIAL DETERIORATION

Pakistan's courts compromised themselves less than a decade after independence. At first they decided to back the army against the civilian politicians, perhaps out of expediency, or perhaps because of disillusionment with the political leadership, or perhaps for both reasons. The partnership with the army did not oblige them to shed their liberal approach toward Islam; it allowed them to stay independent while ruling upon the rights of women and religious minorities. This independence was surrendered, however, as soon as their military allies decided to turn toward "Islamization" in 1977. The judiciary was liberal in matters of religion only in instances where it was prompted to be by the policies of its military masters. The moment political realities changed, so did the judicial outlook.

Pakistan's leaders had promised a parliamentary form of government, but Parliament was only in its infancy when the army took over in 1958. In October 1954 the Parliament had been dissolved by Governor General Ghulam Muhammad. The Federal Court (now known as the Supreme Court) upheld the dissolution based on the "doctrine of necessity," which it described as the underlying principle of both "the law of civil necessity and that of military necessity."[6] This ruling was seen as an invitation to unconstitutional forces to take the reins of power. After a period of political instability, the Parliament enacted the first Constitution of Pakistan in 1956, but in 1958 the army took over, and the Supreme Court legitimized the military coup d'état by ruling that "the revolution, having been successful, satisfies the test of efficiency and becomes a basic law-creating fact."[7]

The courts dropped this "doctrine of necessity" after military rule ended. In 1972 the Supreme Court reviewed its previous rulings and declared the outgoing regime to have been illegal. The judgment sought to justify the delay in the Court's condemnations and made a remarkable confession: "On account of their [the military] holding the coercive apparatus of the state, the people and the courts are silenced temporarily. . . . When the coercive apparatus falls from the hands of the usurper, he should be tried for high treason and suitably punished."[8]

The state's co-optation of the judiciary for its own ends had compromised its position. By the mid-1970s, it did not even pretend to uphold the rule of law, and the government of Zulfikar Ali Bhutto had become increasingly autocratic.

During this period, those addressing political and human rights issues were few, but they kept a section of public opinion alive at a time when democratic norms were being undermined. The bar associations played a pivotal role in providing legal aid to political prisoners. They opposed Zulfikar Ali Bhutto's amendments to the Constitution that eroded the independence of the judiciary and political rights of the people. The Prisoners' Release and Relief Committee campaigned to secure the release of political prisoners. Trade unions, particularly of journalists, kept their issues alive even at the cost of personal freedom and livelihood. The Pakistan Federation of Union of Journalists (FPUJ) risked arrests in acting against Zulfikar Ali Bhutto's antipress laws and policies. Many leading journalists and political cartoonists were arrested for criticism of the government. Some leading newspapers, including the *Sun* and *Punjab Punch*, were forcibly closed down. As political oppression increased by the middle of the 1970s, activists were jailed or isolated. The only political forces that survived and retained control of their own fates were the religious political parties. Having had a taste of victory over the "Ahmadi problem," they were in no mood to retreat.[9] Rather, they mobilized with greater force, seeking the support of the orthodoxy and conservative Muslims. Thus, by the time Zia ul Haq took over in 1977 and established a military dictatorship, religious parties and their allies were an organized, vocal, and entrenched force.

When the 1977 military coup disrupted the transition to democracy, the legality of the new government was challenged on the basis of the Supreme Court's own 1972 ruling that had declared martial law contrary to Pakistan's Constitution. This time around, however, the courts ignored these previous decisions and once again "legitimized" martial law.[10] It was during this period that Pakistan's judiciary turned orthodox in matters of human rights.

Today the judiciary is on trial once again, as it has been asked to decide the constitutionality of the October 1999 coup. The courts are under pressure to pronounce their judgment. If the judiciary legitimizes the coup, it undermines its own image and further erodes its independence, generating expectations that it will follow the military's agenda to the end and allow history to repeat itself.

JUDICIAL AMNESIA

The steady loss of judicial independence in favor of Islamization was not just a consequence of state coercion but was also due to the acts of individuals who were more concerned with career enhancement through politics than with the exercise of justice. Thus judges changed their public postures according to what they saw as the direction of the political wind. For example, in 1960 the government had banned a book for containing material that would "outrage the feelings of Muslims." Written by a Christian, the book argued that Christianity is superior to Islam. The High Court set aside the ban because it saw the book as a work of research and not intended to injure the feelings of Muslims. It further said that the executive order banning the book did not find that the book insulted Islam or the religious beliefs of Pakistani Muslims, but rather that it was calculated to "outrage" the religious feelings of the Muslims of Pakistan. It did not, therefore, violate the law, as its intention was not to "insult." This outcome may have incensed some Muslims, but not most.[11]

One of the judges who rendered this opinion later changed his views. By 1976 it was evident that the government of Zulfikar Ali Bhutto would fall and that the religious parties were gaining the support of the military. This judge, now retired, filed a petition in the High Court in 1976 to enforce Islamic law. He had come far from his earlier stance, when he could discern the subtle distinctions between the intent to "insult" and the intent to create "outrage." The superior courts, however, were at this time still willing to resist this attempt at Islamization, ruling that it was the Constitution, not divine law, that bound the courts in Pakistan.[12]

In the early years of Zia's rule, the superior courts moved with caution. To begin with, they held that "law" did not include Islamic injunctions unless specifically enacted by the Parliament.[13] At the same time they urged the government to bring all laws in conformity with the injunctions of Islam so that the courts could deliver complete justice.[14] A petition was filed requesting that the Supreme Court declare Shariah (Islamic) law as the supreme law of Pakistan. The Supreme Court did not accept the petition but pointed out that "a scheme and procedure for Islamization of laws" based on the 1973 Constitution was being developed by Zia ul Haq's government.[15] In their judgments, the courts indicated their willingness to uphold the process toward Islamization. They began to place Islamic laws above any other form of legislation. In August 1980 the High Court of Quetta stated that, "According to the holy Prophet (peace be upon him) every person is equal before law, therefore, the right of equality before law and equal protection of law cannot be suspended by any law whether it is by way of Constitutional amendment, extra-Constitutional amendment or supra-Constitutional Amendment. Such an act would be a negation to the Islamic system of Justice."[16]

In March 1981 the Chief Martial Law Administrator, Zia ul Haq, issued a Provisional Constitutional Order requiring the judges of the superior courts to take a fresh oath under the new order.[17] The Constitution of 1973 was to be held in "abeyance." The grand claims of the courts to uphold their divine duty to God by upholding equality soon disappeared, and the courts followed the narrow path of Islamization paved by Zia ul Haq. This was a crucial blow to the rights of women and religious minorities.

WOMEN'S HUMAN RIGHTS

Pakistani women had the right to vote since independence. This right was extended by law for the first general elections to be held in Pakistan.[18] The first Constitution of 1956 retained this right. As an affirmative action, certain seats were reserved for women to the Parliament.[19] Discrimination in law, however, was inherent in family laws designed to protect women rather than grant them equal status in the family. Citizenship laws deprived the children and spouse of a female citizen from seeking citizenship.[20] This law was based on a principle of common law, where private international law presumed that the domicile of a wife followed that of her husband. Gender bias in the judiciary was based on the belief that women were different rather than inferior; they were vulnerable and therefore needed protection.

This protectionist approach was not opposed by women themselves. The first women's organization, All Pakistan Women's Association (APWA), was founded soon after independence under founding president Rana Liaqat Ali, the wife of the prime minister.[21] APWA members began their work by addressing the needs of refugees arriving from India. Gradually, by the early 1950s, their attention was drawn to the unequal status of spouses within family laws. For example, polygamy was legal; APWA demanded that it be banned. In response to the demand of APWA, the government set up a commission to inquire into the status of Muslim women under family laws.[22] On the recommendations of this commission, reforms in family laws were introduced in 1961.[23] They were insufficient and did not grant women equal social or economic rights. The commission went further than the reforms introduced by the government, but confined itself within religious norms and applied a protectionist approach rather than presuming that women should have equal status within the family. It did, however, recommend a ban on polygamy, based on a liberal interpretation of Islamic injunctions.

Women welcomed the 1961 reforms. However, the Muslim Family Laws Ordinance of 1961 did not even ban polygamy, which had been the central demand of APWA, but merely regulated it.[24] Apart from the minor reforms introduced in family laws in 1961, the legal status of women did not undergo any change until 1973 when the 1973 Constitution stated that there should be no discrimination on the basis of sex.[25] Nevertheless, the laws that were discriminatory against women were not repealed. The government took no initiative to do so. Only a few women were prepared to challenge these laws, and those who did so had little success. Women's organizations accepted this slow pace of recognition of their rights; it was not until early 1980 that women became politically aware and began to protest against discrimination.

In the pre–Zia ul Haq period, Pakistan's courts were patronizing toward women. They accepted that women were "equal but with a difference." Women had rights but these had to be in conformity with the moral and religious norms of society. Occasionally the courts ruled in favor of women by interpreting Islam to their advantage. Their decisions were based not on equal rights but on religious laws. On such a basis, in a landmark judgment, the Supreme Court of Pakistan granted women the right to dissolve their marriage on the grounds of incompati-bility.[26] Islamic law accepts this form of dissolution of marriage, called khula.[27] A Muslim woman's grounds for dissolving her marriage were thus expanded, but she still did not have rights equal to those of men in the same area of the law.

A few women tested the courts on gender equality. A female candidate to local elections challenged gender discrimination in the election rules. The candidates and the electorate were divided on gender lines. The number of seats fixed for female candidates was lower than for male candidates in all respects. The petitioner won her case at the High Court but lost it in the Supreme Court.[28] The Court concluded that the rules were not made with bad-faith intent to harm women's interests, and thus discriminatory treatment could not be proven.

In the early 1980s, women's rights were threatened through the policies and laws adopted by military dictator Zia ul Haq. He was a brilliant political strategist who realized that enlightened and democratic Pakistanis would never support him. However, the orthodox segment of society was looking for official patronage. Fortunately for Zia, international geopolitics were such that the West was keen to have an ally on the border of Afghanistan. Thus General Zia killed many birds with his one stone of brute Islamization, and he would rule Pakistan for eleven years, until his death in 1988.

In order to legitimize his presence, he brought about fundamental institu-tional changes. The first laws to be introduced were a collection of five criminal laws, collectively known as the Hudood Ordinances. They remain controversial to this day, but no politician has had the courage to amend or repeal them. The "Offenses against Property" ordinance deals with the crime of theft and armed robbery. The "Offense of Zina" ordinance relates to rape, abduction, adultery, and fornication.[29] The "Offense of Qazf" ordinance relates to a false accusation of zina. The "Prohibition Order" prohibits use of alcohol and narcotics. The "Execution of Punishment of Whipping" ordinance prescribes the mode of whipping for those convicted under the Hudood Ordinances.

The Hudood Ordinances were promulgated ostensibly to bring the criminal legal system of Pakistan into conformity with the injunctions of Islam. Thus the ordinances introduced the forms of punishments recognized by Muslim jurists. Two levels of punishment and, correspondingly, two separate sets of rules of evidence are prescribed. The first level or category of punishment is called *hadd*, which literally means "the limit" ("Hudood" is the plural of "Hadd"), and imposes stringent standards of evidence. The other is called *tazir*, which means "to punish." Hadd punishments are fixed, leaving no room for the judge to take account of mitigating or extenuating circumstances.[30] Hadd for theft is amputation of a hand; for armed robbery it is amputation of a foot, thirty whippings, or the death penalty, under specific circumstances enumerated in the law. For rape or zina committed by an adult married Muslim, Hadd punishment is stoning to death; for adult non-Muslims and adult single Muslims, it is a hundred lashes of the whip. Hadd for committing Qazf and for the drinking of alcohol by Muslims is eighty lashes. Tazir is a fallback position from Hadd. For instance, lack of evidence to uphold Hadd does not exonerate the accused of criminal liability: The accused is still liable for tazir. Hadd punishments have never been carried out, due to the very high evidentiary standards. The tazir punishment for zina has been the most used part of the law; thousands of women and men have been imprisoned under it.[31]

THE IMPACT OF HUDOOD ON WOMEN

The pre–Hudood criminal legal system of Pakistan was by no means an ideal criminal code for women, but it was not repressive and it afforded certain protections to women and children. Women received special consideration in granting of bail (and still do). Adultery under the pre–Hudood legal system was a crime for which only men could be punished; women could not be charged with this offense. Any intercourse with a child under the age of fourteen was treated as rape; consent was immaterial. Rape of a minor wife was an offense.

The Hudood laws have drastically changed most aspects of the law.[32] Today women can be charged with the offense of zina. Raping of a wife is no offense under the law; and children, regardless of age, can be convicted of zina or rape. A victim of rape can be prosecuted for zina if the police or the magistrate doubt her story and believe she "consented" to an act of zina. Hence complaining of rape is risky for women. Moreover, silence is as risky as making a complaint of rape. While the question of consent has raised serious questions in all systems of jurisprudence, the Hudood Laws go much further. Under the Anglo-Saxon systems of law, consent would lead to acquittal of the accused, but under Hudood, consent would amount to zina and lead to punishment of the victim. While the alleged rapist is innocent in the eyes of law until proven guilty, the victim is presumed to be guilty until she proves her innocence.

One notorious case is that of Safia Bibi, a blind girl. She allegedly got pregnant as a result of rape, which came to light only once she was admitted into a hospital for delivery. Her father then filed a complaint of rape. The trial court convicted Safia Bibi of zina but acquitted the persons accused of rape.[33] This particular case aroused public sympathy, and the Federal Shariat Court ultimately acquitted her, but the judgment laid down no principle of law to guide similar circumstances in the future, calling it "an unfortunate case which received considerable publicity in the national and international press." It was clearly a judgment in response to national and international public opinion. Safia was hurriedly acquitted on technical grounds, making no reference to the peculiarity of the law under which the onus of proof shifts to the victim of rape to explain her pregnancy.

In another case, a woman named Tasleem Bibi filed a complaint of rape. She was pregnant as a consequence of the rape. The alleged rapist in turn accused Tasleem of being "a woman of easy virtue." The trial court converted the offense of rape to zina and convicted Tasleem and the alleged rapist. The appellate court acquitted the alleged rapist for lack of evidence. He was afforded the benefit of doubt, but the complainant was not.[34] Since Tasleem did not appeal her conviction, she remained in jail, and her baby died there at the age of two months.

A man named Allah Bux and a teenage girl named Fehmida were sentenced under the harsh rules of Hadd on charges of zina. Allah Bux was sentenced to be stoned to death and Fehmida to a hundred lashes since she was a minor.[35] Their offense was that they eloped to marry. There was a public outcry against the sentence; the couple appealed and were finally acquitted.

Fifteen-year-old Jehan Mina, a victim of rape, was sentenced to Hadd for zina on account of her pregnancy. Her story of rape was not believed, and those she accused of the rape were acquitted. She was convicted instead and sentenced to suffer a hundred lashes of the whip. Jehan Mina's "unexplained" pregnancy was taken as an automatic confession of zina. Her conviction was upheld by the appellate court, but the sentence was converted to tazir, because she was a minor and could not be sentenced under the standards of Hadd. The court said that "failure to explain is sometimes the most incriminating circumstances against [the accused], and it may be injurious to [the accused] if a false and *unsatisfactory* statement is given." The same principle is, however, never applied to those accused of rape or any other offense.

Such horrific cases are a legacy of Zia's tactics of using Islam to brutalize an entire society. Whereas earlier the focus had been on general strictures, such as bans on alcohol and gambling, the Hudood laws reflect an almost obsessive hatred of women. One can only speculate what would have happened if Zia ul Haq had ruled any longer. Orthodoxy and a very twisted view of women and Islam had begun to permeate every institution. Forced veiling and restriction of movement were on the agenda and are now part of the discourse of most religious parties.

WOMEN REACT

Most political parties did not take seriously the terror and injustice unleashed on women through the Hudood laws. The first active group that demanded human rights was the Women's Action Forum (WAF). WAF was founded in 1980, soon after the promulgation of the Hudood Ordinances. Its members were a mixture of women, mostly the educated elite along with some belonging to trade unions and others with a history of political activism. Many of its leaders avoided direct political confrontation with the state, believing that the rights of women were not a political issue. Thus, from 1980 to 1983, they at first refused to ally themselves with any political, pro-democracy party. Instead, WAF described itself as a lobby-cum-pressure group. However, driven by the activists, it soon found itself in the middle of the main political debate over the Islamization process. On February 12, 1983, WAF members joined a demonstration at Lahore organized by women lawyers demanding the withdrawal of a draft law of evidence; the rally brought many women together and politicized WAF.

The government was about to introduce a new law of evidence based on what many viewed as a particularly blatant misreading of the Qur'an. Under the proposed law, the evidence of two women would have the same weight as the evidence of one man in every matter. The activists in WAF enthusiastically joined and organized public demonstrations to protest against Zia's misogynist policies and laws. It was perhaps the first time in the history of Pakistan that women without official patronage staged public protests demanding equal rights for women. The government overreacted by using violence and arresting women activists. Its high-handedness brought international attention to women's rights issues in Pakistan. In the process, a public debate emerged about Islamization. The Islamists stridently denounced the women activists as "Westernized women fit for the fire" and issued fatwas (legal statements issued by a mufti or a religious lawyer) condemning them.

The women's struggle against the proposed law of evidence gained them some advantages. First, by mobilizing, they gave voice to what was until then a silent public opinion. Second, even though the proposed law was enacted, it was diluted by limiting the gender-based discrimination in the law to monetary transactions alone.[36] Third, by compromising and making changes in the law, the government essentially conceded that the law was not truly determined by Islamic doctrine.

However, this victory divided WAF's own ranks. The activists wanted to have nothing to do with religion; they had a secular agenda. For them, women's rights were a political issue linked to the mainstream movement of civil liberties as articulated by many political parties. The more cautious members of WAF feared that the movement might be overtaken by political opportunists and that therefore it should remain aloof from any form of pro-democracy movements. They also preferred to use the strategy of advancing the rights of women within the framework of Islam. The two groups parted ways for couple of years but regrouped in 1985, deciding to adopt the secular approach and to stop describing WAF as "nonpolitical."

THE RIGHTS OF RELIGIOUS MINORITIES

Pakistan was to be a country for Muslims of India to live in peace, a place where they could practice their religious beliefs freely and without fear from the Hindu majority of the subcontinent. It could never be a country with an exclusive Muslim population. Hindu, Parsi, and Christian communities living in East and West Pakistan were allowed to stay on after partition of the subcontinent. They were assured protection by the state. They could acquire Pakistani citizenship on the same basis as the Muslim population living in or migrating to Pakistan.

Prior to partition of the subcontinent, the Muslim League had demanded and been granted separate electorates for religious minorities of India. Thus Pakistan inherited a system of separate balloting. In 1956 this was changed in East Pakistan, and joint electorates were held there.[37] In 1973 the Constitution introduced the scheme of joint balloting for the entire country. This had one immediate impact on Pakistan's politics: It brought religious minorities to mainstream politics, thus marginalizing orthodox Islamic parties. Until early 1980, although religious minorities suffered some social discrimination, the laws of Pakistan were, on the whole, not oppressive for them.

The most severe human rights abuses against religious minorities (except the crimes against humanity committed by the army in 1971 in East Pakistan) were conceived and implemented during Zia's rule and remain in force today. In 1985 the 1973 Constitution was "Islamized" to give the president more power.[38] Wide-ranging amendments were made to the Constitution. A new system of elections was introduced, whereby non-Muslims could vote only for non-Muslim candidates to the Parliament; thus the country was divided into Muslims and non-Muslims for the purposes of all elections and political representation. Since a non-Muslim candidate had to capture votes from all across the country, only government-sponsored candidates could run an effective campaign and hope to win. Thus non-Muslims were cut off from the political mainstream and their votes rendered irrelevant to major parties.

The Objectives Resolution, which declared that Pakistan would be "a democratic state based on Islamic principles of social justice," was added to the substantive part of the Constitution in 1985.[39] In 1985 the constitutional right of religious minorities to practice their religion "freely" was curtailed, by removal of the word "freely." Muslim members of Parliament could be disqualified if their religious belief or moral outlook was found to be inadequate.[40] The composition of the Senate was changed in 1985, by requiring a certain number of religious scholars (*ulema*). Also in 1985, the Federal Shariat Court (FSC) set up by Zia in 1978 received constitutional protection.[41] It could declare any law "repugnant to Islam" and therefore void, except the Constitution, fiscal laws, and personal laws. While he institutionalized Islamization in key areas, Zia shrewdly postponed placing fiscal laws under the Federal Shariat Court's jurisdiction during his own rule. He left it to future governments to handle resulting conflicts of interest, such as the FSC challenging the charging of interest in the banking system. All subsequent governments and the judiciary have been under pressure to declare it un-Islamic. If they resist, Pakistan's Islamists will protest strongly, but if it is outlawed the country faces a financial crisis.

A set of antiblasphemy laws was added to the penal code in 1984.[42] These laws had the effect of prohibiting the members of the Ahmadi community from calling themselves Muslims or from doing, saying, or writing anything that would even indirectly suggest that they belonged to the Islamic faith. In addition to denying the Ahmadis the right to practice their religion, these laws were used to persecute the community.[43]

In 1986 another set of antiblasphemy laws was enacted that impose a mandatory death sentence for insulting the holy Prophet of Islam.[44] Insults included blasphemy committed "by visible representation, or by imputation, innuendo, or insinuation, directly or indirectly." Although this law was not specifically directed at any specific community or non-Muslims, non-Muslims have mostly been its victims.[45] This set of blasphemy laws continues to be the bane of minorities. The only opposition to it has come from human rights groups, which have undertaken the legal defense of many of the accused under these laws. This defense has brought the groups into direct confrontation with the Islamists and the state. After one acquittal on appeal, the Islamists vowed to take "better care" of such cases in the future by simply killing the alleged blasphemer.

One case illustrates the dangers.[46] In 1994 three Christians, including a fourteen-year-old boy named Salamat Masih, were arrested on charges of blasphemy. It was alleged that Salamat had written some words with a piece of coal on the outside the wall of a mosque. These words, it was alleged, were blasphemous and therefore could never be disclosed since to utter them would be blasphemy. The complainant (a *khatib,* or chief cleric of the mosque) washed the words away and stated that he had found pieces of paper with blasphemous words that he had reason to believe were thrown inside the mosque by Salamat

Masih at the behest of the other two coaccused. One of the accused was murdered during trial near the court premises. Throughout the trial, the court was surrounded by religious fanatics calling for death to all of the accused. Three eyewitnesses including the complainant appeared in the trial court to testify against the accused. None of them saw the person who wrote or possessed the pieces of paper found in the mosque. The complainant refused to give any testimony. He expressed fear for his life, but he added that he did not fear this danger from the accused. The two other witnesses had no knowledge of the pieces of paper. They did not mention the words written on the wall, and their testimonies did not corroborate each other in the sequence of events. Despite the flimsiness of the evidence, the trial court awarded death penalty to the two surviving accused to the death penalty.

On appeal, the scene around the courthouse was even uglier, with calls to put to death the lawyers and human rights activists attending court hearings. The accused were finally acquitted. The government could not vouch for their security. Therefore it escorted them out of prison in strict security and took them to a flight for Germany, where they were granted political asylum.

One of the judges who acquitted the accused was later murdered in broad daylight by a religious fanatic, and the lawyers remain on the extremists' "hitlists." As a result of such terror tactics, only a few who are accused of blasphemy receive legal assistance, and even judges are hesitant to hear such cases.

The institutionalization of Islam into state and judicial mechanisms has not enhanced social justice but rather has terrorized people into submission and silence. The projection of Islam by sundry self-styled "guardians" of Islam has little to do with piety and more to do with power for the sake of power. In this process, the rights of Pakistan's women and of its minority communities have been trampled, frequently with tragic consequences.

THE BATTLE FOR HUMAN RIGHTS

Given the conditions that prevailed during Zia's rule, the few protests by human rights activists were remarkably courageous. Large-scale open support was absent. Political parties were critical of the changes in laws, but only so far as they curtailed political activity. Most politicians preferred to avoid any reference to religion. While recognizing that Zia ul Haq was misusing religion for political expediency, few risked making this a public issue. Many opportunists were intent on retaining the petty privileges accrued to them through Zia's pseudo-Parliament.

Although movements for political rights had always been active in Pakistan, they were mostly affiliated with political parties and confined their activities to issues around the restoration of democracy. The decline of human rights brought out new voices that collectively called for a national convention in 1986 to discuss the human rights situation in Pakistan. The response was enthusiastic; over 500 leading figures in the civil rights movement from across the country attended. All the participants had one common concern: the consequences of rising religious intolerance in Pakistani society on people's rights.

The national convention ended with a resolution calling for a commission to monitor human rights violations. A group, nominated to give the organization shape, was to include members from all four provinces of Pakistan; and women and religious minorities were to be well represented. The organization espoused equal rights for all citizens without any form of discrimination. Later named the Human Rights Commission of Pakistan (HRCP), it remains at the forefront of Pakistan's civil liberties movement.[47]

The HRCP helped to fill the need for a broad-based organization that focused on all human rights issues. It highlighted human rights violations against women and religious minorities; called for abolition of the capital punishment and forced labor; and declared its belief in secular politics as imperative for the promotion of human rights. It set the pace for civil society to make linkages between human rights and democratic development. During this period several groups emerged that vastly contributed toward the promotion of human rights. WAF was active in promoting the rights of women. Some existing organizations became more aware of human rights issues as a political struggle rather than a mere social neglect.[48] Others that had worked in isolation became more visible and assertive.

Pakistan's human rights organizations have played a pivotal role in bringing human rights issues to the national agenda. They work together closely and coordinate their activities. Each organization leads campaigns concerning vital issues. The Aurat Foundation, for example, has consistently kept alive the issue of women's representation in the Parliament. This issue has been adopted by all major political parties, which promise better representation of women to the elected bodies. Sanghi and South Asia Partnership have been able to mobilize men and women in remote areas of Pakistan to support human rights issues. AGHS Legal Aid Cell and Lawyers for Human Rights have provided free legal aid to victims of human rights violations.[49] The HRCP and other groups have, for example, managed to get thousands of forced laborers released from private jails in Sindh and from captivity in Punjab. For example, in Punjab's brick kiln industry, laborers (mostly Christians) skilled in kneading and baking bricks were entrapped through debt-bondage and then kept as virtual slaves. AGHS Legal Aid Cell provided them legal assistance and HRCP was able to get a law passed punishing anyone indulging in such slavery-like practices. In Sindh, hari ("untouchable") peasants are kept like slaves by affluent landlords. The HRCP has managed to get over 7,000 freed, but many more remain enslaved.

Human rights organizations contested the issues of the law of blasphemy, killing of women for "honor," and denying to women the right of marriage of their choice, bringing these issues to public attention, both domestically and internationally. Some gains have been made. The situation in some areas has improved, and in others the violations at least do not go unnoticed.

In 1988 General Zia died in a plane crash. New elections were held on a party basis, and there was a sense of hope and optimism. Most people assumed that the return to electoral democracy would result in the elimination of the oppressive practices and laws of the dictatorship. In fact, however, Pakistan's transition to democracy has been slow. It brought new challenges for those supporting even weak forms of democracy in place of a military dictatorship. They had to work on many fronts: exposing the prevailing oppression in the system, seeking to rebuild institutions, and at the same time sustaining an informed public opinion in support of the process of democracy.

The ghosts of Zia's era haunted the new democratic process. Four governments in a row were dissolved, and eight prime ministerial changes were made between 1988 and 1997. And in October 1999 General Pervez Musharraf staged another military coup. Barely able to stay in office, no government has been able to undo Zia's constitutional or legislative changes. Meanwhile, the orthodoxy has lost no time in taking advantage of this political instability. Zia had managed to control his own creations, but since his death they have begun to assert their form of politicized Islamization on the entire society. A culture of *jihad* (religious war) prevails. Evil is to be conquered through violence. Hundreds of religious schools, called Deeni Madras, teach children the virtues of jihad and to identify "evil."

The Federal Shariat Court ruled that the laws on murder and bodily harm were to be changed.[50] The victims or their families can forgive the offenders and accept compensation (*diyat*). Thus these crimes have been personalized and are not crimes against the state. Therefore, the state has no responsibility to ensure punishment for those who use violence against fellow citizens. The change has given rise to large-scale impunity for those who can intimidate or buy off their opponents. The victims and their families are left vulnerable to the pressures of criminal gangs and militants, often supported by the police and influential local political leaders. Criminal mafias and religious militants murder with impunity.

The governments have made no effort to control the situation by strengthening the legal and justice system. Instead they have embarked upon a systematic cleansing of "criminal" elements. The HRCP reported 566 people killed in over 400 so-called encounters in 1998 in Punjab Province alone. Official figures produced in the Lahore High Court for January to April 1998 admitted to 20 encounters in the city of Lahore, during which 26 "criminals" were killed. Deaths in police custody are common. The government denies these figures and argues that such killings were carried out while police were defending themselves, but at least 15 cases were reported in 1998 where those shot dead were handcuffed.

Violence against women has increased. The new law of Qisas and Diyat allows the victim's family to "forgive" the offender. People kill women in their own families with impunity, because they will be forgiven by the family if they are ever brought to trial and convicted. In the Punjab Province, 885 women were killed in 1998, 595 by their relatives; at least 286 were murdered for "dishonoring" the family.

During Zia's era, the Federal Shariat Court had ruled that an adult Muslim woman could contract a marriage according to her own wishes; the superior judiciary also supported this view. In early 1990, however, some judgments took a contrary view. Young couples marrying against the wishes of their parents were harassed by the police, and many were arrested on charges of zina. In other cases, courts sent young wives to "custody homes" while the husband stood trial on charges of having kidnapped the young woman who was his wife. These custody homes are mostly run by the government, and their conditions are worse than ordinary prisons. The confined women are not permitted to see anyone without the approval of the warden; they have no communication with the outside world.

A group of women opened a model shelter home as an alternative; it became the target of threats and criticism, and was seen as an incentive for young girls to rebel against their families. Thanks to dangerous and sustained battles, women and human rights activists recently have won a round of litigation asserting the right to choose one's own marriage partner. A recent court opinion admits the follies of the past:

> Behind the evangelistic facade there was a certain culture at play. It is that culture which needs to be tamed by law and an objective understanding of the Islamic values. Let us do a little self-accountability and little soul searching both individually and collectively. Let there be no contradiction in our thoughts and actions. Male chauvinism, feudal bias and compulsions of a conceited ego should not be confused with Islamic values. An enlightened approach is called for otherwise an obscurantism in this field may break the social fabric.[51]

The confusion between religion and traditions will always remain. Religion and customary practice are in most cases interlinked. Therefore, in Pakistan women's rights advocates have to reconcile religion to human rights norms or else adopt a secular agenda.

GLOBALIZATION AND DOMESTIC REALITIES

To the extent that numerous developing countries are in the throes of what may well become a global crisis, the current tensions in Pakistan are not exceptional. However, globalization, particularly its implications for human rights, is an issue for Pakistan. While there can be no denying that globalization has its advantages, it also creates its own tensions. Living in closer proximity than ever before, people are exposed to a multiplicity of cultures and values. An increased flow of information enables marginalized and minority groups to become more conscious of their rights and to coordinate their grievances in a more effective fashion. This diversity of voices and growing awareness is both a strength and a weakness. It has the potential to promote tolerance, but it can also fragment any society that cannot sustain and accommodate human diversity. Nations that have established a bedrock of common values and pluralistic systems find it relatively easier to adapt to new globalization.

There appears to be no genuine homogeneity in any society today. Nevertheless, many societies lay claim to it, and some countries persist in ignoring the diversity within their borders. Countries that categorically refuse to face the realities of their diversity will remain ill at ease in a globalized world, and their development and future will be unstable.

The transition to globalization also has reopened questions of universally acceptable values and standards. Among the most salient issues of our times is whether, along with diversity, there exist any universal values and norms by which humanity as a whole can or should abide. As its very name suggests, the Universal Declaration of Human Rights bases itself on the premise that cultural diversities as such are not a barrier to the acceptance of a core of common human values, especially those relating to matters of political, social, and economic justice. Certain people, in Pakistan and elsewhere, often those inclined toward, or party to, autocratic systems, would like to reject the possibility of such a vision of human rights. In Pakistan and elsewhere, there is a concerted move to create a controversy over international laws regarding human rights. Arguing that such norms should be tailored to suit cultural and traditional sensitivities, autocratic rulers and Muslim religious leaders propose to redefine "universal human rights."

Such antidemocratic forces have gained strength especially in Muslim societies, as a direct result of recent political events such as the wars in the Persian Gulf and the wars in the Balkans. These developments are perceived as betrayals: The perception is that the West selectively uses human rights (or their violation) as a mere cover for its prejudice against Muslim societies. "Human rights" is said to be a Western concept that the West is using in a calculated manner to erode indigenous values. As a result of these views, liberal movements in the developing world, particularly in Muslim countries, have become isolated. They support the West in its promotion of the universality of human rights but cannot justify many of the West's actions taken under the banner of human rights. As secular and democratic liberals, they are committed to opposing autocratic rulers and militant Islamic groups. However, both secular and Islamist groups cannot help but share suspicion of deep-seated Western prejudices against Islam. Thus, even while opposing rigid Islamists, the liberals cannot approve of the often-violent methods the West is using to quell them.

Pakistan finds itself in the eye of the storm of these controversies. Islamic movements are acquiring considerable momentum as the countervailing force to Western hegemony. This trend has heightened the insecurity of the nonorthodox and nonmilitant segments of society. That they are a majority is evident from the fact that no religious party in Pakistan has ever managed to do well in national elections. Nevertheless, this majority of nonorthodox, nonmilitant, secular, liberal, and moderate citizens finds itself increasingly vulnerable, particularly in the absence of a common national ethos or a sense of values that would provide protection from Islamists making a bid for political power and in a state that continues to try to impose a homogenous idea of Islam at the cost of the rights of ethnic, religious, gender, and linguistic minorities.

A democratic process can grow only if some basic guarantees exist: mechanisms to ensure free and fair elections, a multiparty system, an independent judiciary, free press and media, laws guaranteeing fundamental rights, and a minimum level of transparency in decision making. Multiple political parties and a relatively free press were all that the new democratic system had in 1988, and this is still the case. The political parties have weak structures, since very few hold elections. Party leaders are surrounded by relatives and sycophants, who themselves often become candidates on the basis of personal loyalty, not substantive issues.

Pakistan remains a deeply fragmented society, but during the 1990s a semblance of democracy has been restored. The press is freer, political parties are more active, Parliament is operational, and there has been a gradual awareness of human rights issues. These changes are reinforced by more efficient and widespread national and international communications. Marginalized groups are able to express their disaffection with the current workings of the state. During this period of transition, Pakistani governments have been unable to deal with a long-standing crisis of identity, which is complicated further by a crisis in the economy and deteriorating social conditions.

Rather than rectifying past mistakes, governments seek to avoid unpleasant confrontations by continuing to take cover behind Islam, giving it official status as the only unifying force among Pakistanis. Any demands for alternatives are dubbed "anti-Islamic" and hence unpatriotic. This political gimmick strengthens those movements that use Islam for their own ends. They continue to maneuver in such a way that, despite being a minority, they set the national agenda. Directly or indirectly, they have gained control over most institutions of the state, pushing it toward increasingly extremist positions. Movements of minority emancipation are trampled on the pretext of imposing "true" Islam in Pakistan. The ordinary person remains confused and insecure. The army has taken advantage of this confusion, staging a takeover premised on removing the very hurdles it has placed before the democratic process. Yet again the ordinary person has fallen into the trap of believing the army's promise of a fresh start. But soon the military "honeymoon" period will end. Its autocratic practice will likely fail to match its democratic promise, and it will marginalize and muzzle organized movements that oppose military rule and demand power sharing. The pattern is familiar; some civilians will be co-opted by the army, while others will be victimized and silenced.

The great challenge to civil society is to build a consensus on the basic principles of human rights in a manner that will be acceptable to most Pakistanis, including minorities. Doing this will not be easy, yet it is vital that such a consensus be reached if the democratic process is to be restored. In such a time of economic insecurity as this, people can behave in unpredictable ways—perhaps with greater religious fervor, but perhaps also with a more tolerant view of each other. For the average Pakistani, the choices are limited: Political parties have failed to deliver, and the liberal elite remains disorganized and apathetic in the face of brazen social and economic injustices. In the absence of enlightened leadership, Pakistan's current drift toward further Islamization or militarization threatens not only to harm its own citizens, especially its women, but also to poison the region's political atmosphere.

CONCLUSION

Strong forces in Pakistan wish to see the end of the process of democratization, some for reasons of their vested interests, while others genuinely believe that a cleansing period can give birth to a new process of democracy. Human rights activists and intellectuals are divided over the issue. Some support the "cleansing" theory, while others want to see the process continue but feel the urgency to give it some direction. These forces won out in October 1999 with General Musharraf's coup. Musharraf appointed a civilian cabinet, but it has too little say in decision making. In the initial days of military rule, a populist agenda of accountability and reorganizing democracy won the people's support. When the new regime arrested dozens of the largest bank defaulters in November 1999 for instance, Pakistanis widely applauded.

However, while many Pakistanis are pleased that the corrupt government of Prime Minister Nawaz Sharif has been forced out, many involved in Pakistani human rights nongovernmental organizations are concerned about the extraconstitutional means used to oust him. For example, the Human Rights Commission of Pakistan has argued that the country should be brought back to the constitutional framework by the holding of fresh elections. In addition, along with the Constitution, the federal and provincial parliaments were suspended. The superior judiciary was administered an oath to be loyal to the new legal order rather than the Constitution. Six Supreme Court judges—including the Chief Justice of the country—refused to take a fresh oath. They were dismissed. Political rallies were banned. Arbitrary detentions and torture continued. The economy continues to suffer and tensions with neighboring India have increased. In the international community, Pakistan stands quite alone.

While Sharif's rule represented a failure of political leadership, it is becoming increasingly apparent that Pakistan's institutions cannot be revived through the barrel of a gun. More democracy is needed to improve the health and wealth of the country, not strong-armed tactics that only auger more of the autocratic rule to which Pakistanis have become accustomed. Human rights NGOs will have to find space to maneuver in this new regime and to encourage the education of the populace to move beyond support of "quick fixes" that the coup was supposed to bring.

In order to place human rights on the political agenda, civil society has to strengthen and broaden its base among ordinary Pakistanis. The issues of the ordinary person stem from economic poverty. Activists have to be articulate and clear in demonstrating that the politics of poverty is linked to denial of human rights across the board. Economic and political rights have a relationship in improving the quality of life for Pakistan; peace in the subcontinent will open avenues for economic growth.

In a population of 130 million people who are mostly illiterate, campaign and mobilization is difficult. Electronic media are government controlled, and education receives a low priority in the national budgets.[52] The government and political parties have to be persuaded to deregulate the media and to spend more on education. Such demands have to be made in a coordinated manner by the NGOs and with the vocal support of their grass-roots partners in the field.

Electoral politics can turn into domination by the majority or by a few influential rulers unless the norms of justice are upheld. Pakistan's judicial system has failed to deliver justice. Constitutional amendments to make it independent are necessary but not enough. The bar associations must be strengthened and legal education improved. More emphasis has to be laid on human rights law and international standards if Pakistan is to compete in the new globalized world.

The continuing political process will mature political parties. Their claim to power depends on the certainty of the electoral process. Pakistan's Election Commission is vulnerable to political pressures and is not a permanent institution. Its independence and resources have to be ensured.

Pakistan's foreign policy has a critical effect on the economic and political rights of people. Defense expenditures have impoverished the country. The support to the Talibans of Afghanistan has given rise to religious intolerance. The continuing struggle of the Kashmiri freedom fighters has failed to bring peace in the subcontinent. Its resolution is imperative but not enough. A large minority of Muslims (in addition to the predominantly Muslim Kashmiris) live in India, but India, like Pakistan, has a poor record of upholding the rights of religious minorities. The rights of India's Muslims are also often violated by the state and by Hindu militants. While such violations usually are followed by a reaction in Pakistan, the orthodox continue to find an excuse to continue oppressing Pakistan's religious minorities, including a vulnerable minority of Hindus. As a first step toward improvement, Pakistan and India must be brought together to sign a treaty to protect their religious minorities.

The rights of women in Pakistan will continue to be violated unless the state demonstrates political willingness to address the issue. Women cannot expect to gain rights in a system of arbitrary rule. Only with the revival of democracy do they stand a chance of advancing their cause. Only then can they begin to address state-sponsored and society-enacted injustices perpetrated against them and to end gender discrimination at all levels. As a first step all discriminatory laws against them should be repealed. Women must be appointed to positions of power and be adequately represented in the elected parliaments and local bodies.

These measures are only small initial steps toward extracting the country from its vicious circle of perpetual injustice and conflicts. To achieve any respect for human rights, Pakistan's institutions must be rebuilt rather than strengthened. The ordinary person has to be empowered through education and active participation in the political process in order to secure his or her rights. The country is in a deep crisis. The democratic process must be resurrected, the judicial system has to become independent, and organizations within civil society must unite to force these developments. Pakistani citizens are searching for the way to live a dignified life, but doing so requires a healthy democratic system that remains elusive.

NOTES

1. "National Islamization" is now an official term and is treated as "the ideology of Pakistan." It has never been defined but is used frequently in all laws, stated as a creed by which all Pakistanis must abide.

2. Just 25 percent of girls in Pakistan receive primary education, compared to 76 percent in India, 78 percent in Bangladesh, 46 percent in Nepal, 100 percent in Sri Lanka, 47 percent in Bhutan, and 100 percent in the Maldives. *Human Development Report 1995* (New York: Oxford University Press, 1995) published for the United Nations Development Programme.

3. Female newscasters must cover their heads. Television plays are heavily censored, and men and women appearing in them are instructed to keep a distance from one another.

4. The only religiously based laws were those concerned with personal matters such as family law and inheritance.

5. Zia Ul Haq took over in July 5, 1977.

6. PLD 1955 Federal Court 435. Reference by His Excellency the Governor General.

7. *The State v. Dosso*, PLD 1958 SC 533.

8. *Miss Asma Jilani v. the Government of Punjab*, PPL 1972 SC 139.

9. At the instigation of the religious political parties, Zulfikar Ali Bhutto's government declared Ahmedis to be non-Muslims through a constitutional amendment. The Ahmadis are followers of Mirza Ghulam Ahmad (1835–1908), who claimed to be the promised Messiah or Mehdi and a successor to Muhammad, the prophet of Islam (peace be upon him). While the Ahmadis claim to be a reform movement within Islam, many mainstream Muslims, for whom the finality of prophethood of Muhammad is a cardinal article of faith, consider them heretics. See, for example, Human Rights Commission of Pakistan, *State of Human Rights in Pakistan 1993* (Lahore: Human Rights Commission of Pakistan, 1994); Tayyab Mahmud, "Freedom of Religion and Religious Minorities In Pakistan: A Study of Judicial Practice," *Fordham International Law Journal*, Vol. 19, No. 40 (1995), p. 44, n. 7; M. Nadeem Ahmad Siddiq, "Enforced Apostasy: Zaheeruddin v. State and the Official Persecution of the Ahmadiyya Community in Pakistan," *Law & Inequality Journal*, Vol. 14, No. 275 (1995), n. 18. .

   Under Zulfiqar Ali Bhutto, the 1973 Constitution had declared Islam to be the state religion. Almost simultaneously, certain clerics demanded that the Ahmadis be declared non-Muslims, and by 1974, the government had done so by means of a constitutional amendment. In a bid to bolster his flagging popularity, Bhutto declared that he had thus "solved the Ahmadi problem."

   In 1984, a law was introduced forbidding Ahmadis to call themselves Muslims. So vague and open-ended as to invite all manner of abuse, this law was challenged in the Federal Shariat Court and ultimately in the Supreme Court of Pakistan. Both Courts upheld the law as constitutional. The law, it was argued, had to be imposed because the Ahmadis insisted on considering themselves Muslims and this offended the belief of "true" Muslims. The Supreme Court declared that "The Ordinance . . . does not amount to interference with their right to profess or practice their religion . . . [It is simply a] restraint against their posing as Muslims."

   Ahmadis have frequently been arrested under this law for a variety of reasons. In 1998 criminal cases were registered against 106 Ahmadis for violating this law; over 300 Ahmadis were in prison as of February 1999. Such arrests have been upheld by the Supreme Court.

10. *Begum Nusrat Bhutto v. Chief of Army Staff*, PLD 1977 SC 657.

11. The Punjab Religious Book Society, Lahore, PLD 1960 (WP) Lahore 629.

12. Mr. Badi-uz-Zaman Kaikaus, PLD 1976 Lahore 1608.

13. Abdur Rahman Mobashir, PLD 1978 Lahore 113.

14. Ibid.
15. B.Z. Kaikaus, PLD 1980 SC 160.
16. Yahya Bakhtiar, NLR 1980 Criminal Quetta 815.
17. CMLA's Order 1 of 1981; Provisional Constitution Order, 1981.
18. Constitution (Amendment) Act, 1951; March 19, 1951.
    Delimitation of Constituencies (Adult Franchise) Act, 1951.
19. Constitution (Amendment) Act, 1951.
20. Pakistan Citizenship Act, 1951.
21. APWA was formally registered on February 1, 1949.
22. The Commission was established in August 1955 and its report was submitted in June 1956.
23. The Muslim Family Laws Ordinance, 1961.
24. This law continues to be in effect today.
25. Women of Pakistan were guaranteed equality before the law in all constitutions of Pakistan. The 1956 and the 1962 Constitutions entitled all citizens equal protection of the law. The 1973 Constitution prohibited discrimination on the basis of sex and at the same time made exceptions for affirmative action for female citizens. It states in Article 25: "All citizens are equal before law and are entitled to equal protection of law. (2) There shall be no discrimination on the basis of sex alone. (3) Nothing in this Article shall prevent the State from making any special provision for the protection of women and children."
26. *Ms. Khurshid Bibi v. Baboo Muhammad Amin*, PLD 1967 Supreme Court 97.
27. *Khula* means that a woman's testimony declaring aversion for her husband is sufficient ground for dissolving the marriage.
28. *Ms Parveen Zohra v. Province of W. Pakistan*, PLD 1957 (WP) Lah 1071. *Ch. Atta Ellahi vs Ms. Parveen Zohra*, PLD 1958 Supreme Court (Pak) 298.
29. A man and a woman are said to commit zina if they willfully have sexual intercourse without being validly married to each other. The word "zina" covers adultery as well as fornication.
30. See, e.g., Anika Rahman, "A View Towards Women's Reproductive Rights Perspective on Selected Laws and Policies in Pakistan," 15 *Whittier Law Review* 981 (1991), pp. 999-1000: "Because of the difficulty of obtaining four male Muslim witnesses, men accused of zina-bil-jabr have in reality become exempted from the maximum punishment. Although maximum Hadd punishments have been imposed, none have ever been carried out. The majority of zina or zina-bil-jabr cases are thus heard at the lesser Tazir punishment level." David F. Forte, "Apostasy and Blasphemy in Pakistan," 10 *Connecticut Journal of International Law* 27 (Fall 1994), pp. 37-38: "The hadd crimes of the Shari'a are those purportedly derived from the Qur'an [or Sunnah (i.e., the traditions which record the sayings or acts of Prophet Mohammed)], whose penalties are fixed and from which no judicial deviation is allowed. The brake on the application of the Hudood Ordinances has been that they must be tried before the ordinary courts, no qadi courts yet having been established, and the judges retain the option of trying the offense under the secular penal code."
31. Between 1980 to 1987 appeals against convictions of zina numbered 3399.
32. Over 5000 people are in Pakistan's jails in February 1999 awaiting trial.
33. *Safia Bibi v. The State*, NLR 1985 SD 145.
34. *Shabbir Ahmed v. The State*, PLD 1983 FSC 110.
35. *Allah Bux and Ms. Fehmida vs. The State*, PLD 1982 FSC 101.
36. Presently the law says that in case of "future" monetary transactions the evidence of two men or one man and two women will be acceptable.
37. Act XXXVI of 1956, Electorate Act, 1956.
38. Revival of the Constitution of 1973 Order, 1985 (P.O. 14 of 1985).
39. The Objectives Resolution was passed by the first Constituent Assembly in 1949. It promised parliamentary democracy and rights as "enunciated by Islam." Until 1985 it remained in the Preamble of the Constitution and therefore was not enforceable in court.

40. They can be disqualified by a complaint to the Election Commission of Parliament. The member then can appeal against the decision of the Commission to the High Court and subsequently to the Supreme Court. Article 62 of the Constitution says that a person shall not be qualified to be elected or chosen as a member of the Parliament unless "he is of good character and is not commonly known as one who violates Islamic injunctions... has adequate knowledge of Islamic teachings and practices obligatory duties prescribed by Islam as well as abstains from major sins . . . he is sagacious, righteous and non-profligate and honest and pious."

41. In 1978 Zia established Shariat benches in Pakistan's superior courts (President's Order 22 of 1978, Shariat Benches of Superior Courts Order, 1978) as part of the process of Islamization of Pakistan. In 1980 these benches were replaced by a stronger Federal Shariat Court, having jurisdiction, "notwithstanding anything in the Constitution," to examine whether any law was repugnant to Islam.

42. Sections 298-A, 298-B, 298-C of the Pakistan Penal Code inserted by Ordinance XX of 1984.

43. According to the 1998 Human Rights Commission of Pakistan report, 106 cases have been filed against Ahmadis under these laws in 1998 alone.

44. Pakistan Penal Code, section 295-C.

45. So far no one has been executed under this law, but detention starts virtually with the making of the complaint by almost anyone. During trials, public pressure is intimidating. Courts are under a kind of siege by zealots. Lawyers are often threatened, and one judge was murdered for acquitting the accused. As of 1996 thirty-one people were being prosecuted under this law.

46. *Salamat Masih and another v. the State,* 1995 PCrLJ 811 (Lahore).

47. I am a founder of HRCP and was its Secretary-General for two terms (six years). I was then its Chair for two terms and retired in 1998. As a former Chair, I remain a member of its Executive Council.

48. Prominent organizations are: Aurat Foundation, Pakistan Women Lawyers Association, Punjab Women Lawyers Association, Sahil, Shirkat Gah, Sanghi, Piler, Simorgh, ASR, Shehri, Lawyers for Human Rights, AGHS Legal Aid Cell, South Asia Partnership, and Democratic Commission for Human Development.

49. AGHS Legal Aid Cell was founded by four women lawyers: myself, Gul Rukh Rehman, Hina Jilani, and Shehla Zia.

50. Criminal Law (Amendment) Act No. II of 1997 (the Qisas and Diyat law).

51. Humaira Mehmood, 1999 PCr.R. 542 Lahore.

52. Just 2.7% of Pakistan's GNP is spent on education.

NINE

Advancing the Cause of Human Rights: The Need for Justice and Accountability

RICHARD J. GOLDSTONE[*]

Justice of the Constitutional Court of South Africa and former judge of the Appellate Division of the Supreme Court of South Africa, Richard Goldstone served as the Chief Prosecutor of the International Criminal Tribunals for the former Yugoslavia and Rwanda from August 1994 to September 1996. He was the Chairperson of South Africa's Commission of Inquiry regarding Public Violence and Intimidation (the Goldstone Commission) from 1991 to 1994 and is a member of the International Panel established in August 1997 by the Government of Argentina to monitor the Argentine Inquiry into Nazi activities in the Argentine Republic since 1938.

The horrors of the Holocaust were enough to make even the most optimistic observer question basic human morality. Perhaps it was comforting then to believe that the commission of such crimes was unique—that they constituted a horrible and isolated deviation on the road to civilization and a scope and savagery of atrocity that would surely never be repeated. An examination of these crimes led to noble promises by international leaders and to a resolve that such atrocities would "never again" occur. This is the message that the Nuremberg trials supposedly carried; this is the genocide-free future the landmark trials supposedly guaranteed. Yet a half century later, the world found itself again shocked by images and crimes in the former Yugoslavia, Rwanda, and Congo horribly reminiscent of those humanity once hoped to banish.

Wars of aggression, genocide, mass rape, torture, disappearances, forced removals, and innumerable other human rights violations have occurred repeatedly in the years since Justice Robert Jackson announced that the Nuremberg trials would "do away with domestic tyranny and violence and aggression by those in power against the rights of their own people."[1] Since this pledge, nearly one hundred wars have raged—some 90 percent of them civil wars—leaving almost 200 million people dead. Yet the perpetrators of atrocity and abuse in Cambodia, Chile, Iraq, and elsewhere went unpunished.

At the end of the cold war in 1989, the optimism of the late 1940s returned. Many believed that the thawing at the United Nations Security Council and the end of ideological showdowns would bring an era of wars to an end, would ensure that democracy would reign supreme, and would bring an increase in respect for human rights around the world. This hope, however, proved short-lived. A number of states were overwhelmed by ethnic nationalism and torn apart by civil war and strife, which resulted in death and that dreadful euphemism, "ethnic cleansing." Ironically, it was during this same period that states signed on in droves to international human rights conventions and treaties.[2] Although atrocities and abuses appeared to multiply, we saw the first international efforts since Nuremberg to confront perpetrators as well as the establishment, nearly fifty years after the passage of the 1948 Genocide Convention, of an international criminal tribunal designed to act upon the Convention's early promise to punish individual perpetrators.

What then is the true legacy of Nuremberg? How do we account for fifty years without any prosecutions of such international crimes followed by the recent, seemingly sudden creation of the two ad hoc UN War Crimes Tribunals for the former Yugoslavia and Rwanda as well as the passage of a treaty for the new International Criminal Court (ICC)?[3]

In this chapter I explore these questions, with a brief review of the way in which notions of sovereignty traditionally precluded investigation or punishment of human rights violations within a state by any state or entity beyond its borders. I note the changes in international law brought about by the postwar Nuremberg and Tokyo war crimes trials, by which the victorious allies brought war criminals of the vanquished nations to justice and the crime of "genocide" was recognized and established. Yet, as I explain, enforcement lagged behind these legal developments until relatively recently, when national "truth commissions" were established, and then, in 1993, the UN Security Council established the International Criminal Tribunal for the former Yugoslavia, soon followed by the International Criminal Tribunal for Rwanda. I examine the different forms of justice and the benefits of truth as a component of justice. Then I explore the recent progress and lessons and achievements of these tribunals, and of South Africa's Truth and Reconciliation Commission, for further development of the international law of human rights, especially as it affects the establishment of the proposed International Criminal Court. I conclude that justice and accountability are indispensable to lasting peace and that the International Criminal Court is the culmination of all our previous efforts and represents our best chance to date for meaningful enforcement of the international law of human rights against war crimes, crimes against humanity, genocide, and crimes of aggression.

SETTING THE STAGE

Prior to World War II, neither the League of Nations nor individual states were concerned with the investigation and punishment of human rights violations. What occurred within a state's borders was, generally speaking, a state's business.[4] International law traditionally focused on the rights of nations but ignored those of individuals. It said little—and did less—to protect civilians, that is, noncombatants, during times of war. Even the provisions of the Laws of War, set out in the Hague Conventions of 1899 and 1907 and the Geneva Conventions of 1949, did not confer any jurisdiction upon national courts to bring war criminals to account for violations committed in other countries. When Nazi Germany passed its Nuremberg laws, stripping Jewish citizens of basic rights, neither international law nor the "international community," such as it was, was empowered to act.

Perhaps the most significant consequence of the Nuremberg trials of 1945–1946 and the 1946–1948 Tokyo trials was that they created universal jurisdiction over individuals who were suspected of committing crimes against humanity, which was first recognized in the Charter establishing the Nuremberg Tribunal.[5] The postwar trials also gave rise to the articulation and prohibition of the crime of "genocide," a word invented to describe the systematic destruction of individuals based on their group identity. By recognizing the existence of "crimes against humanity," the postwar trials announced to the world that certain crimes were so egregious that international law would consider them committed against the whole of humanity, not just against a particular individual, people, or nation. Doing this empowered the whole of humanity, and not simply representatives of the state where the crime was committed, to claim the right and the jurisdiction to put the worst perpetrators on trial. The Genocide Convention, adopted in 1948, broadened this concept further, obliging signatories to prosecute the crime of genocide no matter where it was committed. Universal jurisdiction was also established under the "grave breach" provisions of the 1949 Geneva Conventions as well as the Apartheid Convention of 1973, which declared apartheid to be a crime against humanity. Building on the foundation laid in Nuremberg and Tokyo, international law gradually broadened the class of egregious crimes that, whether committed within or between states, would be treated as international crimes.[6]

The significance of these developments should not be underestimated. The recognition of universal jurisdiction marked a critical inroad into state sovereignty. Even at a purely theoretical level, when states committed to these international conventions, they were giving up part of their sovereignty. Legally speaking, the perpetrators of war crimes and crimes against humanity could no longer be saved by, or hidden within, national borders.

Yet notwithstanding these monumental *de jure* advances, most of this law went unenforced, causing many to question its practical significance. Because it was not enforced, it had little, if any, influence on the conduct of political or military leaders in respect of the way in which wars were fought. Skeptics justifiably questioned the value of humanitarian law, citing John Austin's maxim that law lacking an adequate enforcement mechanism "was not law properly so-called." It appeared that, whatever the strong moral, legal, or historical imperatives that might have demanded an accounting for human rights abuses, the major powers that composed the appropriate international institutions lacked the political will to prosecute those responsible for committing abuses. Cambodia's Pol Pot and Iraq's Saddam Hussein were left unhindered to commit abuses within their borders.

Contemporaneous with these developments in international law, another phenomenon was occurring: Countries that had experienced long periods of repression and citizens who had suffered massive violations of human rights were democratizing. As countries in Latin America, Eastern Europe, and Africa struggled to move forward from pasts rife with injustice, many of them decided to establish "truth commissions" they hoped would facilitate the transitions to democracy by documenting sins of the past and permitting an airing of grievances. Since 1974 approximately twenty such commissions have been set up. In the 1990s, however, these commissions not only proliferated but also became the subject of a widespread public and scholarly inquiry. The more recent wave of interest was spurred by the highly publicized UN Commission on Truth for El Salvador, which was established in 1992. However, the first to receive major international attention was Argentina's truth commission a decade earlier. In 1983 Argentine President Raul Alfonsín introduced a two-stage process: He established the Sábato Commission on the Disappeared, which would investigate and document the disappearances, and then military trials would be held to prosecute those responsible for the atrocities outlined in *Nunca Mas* (Never Again). This report by the Sábato Commission detailed the atrocities committed by the military in Argentina from 1976 to 1979 and formed part of the evidentiary basis for the subsequent military trials.[7]

The principle that underpinned many of these truth commissions was that certain crimes should not—and indeed could not—go unaccounted for, regardless of the form of that accountability. Those who assumed positions in new governments, and even those who were relics of past regimes, appeared to recognize the importance of truth and accountability, and many did so of their own accord and without international prompting. These leaders made a link between exposing individual suffering and individual responsibility on one hand and creating a stable, enduring peace in their new democracies on the other.

However, while these national governments considered truth a prerequisite to peace, it was the international community that made the formal link between justice and international peace and security. The UN Security Council, acting under Chapter VII of the UN Charter, created the first ever ad hoc International Criminal Tribunals for the former Yugoslavia (ICTY) and Rwanda (ICTR).[8] Under Chapter VII, the Security Council could create jurisdiction by recognizing that the conflicts and widespread violations of international humanitarian law in the two regions constituted threats to international peace and security. Because the wars in the former Yugoslavia could be judged as partly internal and partly international, the Security Council could make the link to international peace more easily than in Rwanda, where militants close to the former Hutu regime organized a genocide against some 800,000 minority Tutsi and moderate Hutu citizens in Rwanda itself. Still, the Security Council forged ahead and established that even crimes that remained confined within a member state of the United Nations could indeed constitute a threat to international peace and security.

The political will to take this most important first step had, until the creation of the tribunals, been absent. How then can one account for the Security Council's decision to act in response to the conflict in the former Yugoslavia, when it had so obviously failed to take similar steps in response to other egregious abuses, such as those committed in Cambodia or Iraq? First, the members of the Security Council found events in the former Yugoslavia reminiscent of the Holocaust. The photographs of gaunt men trapped behind barbed wire reminded many of Nazi concentration camps. Second, before the outbreak of war in the Balkans, Western leaders had not conceived that such crimes would ever be repeated in Europe in the post-Nuremberg era. The crimes committed in Bosnia, which were televised directly to European and American leaders and their constituents, forced the international community to admit the cold truth that the world system had failed to fulfill the promises made after Nuremberg. Third, because the international media were present and able to witness, report, and film the events in question, politicians could not deny these atrocities or remove them from their—or their constituents'—daily lives. The historical resonance, the perception that international coping mechanisms had failed, and the staying power of the images together provided national and international human rights organizations with a platform for bringing pressure against the Security Council and demanding appropriate action to punish the perpetrators. Fortuitously, this pressure arose at a time in which the major international players, the permanent members of the Security Council, did not oppose the creation of an ad hoc international criminal tribunal and even welcomed an opportunity to be seen to be doing something to respond to the horrors on the ground. Despite all of these forces, the mechanism that was finally employed and the manner in which it was put in place were by no means obvious at the time.

THE LINK BETWEEN PEACE AND JUSTICE

Human rights activists and lawyers who believed in the importance of fulfilling Nuremberg's promise had assumed that if an international criminal court were ever to be established, it could be created only by treaty. They did not anticipate that the Security Council of the United Nations would take advantage of the powers conferred by Chapter VII of the UN Charter to create a judicial suborgan as a measure to restore "international peace and security." This decision was predicated on the recognition of a direct link between justice and peace.

Chapter VII authorizes the Security Council to pass resolutions binding on all states if it decides that enforcement measures are necessary to bring an end to a situation that constitutes a threat to international peace and security. In September 1991 the Security Council already had determined that the situation in the former Yugoslavia constituted such a threat when, acting under its Chapter VII powers, it imposed a complete arms embargo on the former Yugoslavia. UN Resolution 827, which was passed twenty months later in May 1993, explicitly acknowledged that the widespread violations of humanitarian law and human rights occurring in the region constituted a threat to international peace. The

Security Council resolution based the creation of a tribunal on the following grounds:[9]

- *Expressing* once again its grave alarm at continuing reports of widespread and flagrant violations of international humanitarian law occurring within the territory of the former Yugoslavia, and especially in the Republic of Bosnia and Herzegovina, including reports of mass killings, massive, organized and systematic detention and rape of women, and the continuance of the practice of "ethnic-cleansing," including the acquisition and holding of territory;
- *Determining* that this situation continues to constitute a threat to international peace and security;
- *Determining* to put an end to such crimes and to take effective measures to bring to justice the persons who are responsible for them;
- *Convinced* that in the particular circumstances of the former Yugoslavia the establishment, as an ad hoc measure by the Council, of an international tribunal and the prosecution of persons responsible for serious violations of international humanitarian law would enable this aim to be achieved and would contribute to the restoration and maintenance of peace;
- *Believing* that the establishment of an international tribunal and the prosecution of persons responsible for the above-mentioned violations of international humanitarian law will contribute to ensuring that such violations are halted and effectively redressed. . . .

The Council resolved that the establishment of the International Criminal Tribunal for the former Yugoslavia was the most appropriate way of dealing with such a threat. In November 1994, at the request of the Rwandan government, the Security Council made a similar decision with respect to Rwanda, where an internal armed conflict leading to genocide had killed nearly half of the country's Tutsi populace.[10] The Security Council decided that justice would help restore peace in both the former Yugoslavia and Rwanda and hasten the return of refugees to their former homes. The Nuremberg court had been set up after the conflict as a consequence of the peace secured by the victorious allies, while the ICTY had been created during an ongoing conflict in the hopes of restoring peace.

The Security Council thus expanded conventional interpretations of "security." Henceforth the term would constitute more than just the military security of a state and would encompass "human security": both the security of the individuals within the state and the ripple effects that their insecurity would have upon the region and upon the international system as a whole.[11]

PEACE VERSUS JUSTICE

The notion that justice would enhance the prospects for peace and security was a novel one. The traditional understanding of the relationship between peace and justice viewed the two concepts as mutually exclusive: Both terms were defined narrowly, with peace understood simply as the absence of manifest conflict and justice seen as inherently necessitating prosecutions. While the search for peace was more forward-looking, the search for justice was seen as a process that dwelt on the past and thus hindered attempts to put the conflict to rest and get on with life. However, both the recent proliferation of truth commissions and the creation of war crimes tribunals have demonstrated the inextricable and positive link between these two concepts.

It is easy to see why forgetting the past in the quest for a better and more peaceful future appears attractive. People who have lived through and survived the trauma of gross human rights abuses have many needs apart from psychological healing. They may require medical treatment; they may need to find loved ones from whom they have been separated; or they may simply wish for the absence of the daily dread and fear that so frequently accompanies life in repressive and autocratic regimes. Thus it is not surprising that building a future takes precedence over belaboring the past.

However, the most serious challenge to this narrow view of peace and justice can be found in history itself. While I traveled around the former Yugoslavia and Rwanda as prosecutor from 1994 to 1996, I was often given lengthy and detailed accounts of past human rights abuses that had been allowed to fester. In Belgrade I was told of Serb grievances that could be traced back to Croatia's collaboration with the Nazis during World War II and even to the Battle of Kosovo in 1389. On all sides a litany of historical abuses had gone unaccounted for, and calls for justice had gone unanswered. In Rwanda, the Hutu and Tutsi inherited an unresolved history of precolonial and colonial repression, and militant leaders were able to play upon the fear and the competition between the two ethnic groups in order to create the fiction that the two could not live together in peace. Amid historical grievances—some real, others imagined—many quickly and tragically overlooked the fact that in many parts of Bosnia and Herzegovina and Rwanda people from different ethnic groups had lived together and intermarried for centuries.

Without justice, any peace in these parts is likely to be only a deceptive, short-term peace, which is not the kind that we should be seeking. Beneath such superficial calm can lie unsettled scores that are easily exploitable and that can tear countries and neighborhoods apart. Regimes intent on grabbing resources or achieving ethnic exclusivity can employ propaganda in order to capitalize on these old scores and to instill fear and hate.

In order to ensure that the peace that follows a period of conflict is meaningful, lasting and effective, nations must strive for some kind of justice and accountability, which can help break the cycles of violence that depend for their very existence on unsettled scores and the manipulation of history.

Truth as Justice

Although criminal prosecution is probably the most common form of justice, it is not the only or necessarily the most appropriate form. The public and official exposure of the truth is itself a form of justice. By truth, I refer to the experiences of the victim and the deeds of the perpetrator; and by justice, I mean some form of punishment for the perpetrator. A public trial and appropriate punishment for those convicted is what most victims justifiably demand. In the case of widespread criminality, no criminal justice system has the resources to afford this form of justice. It is in this context that truth commissions provide an alternative, if limited, form of justice. The public exposure of the perpetrator's deeds affords important acknowledgment for the victim, and the public admission of criminal conduct by the perpetrator is a significant punishment. By liberating ourselves from the narrow view of justice as punishment, we can see that justice may take the form of national or internationally sponsored truth commissions as well as national or international prosecutions. A country may well opt for both prosecutions and a truth commission, as in South Africa, provided they do not undermine each other and are part of a coherent and consistent approach to justice.

Justice, in whatever form, has much to do with retribution and the past, but to be really just, a process also must help secure lasting peace for the future. It can do so in the following ways. First, justice helps establish the truth, the most important element of which is that it is not entire groups—ethnic, racial, or otherwise—that commit genocide or crimes against humanity but a finite number of individuals. In the Balkans, where few in history have been held accountable for violence, blame was ascribed not to the particular leaders who sponsored the violence but to the communities represented by those leaders. Instead, a trial or a truth commission hearing could bring the truth of individual responsibility to light and thereby help to individualize the guilt so that collective guilt is not ascribed to "Serbs" or "Muslims" as such but instead to particular individuals. In this respect, perhaps the most important benefi-ciaries of the Nuremberg trials were the German people themselves. The trials focused on the accused as individual criminals and not as representatives of the German people.

In 1995 South Africa opted for a combination of national prosecutions and the Truth and Reconciliation Commission (TRC) in its effort to achieve justice and accountability.[12] The TRC has established that certain leaders in the security forces were responsible for the worst evils of apartheid. In implementing the apartheid policy of the former South African government, these security figures ordered the murder of political opponents as well as the bombings of office buildings of the antiapartheid organizations in South Africa and England. They did so with the explicit intention of sowing hate among black political rivals. In addition to identifying individual perpetrators, the TRC also demonstrated that its commissioners, and the victims who appeared before the commission, came from all sectors of our society. If the TRC had not exposed the truth, future generations of black South Africans would inevitably have blamed the human rights abuses committed during the apartheid years on all white South Africans or to Afrikaners who, as a group, were identified with the apartheid government. The fact that the African National Congress (ANC) has admitted before the TRC that its members also committed human rights abuses is a powerful reminder to all South Africans that criminality is not the preserve of any particular group but a human weakness that can afflict any people anywhere. This fact is underscored by the words of Archbishop Desmond Tutu in his foreword to the TRC's Final Report: "A venerable tradition holds that those who use force to overthrow or even to oppose an unjust system occupy the moral high ground over those who use force to sustain that same system. . . . this does not mean that those who hold the moral high ground have carte blanche as to the methods they use."[13]

Second, by exposing the truth, a commission hearing or a trial can bring public and official acknowledgment to the victims of abuses. It gives victims the opportunity to articulate their own experiences, thereby making others understand what they have suffered. Doing this breeds greater sensitivity and awareness in the public, and to the extent that it engenders collective action against such human rights abuses, or even collective moral condemnation, it constitutes an important element of justice.

A third benefit that flows from exposing truth through a process of justice is that history is recorded more accurately and more faithfully than would otherwise have been the case. Cover-ups and denials are common in the wake of gross human rights violations, but the Nuremberg trials, for example, render impotent the efforts of those who would deny the Holocaust.

Similarly, the work of the ICTY has made fabrications by Bosnian Serb spokespersons less plausible. In July of 1995, the now-infamous slaughter of some 8,000 civilian men and boys took place outside the UN "safe area" of Srebrenica. There was the usual denial by the Bosnian Serb army, but some months later one of the perpetrators, Drazen Erdemovic, confessed to having murdered over 70 of those civilians as a member of the Bosnian Serb army. His evidence enabled the prosecutor to identify the site of the mass grave to the U.S. government. The United States then found satellite photos that showed bodies lying in the vicinity of a mass grave around the fallen "safe area," and photographs taken the following day that showed the grave freshly covered with earth. A Bosnian Serb army spokesperson claimed that the grave contained the bodies of soldiers killed during battle, but Erdemovic's testimony helped to verify the fact that mass murders had been committed at Srebrenica. Exhumations conducted by the Office of the Prosecutor in the summer of 1996 showed that the people buried in the grave had each been killed by a single gunshot to the back of the head. Most had been shot while their arms were bound behind their backs, refuting Serb claims that the men had been killed in the course of battle. Thus the massacre of thousands of innocent Muslims who had sought safety in the United Nations "safe haven" of Srebrenica was established through the ICTY with a degree of certainty that would otherwise have been impossible to achieve. Without this truth, many people, especially in the former Yugoslavia, might have believed the denials of the Bosnian Serb army or suspected that the Bosnian government had concocted the story of massacres as a form of propaganda.

A fourth benefit is that exposing the nature and extent of human rights violations frequently reveals a systematic and institutional pattern of gross violations of human rights. This revelation often helps successor governments to identify and dismantle the criminal institutions, which in turn helps prevent future recurrences. If left unchallenged, these institutions retain their organized culture of unaccountability and may be relied on by the successor regime. For example, in the Democratic Republic of Congo, President Laurent Kabila has been able to continue the country's tradition of prohibiting political parties, apprehending democratic opposition leaders, arresting journalists, establishing military tribunals empowered to judge civilians, and barring certain citizens from political activity.

Finally, just as the existence and efficacy of a national criminal justice system acts as a deterrent to national crime, an effective international criminal justice system also may deter would-be criminals around the world. It can hardly be questioned that there is a direct link between the effectiveness of policing and the crime rate. In the international arena, there has never been any policing of war criminals, efficient or otherwise. The lack of political will in respect to the arrest of Serbian warlords Radovan Karadzic and Ratko Mladic has no doubt weakened any deterrent effect that the ICTY might have exercised. Nonetheless, some commentators have pointed out that the war crimes committed in Kosovo in 1998 and 1999 are far less egregious than those committed by the Bosnian Serb army in Bosnia between 1991 and 1995, and this may be a result of deterrence. However, although there have been no "death camps," there have been attempts at "ethnic cleansing" by more direct means, and in this respect there are similarities between the conduct of the Croatian army in Krajina and that of the Serb army in Kosovo. It is difficult and hardly relevant to quantify the extent of the war crimes in Kosovo for the purpose of comparing them to those perpetrated in Bosnia. What is relevant is that the "death camps" that were a feature of the Bosnian "ethnic cleansing" were absent in Kosovo. Further, in Kosovo, the Serb forces attempted to remove evidence of many mass graves by removing the corpses. To suggest that the ICTY acted as a deterrent in Kosovo would not appear to be justified. However, that many of the perpetrators of war crimes in Kosovo were aware of the possibility of later prosecutions cannot be doubted.

With its recent attempts to bring justice to individuals, the international community has sent out a strong moral message that the culture of impunity in which the world has winked at atrocity since Nuremberg is no more. Indeed, while seeking medical treatment in Britain, General Augusto Pinochet of Chile was arrested on a warrant issued by a Spanish judge on charges of having committed crimes against humanity, including systematic executions and "disappearances" against the Chilean people while he was in power. In extensive legal battles over the applicability of the general principle of international law that a head of state is immune from prosecution for acts committed while in office, England's House of Lords and the Home Secretary found Pinochet subject to trial in Spanish courts.[14] Nonetheless, despite a British medical evaluation which prevented Senator Pinochet's extradition to Spain, the acts of the British and Spanish governments and courts have added strength to the message that the age of impunity is over.

Thus, a link exists between justice and truth as well as between truth and reconciliation. However, it is not always clear why an international forum is preferable to a domestic one in aiding the process of rebuilding a society ravaged by gross violations of human rights. It is to this question that I now turn.

WHY INTERNATIONAL TRIBUNALS?

There can be no question that, at least in theory, national trials are to be preferred. They take place in the country where the crimes were committed, and the victims can observe, understand, and participate in them. Their own prosecutors and defense lawyers participate in the proceedings, and the perpetrators are judged by their own judges.

However, international tribunals may be preferable to domestic courts for securing justice under three circumstances. The first is a situation in which the national government is unable or unwilling to take this responsibility. The second is one in which the complicity, or even partiality, of the national government makes it undesirable for such a government to take this responsibility because of a perceived or actual conflict of interest. The third is one in which the gravity of the crime triggers such a significant international or human stake in the case that it would be better to settle it on an international stage.

Since World War II, many states have been unable or unwilling to punish war criminals and perpetrators of gross human rights abuses. Dealing firmly with the past requires a high degree of political stability, which is not always present in a transitional society. War crimes and other human rights abuses are carried out most often by government agents operating in a brutal culture of unaccountability. The transition often leaves a delicate balance of power between the outgoing and the incoming forces. The new leaders or their supporters may thus fear destabilizing their fragile hold on power by prosecuting those who still hold considerable influence.[15] Further, even in cases where the political will is present, the national justice system often is too weak, too discredited, or too lacking in resources to be able to apprehend the offenders, investigate the crimes, or conduct fair trials.

The second scenario is one in which implicated parties retain power. Examples include Iraq, where Saddam Hussein maintains tight control, and the former Yugoslavia, where President Slobodan Milosevic still runs the show in Serbia, and where the Bosnian Serbs, who committed the bulk of the atrocities in the war, were granted their own little republic. In neither instance could local Iraqi or Serb court systems be counted on to bring perpetrators to justice. Similarly, after World War II, the victorious powers certainly would not have left it to German courts to bring the Nazi leaders to justice. Indeed, it was not until 1955 that the United States, France, and the United Kingdom allowed the courts of West Germany to try Nazi war criminals.

In these first two circumstances, therefore, an international tribunal probably would have greater success and may even offer victims the only hope of securing justice. The third scenario is one that involves crimes against humanity—those crimes that represent such serious violations of the laws of humanity that national courts should allow international involvement in their prosecution. One reason for the state being the vehicle for conducting domestic criminal prosecutions is that society as a whole suffers when crimes go unsolved and unpunished. Since society-at-large is a victim, society-at-large brings the complaint against the accused through the state acting as society's agent. In this third scenario, the crime is of such magnitude—be it in horror or in territorial impact—that international society is a victim of that crime and should therefore be able to bring its claim in the international arena acting through international agents. When crimes are committed of the magnitude of those perpetrated in Nazi Germany, the former Yugoslavia, or Rwanda, all of humanity has an interest in bringing those responsible to account. As Justice Jackson said, "the wrongs which we seek to condemn and punish have been so calculated, so malignant and so devastating, that civilization cannot tolerate their being ignored."[16]

ACHIEVEMENTS OF THE TRIBUNALS
IN THE FORMER YUGOSLAVIA, RWANDA, AND SOUTH AFRICA

Having opted for the international approach to justice in the former Yugoslavia and Rwanda, the Security Council made possible a number of powerful achievements. First, the work of the tribunals has substantially advanced the norms of international humanitarian law. The decisions handed down by the judges of both the Appeals and Trial Chambers have begun to create a new international jurisprudence that eventually will exert a positive influence on national systems of law. The problematic gaps in humanitarian law—in particular the artificial distinction between international and internal wars—have been reduced considerably. The Appeals Chamber of the ICTY, in the *Tadic Jurisdiction Motion* case, made clear that this distinction could no longer be sustained.[17] In the twentieth century, millions of people were killed, raped, tortured, or displaced as a result of internal wars. These internal wars are often the most brutal and have the most devastating effect on civilian populations. As the Appeals Chamber held, it makes little sense to protect people from murder, rape, and wanton destruction of their property in the case of an international war and not do to the same merely because the war does not cross any borders. The court emphasized that international humanitarian law is moving away from the traditional state-centered approach and toward a human rights–oriented approach. Thus the work of the international tribunals in clarifying and developing the norms of international humanitarian law represents a positive step toward achieving international peace and justice.

A further important development is that the prior invisibility of mass rape in international humanitarian law has been significantly transformed by the recognition that such abhorrent conduct constitutes not only a war crime but also a crime against humanity, and perhaps even genocide.[18] Even a cursory reading of the Laws of War and the relevant International Conventions make it plain that these were conceived and written by men, for men. How else can one explain the complete omission of gender-specific crimes, even though rape as an incidence, if not a weapon, of war is not a new phenomenon? Sexual crimes had faced a double exclusion at the hands of international humanitarian law: excluded first on the grounds that they belong within the purview of *domestic* law and again on the grounds that they belong within the *private* sphere of domestic law. Traditionally, if rape were to be considered an internationally justifiable act when committed during times of conflict, it would have had to be treated as an instance of "inhuman treatment" or, in some cases, "torture." However, prior to 1995, the crime of rape had never been charged under the auspices of international law. Indeed, although witnesses recounted their experiences of rape in their examination-in-chief at Nuremberg, the Tribunal failed to refer to it even once in the judgment.

It required some persistence and ingenuity to ensure that indictments in the ICTY and ICTR appropriately charged mass rape as a war crime. Following the genocide in Rwanda and the Balkans, women's groups and human rights groups in Europe, the United States, and Canada, as well as nongovernmental organizations in the former Yugoslavia, launched such a campaign. Letters, petitions, and *amicus curiae* briefs called for attention to be given to gender-related crimes, especially systematic rape as a war crime. In heeding these calls, the tribunals set important precedents, as this marks the first time that systematic rape ever has been charged and prosecuted as a war crime in itself. The *Foca* indictment in the ICTY related to a number of alleged perpetrators, and all of the crimes charged were related to rape and other forms of sexual assault. In addition, the Rwanda Tribunal has handed down a verdict of guilty that deemed rape a crime against humanity.[19] Thus victims of human rights abuses who were once denied access to justice have been recognized by international law at last.

Second, the tribunals have brought about a resurgence of international interest in humanitarian law. It is now written about and discussed in the media on a daily basis in many countries, and it is taught to crowded classrooms in law schools and elsewhere. Perhaps most important, political and military leaders in a number of countries now are paying it some attention. This was seen in 1996, when the Croatian government launched Operation Storm in Krajina. Croatian leaders made public statements exhorting the Croatian army to protect civilians and to not breach international humanitarian law. That the Croatian troops nonetheless violated international humanitarian law emerged from many reports of war crimes committed by them, although whether even more egregious violations would have been committed in the absence of the ICTY is impossible to judge. These might be seen as small successes, but for the first time the law of war is present in the minds of some, if not all, political and military leaders who are waging war.

Third, as a consequence of the work of the tribunals, individual governments are taking a serious interest in international humanitarian law. Three permanent members of the Security Council—the United States, France, and the United Kingdom—have passed national legislation recognizing their international obligation to comply with the statute under which the tribunals operate. In addition, the Russian Federation has notified the ICTY formally that it does not require national legislation in order for it to comply, and has confirmed that it will do so. Under tremendous international pressure, Croatia amended its constitution to enable it to comply with the statute; however, it has done little to comply with the amendments.

A fourth achievement of the tribunals has been the marginalization of indicted war criminals who have not yet been arrested. Karadzic and Mladic, for example, were removed from office as a result of being indicted. Karadzic's status as an indicted war criminal also kept the Bosnian Serb leader from attending the Dayton Peace negotiations, which made it easier to reach agreement there. The indictment of Milosevic in May 1999 did not stop him, immediately afterward, from accepting the terms of the North Atlantic Treaty Organization (NATO) peace agreement.

Finally, in establishing the tribunals, the Security Council has struck a meaningful blow against impunity. It has sent out the message to would-be criminals that the international community is no longer prepared to let war crimes go unaccounted for. The international community may be in a stronger position than ever before to send this message. International humanitarian law has been modified substantially in the last fifty years to remove the obstacles that stood in the way of effective international policing. The result is that we have universal jurisdiction, acknowledged crimes against humanity, and the effective removal of the distinction between crimes committed in international as opposed to internal conflicts.[20] All this means that sovereignty, which was previously a state's best shield against any international intervention, is no longer absolute. The international community demonstrated its resolve to implement this body of international humanitarian law with the establishment of the ICTY and the ICTR. The link between justice and international peace and security provided a strong moral, political, and legal justification for such tribunals.

The tribunals played a significant role in creating momentum for the establishment of a permanent International Criminal Court (ICC). The experience of the ad hoc tribunals showed that an international body could hold efficient investigations and fair trials. In addition, with humanitarian law strengthened and a greater measure of justice secured for both the victims and the international community, people came to accept that war crimes, crimes against humanity, and associated human rights violations could be curbed only by enforcing humanitarian law. The experiments with the ad hoc tribunals worked sufficiently well to inspire confidence in at least the close to one hundred signatory states that a permanent body could function and prosper.

For all of these achievements, it is important to note the deficiencies and to realize that no perfect model of justice can be imported blindly into any country. The three countries with which I have had some experience—South Africa, Yugoslavia, and Rwanda—demonstrate the importance of assessing the particular political, financial, and social circumstances of a country when deciding whether to opt for national prosecutions, a truth commission, or an international tribunal.

South Africa

In South Africa, the decision to establish the Truth and Reconciliation Commission was a political one and itself an important compromise. The former apartheid government wished to forget the past and get on with building a new South Africa, but doing so would have meant forgetting the legitimate claims of the millions of victims of apartheid. At the other end of the political spectrum, the African National Congress and other liberation organizations wished to hold Nuremberg-style trials of the apartheid leaders. Without an acceptable compromise, this dispute alone would likely have prevented a peaceful transition. The TRC represented a compromise: The Commission would be empowered to grant amnesty for politically motivated crimes that constituted gross violations of human rights only in instances in which the perpetrators made individual applications for amnesty and disclosed full details of the crimes for which they sought amnesty.

No important endeavor in the life of a people is without cost. The cost of the TRC is that many victims of the worst human rights abuses will be denied full justice. Some of the families of people murdered by the former South African security personnel are today outspoken opponents of the Commission. They demand punishment of the police officers who have come forward and admitted guilt, and one cannot but have sympathy for them. However, those families would never have known the identity of most of those murderers had there been no TRC, and no criminal prosecutions could have been instituted. The TRC at least made possible discovery of the perpetrators' identities. Thus the real choice that faced the country was not one between indemnity and prosecution, the choice was to fashion a remedy for as much justice as the country could afford, politically, to demand. Many perpetrators have felt compelled to come forward and publicly admit their part in the commission of gross human rights violations, and this type of public humiliation is in itself a form of punishment. Criminal prosecutions could have uncovered no more than a few of the human rights abuses committed in South Africa over the last half century, but in a period of two and a half years, the TRC has received more than 20,000 depositions from victims detailing gross human rights violations over a period of three decades.[21] Over 8,000 amnesty applications also were received.

The South African option has unique features, the most notable of which is that it encompasses both amnesty and prosecutions. In this way it has tried, within the given political constraints, to maximize the degree of justice that will be secured for present and future generations. Within the TRC, amnesty is granted only in exchange for full disclosure. Victims are able to tell their stories and have public confirmation and acknowledgment of their experiences. Many people are able, for the first time, to find or confirm the truth about what happened to their loved ones and to learn or confirm who was responsible for their suffering. Moreover, the process does not preclude prosecutions outside the TRC, which may be, and have been, instituted against people who choose not to seek amnesty.

The Former Yugoslavia and Rwanda, and Lessons for the Proposed ICC

In the former Yugoslavia, any justice mechanism had to operate amid an ongoing conflict, which almost ruled out the options of a truth commission or a set of national prosecutions. It would have been impossible for local authorities to conduct meaningful investigations into massive human rights abuses, to enforce arrest warrants, or to obtain custody of suspected war criminals. Each of the warring factions would have protected its own perpetrators, and their denials and cover-ups would have exacerbated the grievances already lurking in the region.

In Bosnia today, a number of organizations have called for a nonamnesty truth and reconciliation commission that would provide a credible and official platform for victims to tell of their victimization. If such a body were to develop an efficient investigation department and could avoid being used as a political platform, it would help reveal the truth concerning the human rights violations that were committed to different degrees by all sides and therefore would probably be worth pursuing. Indeed, although citizens in the former Yugoslavia possess a high degree of awareness of human rights violations, one's ethnic affiliation tends to dictate which facts one sees or acknowledges. Although the ICTY can assist in obtaining a record of the violations committed by all sides, a truth commission might be able to reach those beyond the grasp of criminal justice processes. The proceedings of the ICTY will never investigate or make public more than a fraction of the history and should not claim a monopoly over truth-telling. A growing call for such a commission from a significant number of Bosnian human rights organizations has received support in the local media.

The situation in Rwanda had marked differences from that of Bosnia, where perpetrators of wartime atrocities have been able to live comfortably in territory under the control of their own ethnic groups. In contrast, by the time the army of the present government of Rwanda was able to stop the Hutu militants who had killed nearly one-seventh of Rwanda's population, the criminals responsible had fled the country, in many cases with millions of dollars of state funds. The Rwandan government requested the creation of an international tribunal for Rwanda for a number of reasons. Some of these related to matters of principle, such as its belief that genocide is a crime against humankind as a whole and therefore should be suppressed by the international community as a whole.[22] Most important, perhaps, it sought to eradicate the culture of impunity that had been rife in Rwandan society, knew it could not grapple with the consequences of a slaughter of such magnitude on its own, and understood that the masterminds of the genocide might be apprehended in neighboring states, necessitating international cooperation to obtain custody of them.

Having already created a court for crimes committed in the former Yugoslavia, the Security Council did not hesitate to establish the International Criminal Tribunal for Rwanda. The Rwandan government, however, did find fault with the Tribunal, and ultimately voted against the resolution that established it, out of concern that justice would not be done if the ICTR possessed only limited resources and shared an Appeals Chamber and Prosecutor with the ICTY. The Rwandan government objected to the fact that some of the proposed judges were nationals of states that had taken "a very active part in the civil war."[23] In addition, it opposed the establishment of a UN court outside Rwanda (the ICTR was set up in neighboring Tanzania) as well as the fact that the Tribunal precluded the death penalty for any perpetrators. The Security Council disregarded the latter two objections on the grounds that fair trials could not have been held in Rwanda itself, where millions of survivors and relatives of the deceased would have called for bloody revenge, and that international law prohibited the death penalty. The Rwandan government decided to conduct national prosecutions simultaneously with the operation of the ICTR, creating an inconsistency in which the genocide's masterminds are treated less harshly by the international tribunal than those under their command have been treated by Rwandan courts.

Indeed, the concerns of the Security Council about bloody revenge appear to have been borne out. In April of 1998, tens of thousands of Rwandans gathered at the Tapis Rouge soccer field to watch the first executions, by firing squad, of people convicted of genocide before Rwandan courts. None of the twenty-two people executed was a leader or mastermind of the genocide, and human rights advocates objected that many of the trials resulting in the executions had been conducted well beneath international standards for fair trials. Since then there have been many further trials and sentences passed, including the death sentence. As far as I am aware, only one leader, Froduard Karamira, was tried in a Rwandan court and executed.

The troublesome discrepancies of this dual justice system highlight the need for consistency when different forms of justice operate simultaneously but under the control of different bodies.

The experience of these two international tribunals will prove very instructive for the ICC. It has highlighted the kinds of problems that arise with the creation of ad hoc courts by resolution rather than treaty—for example, the difficulty of getting states to give up part of their sovereignty and the problem of compelling them to fulfill their obligations in arresting indictees. However, states that have ratified the ICC treaty are more likely to fulfill the obligations they have thereby accepted, and when a significant number of states have ratified the treaty, those that ignore their international obligations are more likely to be treated as pariahs. International opprobrium will add to their incentive to comply.

To date the ICTY has issued ninety-four public indictments since its inception. Currently there are thirty outstanding public indictments against sixty-seven people; thirty-eight of them have been arrested and brought to The Hague. The rest are still at large in various parts of the former Yugoslavia, Bosnia, the Federal Republic of Yugoslavia, and possibly Croatia.[24] The primary obligation to arrest these people rests on the governments of the former Yugoslavia and on authorities outside Yugoslavia who know that indictees are passing through or inhabiting territory under their control. Outside governments such as Germany and Austria have fulfilled this duty, arresting war criminals in their midst. Ever since the signing of the Dayton Peace Agreement in 1995, outside powers also have had the opportunity to use their forces within Bosnia to make arrests. In December 1995 an Implementation Force (IFOR), consisting of 60,000 troops from both NATO and non-NATO powers, was deployed in Bosnia specifically to assist parties to the Dayton Agreement fulfill their obligations, including compliance with the orders of the ICTY. However, the North Atlantic Council (NAC), the political body controlling IFOR, decided at first that it would be too dangerous to pursue indicted war criminals and that IFOR troops should detain only people the troops come across in the ordinary course of their activities. Not surprisingly, indicted war criminals went to great lengths to avoid IFOR checkpoints, making the NAC mandate to arrest war criminals next to meaningless.

Later, the NATO allies began to take a slightly more robust view of their mandate. In July 1997 British troops struck for the first time, arresting one suspect—Milan Kovacevic—and shooting dead another, Simo Drljaca. Although NATO claimed that the arrests did not represent a change in policy, NATO has since then made more than a dozen arrests, which in turn has led to a series of voluntary surrenders to the tribunal.

Despite these improvements in enforcement of the tribunal's will, the two men believed to be most responsible for atrocities in Bosnia—the wartime political leader of the Bosnian Serbs, Radovan Karadzic, and military leader Ratko Mladic—remain at large. It is not difficult to imagine the sense of disillusionment and abandonment that victims must feel. The injustice they suffered was given official recognition when the international tribunal was set up, and the victims were promised justice and told that sufficient evidence existed for the issuance of indictments against those thought to be responsible for these crimes. However, they saw these same individuals remaining free, as governments lacked the political will to have them arrested.

As nations around the world cooperate in the establishment of a permanent International Criminal Court (ICC), we need to look long and hard at whether such a court is really the best it can do. First and foremost, the problems of the ICTY with regard to enforcement demonstrated unequivocally that if the ICC intended to make significant inroads into state sovereignty, it could not do so by attempting to impose its will on states by mere resolution, no matter how compelling its justification. If the ICC is to muster the support it needs to make this endeavor successful, states will have to commit themselves to the process freely and voluntarily, but states are not likely to do so without a forum in which to voice their concerns and collectively seek appropriate ways to address these concerns. Such a forum was the Rome Conference of June/July 1998. 120 of the 150 states represented accepted the terms of the Rome Statute that they had helped draft in the five-week, intensive negotiation.[25] The inclusiveness of this process bodes well for the future and improves the likelihood that states will honor their obligations under the ICC Treaty and that they will cooperate in enforcing it—including making arrests, as they have not in Bosnia—because of their participation in the initial decision-making processes. The Rome process also gives the international community more leverage to compel compliance should some states fail in this regard. Apart from the combined pressure that can be brought to bear by the sixty or more states that will have ratified the Rome Statute to bring it into effect as a treaty, in cases of serious violations giving rise to threats against international peace and security, the Security Council will, under the Treaty, be able to confer its Chapter VII peremptory enforcement powers upon the ICC and impose peremptory sanctions on noncomplying states. (It is highly unlikely that military measures would be used.)

While there is much to commend this process, it is not without its difficulties. Many states still resist giving up part of their sovereignty to a new international body. Many fear the independence of the ICC and seek assurances that the Court's affairs will be conducted fairly and legitimately. In addition, in instances where states are able and willing to try criminals themselves, they want to make sure that they will not be compelled to hand them over to the ICC. Although these concerns are understandable at a general level, they are in fact misplaced in this instance. All those involved are aware of the fact that this is a bold new step for the international community and thus are sensitive to the need for caution. Safeguards have been built into the process to prevent the kind of arbitrariness or bias that concerns some states. Investigations for the purpose of prosecutions will be launched only after a two-step process has been completed, satisfying both the prosecutor and the pretrial chamber that a reasonable basis exists upon which to launch an investigation into a case. The state concerned also has the right to be heard by the pretrial chamber if it challenges whether that reasonable basis exists.[26] The ICC's power is further checked by the fact that the Security Council may, in effect, order that an investigation or prosecution be deferred for up to twelve months, by resolution acting under its Chapter VII powers.[27]

It is also clear from the Rome Statute that the ICC is not intended to be an automatic substitute for any national system. The ICC is given jurisdiction only where the national system is deemed by the Court to be unwilling or unable to carry out the investigation or prosecution, in accordance with guidelines agreed to by all.[28] This decision will be made following arguments by the state or states affected, and can be appealed to the Appeals Chamber by the state concerned or the prosecutor, if the state concerned is investigating or prosecuting, or has investigated or prosecuted, the case.[29]

Contrary to the cries of many alarmists in the United States, the election procedures for the eighteen judges also help ensure the independence and integrity of the ICC. Any state party to the Rome Treaty may nominate one candidate, whether the candidate originates in its own state or not, and no two elected judges may be nationals of the same state.[30] Judges are elected by a two-thirds majority of the Assembly of State Parties wherein all states who have signed the treaty participate.[31] Thus states are both represented and closely involved in the Court's processes.[32]

The ICC will, at least initially, be given a limited jurisdiction extending only to war crimes, crimes against humanity, genocide, and, once a definition has been agreed upon, crimes of aggression.[33] With the exception of crimes of aggression, the rest of these crimes already have very wide, comprehensive definitions in the treaty, thus ensuring that the worst crimes will fall within the jurisdiction of the ICC.[34]

A permanent international criminal court to which states have voluntarily given their support is probably what the drafters of the international human rights treaties and conventions envisaged after World War II. However, it is safe to say that none thought that the creation of a permanent international criminal court would take as long as fifty years. After the Nuremberg trials, it seemed that it would follow naturally and not too far behind. Yet it has taken half a century to fill the gaps in humanitarian law, to galvanize political will around the world, and to realize that enforcing humanitarian law is crucial to securing justice, which is in turn indispensable to creating a lasting, stable peace.

CONCLUSION

It should never be forgotten that it is the victims who are central to the pursuit of justice. When the dust settles and the power plays and politicking end, the success or failure of any international tribunal will be judged by the victims themselves. When the ad hoc tribunals were first set up, they were harshly criticized as "fig leaves" designed for no greater purpose than to mask the international community's failure to prevent these crimes in the first place. However, the courts have, against stiff odds, accomplished an immense amount and brought us to the threshold of a new era in the development and enforcement of international humanitarian law.

The tribunals have served different purposes for different people, and their successes also must be judged accordingly. Some may argue that victims do not benefit from developments in international humanitarian law, the establishment of the ICC, or the possibility of lasting peace that comes when justice and accountability help break cycles of violence. I disagree; the need to feel secure is central to human existence, and, to the extent that the enforcement of international humanitarian law can make the world a safer place, it is of the utmost importance to victims. The value of truth, which can bring the added benefits of closure and healing also, should not be underestimated.

In the final analysis, success will, to a large extent, be measured by the number of arrests, prosecutions, and convictions that the international courts secure and ultimately by their deterrent effect on would-be human rights violators. Protecting human rights at an international level is fraught with difficulties and dependent on so many factors beyond the control of any state or individual—political will being the foremost—that it is easy to become disillusioned and cynical. Still, one should always keep in mind that this is an area in which we do not have time to perfect the solutions. We learn from our mistakes, and we try with each new endeavor to save more lives and prevent more destruction.

The world invests high hopes in the ICC, but I would like to sound a word of caution. The protection of human rights at an international level is a collective responsibility and will succeed only as a collaborative effort. This effort requires the commitment of every state and the support of people in every country. When one sees the human capacity for evil in the extreme manifestations that we have witnessed in this century, it is easy to forget the human capacity for compassion. In the tribunals, I have been proud to work with people whose strength of character, moral courage, and conviction have fed my own strong belief that we must work hard to ensure that the next century is not a repeat of the last.

NOTES

*   I would like to express my sincere appreciation to my research assistant, Tashia Jithoo, for the substantial contribution she has made to this chapter. In writing this chapter, I have drawn substantially on the following addresses I delivered, which are used by permission of the publisher: "Justice as a Tool for Peace-Making: Truth Commissions and International Criminal Tribunals" at New York University, January 1997, published in the *New York University Journal of International Law and Politics*, Vol. 28, No. 3 (Spring 1996), pp. 485-503; "The United Nation's War Crimes Tribunals: An Assessment" at the University of Connecticut School of Law, October 1996, published in the *Connecticut Journal of International Law*, Vol. 12, No. 2 (Spring 1997), pp. 227-40; and "50 Years after Nuremberg: A New International Criminal Tribunal for Human Rights Criminals" at Nuremberg, public address, September 1995.

1.   Mr. Justice Robert Jackson, opening speech, in International Military Tribunal, *Trials of the Major War Criminals* (Nuremberg: International Military Tribunal, 1947–1949) Volume 2: *Proceedings 11/14/1945-11/30/1945,* p. 102.

2.   In the period between 1989 and 1996, twenty-two states signed the Genocide Convention, forty-seven states signed the International Covenant on Civil and Political Rights (ICCPR) and thirty-seven signed the First Optional Protocol to the ICCPR. The ICCPR outlines the major civil and political human rights norms. It also provides for enforcement of those norms, setting up a system by which states can bring complaints against other states before the UN Human Rights Commission. The First Optional Protocol allows individuals to bring complaints against states that have ratified the Optional Protocol.

3.   After World War II, the International Law Commission began work on the first of several draft treaties for a permanent international criminal court. The process continued intermittently over the next half century until June 1998, when the United Nations convened the Rome Diplomatic Conference for the Establishment of an International Criminal Court to debate the latest initiative. The following month, a coalition of more than sixty "like-minded" states from all continents, bolstered by partnerships with nongovernmental organizations, brokered a successful conclusion to the five-week conference in the form of a treaty for the statute of an international criminal court. As of April

12, 2000, ninety-six countries have signed the treaty, and eight—Senegal, Trinidad and Tobago, San Marino, Italy, Fiji, Ghana, Norway, and Belize—have ratified it, according to the Coalition for an International Criminal Court, <http://www.igc.org/icc/rome/html/ratify.html>, which tracks signatures and ratifications. The treaty will enter into force the day after the sixtieth instrument of ratification is deposited with the UN Secretary General. Rome Statute of the International Criminal Court, art. 126(1).

4. Exceptions to this general rule did exist, such as the Minority Protection Regime of the interwar period, which obliged signatories to provide minorities with, inter alia, cultural and educational autonomy. The treaties guaranteed minorities protection of life, liberty and religious freedom, and equal treatment before the law. They also made explicit provisions for minorities' rights to establish their own religious, educational, and social institutions. The treaty regime comprised a system of bilateral treaties between the Allied and Associated Powers on the one side and the newly reconfigured states of Central and Eastern Europe and the Balkans on the other side. These treaties, entered into after the end of World War I, were incorporated into the League of Nations regime, providing access to the League's procedures, such as petitioning the League's committee on minorities or gaining access to the advisory opinion jurisdiction of the Permanent Court of International Justice. In this way, although the norms were expressed in terms of bilateral treaties and declarations, they took on a multilateral aspect through their incorporation into the League of Nations (see Henry J. Steiner and Philip Alston, *International Human Rights in Context: Law Politics Morals* [Oxford: Clarendon Press, 1996], p. 89), and could be considered interference by the "international community" within a state's borders.

5. See Airey Neave, *On Trial at Nuremberg* (Boston: Little, Brown, 1979); Telford Taylor, *The Anatomy of the Nuremberg Trials: A Personal Memoir* (New York: Knopf, 1992); Geoffrey Best, *Nuremberg and After: The Continuing History of War Crimes and Crimes Against Humanity* (Reading: The University of Reading, 1984); and Arnold C. Brackman, *The Other Nuremberg: The Untold Story of the Tokyo War Crimes Trials* (New York: Morrow, 1987).

6. After the Nuremberg and Tokyo trials, international criminal law expanded to incorporate new crimes and existing crimes, such as trafficking in people for prostitution in 1950; slavery in 1956; drug trafficking in 1961; and aircraft hijacking in 1970. These offenses were codified and refined partly due to the increased legitimacy of individual responsibility under international law, and partly to respond to the changing needs of the international community because of changing societal conditions.

7. Following a 1987 military rebellion in Argentina, however, Alfonsín limited prosecutions to military officers who held commanding authority (some thirty-four officers) during the period in which the alleged crimes had taken place and pardoned all those convicted for "obeying orders" (more than 1,000). Alfonsin's successor, President Carlos Menem, assumed power in July 1989, and promptly granted a blanket pardon to officers imprisoned for repression in the Dirty War (including all junta members) and those who led uprisings under the Alfonsín government.

8. The two tribunals are separate entities charged with distinct mandates. While both have the power to investigate and prosecute serious violations of international humanitarian law, the jurisdiction of the ICTY is limited—mainly territorially—to violations committed in the former Yugoslavia since 1991 (ICTY Statute, art. 1), whereas that of the ICTR is limited to violations committed in Rwanda between January 1, 1994 and December 31, 1994 (ICTR Statute, art. 1). The ICTY, based in The Hague, Netherlands, and the ICTR, based in Arusha, Tanzania, have separate staffs and trial judges but share a chief prosecutor and appellate judges. While their statutes are almost identical, their substantive provisions refer to different provisions of international humanitarian law, since the ICTY is dealing with an international conflict and the ICTR is concerned with an internal conflict. The European Union and the United States were leaders in the call for the ad hoc tribunals. See Antonio Cassese, "Introduction," *The Path to The Hague*, available from <http://

www.un.org/icty/path.htm#a>. See also, for example, Mirko Klarin, "Nuremberg Now!" *Borba* [Belgrade, Yugoslavia], May 16, 1991.

9. UN Resolution 827, May 25, 1993, reprinted in 14 *Human Rights Law Journal* 197 (1993), p. 127.

10. The Rwandan government, at that time, held one of the nonpermanent seats on the Security Council. With the precedent of the ICTY still recent, there was no difficulty in the Security Council acceding to the request.

11. Conflict in one country may spill over, forcing neighboring countries to deal with many displaced people and refugees. This places a strain on resources and may lead to further violence in the host country.

12. See South Africa Truth and Reconciliation Commission, *Truth and Reconciliation Commission Report* (Cape Town: Truth and Reconciliation Commission, 1998); Kader Asmal, *Reconciliation Through Truth: A Reckoning of Apartheid's Criminal Governance* (Cape Town, South Africa: Mayibuye Books, 1996); Paul Lansing and Julie King, "South Africa's Truth and Reconciliation Commission: The Conflict Between Individual Justice and National Healing in the Post-Apartheid Age," *Arizona Journal of International and Comparative Law*, Vol. 15 (1998), p. 753; and Emily H. McCarthy, "South Africa's Amnesty Process: A Viable Route Toward Truth and Reconciliation," *Michigan Journal of Race and Law*, Vol. 3 (1997), p. 183.

13. TRC Final Report, Vol. 1, paragraph 54, available from <http://www.truth.org.za/final/execsum.htm>.

14. Although the decision was generally well received, human rights organizations have criticized the decision on the basis that the House of Lords found that Pinochet was only liable for acts committed after 1988, the date on which Great Britain adopted the UN Torture Convention. But Human Rights Watch hailed the October 8, 1999, decision of a British magistrate to commit Pinochet to extradition to Spain. The decision strengthened the conspiracy to commit torture charge. London Magistrate Roland Bartle specifically ruled that Pinochet's conduct before 1988—which would include the creation of the secret police and the establishment of Operation Condor targeting Pinochet's opponents abroad—could be examined in proving the conspiracy. See the Human Rights Watch Pinochet Decision Update No. 2, <http://www.hrw.org/press/1999/oct/update1099.htm >.

15. An example is Guatemala, after a peace treaty between the government and the armed opposition was signed in 1996.

16. Jackson, opening speech, *Nuremberg Trials,* p. 98.

17. *Prosecutor v. Tadic,* No. IT-94-1-T (Yugo. Tribunal, Trial Chamber, August 10, 1995).

18. In the former Yugoslavia and Rwanda, rape was used as an instrument of genocide, with the intent of demoralizing and destroying communities, impregnating victims in the hope of "diluting" their ethnicity and driving people away from their homes.

19. *Prosecutor v. Jean-Paul Akayesu,* September 2, 1998, ICTR.

20. The ICTR makes this clear.

21. The apartheid era in South Africa can be dated from the late 1940s, when the government began enacting legislation aimed at entrenching white supremacy in South Africa, starting with the Prohibition of Mixed Marriages Act 1949. The TRC's mandate, however, ran only from 1960 to 1994; see the Preamble to the Promotion of National Unity and Reconciliation Act, No. 34 of 1995. This period encompasses the last—and possibly the bloodiest—chapter of South Africa's struggle for decolonization and equality, which began with the Sharpeville Disaster of March 21, 1960, where many people were killed by government forces for protesting the pass laws, which required nonwhites to carry passbooks and present them on demand to the police. It ends with Nelson Mandela's inauguration as president of South Africa on May 10, 1994.

22. UN Doc. S/PV.3453, p. 14 (1994).

23. The Rwandan representative said that these countries "need not be named"; Ibid., p. 15.

24. The ICTR has had more success, with forty-four of the fifty-two persons indicted by the Rwanda Tribunal brought into custody by early 2000. This may be attributable to two factors: The military defeat of the perpetrators of genocide in Rwanda made it much easier to arrest those remaining in Rwanda, and the cooperation of the Rwandan and neighboring governments with the ICTR aided extradition.

25. Although the Rome Statute was accepted, in principle, by 120 states, there were only ninety-six signatories, as of April 12, 2000.

26. Rome Statute of the International Criminal Court, July 17, 1998, art. 15.

27. Ibid., art. 16.

28. See ibid., arts. 17 and 18. Article 17(2) provides that state is considered unwilling if its decision not to prosecute or investigate is made for the purpose of shielding the person; if there is an unjustified delay that is inconsistent with an intent to bring the person concerned to justice; or if the proceedings are not being conducted independently or impartially. In deciding whether a state is considered unable to investigate or prosecute, the Court considers whether, due to a total or substantial collapse or unavailability of the national judicial system, the state is unable to obtain the necessary evidence and testimony or to otherwise carry out its proceedings.

29. Ibid., art. 18(2)(b), (6).

30. Ibid., art. 36.

31. Ibid., art. 36(6)(a).

32. Ibid., art. 36(2), provides that the eighteen elected judges should represent the major legal systems of the states that are party to the Treaty and should display an equitable geographical representation as well as a fair representation of both genders.

33. Ibid., art. 5.

34. Ibid., arts. 5 to 8.

PART III

Human Rights Policy Ideas, Institutions, and Instruments

Human Rights Organizations:
A New Force for Social Change

KENNETH ROTH

Kenneth Roth is the Executive Director of Human Rights Watch, a post he assumed in 1993 after serving as the organization's deputy director since 1987. Human Rights Watch monitors and promotes human rights in some seventy countries worldwide. Mr. Roth, a lawyer and former prosecutor, has conducted numerous human rights investigations and published widely on human rights issues.

Although the language of the Universal Declaration of Human Rights has not been altered in the half century since its adoption, its operational significance has changed dramatically. [1] The role of governments, the scope of beneficiaries, and the strength of rights defenders today have been expanded considerably from what they were half a century ago. Indeed, they have grown significantly in the past decade alone.

No longer can governments claim to be the sole judge of their human rights record; rights are now understood to permit independent scrutiny of governmental conduct. No longer are the holders of rights understood as limited to political elites; rights are now understood to embrace all people, including those outside the political mainstream.

Much of this evolution in the strength and scope of rights is due to the rapid proliferation of nongovernmental organizations (NGOs) devoted to the defense of human rights. Far more than simple collections of concerned citizens, these groups have developed considerable expertise in mobilizing information and coordinating alliances across national boundaries to build intense pressure on governments to protect human rights in their foreign and domestic policies. Examples of their power include recent work to highlight atrocities in Kosovo and the Democratic Republic of Congo, as well as campaigns to ban antiper- . sonnel land mines and create an International Criminal Court.

RIGHTS AS LIMITS ON GOVERNMENTAL ACTION

So much has changed that it is difficult to read the Universal Declaration now and recall the far more limited meaning that most attributed to it at its adoption. For example, while the Declaration imposes certain obligations on governments, many governments claimed for years that they alone were the judges of their own compliance. Dictatorial governments regularly rejected criticism of their human rights records as "interference" in their "internal affairs." Pressure to end abuse from other governments was, at first, rare. Even the United Nations (UN) Commission on Human Rights, for much of its early existence, would not publicly name the governments that violated international standards. Under this original, narrow conception, the Universal Declaration was effectively unen- forceable—a set of duties that each government, if so inclined, upheld on its own.

Today human rights are well established as the legitimate concern of all humanity. Governments regularly comment on each other's human rights practices and make respect for human rights an important factor in their aid relationships. Regional human rights bodies have been set up in Europe, Africa, and the Americas.[2] Major UN operations to protect rights are mounted, if belatedly, in places such as Bosnia, Kosovo, and Rwanda. Even international financial institutions and multinational corporations have shown increasing sensitivity to human rights concerns. Sovereign governments retain the primary duty to respect rights, but it is widely accepted today that any failure on their part is the legitimate concern of the international community.

Governments sometimes still claim that human rights criticism interferes in their internal affairs. Yet even China, once a frequent proponent of that argument, has accepted the legitimacy of international scrutiny by signing the two major treaties that codify the rights of the Universal Declaration. China has even criticized human rights violations by other countries.[3] Similarly, within the Association of Southeast Asian Nations (ASEAN), traditionally a stalwart partisan of "noninterference" on human rights matters, President B. J. Habibie of Indonesia and President Joseph Estrada of the Philippines protested the detention of former Malaysian deputy premier Anwar Ibrahim.[4] These developments demonstrate the growing recognition that people have a legitimate interest in upholding human rights standards everywhere.

THE RIGHTS OF "EVERYONE": WHO IS PROTECTED?

Since its inception, the Universal Declaration has come to protect the rights of an increasingly broad range of people. The Declaration was deliberately written in sweeping language. Article 2, for example, affirms that "everyone" is entitled to its rights and freedoms. For many years, however, the international human rights movement understood its cause more narrowly. Although the Declaration was born of the horrors of the Holocaust, it was implemented at the height of the cold war and, in its early years, was applied primarily for the benefit of political dissidents and governmental opponents. The human rights movement embraced the Soviet intellectual battling a monolithic and repressive system, the Latin American or Asian opposition figure standing defiant against the generals, or sworn enemies of apartheid threatened by a pariah regime. Yet it said little about the great mass of people who suffer violation of their rights not because of their immersion in politics but because of discrimination, police abuse, mistreatment in custody, indiscriminate warfare, and the like. The broad language of the Universal Declaration fairly embraces these people, but for many years it was rarely invoked for their defense. In this sense, the Declaration was for a long time "universal" far more in the breadth of governments it addressed than in the range of people it protected.

Expanding the scope of human rights protection has not been easy. For example, when the human rights movement began to address the rights of women or to defend civilians from indiscriminate violence in time of war, some critics within the movement feared that this risked diluting the stigma of being identified as a human rights violator. They argued that taking on issues of land mines, violence against women, or indiscriminate shelling of civilians might weaken the movement's ability to defend the jailed newspaper editor or the tortured opposition figure.[5]

Today the claim that the Universal Declaration indeed embraces "everyone" is far more credible, but the turning point came relatively recently. It was not until the Vienna World Conference on Human Rights of 1993 that many in the human rights movement genuinely endorsed the slogan that "women's rights are human rights."[6] It was not until the horrors of the genocide in Bosnia that the movement broadly accepted that the Universal Declaration's assertion of the "right to life" could be understood to incorporate international humanitarian law and thus impose limits on military force in time of war.[7] It was not until the advent of the global economy that many international groups began defending the right of workers to organize.[8] It was only in recent years that the international movement devoted serious attention to the rights of children, common prisoners, and gays and lesbians, and to economic, social, and cultural rights.[9]

THE HUMAN RIGHTS MOVEMENT: WHO ARE THE PROTECTORS?

The expanded scope of human rights protection has been driven largely by a third major development since the adoption of the Universal Declaration: the growth of the human rights movement itself, that is, of nongovernmental organizations (NGOs) devoted to developing and applying international standards on human rights. The human rights movement did not begin with the Declaration. Precursors can be found in the campaigns to abolish slavery, to grant women the right to vote, and to alleviate suffering in time of war. Among the earliest human rights groups were the British and American Anti-Slavery Societies of the nineteenth century, the International Woman Suffrage Alliance of the early twentieth century, and the International Committee of the Red Cross, established in 1863. Following World War II, NGOs lobbied for the inclusion of language on human rights in the UN Charter and for the adoption of the Universal Declaration, but there was as yet little in the way of a formal human rights movement.

Since then, however, there has been a veritable explosion in the number and breadth of organizations devoted to human rights, particularly since the 1970s. That is when human rights groups began to emerge in Asia in reaction to repressive governments in Korea, Indonesia, and the Philippines. The Helsinki Accord of 1975, affirming "the right of the individual to know and act upon his rights," helped launch the human rights movement in the Soviet bloc.[10] Human rights groups emerged throughout Latin America in the 1970s and 1980s in opposition to death squads and "disappearances" under right-wing dictatorships. Much of Asia in the 1990s has seen a stunning proliferation of human rights groups. While growth has been slower in Africa and the Middle East, human rights organizations have established a firm presence in all but the most repressive countries. In many places human rights defenders still face persecution, often severe. Ten were killed for their work in 1999 alone, and in one of these cases, two family members were killed as well.[11] Yet despite the danger, this growing movement has become a powerful new source of pressure to uphold human rights. It is the major reason why today the Universal Declaration has so much greater practical breadth and significance than it did fifty years ago.

Over time, the human rights movement has helped create a new kind of NGO. Many human rights organizations today serve not just to amplify the voice of their members but also to collect and deploy information strategically. This role would not have been possible if human rights ideals did not speak so directly to the people of the world. It is only against the backdrop of popular values that human rights information has an impact. Because of these widely shared values, the human rights movement has an influence far beyond its numbers: By uncovering human rights crimes, it can expose their authors to public condemnation.

Moreover, in the 1990s, new communications technologies such as the Internet helped human rights organizations go beyond addressing countries one by one, enabling them to launch global campaigns such as those to ban land mines, establish an International Criminal Court (ICC), end the use of child soldiers, and curb the transfer of small arms.[12] The coalitions thus assembled have transcended national boundaries and built a genuinely worldwide movement for human rights.

The reality that people around the globe now assert their rights has helped to underscore the universality of the rights proclaimed in the Universal Declaration. As the "interference in our internal affairs" argument loses its punch, many governments have sought to take refuge in the claim that human rights are a concept that is alien to their cultures. Variations of this argument can be found in the assertion of an "Asian concept of human rights," the appeal for "African solutions to African problems," the argument that Islam provides the only true basis for human rights, and the U.S. government's distrust of international standards.[13] The emergence of human rights organizations in all parts of the world undercuts these arguments. It shows that rights are not a "foreign imposition" but that people everywhere aspire to the same basic dignity and respect that the rights of the Universal Declaration protect.[14]

THE CHALLENGES AHEAD

Despite its growing strength, the human rights movement has hardly ended serious human rights abuse. There has been much improvement in the last fifty years in most countries of the former Soviet bloc, Latin America, and southern Africa, as well as parts of Asia. But serious problems persist: many governments still resist applying the Universal Declaration to all their people. Repressive governments continue to run such countries as Burma, China, Iraq, North Korea, Saudi Arabia, and Turkmenistan. Abusive warfare is carried out in such places as Afghanistan, Algeria, Colombia, Kosovo, and Sudan. Even genocide, that most universally condemned crime, has been committed in the last decade of the twentieth century, in Bosnia and Rwanda.[15]

It is a sad truth that governments and warring parties always will be tempted to violate human rights as a means to secure power. Why tolerate a nettlesome opposition when it can be jailed? Why suffer criticism of poor political performance when it is possible to divert public attention by attacking an unpopular minority? Why risk losing social or economic privilege if discrimination can keep challengers down? Why spare civilians the hazards of war if slaughtering them might weaken the enemy's will to fight? The human rights movement cannot promise to end such abuse, but it can generate pressure on governments and insurgents to resist the temptation to violate rights. The goal is to increase the cost of abuse and thus to alter the political calculations that might lead to human rights violations.

There will never come a time when the human rights movement can afford to "wither away"; that is no more likely than finding a permanent solution to the problem of crime. The temptation to violate rights always will exist. Vigilance and activism always will be necessary to counter that threat. But the remarkable growth of the human rights movement means that the defense of human rights will be far more vigorous and effective than it was when the Universal Declaration was adopted.

THE HUMAN RIGHTS MOVEMENT: SOURCES OF STRENGTH

In the last half of the twentieth century, seven factors have enabled the human rights movement to become such a substantial force: the human rights ideal, better communications technology, the press, the policies of influential governments, the development of international standards, the partnership between local and international human rights groups, and the growing professionalism of the human rights movement itself.

The strength of the human rights ideal is a necessary starting point in analyzing the power of the human rights movement. The values codified in the Universal Declaration are at the core of what it means to lead a complete and fulfilled human life. People fortunate enough to live in countries that respect the Universal Declaration in all its dimensions enjoy the freedom and means to live life to its fullest. They are able to speak their minds, practice the religions of their choosing, meet with their compatriots, be treated fairly by their government, and enjoy access to the necessities of life. These ideals are universally sought.

Second, modern communications technology is essential for human rights activists to be able to inform the public of events in faraway places. Earlier human rights movements needed decades to build public consciousness of even such a broadly condemned evil as slavery. It would have been impossible to mobilize public outrage against isolated atrocities, such as a massacre on distant shores, if word could travel no faster than the speed of a sailing ship. Technological developments such as the telegraph, the telephone, radio, television, fax machines, and the Internet have successively enhanced the ability of human rights activists to scrutinize distant conduct and generate a popular response quickly enough to make a difference.

New communications technology also has rendered governmental efforts to restrict the flow of information increasingly futile. Just a decade ago, Western human rights groups were smuggling primitive fax machines to Soviet dissidents who wanted to disseminate their reports more efficiently. Today the Internet is rendering traditional forms of censorship obsolete. For example, in September 1998 Human Rights Watch put a bulletin on its Web site about the political crackdown in Malaysia, including information that was not widely available in the Malaysian press. In the next two weeks 28,000 people visited the page, mostly from Malaysia itself. By allowing cheap and efficient communication, the Internet also enhances cooperation among human rights activists worldwide, a key factor in the global campaigns to ban antipersonnel land mines and to establish an International Criminal Court.[16]

Third, and related, growing press interest has played a significant role in advancing the human rights cause. It is a sign of the strength of the human rights movement that, today, no government wants to be known as a human rights violator. That is hardly to say that no government violates human rights, but every government does try to hide its abuse. Being seen to respect human rights has become an important part of a government's legitimacy before its own people and the international community. Press coverage of abuses can stigmatize and delegitimize a government before its public and peers. Governments will go to great lengths to avoid that fate.

The press is also important for mobilizing action to curtail human rights violations. It does little good for activists to learn of serious abuse if they cannot disseminate that information widely to stimulate action by the general public and sympathetic governments. When the press covers atrocities, the exposure tends to elicit demands from the public that its representatives in government use their influence to end those atrocities. Indeed, government officials often treat press coverage as a surrogate for the public's reaction and may be moved to action even before the public itself actually demands it.[17]

The press has proven a reliable ally of the human rights movement. In the movement's infancy, the press was willing to report on the investigations and concerns of human rights organizations. Over time the press itself began looking into and reporting on human rights problems. Today human rights issues comprise a substantial part of international press coverage and an increasing part of local news.

Human rights organizations themselves have aided and encouraged this expanding press coverage. Most effective is human rights reporting that personalizes an issue, analyzes its context and causes, and suggests a solution; these are both interesting angles for the press and important ways of demonstrating to the public that something can be done to stop human rights abuse. Human rights activism on behalf of the right to a free and independent press also has helped to give journalists in some countries the freedom they need to address controversial issues, including human rights.

Indeed, it is ironic that human rights reporting has become so common that some press outlets no longer consider many accounts of human rights abuse to be "newsworthy" in themselves. A challenge facing the human rights movement is that of finding new ways of making human rights concerns seem newsworthy, for example, by linking them to the policies of governments closer to home. Someday the Internet may allow the human rights movement to communicate with and mobilize large numbers of people directly, without the need to operate through formal press channels. Yet even with the Internet's many benefits, the greater visibility of the traditional press—its ability to demonstrate to government officials that the public is learning about important human rights issues—remains a big advantage.

A fourth key asset in the fight for human rights has been the willingness of many influential governments to make the protection of human rights an important part of their foreign policy. For example, in part in response to U.S. support for the brutal 1973 coup in Chile, the U.S. Congress enacted laws in the 1970s requiring many forms of government-to-government assistance (other than those serving basic human needs) to be cut off or redirected if a government engages in a systematic pattern of gross violations of human rights.[18] These laws have been honored more often in the breach than in the observance, as is evinced by the fact that Israel, Egypt, and Turkey are among the largest recipients of U.S. aid, despite their systematic practice of torture and other serious abuses. Nonetheless, the laws set standards by which U.S. aid policy can be judged.[19] At times campaigns by human rights organizations have led the United States to end aid relationships with abusive governments or to exert pressure on governments to curtail abuses in order to maintain their aid. The gradual diminution of U.S. aid to various African tyrants in the 1990s—Mohamed Siad Barre of Somalia, Samuel Doe of Liberia, Mobutu Sese Seko of Zaire—was due at least in part to pressure from human rights groups. So was the gradual cutoff of U.S. aid to the UNITA rebel group in Angola. Even when U.S. aid to an abusive government persisted, as it did to El Salvador in the 1980s, pressure from human rights groups to comply with U.S. law forced the U.S. government to put pressure on the Salvadoran government to curtail abuses in order to minimize the political scandal in the United States surrounding El Salvador's receipt of military assistance.

In addition, the U.S. State Department's *Country Reports on Human Rights Practices,* a global survey of human rights conditions produced under congressional mandate,[20] has been a useful tool for putting the U.S. government on record about human rights abuses and stigmatizing offending governments (although these reports have been too little heeded in making U.S. policy). The European Union, too, has adopted the practice of making its aid and cooperation agreements formally conditional on the beneficiary's respect for human rights,[21] while the Japanese government's declared policy is that human rights are a factor in determining its overseas development assistance.[22]

International human rights organizations therefore devote much time and energy to exerting pressure on these influential governments to live up to their declared policies and to use their diplomatic and economic clout on behalf of human rights. If these governments refuse, they can be subjected to the same stigmatization efforts as are used against abusive governments. Moreover, if an influential government turns its back on serious human rights abuse, that policy itself can become news, and the debate about the policy can be used to spotlight the abuses far more effectively than if the press were asked to report on them without a local "news hook."

A fifth factor in the effectiveness and credibility of the human rights movement has been the elaboration of international human rights law and standards. Why, one might ask, should an abusive government listen to the demands of an international human rights organization that may be located a continent or an ocean away? What legitimacy does an international human rights organization have to address distant human rights concerns? The answer lies in the movement's application of internationally recognized human rights standards.

While the Universal Declaration of Human Rights speaks in nonbinding language, its principles have been codified in two binding treaties introduced by the United Nations in 1966: the International Covenant on Civil and Political Rights and the International Covenant on Economic, Social and Cultural Rights. These Covenants entered into force ten years later, making many of the provisions of the Universal Declaration of Human Rights binding on the scores of countries that have ratified them. Regional treaties also have been adopted for Africa, Europe, and the Americas, as have specialized treaties addressing the rights of women, children, refugees, and workers, and the problems of torture, racial discrimination, and wartime abuses.[23] This legal framework enables international human rights organizations to point not just to their own values but to standards that have broad international endorsement.

Human rights groups deserve some credit for the development of international human rights law. They have helped to draft treaties and have been instrumental in interpreting them and giving them life. Because international law is relatively underdeveloped in comparison with most domestic systems, its violation does not yet always carry the same stigma: Whereas a domestic criminal offense usually is regarded as cause for opprobrium, violation of international law may seem less wrong because of the complexity and novelty of the international legal order. By portraying publicly the devastation caused to individual victims of abuse, however, human rights groups add a human dimension that gives flesh and urgency to the legal abstractions of international law.

Human rights organizations also have helped to extend moral judgments beyond the obvious original meaning of a law. For example, the drafters of the Universal Declaration probably would have said that common crime falls outside its scope. However, human rights organizations, looking at the problem of domestic violence against women, saw a link.[24] While an act of domestic violence might not itself violate human rights standards, official indifference to the problem on the part of police, prosecutors, and judges can be said to violate international standards against discrimination on grounds of gender. By suggesting that this official indifference amounted to complicity in the abuse, the human rights movement helped to expand the meaning of international law to embrace this important but neglected problem. Similarly, years of campaigning by the human rights movement has promoted acceptance of the view that the right to an "effective remedy" for human rights violations requires not simply granting the victim the opportunity to pursue civil damages but, for the most serious abuses, official investigation of the crime, followed by punishment of the perpetrators.

The human rights movement has also led the lawmaking effort by bringing humanitarian problems to international attention and proposing new laws to address them. The successful campaign to ban antipersonnel land mines and the current campaign to end the use as soldiers of children under eighteen years of age are good examples.[25] The tremendous strides made in recent years in convincing the public that multinational corporations should respect human rights standards—although the relevant international standards apply formally only to governments, not to the corporations themselves—illustrate the human rights movement's capacity to build moral consensus even in the absence of law.[26]

A sixth key factor in the growing success of the human rights cause has been the effective partnerships forged in dozens of countries between international and local human rights organizations.[27] Local organizations are best positioned to mobilize local opposition to human rights abuse and to insist on change. Given governments' preoccupation with maintaining power, these local voices tend to have the greatest resonance. An abusive government wants to avoid being denounced before its citizens or having its disregard for human rights spark demonstrations and public protests. For that reason, however, many local activists have themselves become targets of abuse and repression: Many have been killed, and many more have faced persecution.

Because of this danger, international human rights organizations place their highest priority on trying to protect the local human rights activists who are on the front line. Any attack on a human rights monitor gives rise to fierce denunciations and intense pressure on the offending government. In this way, international human rights organizations work to create and maintain the political space that local activists need to function.

As local organizations are able to operate more freely, they, in turn, provide invaluable assistance to international groups, ranging from logistical assistance in identifying witnesses and navigating difficult terrain, to strategic assistance in selecting topics for inquiry, shaping investigations, fashioning recommendations for policymakers, and planning advocacy campaigns. The partnership between local groups, with their superior knowledge of local conditions, and international groups, with their global perspective and access to the international press and policymakers, has been a powerful one.

The final important ingredient in the success of the human rights cause has been the growing professionalism and expertise of the movement itself. It has not been enough for human rights organizations simply to express outrage at abuse or to issue calls for others to rally to the cause. Abuses are usually too distant from the lives of people outside the country where human rights violations are committed to be much of a priority. Even if people are moved to address abuses, few know what can be done to curtail them. The human rights movement has had to build and channel outrage, which are tasks of considerable complexity.

Generating outrage is, of course, not a matter of creating opinions out of thin air, because, as noted, widely shared values underpin the human rights ideal. But making potential outrage manifest can be complicated: Human rights activists must identify and speak with victims of abuse, analyze their plight under relevant standards, determine who is responsible, suggest ways to improve the situation, and generate the political will to see these steps taken. Doing this requires linguistic skills, familiarity with the country, competence in conducting investigations, knowledge of human rights standards and issues, links with others in the human rights movement, analysis of policy options in various capitals, experience in dealing with the press, and the ability to mobilize popular demands for action.

An example is the problem of bonded child labor in India. Investigations must be conducted in the face of considerable resistance from local businesses and governments. Local and international journalists must be convinced to write about an issue that may seem intractable and thus not "newsworthy." Only by enabling the general public to "meet" specific children who are victims of this terrible practice can the human rights movement transform a general dislike of an abstract concept into active repulsion and a desire to do something about it.[28] Even then it is not obvious what should be done. Who can generate pressure on the Indian government to confront the problem? How can remedies be devised that will not make things worse for the children? Who will finance these remedies? How can external pressure be mobilized? In short, even after exposing a human rights violation, extensive policy research must be done so that the outrage of the general public and sympathetic governments can be channeled in useful directions.

To complicate matters further, a single investigation and report is rarely enough to make a difference. Often governments will decide simply to ride out a wave of bad publicity, unless a second, third, or fourth report is issued and the government realizes that its public relations problem will not go away until it addresses the human rights problem at its core. Often governments will attack the messenger, which is why careful, scrupulously objective reporting is so important. Even when a government agrees to change, ongoing monitoring is needed to ensure that officials live up to their promises. This scenario is repeated for each country and each issue that a human rights organization takes on.

Sustaining this effort is a complicated, expensive endeavor. It can be done only by attracting and training a staff of professionals willing to devote their talents to the cause. It also requires the financial support of those who recognize that just adding their voices on behalf of human rights is not enough, since without the expertise of the modern human rights movement it would be difficult to direct those voices effectively. In this way, the human rights movement has helped to create a new kind of NGO: not simply an organization that amplifies the voices of its members by enabling them to speak in unison, but an organization that allows its members and supporters to collect and deploy information strategically in a way that would have been beyond the capacity of any of them individually.

Some have asked whether, in contrast to an NGO that simply directs the voices of its members, a human rights–style NGO presents a problem of accountability. To whom is such an NGO accountable, if not to its members? The answer lies in the nature and source of its power: Because such an organization can use the process of stigmatization only against the backdrop of broadly shared values, and because the stigmatization process must be highly visible to be effective, human rights NGOs cannot stray far from the basic values of the human rights cause without losing their effectiveness and subjecting themselves to public criticism. Indeed, this highly public form of accountability is arguably stronger than the theoretical accountability exerted on a classic NGO by its members, many of whom may not have the time, inclination, or knowledge to scrutinize lower-profile activities.

HOW A MODERN
HUMAN RIGHTS ORGANIZATION OPERATES

Recent work by my organization, Human Rights Watch, on the Democratic Republic of Congo (DRC) and Kosovo, and recent international campaigns in which we have been involved opposing antipersonnel land mines and promoting the creation of an International Criminal Court serve to illustrate the role of the modern human rights organization.

The Democratic Republic of Congo (Former Zaire)

The Rwandan-led invasion of Zaire that brought President Laurent Kabila to power in Kinshasa was accompanied by attacks on Rwandan Hutu who had taken refuge in camps in the eastern part of the country. The camps housed not only genuine refugees but also *génocidaires*—those responsible for the 1994 Rwandan genocide. The attacking forces allowed safe passage back to Rwanda for those who agreed to repatriation but attacked all those who fled west across Zaire, including many women, children, and elderly people, without regard to whether they were armed or not, and without any proof of their involvement in the Rwandan genocide.[29] An estimated 200,000 people were missing after the attacks and presumed dead.[30] Most Western governments, including the United States, were eager to make peace with the new Congolese government, which was seen to offer stability and economic opportunity. They were disinclined to allow concern with the slaughter of exiles and refugees to stand in the way of warm relations. However, human rights organizations, including Human Rights Watch, were determined that those responsible for this slaughter be held accountable.

Human Rights Watch pursued two different approaches to the problem, one involving international policy, the other on-site fact-finding. The first is illustrated by the story of Roberto Garreton, the UN Special Rapporteur for Zaire since 1994.[31] A respected human rights lawyer from Chile, Garreton was, in April 1997, outspoken in calling the world's attention to the massacre of Hutu refugees from Rwanda, even as the killing was under way. His efforts exemplified the early warning function that the United Nations (UN) says it aspires to provide. Garreton's effectiveness drew the ire of Kabila's new government, which insisted that he be replaced. Seeing the entire matter of the refugee massacres as an unwelcome complication, the U.S. government agreed and encouraged the UN to oust Garreton. Apparently neither the United States nor the UN saw any reason to insist that Kabila respect the principle that abusive governments not select their own investigators, even though several months later the United States would almost go to war with Iraq over its attempt to replace UN arms inspectors.[32]

Upon learning of the plans to dismiss Garreton, Human Rights Watch publicized and denounced the move. The European and U.S. press, able to connect distant events in Congo to policies closer to home, gave the story a high profile. The United States and the UN backed down, and Garreton retained his position. Revelation of this weak commitment to establishing accountability for the slaughter of refugees forced the U.S. government and the UN to adopt a more supportive posture toward investigation of the killing.

Kabila still refused to cooperate, denying that killings had occurred. UN investigators sent to Kinshasa faced numerous governmental obstacles to their work. While the UN investigation stalled, Human Rights Watch quietly sent its own investigator into the country. With the unobtrusive help of local activists, he was able to retrace part of the path of the westward-fleeing Hutu. Speaking with witnesses and photographing remains, he assembled a detailed chronology of the massacres along a particular stretch of road.[33] When published, this account—the most complete to date—made headlines.[34] Because primary responsibility for the killing seems to lie with the invading forces of the current Rwandan government—a close U.S. ally—progress remains slow. But because it is now undeniable that massacres occurred, pressure persists for those responsible to be brought to justice.

Kosovo

Attacks by Yugoslav and Serbian forces on ethnic Albanian villages had, by September 1998, led to the forced displacement of more than 250,000, including some 50,000 who had taken refugee in Kosovo's hills and forests and faced death by starvation and exposure if they could not return home safely before winter descended. However, it had become clear that the international community would feel little pressure to end the violence against civilians unless the attacks could be shown to have exceeded what was necessary to combat the rebel Kosovo Liberation Army. Two Human Rights Watch investigators were sent to Kosovo at the time with the aim of investigating the tactics of this counterinsurgency effort. Traveling through the war zones, they uncovered two massacres. In one, eighteen people, mostly women, children, and elderly people, had been slaughtered near a stream where they had taken refuge. The other involved the interrogation, torture, and execution of thirteen unarmed men who had been lured down from the hills. As a result of Human Rights Watch's investigation, these massacres, too, made headlines and helped to change the public image of the war.[35] The public outrage helped to push the North Atlantic Treaty Organization (NATO) to threaten Yugoslav President Slobodan Milosevic with military force, which in turn convinced him, temporarily, to pull back his troops and permit the insertion of an international monitoring force.

But this shaky stalemate quickly broke down. After the failure of the Rambouillet peace accords, NATO launched its bombing campaign against Serbia on March 24, 1999. The Yugoslav army and Serb special police in Kosovo intensified their policy of "ethnic cleansing" in the region, provoking the flight of some 800,000 Kosovar Albanians before a peace deal was struck; NATO bombing was halted, and Yugoslav troops withdrew in June. Human Rights Watch researchers were among the first independent observers to document massacres and other atrocities committed by Yugoslav forces. Within three days of the onset of NATO bombing, the researchers began interviewing Kosovar refugees as they fled across the Albanian and Macedonian borders. By interviewing independent refugees separately about the atrocities they had experienced or witnessed, the researchers were able to assemble the most complete accounts then available of the slaughter, rape, and massive displacement being carried out by Yugoslav and Serbian troops. The disclosures helped to generate pressure on the international community to come to the assistance not only of the relatively fortunate ethnic Albanians who had found refuge outside Kosovo but also of those left behind whose lives were in profound jeopardy.[36]

The evidence collected also was forwarded to the International Criminal Tribunal for the Former Yugoslavia. In April 1999 the Tribunal indicted President Slobodan Milosevic for war crimes and crimes against humanity committed by troops under his command in Kosovo, the first indictment by an international tribunal of a sitting head of state. Of the seven episodes of mass murder listed in the indictment, six had already been investigated and reported on by Human Rights Watch researchers.

Land Mines

While most human rights work focuses on one country at a time, human rights NGOs have shown themselves increasingly able to address global issues as well, as the campaign to ban antipersonnel land mines illustrates. The land mine campaign was launched when several NGOs, including Human Rights Watch, Handicap International, and the Vietnam Veterans of America Foundation, began collecting data on the devastation that land mines inflict on noncombatants even long after armed conflict ceases. Each year these indiscriminate weapons kill or maim thousands of civilians in such war-torn countries as Angola, Bosnia, Cambodia, and Mozambique.[37] Human Rights Watch and others began documenting the appalling scope of the problem and encouraging the press to write about it.[38] Eventually a surge of popular outrage was generated. Unlike most human rights work, which proceeds one country at a time, banning antipersonnel land mines required a global solution; an active outreach effort ultimately brought together more than 1,000 NGOs in some sixty countries under the banner of the International Campaign to Ban Land Mines (ICBL).

The ICBL was opposed by the governments of the United States and other major powers, which were not eager to give up a widely used weapon despite its humanitarian costs. The Clinton administration sought various exceptions to an absolute ban that would have allowed it to continue deploying land mines.[39] Ordinarily, given the influence of the United States, it would have prevailed. NGOs, however, worked to bring together an unprecedented coalition of small and medium-sized governments from the developed and developing world, dedicated to an unconditional ban on antipersonnel land mines. Some were governments that traditionally had a strong moral component to their foreign policy, such as Canada, Norway, and Austria. Others were from lands that had been blighted by land mines, including Mozambique and South Africa. NGOs provided these allied governments with the expertise and public outreach needed to defend an unconditional ban. In recognition of this important role, governmental proponents of a land mine ban insisted that representatives of the ICBL be granted access to final treaty negotiations and the right to comment on deliberations, the first such involvement by an NGO in any arms control or humanitarian law negotiation.

NGO participation significantly affected the terms of the debate. For example, when the Pentagon claimed that land mines were necessary to save the lives of American soldiers, NGOs issued a report showing that one-third of

American casualties in the Vietnam war were caused by land mines;[40] when the Pentagon sought to exempt as "submunitions" certain antipersonnel land mines that were used in combination with antitank mines, NGOs revealed that the Pentagon had already classified these weapons as antipersonnel mines in its own internal communications; when the Pentagon claimed that land mines were necessary to defend South Korea, NGOs recruited fourteen retired American generals and an admiral to rebut this claim; and when the Clinton administration sought to change the subject by pledging money to remove mines already in place, NGOs highlighted the inadequacy of the plan: without a ban, land mines could still be produced for as little as $3 each, while removing a single land mine costs as much as $1,000.

As of early 2000, these arguments have not yet convinced the U.S. government to support a land mine ban, but they provided ample reason for most of the rest of the world to leave Washington behind on this issue. In December 1997, at a conference in Ottawa, Canada, a broad coalition of governments adopted the Mine Ban Treaty.[41] Since then more than 130 governments have signed the Treaty, and when it entered into effect on March 1, 1999, 65 governments had ratified it, far more than the 40 needed for it to take effect. Washington, feeling the heat, has begun to destroy some of its stockpiled land mines and has made a conditional pledge to sign the treaty by the year 2006, but it still refuses a closer embrace of the Treaty. Meanwhile, many of the NGOs that campaigned for the land mine treaty have launched a new global partnership to monitor compliance with it.[42]

The International Criminal Court

A similar tale of global NGO cooperation lies behind the treaty concluded in Rome in July 1998 to establish an International Criminal Court (ICC). The ICC, which will be launched once sixty governments ratify the Rome Statute, will be available to prosecute and to punish the world's most ruthless human rights criminals—those responsible for genocide, war crimes, and crimes against humanity—whenever national judicial systems fail.[43]

As in the case of land mines, the U.S. government and several other major powers sought to weaken the proposed ICC. Some opponents, such as India and Mexico, objected to any strengthening of mechanisms to enforce human rights. The Clinton administration, while endorsing the ICC in theory, was preoccupied with precluding any possibility, however remote, that an American might be brought before the Court without the U.S. government's consent. The administration went so far as to appeal to militaries with a long history of abuse, in countries such as Guatemala, to inject themselves into the debate. This act was an astonishing demonstration of willingness to undermine civilian rule in fragile transitional states just to forward the parochial goal of protecting American servicemen from a theoretical possibility of prosecution for war crimes.

Washington's obstructionism was far more problematic for the ICC negotiations than for the land mine ban. Even if Washington never joins the land mine ban, a strong norm against the use of these indiscriminate weapons still can be created. But many fear that the ICC cannot succeed without the financial, diplomatic, and military backing of the world's most powerful nation. Building a strong coalition committed to a strong and independent ICC is thus essential.

NGOs have played a central role in this process. As in the land mine campaign, they helped forge a coalition of some sixty governments from the developed and developing world. These governments included not only established democracies that are usually supportive of human rights enforcement, such as Canada and Norway, but also a range of governments, such as South Africa, Argentina, and South Korea, that recently had begun the transition from authoritarian to democratic rule and appreciated the importance of an institution of justice that would remain beyond the coercive reach of abusive forces in their countries.

Maintaining the cohesion of this "like-minded group," as it called itself, was not easy in the face of intense pressure from Washington. NGOs provided crucial expertise, both at a series of preparatory conferences and during the Rome negotiations. By educating delegates from smaller countries, NGOs helped them make their concerns heard, thus breaking the traditional dominance of the discussion by the large delegations of the major powers. By issuing press statements geared toward wavering countries, NGOs also made sure that delegates had popular backing to stand up to U.S. pressure. By revealing that various U.S. efforts to weaken the Court were really efforts to exempt Americans from its reach, NGOs helped to transform the debate into one of principle— equal justice for all—rather than power politics.

While most U.S. efforts to undermine the Court were rebuffed successfully, not all were, and the Court thus will be weaker than it might have been. Still, it is a Court worth fighting for. Over the next several years, NGOs will be at the forefront of efforts to secure the sixty ratifications needed to establish this historic institution.

PERSISTENT CHALLENGES
FOR HUMAN RIGHTS ORGANIZATIONS

As powerful as the human rights movement has become, it is hardly assured of victory in any given case. Certain countries and issues remain stubbornly resistant to the human rights methodology. Some governments are so powerful economically that classic forms of pressure have little impact; Saudi Arabia is an example. Sometimes the human rights movement faces powerful political antagonists, such as the opposition of much of the international business community to forceful advocacy of human rights in China. Geopolitical calculations still lie behind the tolerance of abuses in certain countries, such as the U.S. government's lenient attitude toward persistent atrocities in Rwanda.[44] A cultural tradition of certain forms of abuse can make it difficult to stigmatize a government, as in the case of the repression of women in some Muslim countries.[45] Certain highly repressive governments, such as that of Burma, have prevented the emergence of the local partners that the international human rights movement needs to be most effective. Some elected governments, such as that of Colombia, successfully deflect international opprobrium in part because they are viewed as "democracies" and hence assumed, however falsely, not to commit serious human rights violations. Certain issues are more resistant to the tools of the human rights community—for example, ending repression in Iraq may ultimately require military force—while other issues, such as those involving certain economic and social rights, have complicated causes and solutions and cannot be solved easily even where public pressure creates political will to do so.

Of course, steps still can be taken to overcome these obstacles, but they are not easy. In some cases, efforts at public stigmatization can be stepped up. In other cases, new sources of economic or diplomatic pressure can be generated. New allies can be found and innovative partnerships built. But even with such heightened efforts, the human rights methodology is not foolproof. Indeed, we should not expect it to be. The methodology was developed as a way of enforcing rights when traditional resort to a legal system fails. Given the fallibility of many legal systems in protecting rights, even with the coercive power of the state at their disposal, one would hardly expect the less direct methodology of human rights organizations to guarantee success. But it does greatly increase the likelihood that, even in the absence of a functioning legal system, people will have some prospect of securing their rights.

A SOLID DEFENSE OF HUMAN RIGHTS

Many, many things remain to be done to build a solid defense of human rights. Despite the recent rapid proliferation of human rights groups, most are small, underfunded, and nearly overwhelmed by the enormous tasks before them. With powerful governments and institutions often opposed to its work, the human rights movement desperately needs strengthening.

There is also a need to expand the possibilities for enforcing human rights norms. The ICC is still several years from being established, and it will address only the most severe forms of abuse. More consistent pressure in support of human rights is needed on the part of the most influential governments and institutions, particularly the United States, the European Union, the Japanese government, the World Bank, and the United Nations. The business community, with its rapidly expanding influence in a global economy, also must be convinced to avoid complicity in human rights abuse.

Perhaps most important, further progress needs to be made in mobilizing popular support for the human rights cause. Too many people see human rights as the concern only of others. While the success of the human rights movement in attracting press coverage has effectively turned the press into a surrogate constituency, that very success has, paradoxically, engendered complacency that hampers efforts to mobilize a real constituency. Ways need to be found to teach more people about serious human rights problems and how they can press for their correction. Overcoming the parochial views that today are dominant in Washington is particularly important in this regard. Completing the process of making the Universal Declaration a truly universal document in practice, applied for the benefit of all people, also will help broaden the human rights constituency.

It is remarkable how far the human rights movement has come since the Declaration's adoption, but this is hardly a moment to savor success: The challenges are too great and too urgent. What is needed is much more of the hard work and perseverance that have characterized the work of human rights organizations over the half century since the high ideals of the human rights cause were summarized in the Declaration. There is too much to do ahead to spend much time contemplating the past.

NOTES

1. The United Nations General Assembly adopted the Universal Declaration of Human Rights (UDHR) on December 10, 1948, to codify the rights that the then-new world organization had pledged to promote in its Charter. The document details the proposition, still novel at the time, that there are limits to what sovereign states can do to their people. It describes in broad terms the rights that were later detailed in two legally binding treaties, the International Covenant on Civil and Political Rights (ICCPR) and the International Covenant on Economic, Social and Cultural Rights (ICESCR). Both treaties were adopted by the UN General Assembly on December 16, 1966, and took effect, respectively, on January 3 and March 23, 1976.

2. Regional organizations include the European Commission and Court of Human Rights, the Inter-American Commission and Court of Human Rights, and the African Commission on Human and People's Rights. See chapters 5, 6, and 7 in this volume.

3. China signed the IESCR on October 27, 1997, and the ICCPR on October 5, 1998. In July 1998, at the annual meeting of ASEAN (the Association of Southeast Asian Nations) foreign ministers, Chinese Foreign Minister Tang Jiaxuan raised the matter of violence against ethnic Chinese in Indonesia with Indonesian Foreign Minister Ali Alatas. On August 3, 1998, he expressed his concerns about these attacks on a visit to Hong Kong. On the same date, the front page of the official Chinese *People's Daily* demanded justice for Indonesia's ethnic Chinese population.

4. Habibie and Estrada made their protests at a meeting in Batam, Indonesia, in October 1998.

5. The author learned that key representatives of a major U.S.-based foundation involved in human rights funding, as well as a U.S.-based international human rights organization, subscribed to this view as recently as the early 1990s.

6. This ubiquitous slogan at the World Conference was endorsed by both the governmental and nongovernmental final declarations. See Vienna Declaration and Programme of Action (June 1993); Written Report by the General Rapporteur, Manfred Nowak, as adopted by the Final Plenary Session of the NGO Forum (June 1993).

7. For example, until the Bosnian conflict one major foundation sought to dissuade Human Rights Watch from monitoring violations of international humanitarian law.

8. Human Rights Watch, for example, began its program on the human rights responsibilities of multinational corporations in 1995.

9. Human Rights Watch launched a project to defend the rights of common prisoners in 1988 and a project to defend the rights of children in 1994. It adopted a policy on economic, social, and cultural rights in 1996. Its first full report on abuses against gays and lesbians, *Sexual Orientation and Criminal Law in Romania*, was published in 1998. See also *Human Rights Watch World Report 2000*, pp. 482-485 (chapter on lesbian and gay rights).

10. The Helsinki Accord, in part a security pact among the North Atlantic Treaty Organization (NATO) and Warsaw Pact countries, also included a range of human rights guarantees. For a history of the Accord and the "Helsinki" movement it spawned in the Soviet Union and Eastern Europe, see William Korey, *Human Rights and the Helsinki Accord: Focus on U.S. Policy* (New York: Foreign Policy Association, 1983); Thomas Buergenthal, ed., *Human Rights, International Law, and the Helsinki Accord* (Montclair, NJ: Allanheld, Osmun, 1977); Helsinki Watch, *From Below: Independent Peace and Environmental Movements in Eastern Europe and the USSR* (New York: Human Rights Watch, 1987).

11. Three were killed in Colombia and one in each of Russia, Northern Ireland, Uzbekistan, Sri Lanka, and Cambodia. In Kosovo, one human rights defender was killed along with his two sons. See *Human Rights Watch World Report 2000*, pp. xxvii-xxviii.

12. See <http://www.icbl.org> (land mines); <http://www.igc.apc.org/icc> (ICC); <http://www.child-soldiers.org> (child soldiers); <http://www.iansa.org> (small arms); <http://www.hrw.org/campaigns> (Human Rights Watch's role in these campaigns).

13. An example of a cultural relativist attack on the universality of the human rights cause can be found in Makau wa Mutua, "The Banjul Charter and the African Cultural Fingerprint: An Evaluation of the Language of Duties," 35 *Virginia Journal of International Law* 339 (1995); he argues for African solutions to African problems. David Kelly and Anthony Reid, eds., *Asian Freedoms: The Idea of Freedom in East and Southeast Asia* (New York: Cambridge University Press, 1998), provides an overview of the debate about human rights in Asia. Amartya Sen, "Human Rights and Asian Values," *The New Republic*, July 14, 1997, pp. 33-40, responds to those in the Chinese government who champion "Asian values" to justify authoritarian rule. I discuss the U.S. government's reluctance to be bound by evolving human rights standards and institutions in Roth, "Sidelined on Human Rights," *Foreign Affairs*, March/April 1998; and "The Court the U.S. Doesn't Want," *The New York Review of Books*, November 18, 1998.

14. Further evidence is found in chapter 2 and chapter 4 in this volume.

15.   For a summary of conditions in these countries, see *Human Rights Watch World Report 2000* (New York: Human Rights Watch, 1999); Amnesty International, *Annual Report 1999* (London: Amnesty International 2000); U.S. Department of State, *Country Reports on Human Rights Practices for 1999* (Washington: U.S. Department of State, 2000). For accounts of the Bosnian genocide, see Chuck Sudetic, *Blood and Vengeance: One Family's Story of the War in Bosnia* (New York: Norton, 1998); David Rohde, *Endgame: The Betrayal and Fall of Srebrenica* (New York: Farrar, Straus, and Giroux, 1997); David Rieff, *Slaughterhouse: Bosnia and the Failure of the West* (New York: Simon and Schuster, 1995); Laura Silber and Allan Little, *Yugoslavia: Death of a Nation* (New York: Penguin Books, 1995); Jan Willem Honig and Norbert Both, *Srebrenica: Record of a War Crime* (New York: Penguin USA, 1997); Norman Cigar, *Genocide in Bosnia: The Policy of "Ethnic Cleansing"* (College Station: Texas A&M University Press, 1995); Human Rights Watch, *Bosnia-Hercegovina: The Fall of Srebrenica and the Failure of U.N. Peacekeeping* (New York: Human Rights Watch, 1995); Helsinki Watch, *War Crimes in Bosnia-Hercegovina*, Vols. 1 and 2 (New York: Human Rights Watch, 1992, 1993); and the series of articles by Mark Danner in *The New York Review of Books*, November 20, December 4, December 18, 1997, February 5, February 19, March 26, April 23, and September 24, 1998. For descriptions and analyses of the Rwandan genocide, see Human Rights Watch (Alison DesForges), *Leave None to Tell the Story: Genocide in Rwanda* (New York: Human Rights Watch, 1999); Alain Destexhe, *Rwanda and Genocide in the Twentieth Century* (New York: New York University Press, 1995); Gerard Prunier, *The Rwanda Crisis: History of a Genocide* (New York: Columbia University Press, 1995); Philip Gourevitch, *We Wish to Inform You that Tomorrow We Will Be Killed with Our Families: Stories from Rwanda* (New York: Farrar, Straus, and Giroux, 1998).

16.   The Web site of the International Campaign to Ban Land mines is <http://www.icbl.org>; that of the Coalition for an International Criminal Court is <http://www.igc.apc.org/icc/>. Overcoming the U.S. government's opposition to these efforts required building a global coalition of governments with the confidence and sense of safety in numbers necessary to challenge the world's "sole remaining superpower." Critical to building that governmental coalition was the construction of a parallel global coalition of NGOs. Keeping this coalition informed and engaged might have been prohibitively expensive without the innovation of e-mail.

17.   This was true in the case of Kosovo, as I explain later.

18.   Among the forms of assistance restricted by these laws are military assistance, arms sales, other forms of security assistance, budgetary support, and development assistance made directly through a government that does not address basic human needs. See sections 116 and 502B of the Foreign Assistance Act of 1961, as amended. These laws also require the U.S. representative to international financial institutions to vote against loans to governments that engage in a systematic pattern of gross violations of human rights, again with the qualification regarding basic human needs. See section 701 of the International Financial Institutions Act. See also chapter 12 in this volume.

19.   See the accounts of the human rights practices of Israel, Egypt, and Turkey and other nations in the annual *Human Rights Watch World Report*. One manifestation of the U.S. government's poor compliance with these laws is the so-called Leahy Amendment, which prohibits U.S. military assistance to particular military units involved in human rights abuse. Such aid already is prohibited by general human rights laws, but because of the U.S. government's reluctance to cut off aid to its allies, this narrower prohibition was passed with the hope that at least it would be complied with.

20.   These reports are submitted annually to Congress by the State Department in compliance with sections 116(d) and 502B(b) of the Foreign Assistance Act of 1961, as amended, and section 505(c) of the Trade Act of 1974. *Country Reports* were first submitted to Congress in 1977, covering 82 countries. In 1999 they covered 194 countries. They are available

online on the State Department Web site: <http://www.state.gov/www/global/human_rights/hrp_reports_mainhp.html>.
21. See, for example, chapter 5 in this volume; or Barbara Brandtner and Allan Rosas, "Human Rights and the External Relations of the European Community: An Analysis of Doctrine and Practice," *European Journal of International Law*, Vol. 9, No. 3 (1998). For example, EU Council Regulation No. 443/92 of February 25, 1992, addresses financial and technical assistance to, and economic cooperation with, the developing countries in Asia and Latin America, requiring the Community to attach a high priority to "the promotion of human rights, [and] support for the process of democratization [and] good governance."
22. Japan's Official Development Assistance (ODA) Charter, adopted by the Japanese government at a Cabinet meeting held in June 1992, outlines four basic principles, including: "To pay full attention to efforts for promoting democratization and introduction of a market-oriented economy, and the situation regarding the securing of basic human rights and freedoms in the recipient country." See the Ministry of Foreign Affairs of Japan Web site for the ODA Charter, <http://www2.nttca.com:8010/infomofa/policy/oda/>.
23. The leading regional treaties are the European Convention for the Protection of Human Rights and Fundamental Freedoms; the American Convention on Human Rights; and the African Charter on Human and Peoples' Rights. Specialized treaties include the Convention on the Elimination of All Forms of Discrimination Against Women; the Convention on the Rights of the Child; the Convention and Protocol Relating to the Status of Refugees; the Convention Against Torture and Other Cruel, Inhuman or Degrading Treatment or Punishment; the International Convention on the Elimination of All Forms of Racial Discrimination; and the Geneva Conventions of 1949 and Their Additional Protocols of 1977.
24. See, for example, Americas Watch and Women's Rights Project, *Criminal Injustice: Violence Against Women in Brazil* (New York: Human Rights Watch, 1991); *The Human Rights Watch Global Report on Women's Human Rights* (New York: Human Rights Watch, 1995), pp. 341-409 (describing domestic violence as a human rights issue in Brazil, Russia, and South Africa).
25. In March 1999 the 1997 Mine Ban Treaty became binding international law, having been signed by 135 nations and ratified by 65. The Nobel Peace Prize–winning International Campaign to Ban Land Mines (ICBL) was instrumental in securing this treaty. Human Rights Watch is a founding member of the ICBL and a member of the Coordinating Committee of the Campaign. Human Rights Watch is also helping to lead the International Coalition to Stop the Use of Child Soldiers, which calls for an international ban on the recruitment of children under the age of eighteen into armed forces.
26. For example, manufacturers of footwear and clothing were among the first to respond to pressure, in part because their advertising depends on a corporate image that would be damaged by association with a reputation for exploiting sweatshop labor. See, for example, Arvind Ganesan, "Business and Human Rights—The Bottom Line," a Commentary for Human Rights Watch <http://www.hrw.org/advocacy/corporations/index.htm>. The movement has benefited from advocacy campaigns on college campuses across the United States that have led to much attention in the press. Recent Human Rights Watch reports on the human rights responsibilities of businesses include: *The Price of Oil: Corporate Responsibility and Human Rights Violations in Nigeria's Oil-Producing Communities* (1999); *The Enron Corporation: Corporate Complicity in Human Rights Violations* (1999) (India); and *Columbia: Human Rights Concerns Raised by the Security Arrangements of Transnational Oil Companies* (1998).
27. See, for example, Adhoc, Licadho, and Human Rights Watch, *Impunity in Cambodia: How Human Rights Offenders Escape Justice* (New York: Human Rights Watch, 1999).
28. For an account of the problem, see Human Rights Watch, *The Small Hands of Slavery: Bonded Child Labor in India* (New York: Human Rights Watch, 1996).
29. For a description of the attack, see Human Rights Watch, *Democratic Republic of the Congo: What Kabila Is Hiding* (New York: Human Rights Watch, 1997).

30. The estimate can be found in the UN High Commissioner for Refugees, *State of the World's Refugees 1997*, p. 23.

31. Special Rapporteurs are appointed upon a vote of the UN Commission on Human Rights.

32. For a synopsis of these events, see *Human Rights Watch World Report 1998* (New York: Human Rights Watch 1997), pp. 33-34

33. The photographs can be seen at: <http://www.hrw.org/reports97/congo/photos.html>.

34. See, for example, Scott Campbell, "What Kabila Is Hiding," *Washington Post*, September 22, 1997; Barbara Crossette, "Rights Report Says Kabila's Troops Are Killing Civilians," *New York Times*, October 9, 1997; David Orr, "Massacres Inquiry Could Open Soon after Kabila Agreement with UN," *Irish Times*, October 27, 1997; "UN Must Make Kabila Come Clean," *Chicago Tribune*, October 12, 1997; Associated Press, "Rwanda Denies It Massacred Hutu," *Orange County Register*, October 11, 1997; Alec Russell, "Troops Loyal to Kabila 'Massacred Hutu Men,'" *The Daily Telegraph (London)*, October 10, 1997; Paul Knox, "Kabila Loyalists Hunted Refugees, Report Says," *(Toronto) Globe and Mail*, October 9, 1997; Colum Lynch, "Group Alleges Armies Tied to Zaire Atrocity: Calls for Probe of Role of U.S.," *Boston Globe*, October 9, 1997; "Rights Group Blames Massacres on Rwandan Army, Kabila Forces," *Baltimore Sun*, October 9, 1997.

35. See, for example, Jane Perlez, "Serb Pullback May Forestall NATO Attack," *New York Times*, October 5, 1998; Jane Perlez, "Survivor of Kosovo Massacre Describes the Killing Garden," *New York Times*, October 2, 1998; Jane Perlez, "Massacres by Serbian Forces in 3 Kosovo Villages," *New York Times*, September 30, 1998; Jane Perlez, "Kosovo Death Chronicles, Serb Tactic Revealed," *New York Times*, September 27, 1998. See also Human Rights Watch, *Federal Republic of Yugoslavia: Humanitarian Law Violations in Kosovo* (New York: Human Rights Watch, October 1998).

36. The findings of these investigations were issued in over fifty "Kosovo Human Rights Flashes" that were distributed widely and posted on the Human Rights Watch Web site, <http://www.hrw.org/campaigns/kosovo98/index.htm>.

37. For a comprehensive overview of the problem, see Human Rights Watch Arms Project and Physicians for Human Rights, *Landmines: A Deadly Legacy* (New York: Human Rights Watch, 1993). For a summary of current efforts to abolish antipersonnel land mines, see International Campaign to Ban Land mines, *Landmine Monitor Report 1999: Toward a Mine-Free World* (New York: Human Rights Watch, 1999).

38. See, for example, Africa Watch, *Landmines in Angola* (New York: Human Rights Watch, 1993); Asia Watch and Physicians for Human Rights, *Landmines in Cambodia: The Cowards' War* (New York: Human Rights Watch, 1991); Americas Watch, *Landmines in El Salvador and Nicaragua: The Civilian Victims* (New York: Human Rights Watch, 1986).

39. For example, the United States sought an exception for troops defending South Korea.

40. Human Rights Watch and Vietnam Veterans of America Foundation, *In Its Own Words: The U.S. Army and Antipersonnel Mines in the Korean and Vietnam Wars* (New York: Human Rights Watch, 1997).

41. The Mine Ban Treaty is formally known as the Convention on the Prohibition of the Use, Stockpiling, Production and Transfer of Antipersonnel Mines and on Their Destruction.

42. Human Rights Watch is Coordinator of the new Landmine Monitor initiative of the International Campaign to Ban Landmines. Landmine Monitor monitors and documents the use, production, transfer, and stockpiling of land mines and monitors victim assistance and demining. Landmine Monitor produces annual reports timed to coincide with the meetings of states parties to the 1997 Mine Ban Treaty. For more information, see the Landmine Monitor reports: <http://www.icbl.org/lm/>.

43. As of early 2000, ninety-six governments had signed the Rome Statute, and there were eight ratifications of the Statute.

44. See *Human Rights Watch World Report 1998* (New York: Human Rights Watch, 1997), pp. 59-66; Kenneth Roth, "Course Correction in Rwanda," *Washington Post*, July 31, 1996.

45. See, for example, chapter 8 in this volume.

ELEVEN

Democracy and Human Rights:
An Argument for Convergence

MORTON H. HALPERIN

Morton H. Halperin has served as Director of the Policy Planning Staff at the U.S. Department of State since 1998. Prior to this position, he was the Senior Vice President of the Century Foundation and directed its Washington office. He has been the Senior Director for Democracy at the National Security Council and Director of the Washington Office of the American Civil Liberties Union. He is the author of a number of books, including *Bureaucratic Politics and Foreign Policy*.

Two views prevail about the relationship between democracy promotion and human rights advancement in the United States, as Thomas Carothers of the Carnegie Endowment pointed out in 1994.[1] One view, widely held by those in the democracy movement, is that the two policies are interlinked; that human rights—particularly political and civil rights, such as the rights to freedom of expression, association, and movement—are "defining elements of democracy." By executing a policy that promotes democracy, therefore, a government simultaneously furthers the cause of human rights. The other view, widely held by those in the human rights movement, is that there is not necessarily any "complementarity" between democracy and human rights policies; that, in fact, democracy promotion programs sometimes take a negative toll on the realization of human rights and therefore should be regarded with skepticism. Some in this second camp point out, for example, that the U.S. embargo against the communist regime of Cuba restricts the free expression, association, and travel guaranteed by Article 19 of the International Covenant on Civil and Political Rights (ICCPR).[2] Furthermore, they contend that the establishment of a democracy may not translate into protection of human rights: democratically elected regimes, such as that of Alexander Lukashenka in Belarus and Alberto Fujimori in Peru, sometimes ignore the constitutional limits on their power, depriving their citizens of basic rights and freedoms.[3]

Both accounts of the relationship between human rights and democracy are partly right. It is true that the elected officials of a true constitutional democracy— which by definition enshrines and guarantees basic civil and political rights—are more likely to advance and protect the human rights of its citizens than the nonelected decision makers in a monarchy or autocracy. It is also true that if a regime comprises freely chosen officials bound by a constitution that protects minority rights, it is easier for groups and individuals, both indigenous and international, to advance a human rights agenda. With the end of the cold war and with it the end of the U.S. government's overeager emphasis on checking the expansion of communism, it is hard to see how promoting the establishment of constitutional democracy could hamper the protection of human rights, or why the democracy and human rights movements should not coordinate their efforts. Yet in the United States, the two movements operate independently from each other and remain deeply divided in their methods and prescriptions. A decade after the fall of the Berlin Wall, it is long past the time to end this division and to bring about a unified community of intellectuals and nongovernmental organizations (NGOs) that reflects the shared objectives of the two movements and develops common approaches. Accordingly, in this chapter I review the origins and focus of the democracy movement, contrast these with the origins and focus of the human rights movement, and argue for their merger into a more effective force.

THE DEMOCRACY COMMUNITY

The very different origins of the democracy and human rights communities play a large role in their ongoing divisions. The modern U.S. democracy movement arose out of the cold war and largely out of the decision of the Reagan administration to take the ideological offensive against communism.[4] In his "evil empire" speech before the British House of Commons in 1982, President Reagan laid out a strategy of democracy promotion.[5] The president declared that the Soviet Union "runs against the tide of history by denying human freedom and human dignity to its citizens," and he outlined a long-term plan for the

United States to follow the lead of many of its allies and assist democratic development abroad. In this way, Reagan said, "the march of freedom and democracy" will continue forward and "leave Marxism-Leninism on the ash heap of history." He also said, "[w]hile we must be cautious about forcing the pace of change, we must not hesitate to declare our ultimate objectives and to take concrete actions to move toward them. We must be staunch in our conviction that freedom is not the sole prerogative of a lucky few but the inalienable and universal right of all human beings. . . . The objective I propose is quite simple to state: to foster the infrastructure of democracy."[6]

While Western democratic governments considered themselves at the forefront of this movement, U.S. policymakers in particular took it for granted that the United States, as the leader of the "free world," would lead the charge to promote and extend democracy; nongovernmental groups played limited roles. However, the Reagan administration's democracy promotion policies also embraced a distinction between totalitarian and authoritarian regimes, characterizing Marxist dictatorships as totalitarian and thus incapable of moving in the direction of democracy, and anti-Marxist dictatorships as authoritarian and therefore more likely to evolve toward democracy.[7] Since the primary targets of this new democratization policy were communist states, the U.S. government, at least initially, placed priority on providing support only to those domestic dissident groups challenging the legitimacy of communist rule, primarily in what was then known as Eastern Europe.[8] The U.S. government ignored similar indigenous efforts in authoritarian countries friendly to the United States.

However, with the end of the cold war and the collapse of the Soviet Union, the U.S. government shifted its emphasis from government assistance to anti-Marxist dissident groups to broader support for civil society within the newly created and fragile democratic states. Seeking to strengthen these nascent democracies and to help create the institutions necessary to preserve and fortify them, U.S. programs focused on conducting free elections, creating an independent judiciary, and increasing the responsiveness of the executive branch, while reducing corruption. For example, post–cold war U.S. policy in Eastern Europe included the 1989 Support for East European Democracy (SEED) Act, which authorized the U.S. government to "undertake a range of activities designed to encourage the establishment of democratic institutions, assist in the development of free market economies, and promote an improvement in the overall quality of life,"[9] and called upon U.S. agencies to emphasize democratization and the social sector in economic assistance programs to the region. As a result, President Clinton announced two new initiatives: the Democracy Network to support nongovernmental groups in advocacy and watchdog work, and social sector assistance programs to help governments develop short- and long-term improvements in unemployment, job creation, and basic social services.[10] John Shattuck, then Assistant Secretary of State for Democracy, Human Rights and Labor, later offered this summary of the Clinton administration's overall democratization efforts before the House Committee on International Relations: "Mr. Chairman, the democracy promotion programs of the United States have four main goals: enhancing respect for the rule of law and human rights; encouraging the development of a politically active civil society; promoting meaningful political competition through free and fair electoral processes; and fostering transparent and accountable governance."[11]

In this endeavor, the democracy movement recognized the importance of private organizations, including political parties, in the effective functioning of democracy, and devoted some of its energy and resources to supporting NGOs. For example, recent efforts by the National Democratic Institute for International Affairs (NDI) in Cambodia include work with the Union of Cambodian Democrats (UCD), a coalition of the four political parties working to restore democracy to Cambodia. NDI is assisting the UCD in its efforts to "articulate a unified coalition platform, to communicate its goals to the international community and to develop a stronger network among supporters in Cambodia and abroad." Since 1995 NDI also has assisted two Cambodian coalitions of NGOs, the Coalition for Free and Fair Elections and the Committee for Free and Fair Elections, to organize civic education and election monitoring programs. Likewise, in 1990, NDI helped the Pro-Democracy Association (PDA), an NGO, in Romania. With NDI's assistance and with funding from the U.S. Agency for International Development (USAID), PDA's network of forty-three local clubs has monitored every local and national election, trained citizens as domestic monitors, conducted candidate debates, and disseminated educational materials to voters around the country. Currently, while NDI "provides technical support and access to international experts" in Cambodia, PDA has "diversified its funding sources and is independently conducting nationwide public awareness campaign to promote greater citizen understanding of electoral legislation and practices" in Romania.[12] Thus, in the words of John Shattuck and Brian Atwood, USAID administrator:

> U.S. democracy assistance helps governments and NGOs in Africa, Central America, the Balkans, the Caucasus, Haiti and elsewhere to institutionalize the rule of law and foster greater respect for human rights, which means building independent judiciaries and public support for their role. These and other institutions are essential to safeguarding basic freedoms, protecting ethnic and religious minorities, promoting decision-making according to rules rather than by fiat, and providing social stability and reliable methods of dispute resolution.[13]

In this way, the democracy movement, now free of the cold war context, has begun assisting other countries and movements, particularly those struggling to establish or reestablish democracy. This assistance includes support for new governments and movements that have overthrown regimes of the right as well as of the left. For example, the International Republican Institute (IRI) organizes town hall meetings in Haiti in order to promote dialogue between elected officials and their electorates; in August 1998 IRI also opened a Political Party Training and Information Center there to train democratic parties. In South Africa, IRI offers local officials training in financial management and budgeting as well as campaigning.[14] The movement assists governments in the conduct of "free and fair" elections, in part by providing international election monitoring. The goal of such international assistance is to ensure that elections are free and fair (and thus "legitimate") and to provide an international "certification" that the country is governed by a democratic regime worthy of international and domestic support.[15]

Therefore, although the targets of U.S. support have broadened since the cold war's end, the democracy movement still looks to established democratic governments to promote and defend these new democracies, especially through U.S. government assistance to the new leaders and the NGOs—and most of all, to the political parties—that play a role in helping the state to function effectively.[16]

The contrast between the democracy movement and the origins and focus of the human rights movement could not be greater.

THE HUMAN RIGHTS MOVEMENT

The human rights movement grew not out of the need to sustain or foster certain governments but rather out of the need to protect individuals.[17] In fact, the leaders of the human rights community in the United States and abroad were deeply distrustful of governments, including democratic governments. They felt that states were driven by ulterior goals and were unwilling, if not unable, to give priority to promoting human rights. Specifically, the human rights community saw that democratic states had been so preoccupied with fighting the international communist movement that they had supported nondemocratic regimes such as that of Mobutu Sese Seko in Zaire, François "Papa Doc" Duvalier in Haiti, and Francisco Franco in Spain, simply because they were not communist and despite the fact that they committed gross human rights abuses. The democracy promoters justified this support on grounds expressed in remarks by Jeane Kirkpatrick, ambassador to the United

Nations during the Reagan administration. She differentiated between "traditional" and "revolutionary" (or communist) autocrats, arguing that "Generally speaking, traditional autocrats tolerate social inequities, brutality, and poverty, whereas revolutionary autocracies create them." Furthermore, Kirkpatrick declared, "Only intellectual fashion and the tyranny of Right/Left thinking prevent intelligent men of goodwill from perceiving the *facts* that traditional authoritarian governments are less repressive than revolutionary autocracies, that they are more susceptible of liberalization, and they are more compatible with U.S. interests."[18] Democratic states often failed to press these regimes to respect human rights out of fear that such pressure would alienate noncommunist governments and encourage local Marxists to engineer coups. Thus, in the view of the human rights movement, democratic governments—and especially the United States—could not be trusted to hold friendly governments to human rights standards.

Unlike the democracy movement, which was born largely as a response to the spread of Marxism, the human rights movement looked beyond the context of the battle against communism to provide support for individuals struggling anywhere in the world for human rights. While dissidents in the Soviet empire were important to the human rights movement, so were citizens who had been deprived of their rights in other nondemocratic states, especially human rights workers. The movement's purview extended to citizens living in nominally democratic states, where individuals might be deprived of basic human rights because they were members of a minority, because their political objectives exceeded those tolerated by the regime in power, or because the criminal justice system operated in ways that violated established norms of human rights. Even full-fledged democracies have not escaped the human rights organizations' spotlight. For example, Amnesty International's October 1998 report on the United States, *Rights for All,* marks the first comprehensive review of the state of human rights in any Western country, and its recent campaign—"USA: Land of the Free?"—focuses on issues of police brutality, ill treatment of prisoners, and executions in the United States.[19] Furthermore, Human Rights Watch made prison conditions in the United States a focus of two September 1998 reports.[20] These examinations of human rights abuses in the United States are the most recent and dramatic manifestations of this concern with the fate of those living in fully established democratic states as well as those in struggling new democracies and nondemocratic countries.

For all of these reasons, the human rights community has focused on strengthening and empowering individuals and NGOs, not governments. Today the movement still devotes its resources to arousing and organizing individuals and private groups so that they will provide financial and material support to individuals and organizations who are struggling—usually *against* governments—to advance human rights.

Although the cold war ended in 1990, the U.S. human rights community remains suspicious of all governments, doubtful that democratic reforms will lead to greater respect for human rights, and skeptical both of Western governmental assistance to fellow states or foreign NGOs and of general efforts to design better government programs.[21] Human rights advocates believe, for example, that the credibility of the indigenous recipients of this assistance will be "contaminated" by their link to the U.S. government, thereby affecting their standing in the local political process. This suspicion of state-linked aid leads most human rights groups to refuse to accept government funds, in contrast to democracy groups, which are supported primarily by government grants and contracts. Human rights leaders in the United States further argue that U.S. assistance to certain state institutions, such as the police or the military, will only strengthen a nondemocratic institution's capacity to commit human rights abuses, as occurred in El Salvador during the 1980s.[22] Rather than advocating the provision of government assistance, they tend to lobby democratic governments to suspend aid or to impose sanctions on governments that abuse human rights. This argument appears in the annual debate over China's most-favored nation (MFN) trading status, and in the remarks of Kenneth Roth, executive director of Human Rights Watch, who testified before the Senate: "The U.S. and other nations claiming to uphold human rights must retain the ability to employ limited and targeted sanctions to express their condemnation of violations, press for a change in abusive government policies, and avoid complicity in abuses."[23]

The international human rights community also has given increased attention to strengthening—and creating—international norms and institutions that are geared to protecting human rights. It presses governments to adhere to international human rights instruments, most notably the International Covenant on Civil and Political Rights, and supports the United Nations human rights organs such as the Human Rights Commission, now headed by Mary Robinson. The most remarkable human rights campaign of this sort was the international effort to create a permanent International Criminal Court (ICC). During the long process leading up to the Rome Conference, and at the Rome Conference itself, human rights NGOs struggled to give the ICC as much independence as possible from control by governments. For example, the Lawyers Committee for Human Rights proposed that: "The International Criminal Court should have automatic (inherent) jurisdiction over the three core crimes. . . . No further state consent should be required for the Court to proceed. . . . the Court should be free from pressure or involvement by the Security Council or any other political body. . . . The Statute should include an unequivocal obligation by states parties to cooperate with the ICC at all stages of the proceedings."[24]

Furthermore, human rights organizations made it clear from the start that they viewed the U.S. government in particular as part of the problem rather than as an indispensable part of the solution.[25] For example, Kenneth Roth wrote that in its opposition to the Court as it emerged from the Rome Conference, the United States aligned itself with "such dictatorships and enemies of human rights as Iran, Iraq, China, Libya, Algeria, and Sudan. It was an embarrassing low point for a government that portrays itself as a champion of human rights."[26] Such leaders did not take seriously the concern of the U.S. government that an international criminal court with broad powers—and the authority to try U.S. military personnel stationed overseas—would make it more difficult to gain the necessary domestic support for any U.S. humanitarian interventions, such as Operation Restore Hope in Somalia in 1992.

Additional philosophical differences divide the democracy and human rights communities. For example, as Thomas Carothers wrote, members of the human rights community believe that the legitimacy of their endeavor rests on international law, such as the International Covenant on Civil and Political Rights, and universal principles; they view democracy as merely a political ideology and its promotion as a uniquely American endeavor. Democracy promoters, in contrast, believe that because constitutional democracy protects basic civil rights, one can find an evolving "right to democratic governance" based on the same international laws upon which human rights activists base their efforts.[27] To demonstrate the universality of democracy promotion, they point to international efforts such as the Institute for Democracy and Electoral Assistance, based in Stockholm, and the Organization for Security and Cooperation in Europe (OSCE), whose Office for Democratic Institutions and Human Rights (ODIHR) is active in monitoring elections and developing national electoral institutions.

The two communities also disagree over priority. Many human rights activists believe that the short-term need to address serious abuses such as torture should outweigh the long-term goal of creating conditions that will enable the establishment of a democracy. Democracy activists, in contrast, argue that only a firm constitutional democracy can truly and consistently protect against human rights violations; they thus approach the problem of such abuses from what they perceive as the root cause rather than the symptom.

AN ARGUMENT FOR CONVERGENCE

In arguing that the two communities would strengthen the struggle for democracy and human rights around the world if they sought a convergence of views and cooperated with each other, I start with the assumption that each of the approaches and the critiques each has of the other have some merit.

Although they perhaps overstate the democracy movement's focus on elections, human rights advocates are certainly correct in arguing that the mere staging of democratic elections does not guarantee a respect for rights. They are also right in pointing out that even citizens of mature constitutional democracies are unlikely to enjoy all of the rights that are "guaranteed" to them by international human rights documents or rapidly developing notions of international "common law." It is also true that U.S. democracy promotion policies—particularly those of the Reagan administration toward Central America—have at times paid insufficient attention to the human rights abuses carried out by elected regimes. Three members of the U.S. Congress who visited Central America in January 1981, for instance, agreed that: "We believe very strongly, on the basis of our own conversations with refugees, and after consultation with others genuinely familiar with the recent history of El Salvador, that by far the greatest responsibility for violence and terrorism rests with those forces now receiving U.S. guns, helicopters, grenades and ammunition."[28] More recently, individuals criticized the Clinton administration for confusing support for democracy in Russia with support for Boris Yeltsin, arguing that the U.S. government had been thus "implicitly condoning Moscow's crimes in Chechnya."[29]

Furthermore, human rights activists are wise to suspect the motives of all governments, to recognize that even democratic regimes often give priority to other strategic objectives, and to argue that the U.S. government is less strenuous in objecting to human rights abuses in democratic countries and in nondemocratic countries that are friendly to the United States. For this reason, activists' encouragement of support for NGOs and individuals is certainly important.

At the same time, democracy advocates are correct in believing that there is a fundamental difference between constitutional democracies, no matter how imperfect, and authoritarian governments. Human rights groups make a fundamental strategic error when they write off democratic states, especially the United States, as potential allies in strengthening human rights efforts around the world, as they did far too soon in the development of the International Criminal Court. Today the United States is unlikely to place the undue emphasis on superficial elections that it sometimes did during the cold war. It is not that the United States always takes the "right" position, but surely it often does, and its leadership can be crucial to success.

While the individuals and organizations that make up the democracy movement and the human rights movement almost always see themselves as part of just one movement or the other, and while the level of cooperation and support between the two is low, some individuals are active in both movements. Thus it might be possible for the two movements to engage in extensive discourse, for each to heed the legitimate criticisms offered by the other, and for both to forge agreement on some common elements.

First, for example, the two movements could agree that there is a fundamental distinction between constitutional democracy and all other regimes, and recognize that no state fully respects the individual rights of its citizens or gives the highest priority to protecting human rights in other countries. Over time, the only way to ensure a permanent improvement in the respect for the human rights of any individual or group is to ensure that they live in a constitutional democracy. The key internal elements of such a regime include periodic free and fair elections, the right of political dissent, respect for individual and minority rights, freedom from arbitrary police power, due process in the criminal justice system, and the establishment of an independent judiciary that is capable of enforcing these rights.[30] The key external elements include an acceptance of international guarantees of human rights, including adherence to the various international covenants and membership without reservation in the ICC and in regional judicial bodies.

In this area, the two communities have much more in common than they acknowledge. For example, many of the concerns that human rights activists have expressed with regard to Burma—repression of the National League of Democracy, virtual detention of opposition leader Aung San Suu Kyi, arrest and imprisonment of protesters, and persecution of Muslims—are shared by democracy advocates.[31] The U.S. government also recognized the common goals of democracy promotion and human rights protection, when, in 1994, the Bureau of Human Rights and Humanitarian Affairs was reorganized and renamed as the Bureau of Democracy, Human Rights and Labor, "reflecting both a broader sweep and a more focused approach to the interlocking issues of human rights, worker rights, and democracy."[32]

Therefore, the democracy and human rights movements should unite over the goal of establishing *de jure* human rights for every individual by working to establish a right under international law of all people to live in a constitutional democracy; such a regime would, in turn, accept the growing body of international human rights standards and international, regional, and domestic enforcement mechanisms. In this context, these communities should point to the failure of the United States to respect international human rights norms at home, especially as they relate to children and criminal justice. Both should support U.S. civil rights and liberties groups in raising this issue.

Second, the democracy and human rights movements should agree to accept the importance of strengthening democratic institutions in established democracies, of assisting in their establishment in new democracies, and of supporting efforts to create them in nondemocratic states.[33]

In the short run, the pursuit of constitutional democracy will require different strategies and tactics in different countries. In states that are functioning democracies, the two communities should join together in efforts to strengthen democratic institutions, such as the independent judiciary and legislature, and to provide support to NGOs, including but not limited to human rights groups. International and foreign NGOs should not devote their inevitably scarce resources to major efforts to change the behavior of democratic governments. This does not mean that such states should have a free ride or escape the monitoring called for by international institutions. It does mean, however, that where a state provides relative freedom to indigenous groups that promote civil and minority rights, the primary role of international and foreign human rights and democracy organizations should be to provide support and legitimacy to the local groups.

In states that are struggling to establish and maintain democracy, the two communities should attempt to assist that process by bringing pressure to bear on the transitional governments, by supporting those groups leading the struggle for democracy, and by lobbying on behalf of those issues that will most likely support the transition. We should examine the human rights community's traditional focus on freeing political prisoners with this goal in mind. In some situations, when pressure from abroad to free such prisoners appears to be the most effective way to support the transition to democracy, this issue should be stressed. However, if greater leverage on the transition process can come from stressing other issues in the short run, such as the right to form political parties, then the human rights groups should pursue this approach. Often both routes can be pursued at once, but there are always issues of priority and emphasis.

The two groups also should join forces to prevent armed forces and other groups from "stealing" democratic elections by preventing the election winners from taking power or by removing them in a coup. To this end, the human rights organizations should heed the proposals of democracy promoters, who urge—and who should urge more forcefully—that the crime of "stealing a democratic election" be added to the list of crimes that are considered to be of universal jurisdiction (i.e., slavery, genocide, piracy, etc.), as well as to those that are subject to the jurisdiction of the permanent ICC (i.e., genocide, war crimes, and crimes against humanity).

In states where democracy is not a realistic possibility in the short term, the two communities should emphasize that even authoritarian regimes must respect human rights, while they simultaneously provide assistance, to the degree that it is possible or helpful, to the forces struggling to bring about democracy. Those who tend to focus on democracy rather than human rights need to accept the fact that protecting human rights will not only help human rights in the short term but also will often effectively stimulate a transition to democracy in the medium term, by making it possible for those seeking change to express their views without fear of disappearance or harassment.

Finally, a word needs to be said about the role of the U.S. government. Democracy groups have too easily accepted the notion that the U.S. government is the leader of the democracy movement and needs to be supported in its efforts. They also have shied away from challenging practices in the United States that violate international norms of behavior (i.e., capital punishment for juveniles) and from criticizing the Senate's accustomed practice of lodging reservations to provisions in international human rights covenants that otherwise might be used to challenge the activities of the federal, state, or local governments (i.e., provisions that govern the treatment of juvenile criminals). Clearly, Americans must come to understand that establishing a world of democratic states governed by the rule of law means that the United States must be willing to subject itself and its citizens to the same rules that we seek to impose on others.

At the same time, human rights advocates should call a halt to the dangerous trend of viewing the U.S. government as at best irrelevant and at worst an enemy of the promotion of human rights. For example, Human Rights Watch's Kenneth Roth has argued that by blocking international treaties such as those prohibiting the use of antipersonnel land mines or child soldiers, Washington has become an obstacle to the development of international human rights law.[34] While the human rights movement should call full attention to the American double standard, it also should show that it understands that the degree and type of human rights abuse in any U.S. state is nowhere near as egregious as in Kosovo, China, and Saudi Arabia. U.S. human rights groups should focus their energy and resources to attempting to bring the United States along in support of domestic human rights initiatives, for example by strengthening their Washington presence. Differences of views on how to promote democracy and human rights, whether in China, Burma, Nigeria, or anywhere else, should be treated as just that—disagreements as to the means that will be most effective—and as evidence that the United States *is* interested in the end of protecting human rights.

International bodies devoted to promoting or protecting human rights require the active participation of the United States in order to be their most effective. We must not allow euphoria over the willingness of traditional U.S. allies to challenge the positions of the U.S. government on certain human rights issues (i.e., those associated with establishing the ICC and the ban on land mines) to obscure this fact. Neither armed interventions to protect against the most extreme human rights abuses, as occurred in Haiti and, belatedly, in Bosnia and Kosovo, nor the organization of effective economic sanctions against an oppressive or illegal regime or its leaders will be possible in most situations without the leadership of the U.S. government.

Our objective must be to develop a common human rights–democracy agenda that has the active support of both the human rights and the democracy communities and, to the degree possible, of the U.S. government as well as other governments. We owe no less to those struggling to protect their rights.

NOTES

* This chapter was completed before the author joined the U.S. Department of State as Director of the Policy Planing Staff in December 1998.

1. Thomas Carothers, "Democracy and Human Rights: Policy Allies or Rivals?" *Washington Quarterly,* No. 17 (Summer 1994), pp. 109-20.

2. *Human Rights Watch World Report 1998* (Washington, DC: Human Rights Watch, 1997), p. 112.

3. See Fareed Zakaria, "The Rise of Illiberal Democracy," *Foreign Affairs,* No. 76 (November/December 1997), pp. 22-43; and Robert D. Kaplan, "Was Democracy Just a Moment?" *Atlantic Monthly,* No. 280 (December 1997), pp. 55-80.

4. Groups active in the U.S. democracy movement include: Freedom House, the National Endowment for Democracy, Center for International Private Enterprise, Free Trade Union Institute, International Republican Institute, and National Democratic Institute for International Affairs.

5. President Ronald Reagan, Speech, House of Commons (June 8, 1982), in *Public Papers of the Presidents of the United States: Ronald Reagan 1982,* Vol. 1 (Washington, DC: U.S. Government Printing Office [U.S. GPO], 1983), pp. 742-48.

6. Ibid.

7. See Arthur M. Schlesinger, Jr., *The Cycles of American History* (Boston: Houghton Mifflin Company, 1986), p. 104.

8. The National Endowment for Democracy describes its work thus in its brochure: "With its annual congressional appropriation, it [NED] makes hundreds of grants each year to support prodemocracy groups in Africa, Asia, Central and Eastern Europe, Latin America, the Middle East, and the former Soviet Union. . . . Much of the Endowment's work in the New Independent States of the former Soviet Union is carried out in cooperation with groups in Central Europe that were instrumental in moving previously totalitarian societies toward democracy;" <http://www.ned.org> (October 1998). See also U.S. Public Law 98-164, 98th Cong., 1st sess. (November 22, 1983), for the legislation creating the National Endowment for Democracy.

9. Congress passed the Support for East European Democracy (SEED) Act (PL101-179), November 28, 1989.

10. U.S. Department of State, *Dispatch* (Washington, DC, August 28, 1995), first appearing in U.S. Department of State, *Dispatch* (Washington, DC, July 1994).

11. John Shattuck, Assistant Secretary of State for Democracy, Human Rights and Labor, speaking for U.S. democracy promotion in Asia to the U.S. House of Representatives Committee on International Relations (September 17, 1997).

12. Description of NDI activities in Cambodia and in Romania, <http://www.ndi.org>.

13. John Shattuck and J. Brian Atwood, "Defending Democracy: Why Democrats Trump Autocrats," *Foreign Affairs,* No. 77 (March/April 1998), pp. 167-70.

14. Description of IRI activities in Haiti and South Africa, <http://www.iri.org>.

15. Many elected leaders recognize the importance of democracy and international certification to the flow of international aid. For example, former coup leader Hun Sen publicly recognized that the Cambodian election in July 1998 was a means to win back international aid. Robin McDowell, AP *Worldstream,* July 28, 1998. This relationship between aid and elections is frequently reinforced by members of the international community; in 1997, for example, the Group of Eight concluded its summit by declaring that international aid to the Democratic Republic of Congo would depend on the new leaders "demonstrating their commitment to democratic reform, including elections." "Summit Leaders Clash over Environment," *Deutsche Presse-Agentur,* June 22, 1997.

16. John Shattuck, Assistant Secretary of State for Democracy, Human Rights and Labor, statement before the Committee on Appropriations, Subcommittee on Foreign Operations, U.S. House of Representatives (April 1, 1998).

17. Amnesty International, which was established in 1961, is illustrative of this movement toward the protection of individuals. Its "Brief History" states that "Amnesty International members work on behalf of individuals, not to change political systems." Amnesty International focuses on obtaining the release of "prisoners of conscience," which it defines as people "imprisoned solely because of their political or religious beliefs, gender, or their racial or ethnic origin, who have neither used nor advocated violence;" <http://www.amnesty.org>. Other groups active in the U.S. human rights movement include Human Rights Watch, International Human Rights Law Group, The Lawyers Committee for Human Rights, and Physicians for Human Rights.

18. Jeane Kirkpatrick, *Dictatorships and Double Standards* (New York: Simon and Schuster, 1982), p. 49 (emphasis in the original).

19. Amnesty International, *Rights for All,* <http://www.rightsforall-usa.org>. The report was published on October 6, 1998. See also Amnesty Campaign, "USA: Land of the Free?" <http://www.amnesty.org.uk>.

20. Human Rights Watch, *Locked Away: Immigration Detainees in Jails in the United States,* Vol. 10, No. 1 (New York: Human Rights Watch, September 1998); and Human Rights Watch, *Nowhere to Hide: Retaliation Against Women in Michigan State Prisons,* Vol. 10, No. 2 (New York: Human Rights Watch, September 1998).

21. See discussion in Carothers, "Democracy and Human Rights: Policy Allies or Rivals?" and see, for example, Aryeh Neier, "Asia's Unacceptable Standard," *Foreign Policy,* No. 92 (Fall 1993), pp. 42-51.

22. See discussion in Carothers, "Democracy and Human Rights: Policy Allies or Rivals?"

23. Kenneth Roth testimony before the U.S. Senate Task Force on Economic Sanctions (September 8, 1998), <http://www.hrw.org>. See also Amnesty International's "Brief History," <http://www.amnesty.org>. For an argument in favor of linking human rights abuses to MFN status, see Robert L. Bernstein and Richard Dicker, "Human Rights First," *Foreign Policy,* No. 94 (Spring 1994), pp. 43-47.

24. Lawyers Committee for Human Rights, *Basic Principles for an Independent and Effective International Criminal Court,* May 1998, <http://www.lchr.org>.

25. Lawyers Committee for Human Rights, Amnesty International, and Human Rights Watch have been especially active in the campaign for an independent International Criminal Court. Principle No. 10, "No Politics," of Amnesty International's Sixteen Principles states: "No political body, including the Security Council, or states, should have the power to stop or even delay an investigation or prosecution under any circumstances whatsoever."

Human Rights Watch has issued several press releases supporting the independent ICC. Human Rights Watch, "Non-Governmental Organization Action Alert (No. 3)," February 1998, states: "As the process to create the ICC enters its final and most critical stage, the role played by NGOs will be crucial to ensuring an effective and independent Court. . . . Human Rights Watch believes it is essential for NGOs to make their views known on key issues and lobby their governments to support an effective and independent ICC."

26. Kenneth Roth, "The Court the U.S. Doesn't Want," *New York Review of Books,* November 19, 1998.

27. See Thomas Franck, "The Emerging Right to Democratic Governance," *American Journal of International Law,* No. 86 (1988), pp. 46-91. Franck argues that "both textually and in practice, the international system is moving toward a clearly designated democratic entitlement, with national governance validated by international standards and systemic monitoring of compliance." See also Morton H. Halperin, "Guaranteeing Democracy," *Foreign Policy,* No. 91 (Summer 1993); and Morton H. Halperin and Kristen Lomasney, "Towards a Global Guarantee Clause," *Journal of Democracy,* Vol. 4, No. 3 (July 1993).

28. There has been some debate over whether U.S. military assistance to El Salvador may have contributed to the human rights abuses committed by Salvadoran armed forces. Former U.S. Ambassador to El Salvador Robert White testified in 1981 hearings before the House Appropriations Subcommittee on Foreign Operations: "The security forces in El Salvador have been responsible for the deaths of thousands of young people, and they have executed them on the mere suspicion that they are leftist or sympathize with leftists. Are we really going to send military advisors in there to be part of that type of machinery?" Center for National Security Studies, compiled by Americas Watch Committee and the American Civil Liberties Union, *Report on Human Rights in El Salvador* (New York: Vintage Books, 1982), p. 193.

29. William Odom and Peter Reddaway, "Yeltsin's False Truce," *New York Times,* April 3, 1996.

30. See Morton H. Halperin and David J. Scheffer with Patricia L. Small, *Self-Determination in the New World Order* (Washington, DC: Carnegie Endowment for International Peace, 1992), pp. 88-93.

31. *Human Rights Watch World Report 1998,* p. 157.

32. U.S. Department of State, Preface to *Country Reports on Human Rights Practices for 1997,* released by the Bureau of Democracy, Human Rights and Labor, January 30, 1998, <http://www.state.gov>.

33. See Morton H. Halperin and Kristen Lomasney, "Guaranteeing Democracy: A Review of the Record."

34. Kenneth Roth, "Sidelined on Human Rights," *Foreign Affairs,* No. 77 (March/April 1998), pp. 2-6.

TWELVE

Diplomacy with a Cause:
Human Rights in U.S. Foreign Policy

JOHN SHATTUCK

John Shattuck served as Assistant Secretary of State for Democracy, Human Rights and Labor from 1993 to 1998. He is currently the United States Ambassador to the Czech Republic. From 1984 to 1993 he was Vice President of Harvard University for Government, Community and Public Affairs; Lecturer at the Harvard Law School; and Senior Associate at the Program on Science, Technology and Public Policy at the Kennedy School of Government. His career as a human rights and civil liberties activist included serving as Vice Chair of Amnesty International USA from 1989 to 1992, Washington Director of the American Civil Liberties Union from 1977 to 1984, and ACLU National Staff Counsel from 1971 to 1976.

At the end of the bloodiest century in history, human rights issues were at the heart of an expanding international debate about the conduct of sovereign states within and beyond their borders. The success of North Atlantic Treaty Organization (NATO) air power in the spring of 1999 in forcing the Serbian army out of Kosovo prompted Western leaders such as Prime Minister Tony Blair of the United Kingdom to proclaim "a new internationalism based on values and the rule of law." More graphically, President Bill Clinton asserted in a speech to U.S. troops in Macedonia on June 22 that, "if somebody comes after innocent civilians and tries to kill them en masse because of their race, their ethnic background or their religion, and it's within our power to stop it, we will stop it."[1] In many quarters such pronouncements were greeted with skepticism or outright hostility. What and whose values should be protected? Who should decide where the lines should be drawn? How should the principle of national sovereignty, the traditional mainstay of international relations, be protected? These are among the questions posed by George F. Kennan, the distinguished analyst of twentieth-century American foreign policy, in an August 1999 interview in which he challenged the new Clinton doctrine of humanitarian intervention: "I would like to see our government gradually withdraw from its public advocacy of human rights. . . . What we ought to do at this point is to try to cut ourselves down to size in the dreams and aspirations we direct to our possibilities for world leadership."[2]

The debate over the role of human rights in U.S. foreign policy has been waged in the context of large-scale bloodshed and crimes against humanity in many parts of the world. In my work as a human rights official, I have been a frequent witness to these crimes.

In May 1994 I traveled to Central Africa to investigate the massive killings then spreading like wildfire in Rwanda. As I flew over the lush green hills along the Rwanda-Tanzania border, I could see the Kagawa River below me, choked with what looked like floating logs. Flying lower, I realized that the river was actually filled with human bodies, the product of a ghastly campaign of genocide. When I returned a week later to Washington after a series of meetings with regional leaders, I was frustrated by my inability to generate a response to this distant horror, where more than a half-million Tutsi were slaughtered in less than two months because of their ethnicity.

A year later, in July 1995, I traveled by helicopter to the war-ravaged Bosnian town of Tuzla on a fact-finding mission for Secretary of State Warren Christopher to interview the refugees then streaming in from Srebrenica, a predominantly Muslim town that the Serbs had overrun earlier that month. I had been sent to probe reports of atrocities, and what I learned was staggering. The survivors, including three men who had escaped their own executions, recounted in graphic detail the torture and cold-blooded murder of thousands of unarmed Muslim men by General Ratko Mladic and his Bosnian Serb troops. Srebrenica would prove to be the largest single act of genocide in Europe since World War II.

The White House immediately publicized the findings of my Srebrenica mission. Ten days later in the United Nations (UN) Security Council, Ambassador Madeleine Albright released aerial photographs confirming the existence of mass graves near Srebrenica. By the end of August, NATO was bombing Serb military targets to prepare the way for an intensive and ultimately successful U.S. diplomatic effort, led by Richard Holbrooke, to bring all parties to the negotiating table, more than three years after the Bosnian conflict had begun. By late November an agreement had been hammered out in Dayton, Ohio, that ended the Bosnian war.[3]

When the Balkan conflict later metastasized to Kosovo, Madeleine Albright, then secretary of state, sent me to Pristina in September 1998 with former Senator Bob Dole to report on the rapidly deteriorating human rights situation. Our mission was to travel throughout Kosovo and interview internally displaced persons to find out why more than 250,000 Kosovars had fled their homes. We heard and reported accounts of the systematic shelling of Kosovar villages and unarmed refugees by Serb paramilitary forces, and the rounding up and execution of military-age men: dramatic evidence of an organized campaign by Serbian President Slobodan Milosevic to terrorize and drive out the entire Kosovar population. Our report was one of the factors that contributed to the Clinton administration's series of decisions during the fall of 1998 and winter of 1999 to strengthen the U.S. response to the atrocities being committed by the Milosevic regime in Kosovo. These decisions eventually led to NATO's military confrontation with the regime and its success in forcing the withdrawal of Serb forces from Kosovo, permitting the deployment of NATO peacekeepers, and paving the way for the return of refugees. Again, witnessing had made a difference.

The massive human rights abuses that I witnessed around the world during my five-and-a-half years as assistant secretary of state were not supposed to have been part of the landscape of the post–cold war era. Immediately after the fall of the Berlin Wall, events appeared to be heading in a very different direction. Changes not expected in our lifetimes had transformed the world in a matter of months.

Commentators spoke glibly of "the end of history," as if the continuing expansion of democracy and universal recognition of human rights were inevitable.[4] However, events in Bosnia, Rwanda, and other places of which most Americans then knew little, turned these unrealistic hopes into dust. By the mid-1990s commentators had shifted from proclaiming the end of history to predicting the beginning of global chaos, from the "third wave of democratization" to the "clash of civilizations."[5]

Which was it to be: utopia or chaos? The answer, of course, was neither. The forecasts of inevitable democracy so popular in the months following the collapse of the Soviet bloc and later predictions of endless escalating conflict were both overly simplistic. The reality is that the world is at once better off and more troubled than it was a decade ago. Although we can see a real and measurable trend toward democracy, the tensions and pressures of globalization, modernization, and democratization have generated significant and unprecedented tremors. More democracies have been born, but more ethnic and religious conflicts have also erupted.[6] What political scientist Samuel Huntington calls the "repressive but peaceful order" of the bipolar world has disappeared, and no other international system has emerged to take its place.[7]

This uncertainty has greatly complicated the formulation of U.S. foreign policy. For every Nelson Mandela, there is a Slobodan Milosevic. For every Velvet Revolution, there is a vicious civil war. U.S. human rights diplomacy in the post–cold war era has sought to promote principles embodied in the Universal Declaration of Human Rights, but it also has tried to anticipate and counter the efforts of those who would use the expansion of freedom to instill fear, revive repression, and promote genocide. Over the last seven years this task has presented the Clinton administration with one of its greatest foreign policy challenges. The effort to meet this challenge has had varying degrees of success and has required a new approach, often difficult to implement, of integrating human rights and democracy directly into the mainstream of U.S. foreign policy.

It is this new approach toward human rights diplomacy that I review in this chapter. Although the roots of this diplomacy lie deep in the soil of American constitutional rights and liberties, it is beyond the scope of the chapter to assess how international human rights principles are applied in the United States. The focus here is on the role of the United States, as a preeminent global power, in projecting these principles through its foreign policy. I begin by tracing the roots of U.S. human rights policy in the congressional initiatives of the 1970s that followed the national debates over Vietnam and Watergate. Next I outline the competing strains of human rights advocacy and democracy promotion in the Carter, Reagan, and Bush administrations, and their synthesis in the post–cold war foreign policy of the Clinton administration. Clinton policy simultaneously has emphasized assisting countries that are now in transition to democracy, promoting democracy and human rights in countries still under authoritarian rule, and responding to human rights catastrophes in disintegrating countries. This chapter takes a close look at the evolving strategies for preventing or ending conflicts like those in the Balkans that have caused massive human rights abuses and threatened both U.S. and global security by destabilizing an entire region. I conclude that U.S. leadership—for example, spurring NATO intervention in Bosnia and Kosovo—is crucial to global human rights progress and that exercising such leadership is in the U.S. national interest.

COMPETING VISIONS

Diplomacy is, by definition, a limited tool for the promotion of human rights. Nongovernmental organizations (NGOs) such as Amnesty International and Human Rights Watch frequently criticize human rights diplomacy because it is clouded by other interests and rarely as single-minded as their own advocacy. But human rights diplomacy by governments and human rights advocacy by nongovernmental actors are by definition never the same. Integrating the promotion of human rights into U.S. foreign policy requires the policymaker to walk between practitioners of *realpolitik,* on one side, who believe that human rights diplomacy is an impediment to the pursuit of other national interests, and single-issue proponents, on the other, who would like to exclude all other considerations. In walking this line, Clinton-era policymakers have taken an approach that is different from that of previous administrations.

During much of the cold war, U.S. officials filtered human rights diplomacy through the prism of Soviet containment policy. U.S. diplomacy was often inconsistent, criticizing some countries for specific abuses while remaining silent about similar practices elsewhere. In many cases this double standard reflected a policy decision to cultivate anticommunist regimes even if they were also authoritarian. Meanwhile, there was a growing debate over whether human rights diplomacy could advance U.S. interests—and conversely, whether U.S. interests could advance human rights. In the first three decades after World War II, much of this debate took place in academic settings and among the foreign policy elite, mainly in the executive branch. But in the 1970s, amid discontent over Vietnam, Watergate, and U.S. government support for dictatorships in South Korea, the Philippines, and Chile, Congress began to assert itself with a louder voice in the U.S. foreign policy decision-making process. Although Jimmy Carter was the first American president to give major prominence to human rights, Congress also played a significant role in pressing these concerns.

In 1973 Representative Don Fraser, a Minnesota Democrat, confronted the executive branch with a series of hearings calling for the United States to act as a leader in human rights issues, with particular emphasis on problems in Latin America, South Africa, the Soviet Union, and the Middle East. The hearings paved the way for later efforts to bring human rights into the mainstream of foreign policy. Between 1973 and 1976 Congress enacted a series of legislative provisions requiring the State Department to monitor the human rights records of U.S. foreign aid recipients.[8] Section 32 of the Foreign Assistance Act of 1973 reflected this new congressional focus. It stated that "the President should deny any economic or military assistance to the government of any foreign country which practices the internment or imprisonment of that country's citizens for political purposes." Although the State Department registered concerns about this provision, it also initiated a human rights fact-finding process to comply with it. In April 1974 the Department asked U.S. embassies in sixty-eight countries receiving U.S. aid to begin reporting on their host country's treatment of political prisoners.

In late 1974 the clash between the executive branch and Congress over human rights issues came to a head. Congress added a new section to the Foreign Assistance Act that provided that "the President shall substantially reduce or terminate security assistance to any government which has engaged in a consistent pattern of gross violations of internationally recognized human rights."[9] Congress included a clause that allowed the executive to opt out of this obligation if extraordinary circumstances existed.[10] Nevertheless, Secretary of State Henry Kissinger resisted the new requirement, and the State Department declined to submit individual country reports on security aid recipients, supplying instead a summary document with few specific facts.[11] The summary report advocated "quiet but forceful diplomacy" as the best way to address security and human rights issues.

This lack of cooperation provoked Congress in 1975 to draft a security assistance bill designed to overcome State Department opposition. Although it was initially vetoed by President Gerald Ford, the bill eventually passed in June 1976 as Section 301 of the International Security Assistance and Arms Export Control Act. It required the State Department to issue annual human rights reports on security aid recipients. It also established the post of State Department coordinator for human rights and humanitarian affairs, a position that was elevated the following year by President Carter to the status of assistant secretary of state, when Patricia Derian was appointed the first assistant secretary for human rights and humanitarian affairs.[12]

Despite the promise of the new human rights legislation, its implementation remained uncertain. The *Country Reports* mandated by the Foreign Assistance Act of 1974 gave human rights advocates in the Carter administration the means to raise issues of systematic human rights abuse and in some cases led to a cutoff of assistance to countries with an egregious record of abuses.[13] For example, in 1977, El Salvador, Guatemala, Brazil, and Uruguay responded to critical *Country Reports* and turned down security aid that was made conditional on human rights improvements.[14]

Thus, when President Carter set out to fulfill his campaign pledge to inject human rights concerns into U.S. foreign policy, the ground had already been broken.[15] The Carter administration began to extend human rights reporting and criticism to "friendly" authoritarian states as well as traditional cold war adversaries. Carter's policy reflected not only his ideals but also his pragmatic assessment of the contemporary American struggle over political values. Exhausted by the dual traumas of Watergate and Vietnam, many Americans welcomed a foreign policy that placed a new emphasis on human rights.

The Carter human rights policy helped bring together liberals and conservatives, and for a brief period it reestablished the traditional bipartisan consensus in U.S. foreign policy that the Vietnam War had so severely strained.[16] Carter also permanently increased the influence of human rights in the formulation of U.S. foreign policy, and he made it difficult for future administrations to ignore human rights issues entirely, even if their policies might not reflect them adequately.

But Carter's human rights policy suffered from a flaw, which opened it to sharp criticism from the right. Carter's policymakers focused on abuses and sometimes failed to offer repressive governments a vision of what they could become: democracies with the necessary institutions to guarantee respect for human rights and the rule of law. In at least two cases—Iran and Nicaragua—Carter's approach left him open to the charge that by abandoning repressive but pro-American regimes, his administration had contributed to the rise of even more repressive, anti-American successor regimes.[17]

The challenge to Carter's human rights policy was led by Jeane Kirkpatrick, the U.S. ambassador to the United Nations during the Reagan administration. Kirkpatrick argued that the Carter policy "failed not for lack of good intentions, but for the lack of realism about the nature of traditional versus revolutionary autocracies and the relation of each to the national interest."[18] In the 1980 presidential campaign, Ronald Reagan embraced this critique, rejecting Carter's even-handed approach in favor of the old double standard, which held that the United States should apply different human rights standards to "friendly" and "unfriendly" regimes.

As president, Reagan condemned human rights abuses in the Soviet bloc while tolerating similar abuses by authoritarian regimes, as long as they did not maintain friendly relations with the Soviet Union. When criticism of this approach mounted, Reagan claimed that he was promoting "democracy" as an alternative to human rights, arguing that the focus should be on political systems and not on specific violations. Reagan's critics contended that his efforts to promote democracy were limited to sponsoring elections, and indeed, the administration often seemed satisfied by the mere holding of elections so long as anticommunist politicians emerged victorious. Reagan's policies often ignored the continued systematic abuse of human rights taking place beyond the polling booths. If a communist or left-leaning party won, by contrast, his administration usually contested the results and highlighted the human rights problems.[19]

The end of the cold war should have rendered such distinctions moot. Nevertheless, a foreign policy chasm continued to exist in the United States between those on one side who focused on human rights violations and those on the other who supported efforts to promote democracy. Each side distrusted the other, and each accused the other of ideological bias and hidden political motives.[20] This new democracy–versus–human rights cold war had a constraining impact on U.S. foreign policy in the years after the fall of the Berlin Wall, inhibiting the development of an approach that might have helped maintain the momentum of the revolution for freedom then cresting around the world. For example, the crisis that erupted in the Balkans as Yugoslavia disintegrated was virtually ignored in both its human rights and democracy dimensions by the Bush administration, whose policy in the region was summed up by Secretary of State James Baker's 1991 comment, "We don't have a dog in that fight."[21]

HUMAN RIGHTS AND
DEMOCRACY IN THE POST–COLD WAR WORLD

The Clinton administration set out to bridge the gap between human rights and democracy in its foreign policy. Early on, the administration reminded both sides of the debate that human rights and democracy promotion are not antithetical but complementary, and that the best chance of securing human rights in the long run is through the development of civil society, the rule of law, and democratic institutions dedicated to protecting the rights of citizens. The new administration asserted that elections should be regarded not as an end in themselves but as a means to a more comprehensive objective: the fostering of institutions that would assure the long-term stability of a state committed to protecting civil and political rights. Such institutions included an independent judiciary capable of enforcing the even-handed rule of law and of protecting the rights of women, workers, religious groups, and ethnic minorities; a lively nongovernmental sector; a free and independent press; and an open, transparent, and inclusive political process.[22]

This synthesis was first formally articulated by Secretary of State Warren Christopher in a June 1993 speech to the World Conference on Human Rights in Vienna. As Christopher notes in his memoirs, there was considerable debate within the administration over whether "the traditional human rights approach" or "promoting democracy" should be the primary focus of the speech.[23] Christopher recognized that the correct answer was that the administration should concern itself with both: "The collapse of communism had made the potential for democratic expansion greater than ever before, but . . . we needed to be sure that our human rights policy could address problems in many countries that were unlikely to become democratic anytime soon, . . . [as well as in] functioning democracies that had less-than-adequate human rights records."[24] Christopher's speech to the delegates at the first global conference of governments in a quarter century thus became an important foundation for the policymaking that followed.

The work of post–cold war human rights leaders around the world reflected a broad synthesis of democracy and human rights. Leaders as diverse as Nelson Mandela, Vaclav Havel, Kim Dae Jung, Aung San Suu Kyi, Oscar Arias, and Anwar Ibrahim viewed the schism in the United States separating advocates of human rights from proponents of democracy as largely irrelevant to their own struggles to promote freedom. While Americans squabbled over ideology, those who led the movements for human rights and democracy were risking their lives in efforts to establish governments that would guarantee the rights of citizens. Through this process they were working to discredit both communism and authoritarianism, to defeat apartheid, to challenge corruption, and to demonstrate the power of grass-roots movements for democratic change. Their actions profoundly altered the global political landscape and moved the promotion of human rights and democracy to the center of post–cold war international relations.

Many of these post–cold war human rights leaders argued that democratization and economic development must proceed simultaneously. The Clinton administration adopted a similar approach in formulating its foreign policy, asserting that it is in the U.S. interest to work to help build open societies with democratic governance and legal systems that protect human rights, because they are more likely to produce stable and equitable economic development. Three fundamental freedoms—speech, press, and association—can generate more and better information for free market decision making. Democratic competition can increase the incentive for officials to resist corruption. Greater transparency can serve as a protection against abuse of power and mismanagement. And democratic elections can help leaders build popular support for economic reforms, especially when they require belt-tightening.

Countries in Transition

In the 1990s, the United States provided assistance to transitional democracies in every corner of the world. U.S. aid was aimed at fostering the growth of democratic culture wherever it had a reasonable chance of taking hold. Until recently, U.S. taxpayers had invested over $1 billion dollars annually in these efforts, but current congressional reductions in the foreign aid budget are now threatening to undercut this long-term commitment to promoting democracy and human rights in countries in transition.

Of course, maintaining funding for direct assistance is only half the battle. The United States is also working to establish long-term partnerships with other donors and with developing democracies themselves. At their May 1997 Denver Summit, the Group of Eight countries committed themselves for the first time to coordinating their democracy assistance to countries in transition. One outcome of the Summit was an international democracy assistance conference in Bamako, Mali, which I co-chaired. Building on President Clinton's earlier trip to Africa in March of that year, the Bamako Conference brought together developed and developing countries as well as officials and nongovernmental activists to discuss how donor and recipient countries could improve the process and substance of democracy assistance and wean themselves away from top-down aid. The Conference produced proposals for local democratic development to help donors and recipients design and implement strategies in pilot countries and move to respond more quickly to democratic openings in places such as post-Suharto Indonesia, post-Abacha Nigeria and, when the moment comes, post-Milosevic Serbia.

A democratic transition sometimes can be boosted by massive public demonstrations, but it cannot be sustained without a long-term popular movement to bring about reform. At times, U.S. policy can play a role in supporting such a movement.

Indonesia is a case in point. As late as August 1997, financial analysts touted Indonesia as the next Asian economic tiger. Nine months later, the dreams of many investors—along with the well-being of the Indonesian people—lay in ruins, victims of a corrupt economic policy and authoritarian rule unchecked by democratic institutions or the rule of law. Students, workers, and other Indonesian citizens took to the streets following the financial crisis to demand a democratic future that also would provide economic stability.

As the crisis in Jakarta unfolded, U.S. policymakers had to balance the demands of those who wanted the United States, for reasons of economic stability, to continue supporting the corrupt and increasingly autocratic regime of President Suharto—even if that meant continued repression of human rights and democracy—and those who wanted the United States to end all aid to Indonesia, even if that meant further destabilizing an already tottering social system and plunging the nation deeper into economic crisis. The United States chose instead a third path—an approach that supported the growth of a democratic opposition, a movement toward democratic transition, and deterrence of political violence on the scale that had occurred in 1965, when over half a million Indonesians were killed in civil strife during the notorious "year of living dangerously." Following this approach, the United States provided over $50 million in assistance to human rights and pro-democracy groups in Indonesia beginning in 1995. As grass-roots pressure for democracy grew, so did U.S. efforts on behalf of democratic change. In addition, the United States linked its own bilateral assistance, as well as the role of international financial institutions in Indonesia, to a continuation of the transition process. The road to transition has been extremely rocky and at times nearly impassable: Major human rights abuses have been committed throughout Indonesia, particularly by the military and paramilitary groups against the people of East Timor after a UN-supervised referendum on self-determination in August 1999—but throughout the turmoil U.S. policy has been aimed at assisting the reform process and deterring a return to authoritarianism. Although the long-term outcome in Indonesia is uncertain, policy choices made by the United States have allied it firmly with the popular movement for democratic change.

The events in Indonesia demonstrate the fallacy of a post–cold war shibboleth: that there is a so-called Asian way to prosperity. This view has been expounded most aggressively by the leaders of China, who assert that economic development must always precede—and sometimes even preclude—the development of democracy and human rights. When their economies were booming, President Mahathir Mohammed of Malaysia and several other Asian leaders argued that democratization would be counterproductive until economic development reached a certain level and that human rights were an inherently "Western" concept alien to most Asians. They also asserted that certain societies require authoritarian governments in order to flourish economically.

The Indonesian example demonstrates the opposite: There is no link between prosperity and dictatorship. Although dictators sometimes may move a country toward prosperity, they often drag it backward. Suharto may have improved the economic well-being of some of Indonesia's citizens for a time, but his cronyism, corruption, and autocratic governance ultimately caused the collapse of both his own regime and the Indonesian economy. By contrast, President Kim Dae Jung of South Korea was able to help his country weather its economic storm in the late 1990s by enacting austerity measures that a majority of citizens deemed legitimate because of Kim's democratic mandate.

In the Philippines, South Korea, Thailand, Bangladesh, Taiwan, and now in Indonesia and Malaysia, authoritarianism has come under attack from within. Political reform, economic development, and the protection of human rights are tied together—not in a Gordian knot, but in a golden braid. This is why U.S. policy promotes them simultaneously.

Countries under Authoritarian Rule

What about countries under authoritarian rule where there is little prospect for near-term transformation? Resistance to human rights, of course, is a defining characteristic of authoritarian governments. When these regimes reject all internal and external pressures for democratization and human rights, they are likely to become internally unstable and externally threatening. Moreover, as President Clinton warned President Jiang Zemin of China in October 1997, they "stand on the wrong side of history."[25] The challenge for human rights diplomacy in these situations is to pursue a strategy that encourages internal change by engaging both with the government and with representatives of the broader society, while at the same time avoiding actions that could contribute to the rise of an even more repressive regime.

Because of its sheer size and global importance, China is at once the most significant and the most difficult authoritarian country for proponents of human rights diplomacy. Although it has proven stubbornly resistant to major human rights progress over the past decade, nonetheless China has occasionally been willing to take small positive steps. The challenge is to persuade the Chinese to take more and larger steps toward human rights protection while avoiding pressures that could induce backsliding. The U.S. approach has been to engage with the government on a specific agenda: release of political and religious prisoners, access to prisons by international humanitarian organizations such as the International Committee for the Red Cross, ratification of human rights treaties and covenants, and respect for the religious and cultural autonomy of Tibetans and other minorities. At the same time U.S. diplomats have made contact with diverse elements of Chinese society—religious leaders, legal experts, heads of social service agencies, women's organizations, and others—most of whom by definition are under the control of China's authoritarian government.

To assert its control, the Chinese government frequently arrests or detains those whose activities, although peaceful and protected under international definitions of free speech, are regarded as threatening to the stability of the country. A central feature of U.S. human rights policy toward China in recent years has been to challenge these detentions in individual cases as well as systemically. This challenge has been asserted through public diplomacy, in the State Department's annual *Country Reports* on China; bilaterally, in diplomatic meetings with Chinese leaders at all levels; and multilaterally, in the United Nations Human Rights Commission and other UN forums. The arrest of Chinese dissident Wei Jingsheng following his meeting with me in March 1994 was an example of China's use of detention to control speech; the subsequent U.S.-led international campaign to secure his release, which eventually occurred in October 1997, exemplified the response of human rights diplomacy to this repressive practice.[26]

U.S. engagement with China on human rights is complicated by a wide range of economic and security issues that lie at the center of U.S.-China relations. Obtaining access to China's huge and growing market economy for U.S. products and investment has long been a priority for U.S. policy. Similarly, restraining the development and proliferation of weapons of mass destruction by China is a major U.S. diplomatic objective. For these reasons human rights diplomacy must be coordinated closely with other aspects of U.S. policy toward China. When coordination fails, as it did following the decision by the Clinton administration in 1993 to use human rights progress in China as the sole criterion for extending China's most-favored nation (MFN) trade status, powerful economic and security interests are likely to overwhelm human rights diplomacy—particularly since its domestic sources of support are often diffuse and poorly organized—and make it impossible for even limited progress to be achieved.

Since 1994, human rights issues have been addressed simultaneously with other interests in U.S.-China diplomacy, but the results so far have been minimal. Limited gains in recent years include China's decision to sign the International Covenant on Civil and Political Rights, its willingness to host visits by UN human rights officials and international delegations of religious leaders, its release of a number of prisoners and detainees, and its early efforts to engage in systemic legal reform. China's overall record on civil and political rights remains dismal.

Critics of "engagement" charge that this approach is too soft and sometimes carries with it the appearance of "appeasement." The answer to the critics has been that no other approach has produced—or is likely to produce—more positive results for human rights. Furthermore, as President Clinton noted in Beijing in June 1998, "engagement is not endorsement." Through its annual Human Rights *Country Reports,* the United States extensively documents the human rights situation in China, publicly condemning abusive practices, as the president himself did during his 1998 trip there. The United States encourages internal proponents of reform, as in the case of the growing dialogue between U.S. experts and Chinese law reform proponents following the Washington and Beijing Summits of 1997 and 1998. In short, U.S. human rights diplomacy toward China has been aimed simultaneously at criticizing current abuses and promoting long-term systemic changes.

Countries in Conflict

The post–cold war world has been shaped by competing international trends: the movement toward greater global integration and a simultaneous tendency toward national disintegration and regional conflict.

Today countries are intertwined in a dizzying range of activities that transcend borders. National economies are increasingly interrelated in regional organizations, such as the European Union, the Asia-Pacific Economic Council, and the North Atlantic Free Trade Agreement. Trade, the environment, security, and population issues are all powerful forces for greater global integration. New technologies of communication, transportation, satellite television, and the Internet bring people of different cultures closer together. These developments can induce and support greater political and social freedom, breaking down traditional vertical power structures and creating a global system where information flows freely across borders. Globalization is weakening hierarchical bipolar models of authority while simultaneously strengthening non-hierarchical, multidimensional models. Traditional government controls over information are eroding, and this erosion in turn is changing the relationship between individuals and governments.

But as globalization creates new opportunities for the free flow of ideas, capital, and products, it also produces powerful reactions in the forms of nationalism, religious fundamentalism, and political repression. Those in the throes of disorienting change often seek refuge from an uncertain future in their own national, ethnic, or religious identity.

In these situations, political leaders like Slobodan Milosevic can come to power by preying on popular insecurity and fanning the flames of communal violence. In Yugoslavia and Central Africa, we have seen most graphically where this can lead. Modern genocide of more than half a million people can occur in just a few weeks, as it did in Rwanda. Other violent post–cold war political, ethnic, or religious conflicts in which civilians have been the principal victims have occurred in Nagorno-Karabakh, Haiti, Afghanistan, Northern Ireland, Liberia, Sierra Leone, Sudan, and East Timor, to name just a few. The United States has begun to work with other countries to meet the challenge of deterring or stemming such conflicts.

Countries in conflict are vulnerable to the most severe forms of violent repression. Some of these countries operate as the human rights equivalent of black holes in space, absorbing positive developments and spreading negative influences across entire regions: Serbia, Burma, the Democratic Republic of the Congo, and Afghanistan immediately come to mind. In recent years U.S. policy has sought to develop an approach to countries undergoing human rights crises that over the short run can limit their negative influence on other countries and that over the long run can meet their people's democratic aspirations. Three strategies are emerging for the pursuit of these objectives: early warning, intervention, and justice.

Early Warning   How can the international community develop early warning systems to prevent the outbreak or recurrence of what happened in Rwanda, Bosnia, and Kosovo? One way is to institutionalize the use of human rights and refugee missions as early warning systems. The Offices of the UN High Commissioner for Human Rights (created by a U.S.-led initiative in the General Assembly following the 1993 UN World Conference on Human Rights) and the UN High Commissioner for Refugees have both established field operations to report on human rights abuses, internally displaced persons, and other signs of growing or recurring conflict. These international warning systems have been set up in dozens of pre- or postconflict countries, including Rwanda, Burundi, Congo, Bosnia, Kosovo, Georgia, Colombia, Cambodia, Vietnam, Haiti, and Guatemala. In East and Central Europe, the Organization for Security and Cooperation in Europe (OSCE) has played a similar early warning role through its High Commissioner for National Minorities and its Warsaw-based Office of Democratic Institutions and Human Rights.

Once policymakers have been forewarned of a potential conflict, preventive diplomacy can take a number of forms. Visa denials, arms restrictions, and conditions on international financing and bilateral assistance can be deployed in an effort to put pressure on leaders who are promoting conflict. That is what the United States and its NATO allies have done to punish and isolate Milosevic and his regime in Belgrade for their role in initiating the conflict in Kosovo and ordering the commission of crimes against humanity. U.S. human rights policy on arms export restrictions has been particularly aggressive in recent years, blocking the export of certain arms to some thirty countries because of their poor human rights records.[27]

At times mediation can bring about an end to violent conflict. In Guatemala, El Salvador, and Haiti in 1993, 1994, and 1995, the United States worked with the United Nations and the Organization of American States to mount effective human rights field missions to strengthen civilian control over repressive military forces, and helped negotiate an end to conflicts involving massive human rights abuses.[28] In Estonia the OSCE, backed by the United States, sponsored a series of local open forums on minority rights in 1993 and 1994 that brought together Estonians and Russians and helped to defuse the explosive potential for conflict.

Active Intervention   When a human rights crisis deepens and does not respond to preventive diplomacy, more active intervention may become necessary. One form of active intervention is the deployment of comprehensive economic sanctions. There is a growing consensus in the United States, however, that overuse of this important strategic weapon on a unilateral basis can undermine its effectiveness, doing more harm than good, unintentionally generating sympathy for a human rights abuser or further endangering the very people the policy is trying to help. Multilateral sanctions, on the other hand, can have a significant impact in some situations on notorious regimes that have received broad international condemnation for abusing human rights. Current examples of comprehensive multilateral sanctions designed to isolate rogue regimes are the arms, trade, and international financing measures imposed against the governments of Iraq and Serbia. Often the most effective mechanism for intervening to stop a conflict involving massive human rights abuses and crimes against humanity is the creation of a multinational coalition. In many successful efforts to impose new sanctions, create a diplomatic framework for negotiations, or, as a last resort, to intervene militarily, multinational coalitions have proven to be essential. The Clinton administration generally has followed two criteria for determining where and when active intervention is warranted: first, the situation is causing major regional destabilization; and second, the countries in the region are willing to participate in a coalition to intervene. The larger the number of regional countries that participate, the greater the legitimacy of the intervention and the likelihood of its success. This is particularly true in the case of military interventions.

The most effective but controversial recent military intervention by a coalition of countries was NATO's use of force to back U.S. and European diplomacy over Kosovo in order to achieve the withdrawal of Serb forces from the province, the entry of international peacekeepers, and the return of refugees. Similar but lower-profile peacekeeping coalitions were assembled to help end violent conflicts involving systematic human rights abuses in Haiti, Guatemala, and El Salvador, where the United States worked closely with the United Nations and the Organization of American States. In Mozambique and Namibia, UN and African leaders, backed by international coalitions that included the United States, brokered the settlement of violent conflicts and the transition to democracy.

These success stories, however, are overshadowed by the failure of early international intervention in Rwanda and Bosnia, the two genocidal conflicts of the post–cold war era. Two major lessons stand out from these tragedies. First, traditional peacekeeping by lightly armed troops with severely limited rules of engagement is inadequate when massive numbers of civilians are intentionally targeted by perpetrators of crimes against humanity, as was the case in both Rwanda and Bosnia. UN peacekeeping efforts in Rwanda in 1994 and Bosnia before 1995 were ineffective because the international community failed to grasp and act on the threats to international peace and security that these conflicts were causing.[29] What was needed and lacking in both Rwanda and Bosnia was an early and forceful response to the massive violations of international humanitarian law that were being committed with impunity. The lessons of these two peacekeeping failures have had a strong impact on the planning of subsequent interventions. For example, the United States is now providing logistical and military training assistance to countries in Central and East Africa in support of a regional African Crisis Response Initiative with the capability to intervene early and forcefully in future Rwandas. The need for robust rules of engagement was recognized in planning the U.S.-led multinational force that entered Haiti in late 1994 (five months after the Rwanda genocide), the NATO air and ground forces that intervened in Bosnia in 1995 and Kosovo in 1999, and the Australian-led United Nations force that moved in to restore order on East Timor in 1999. Each of these military interventions was authorized to respond to renewed aggression or violent attacks on civilians, and each did so early and decisively.[30] In these situations intervention requires not only peace-keeping but *peacemaking* by well-trained air and ground forces under rules of engagement that allow them to counter massive violations of international humanitarian law.

Justice   Another lesson to be drawn from early peacekeeping failures in Rwanda and Bosnia is that where genocide or crimes against humanity have been committed with impunity, the underlying conflict cannot be resolved without the involvement of institutions of justice. Revenge may offer the victims fleeting satisfaction, but only at the cost of a perpetual cycle of violence. Institutionalized justice can provide survivors an alternative means of righting the wrongs committed against them, by holding accountable those who were primarily responsible. Justice is equally important to innocent members of national or ethnic groups involved in the conflict, because it can help remove the stigma of guilt by association that settles over an entire group when some of its members have committed war crimes. Justice also can serve as a warning to others who might want to engage in similar acts in the future.

For all these reasons the United States has been the earliest and strongest proponent of the International Criminal Tribunals for the former Yugoslavia and Rwanda, which were established in 1993 and 1994 respectively, following U.S. diplomatic initiatives in the United Nations. By mid-1999 the United States had provided funding to the Yugoslavia Tribunal in the amount of $82 million in payments assessed by the United Nations and $12 million in additional voluntary contributions. In the case of the Rwanda Tribunal, the United States had supplied nearly $65 million for the Tribunal's work. Both Tribunals have been staffed by many U.S. personnel, including prosecutors, defense attorneys, investigators, and other experts, and the United States has turned over substantial evidence for war crimes prosecutions. The United States also has played a leading role in calling for the creation of other tribunals to prosecute crimes committed by the leaders of the Khmer Rouge in Cambodia and by Saddam Hussein in Iraq.

The prosecution of both Yugoslavian and Rwandan war crimes has faced significant challenges. By early 2000 the Yugoslav Tribunal had thirty-nine people currently in proceedings before the Tribunal of the ninety-four people it has indicted, but many key indicted leaders remained at large, including President Slobodan Milosevic of Serbia, the Bosnian Serb leader Radovan Karadzic, and Ratko Mladic, the Bosnian Serb general who carried out the genocide of more than 7,000 Bosnian Muslims from Srebrenica.

The Rwandan Tribunal has had more success bringing indicted leaders of the 1994 genocide into custody.[31] In September 1998 it secured the first-ever conviction of a defendant for the crime of genocide.[32] However, the Tribunal has suffered from major administrative problems that have impeded its effectiveness. The United States has worked with the Office of the Prosecutor to provide additional technical support for the Tribunal, and it has helped establish a witness protection program.

Despite their flaws, both Tribunals represent a groundbreaking attempt to develop institutions of international justice to prosecute genocide and crimes against humanity. What makes them so remarkable is that they are charting completely new territory in international law. Not even the Nuremberg trials attempted to bring justice to an ongoing conflict as a means of ending it, and certainly no other international institution of justice has ever tried to do so. Nevertheless, the movement pioneered by the two UN Tribunals appears to be taking hold. In 1998 a UN conference drafted a treaty to establish a permanent International Criminal Court. Although the United States was unable to agree to the treaty as drafted because it objected to aspects of the new Court's proposed jurisdiction,[33] it is clear that international institutions of justice are becoming a central feature of human rights promotion.

Of course, international justice by itself is not enough. Over the long run, the only way to deter genocide and crimes against humanity is to build indigenous national institutions that foster the rule of law in situations that are ripe for conflict or emerging from it. Truth commissions in South Africa, El Salvador, and elsewhere have played a critical role in promoting peace and reconciliation.[34] National courts must also play a role. For this reason, the United States is now providing substantial amounts of foreign aid to support the rule of law in postconflict and transitional countries. For example, the new Office of Transition Initiatives of the U.S. Agency for International Development (USAID), which focuses on countries emerging from conflict, dramatically increased its spending starting from no budget of its own in 1994 to in excess of $35 million in 1999. In more than twenty countries, the United States now provides support for the training of judges, court administrators, prosecutors, defense lawyers, and the police; legal education; the writing of constitutions; and a wide range of other law reform activities designed to support new national institutions of domestic justice and human rights enforcement.

HUMAN RIGHTS REPORTING AND FOREIGN POLICY

Human rights reporting is the bridge between witnessing and policymaking. Reporting provides the hard evidence that is needed to formulate policies responsive to complex situations. Human rights monitors spotlight abuses, offer hope to those who face repression, and help legitimize the efforts of local leaders and nongovernmental organizations that may be under severe pressure within their own countries. In formulating human rights policies and diplomatic strategies to implement them, it is essential to have an understanding of the facts on the ground and the context in which they exist. There is no "one-size-fits-all" human rights policy, and it is the role of witnesses, monitors, and fact-gatherers to ensure that policy choices are well informed and driven by reality, not uninformed idealism.

The heart of all official U.S. human rights monitoring is the *Country Reports on Human Rights Practices,* which the State Department submits to Congress and publishes annually.[35] Since their inception in 1977, the reports have become an increasingly valuable tool for policymakers. For example, the reports on human rights atrocities in Haiti contributed to the decision in mid-1994 to change U.S. policy concerning the repatriation of Haitian "boat people" and to assemble a multinational force to restore Haiti's democratically elected president to office. Reports on a number of countries, including Turkey, Indonesia, and Nigeria in the mid-1990s, led to decisions to deny arms export licenses for certain types of weapons that had been used to commit human rights abuses. The Dayton Peace Process was facilitated by U.S. reporting on the mass execution in Srebrenica and other crimes against humanity committed in Bosnia during the summer and fall of 1995. The NATO decision to take military action in Kosovo was influenced by human rights reports concerning Serb atrocities against Kosovar Albanians.

In recent years the process of official human rights reporting has been strengthened within the State Department. In August 1993 Secretary of State Warren Christopher issued a worldwide cable establishing a human rights committee in every U.S. embassy to assemble information and corroborate reports of human rights violations. In 1994 the State Department's Bureau of

Human Rights and Humanitarian Affairs was reorganized, expanded, and renamed the Bureau of Democracy, Human Rights and Labor (DRL). The new name reflected a decision to make human rights advocacy and democracy promotion a seamless enterprise and to infuse both areas with issues involving international worker rights. More recently, under the leadership of Secretary of State Albright, DRL has increased reporting on worker rights, women's rights, the rights of the disabled, and religious freedom.

The *Country Reports* are the product of an annual worldwide diplomatic effort. DRL oversees the work of hundreds of individuals, including human rights officers assigned to each embassy and desk officers in each State Department regional bureau. Officials from other U.S. government agencies, such as the Department of Labor, the Department of Defense, and the U.S. Agency for International Development, also contribute to the reports. The State Department gathers information from a wide variety of international sources across the political spectrum, including foreign government officials, judges and lawyers, military officers, journalists, nongovernmental organizations, human rights monitors, academics, and labor leaders. Compiling this information can be hazardous, and local human rights defenders and political activists often face difficult conditions when they provide U.S. embassies with data and documentation on abuses by their governments. U.S. officials then take this information and convert it into a series of uniform and precisely organized reports on every country in the world.

The first set of *Country Reports* was issued in 1977 and ran 137 pages, covering only those countries then receiving U.S. foreign assistance. The most recent report, issued in February 2000, was the largest ever, covering 194 countries and running 6,000 pages. Using the Internet, the State Department is now able to distribute the reports globally to hundreds of thousands of individuals and organizations, as well as governments, within moments of their release.[36] The reports serve to encourage change and give legitimacy to national organizations that are trying to bring it about. In Mauritania, for example, a country with an extremely poor human rights record, the 1998 report cited the creation a new National High Commission for Human Rights and pointed out that "the Government did not censor or seize any newspapers in the second half of the year, following the creation of the High Commission."[37] The reports' reputation for accuracy and thoroughness has grown in recent years, prompting a leading U.S. nongovernmental organization, the Lawyers' Committee for Human Rights, to decide that there was no longer a need for it to publish its annual *Country Reports* critique. Other NGOs increasingly use the reports to support their own work, and the press in foreign countries often reprint the evaluations of their own countries.

The United States has been slow to issue reports on itself, but in 1995 it published for the first time an official self-evaluation of U.S. domestic compliance with international human rights norms. That year, as assistant secretary of state for democracy, human rights and labor, I headed the U.S. delegation that appeared before the United Nations Human Rights Committee to make the first report on U.S. adherence to the International Covenant on Civil and Political Rights (ICCPR), which the U.S. Senate had ratified in 1992. Additional U.S. reports on ICCPR compliance as well as initial reports on compliance with the Torture Convention and International Convention to End Racial Discrimination, both of which were ratified in the early 1990s, are scheduled to be presented next year to the UN Human Rights Committee.[38] In addition the United States recently hosted several visits by UN Special Rapporteurs investigating human rights conditions in the United States.

CONCLUSION

The process of building international human rights institutions for a new millennium is now well under way. Based in the United Nations and regional organizations around the world, these institutions should begin to draw on the experience of those who have worked successfully in recent years to resolve conflicts in southern Africa, Central America, and Eastern Europe, and serve as resources for addressing protracted and continuing regional conflicts, such as those in the Great Lakes region of Central Africa and in the Balkans. These institutions also should begin to serve as an international source of coordination and support for efforts to promote the rule of law, both in countries in transition to democracy and in countries that remain under authoritarian rule, and efforts to bring to justice those who commit genocide and crimes against humanity. In essence, these new human rights institutions should come to symbolize a commitment in the twenty-first century to learn from the terrible mistakes of the twentieth, the bloodiest century in history.

In Montgomery, Alabama, there is a Civil Rights Memorial dedicated to all who have died in the ongoing effort to create full civil rights and equal protection of the laws in the United States. A thin sheet of water flows endlessly over a simple slab of black granite, symbolizing the endless struggle of Americans to achieve equal rights and racial justice. Inscribed above the memorial is the favorite Bible verse of Martin Luther King, Jr.: "Let justice roll down like water, and righteousness like a mighty stream."[39] Until recently no comparable monument has existed to remind the world of the ongoing struggle by people from all nations on behalf of human rights. The emerging new human rights institutions can become a living memorial to their work.

In recent years the U.S. government has begun to place human rights diplomacy in the mainstream of U.S. foreign policy. Continuing this effort will require leadership that combines sober realism with faith in the principles of the Universal Declaration of Human Rights. The quality of such leadership has been eloquently expressed by Vaclav Havel, president of the Czech Republic and a voice for democracy and human rights throughout the world: "I am not an optimist, because I do not believe that all ends well; nor am I a pessimist, because I do not believe that all ends badly. Instead, I am a realist, who carries hope, and hope is the belief that freedom has meaning, and that liberty is always worth the struggle."

NOTES

1. Remarks by the President to KFOR troops, Skopje Macedonia Airport, Macedonia, June 22, 1999.
2. Richard Ullman, "The U.S. and the World: An Interview with George Kennan," *New York Review of Books,* August 12, 1999, p. 6. Similar questions were posed by former Secretary of State Henry Kissinger in "The End of NATO as We Know It?" op-ed Page, *Washington Post,* August 15, 1999.
3. See Richard Holbrooke, *To End a War* (New York: Random House, 1998), pp. 69-70, 188-91.
4. See in particular Francis Fukuyama, "The End of History," in Fukuyama, *The End of History and the Last Man* (New York: Free Press, 1992). In 1995, when events in Rwanda and Bosnia had led commentators as diverse as Samuel Huntington and Robert Kaplan to dispute his thesis, Fukuyama continued to adhere to it: "Today virtually all advanced countries have adopted or are trying to adopt, liberal democratic political institutions and a great number have simultaneously moved in the direction of market-oriented economies and integration into the global capitalist division of labor. As I have argued elsewhere . . . this movement constitutes an 'end of history,' in the Marxist-Hegelian sense of History as a broad evolution of human societies advancing toward a final goal." See Francis Fukuyama, *Trust: The Social Virtues and the Creation of Prosperity* (New York: Free Press, 1995), p. 3.
5. On chaos as a model for foreign relations theory, see, for example, Robert Kaplan, "The Coming Anarchy," *Atlantic Monthly,* 273 (February 1994), pp. 44-76, which is largely credited with popularizing the idea. Other works predate Kaplan and provide a more scholarly approach. See Zbigniew Brzezinski, *Out of Control: Global Turmoil on the Eve of the Twenty-First Century* (New York: Scribners, 1993), and Daniel Patrick Moynihan, *Pandaemonium: Ethnicity in International Politics* (Oxford: Oxford University Press, 1993). Samuel Huntington is perhaps the best example of a scholar whose views shifted rapidly in the short period between the fall of the Berlin Wall and the start of the Yugoslav civil war. In 1991 Huntington called democratization "perhaps the most important political development in the late twentieth century." Samuel P. Huntington, *The Third Wave: Democratization in the Late Twentieth Century* (Norman: University of Oklahoma Press, 1991), p. xiii. By the time his controversial book *Clash of Civilizations* was published five years later (it was based on a 1993 article in *Foreign Affairs*), Huntington regarded "the central and most dangerous dimension of the emerging global politics" as the "conflict between groups from differing civilizations." In *Clash,* Huntington makes no direct

reference to his earlier work, providing only oblique references to a "wave of transitions" to democracy. Huntington, *The Clash of Civilizations and the Remaking of World Order* (New York: Simon & Schuster, 1996), pp. 13 and 192.

6. By one account, there were only 66 democracies in 1988; today there are 117, nearly double the number in less than ten years. See Adrian Karatnycky, "A Good Year for Freedom," in Adrian Karatnycky and Charles Graybow, eds., *Freedom in the World 1998–1999: The Annual Survey of Political Rights and Civil Liberties* (New York: Freedom House, 1999), p. 5. For the rise in ethnic and religious conflicts, see Huntington, *Clash of Civilizations*, p. 254.

7. Huntington, *Clash of Civilizations*, p. 262.

8. For a detailed discussion of the economic and security aid debate between Congress and the executive branch in the 1970s, see Sandy Vogelgesang, *American Dream, Global Nightmare: The Dilemma of U.S. Human Rights Policy* (New York: Norton, 1980).

9. Section 502(b) of the Foreign Assistance Act of 1974.

10. Thus, in the 1970s, "extraordinary circumstances" were found to justify security aid to Indonesia, Iran, South Korea, the Philippines, and Zaire.

11. For a contemporary analysis and excerpts of the report, see Bernard Gwertzman, "U.S. Blocks Rights Data on Nations Getting Arms," *New York Times,* November 19, 1975.

12. In 1994 the Clinton administration renamed and expanded the responsibilities of this position, which became assistant secretary of state for democracy, human rights and labor. This was the position I held from June 1993 until my confirmation as U.S. Ambassador to the Czech Republic in November 1998.

13. See the discussion of the *Country Reports* later in the chapter. They are available at <http://www.state.gov/www/global/human_rights/hrp_reports_mainhp.html>.

14. See Lawyers Committee for Human Rights, "Linking Security Assistance and Human Rights," 1989, reprinted in Steiner and Alston, *International Human Rights in Context,* 837.

15. See Jimmy Carter's chapter in this volume.

16. See comments attributed to Zbigniew Brzezinski and Hamilton Jordan, among others, in John Dumbrell, *American Foreign Policy: Carter to Clinton* (New York: St. Martin's Press, 1997), pp. 17-18.

17. See in particular, the writings of Jeane J. Kirkpatrick, particularly "Dictatorships and Double Standards," *Commentary,* No. 68 (November 1979), pp. 34-45. Kirkpatrick stated that "The goals [of Carter's human rights policy], I thought, were moderation and democracy; and the results, I thought, were Khomeini and the Ortega brothers." Address to the Council on Foreign Relations, March 10, 1981, reprinted as "Ideas and Institutions" in Kirkpatrick, *The Reagan Phenomenon* (Washington, DC: American Enterprise Institute, 1983), p. 39. For a more evenhanded—albeit neoconservative—critique of Carter's foreign policy, see Joshua Muravchik, *The Uncertain Crusade: Jimmy Carter and the Dilemmas of Human Rights Policy* (Lanham, MD: Hamilton Press, 1986).

18. Kirkpatrick, "Dictatorships and Double Standards."

19. The literature criticizing the Reagan and Bush administrations' human rights policies is voluminous; representative examples of contemporary criticism include Alan Tonelson, "Human Rights: The Bias We Need," *Foreign Policy,* No. 49 (Winter 1982–1983); and Charles Maechling, Jr., "Human Rights Dehumanized," *Foreign Policy,* No. 52 (Fall 1983). Jeff McMahan is particularly critical, arguing that "concern for human rights has not only ceased to function as a constraint on U.S. military sales and assistance; the protection of human rights has virtually ceased to be a goal of U.S. foreign policy." Jeff McMahan, "Human Rights in the New Cold War," in McMahan, *Reagan and the World: Imperial Policy in the New Cold War* (New York: Monthly Review Press, 1985), p. 99.

20. See also Chapter 11 in this volume, where Morton Halperin endorses a convergence of the movement to promote democracy and the human rights movement.

21. Laura Silber and Allan Little, *Yugoslavia: Death of a Nation* (London: Penguin/BBC Books, 1996), p. 201.

22. John Shattuck and Brian Atwood, "In Defense of Democracy," *Foreign Affairs*, March 1997.

23. Warren Christopher, *In the Stream of History: Shaping Foreign Policy for a New Era* (Stanford, CA: Stanford University Press, 1998), p. 63.

24. Ibid.

25. White House, Office of the Press Secretary, "Press Conference by President Clinton and President Jiang Zemin, Old Executive Office Building, October 29, 1997, as published on the White House Web site, <http://www.pub.whitehouse.gov/.

26. See Wei Jingsheng's chapter in this volume.

27. See Testimony of John Shattuck, Assistant Secretary of State for Democracy, Human Rights and Labor, Committee on International Relations, U.S. House of Representatives, April 1, 1998.

28. See Testimony of John Shattuck, Assistant Secretary of State for Democracy, Human Rights and Labor, Committee on International Relations, U.S. House of Representatives, February 1-2, 1994, February 22 and March 16, 1995, February 1-2, March 26, May 22, 1996.

29. The growing pattern and scale of ethnic killings in both Bosnia and Rwanda had been thoroughly documented by international human rights investigators. See, for example, Reports of the United Nations Commission of Experts, established by UN Security Council Resolution in October 1992 to investigate war crimes in the Former Yugoslavia; Reports of the International Commission of Inquiry into Violations of Human Rights in Rwanda.

30. For example, two weeks after deployment of the multinational force (MNF) in Haiti on September 19, 1994, U.S. Marines shot and killed a heavily armed group of paramilitary supporters of General Cedras when they attacked civilians outside a police station. In December 1994 the UN Secretary-General reported to the Security Council that "following the arrival of the MNF and the subsequent disintegration of the Forces Armees d'Haiti, the human rights situation has improved. Politically motivated violence and human rights abuses have decreased." NATO's belated intervention in Bosnia was even more forceful. Following the July 1995 mass execution of civilians in Srebrenica by Serb forces and the August Sarajevo market massacre, NATO unleashed a comprehensive bombing campaign against Serb military targets. "It was the largest military action in NATO history.... Unlike earlier air strikes, when the UN and NATO had restricted themselves to hitting individual surface-to-air missile sites or single tanks, these strikes were massive." Holbrooke, *To End a War,* p. 102.

31. As of early 2000, forty-four of the fifty-two persons indicted by the Rwanda Tribunal had been brought into custody.

32. Jean-Paul Akayasu, former Mayor of Taba, Rwanda, was convicted by the International Criminal Tribunal for Rwanda on September 2, 1998, of genocide.

33. The United States supports the concept of a permanent international criminal court and participated in the drafting of the treaty to create such a court. In the end it voted against the text of the treaty that emerged from the Rome Conference in 1998 because it was concerned that the final draft did not provide adequate protection against spurious prosecutions of the large number of U.S. armed forces engaged in international peacekeeping activities. The United States is attempting to resolve this concern through further diplomatic discussion and revision of the treaty. As of April 2000, ninety-six states had signed the treaty but only eight had ratified it. Sixty ratifications are required before the treaty can enter into force.

34. See Richard Goldstone's chapter in this volume.

35. As the 1999 edition of *Country Reports on Human Rights Practices* notes on its cover, it is "submitted to the Committee on International Relations, U.S. House of Representatives, and the Committee on Foreign Relations, U.S. Senate, by the Department of State in Accordance with Sections 116(d) and 502B(b) of the Foreign Assistance Act of 1961, as amended."

36. See, <http://www.state.gov/www/global/human_rights/hrp_reports_mainhp.html>.
37. 1998 *Country Reports,* p. 269.
38. Full-text treaties are available online at the Web site of the UN High Commissioner for Human Rights: <http://www.unhchr.ch/html/intlinst.htm>.
39. Sara Bullard, *Free at Last: A History of the Civil Rights Movement and Those Who Died in the Struggle* (New York: Oxford University Press, 1993), p. 104.

Economic Sanctions
and Human Rights

ARYEH NEIER

Aryeh Neier is President of the Open Society Institute, the parent body of a network of foundations established by George Soros to promote transitions from authoritarian states to more open societies. Previously he served as Executive Director of Human Rights Watch of which he was a founder. Before that he was Executive Director of the American Civil Liberties Union. His books include *Only Judgement: The Limits of Litigation in Social Change* and *War Crimes: Brutality, Genocide, Terror, and the Struggle for Justice.*

In recent years, the use of economic sanctions as a tool of diplomacy has been widely criticized. Spokespersons for the business community complain about a loss of profits or about the advantages gained by competitors in countries that do not impose sanctions. Those concerned with national security lament interference in policymaking by interests that seem to them to lack strategic significance, and many people with humanitarian concerns lament the harmful impact on ordinary citizens who may themselves be victims of the governments that are the targets of sanctions. In this chapter I argue that, although sanctions can be counterproductive or ineffective, in certain circumstances they also may play a significant role in promoting human rights internationally.

Economic sanctions are attractive to human rights advocates on several fronts. They may promote specific reforms, helping bring about a release of political prisoners or a reduction in such practices as torture and disappearances. If kept in place for sustained periods, sanctions may become a factor in political transformations that result in profound improvements in respect for human rights. Even if they do not accomplish these goals outright, however, sanctions may serve useful purposes by manifesting international condemnation, by deterring other governments from engaging in similar abuses, or simply by punishing regimes that persistently engage in gross violations of human rights.

Another part of their attraction that is less commonly articulated is that they help focus and sustain attention to abuses. From this standpoint, the threat of sanctions, or debates about whether sanctions should be imposed or lifted, may be as effective as sanctions themselves. The foremost method by which proponents of human rights advance their goals is by focusing the international spotlight on the victims of abuses and on those responsible for their victimization. When a repressive regime holds on to power for an extended period and engages in steady, relatively unvarying abusive practices, however, violations of human rights become old news (as chapter 16 by Anna Husarska points out), and it becomes difficult to hold the spotlight.

The question of whether the United States or other Western democracies should aid or trade with those governments, and whether multinational corporations should invest in them, is nevertheless likely to remain a matter of continuing interest, especially in the countries from which investments flow. Proponents of human rights have had considerable success in calling attention to abuses that otherwise would be little noticed, by making surrogate villains of the governments and businesses that aid or trade with repressive regimes. That is, because they provide support to such regimes, they are held accountable for its abuses, particularly if they profit directly or indirectly from those abuses. To cite one example, Burma's use of forced labor is known internationally principally as a consequence of debates over whether two giants of the energy industry, UNOCAL of the United States and Total of France, should finance the construction of a pipeline to transport natural gas to Thailand.[1] Regardless of whether rights advocates succeed in persuading governments to impose sanctions on Burma that would prohibit such investments, or whether the bad publicity persuades multinational investors to withdraw from Burma, the effect of their campaign on behalf of sanctions is to help make the Burmese military regime an international pariah by making its forced labor practices notorious.

On the other hand, sanctions have disadvantages that go beyond the economic cost of interrupting or burdening normal trade relations. As critics frequently note, the sectors of the population that are themselves the victims of human rights abuse may suffer most from sanctions while their rulers may be unaffected. Sanctions also may make it more difficult to influence repressive governments because the interruption of commerce may curb or even curtail the contacts with outsiders that could play an important part in promoting greater openness. In certain circumstances, authoritarian leaders may be able to consolidate their hold on power by exploiting sanctions, and the evidence they provide of international hostility, to stoke the fires of nationalist sentiment. Finally, it is possible, as opponents of sanctions against China have argued regularly, that they could inhibit the emergence of a middle class that, over time, will transform the country and produce a less repressive form of government.

Here, now, are brief assessments of the impact of sanctions where the purpose was to promote rights. In this chapter I examine U.S. policy toward China, Burma, Poland, and South Africa, where the motivation for sanctions was solely or predominantly the promotion of human rights. I review the prohibitions on U.S. economic and military assistance that were imposed on several Latin American military dictatorships during the late 1970s and in the 1980s, exclusively in the interest of promoting human rights. I espoused sanctions in each of these cases, and accordingly, the comments that follow do not purport to provide a neutral assessment. Rather, they reflect the perspective of an advocate who is nevertheless aware that this particular weapon in the arsenal of human rights proponents can be a very blunt instrument and that its use can have unintended consequences.

I exclude consideration of cases in which sanctions have been imposed for other reasons. Many of the countries that have been targets of sanctions in recent years are among the most repressive in the world, and those who argue on behalf of sanctions usually make their case by citing the target states' abuses of human rights along with their other sins. Yet when the main purpose of sanctions is to deal with such issues as aggression, subversion, terrorism, drug trafficking, or nuclear proliferation, we must measure the effectiveness of the sanctions by judging their impact on those concerns rather than on human rights. Accordingly, I will not attempt to weigh the impact of sanctions in such well-known cases as North Korea, Iran, Iraq, or Libya, because promoting human rights was not the primary purpose of imposing them. Nor will I make any attempt to consider U.S. sanctions against Cuba, even though for the past several years the stated purposes have been those set forth in the Cuban Democracy Act of 1992 (the Torricelli Bill): to promote a transition to democratic government in which free and fair elections are held under international supervision; opposition parties are permitted to organize and campaign and enjoy full access to the media; the government shows respect for civil liberties and human rights; and movement takes place toward the establishment of a market economy. The effect of that law is to maintain and extend the embargo that was originally imposed by President John F. Kennedy thirty years earlier to punish Cuba for aligning itself with the Soviet Union and for seeking to export its revolution to other countries in Latin America. In the circumstances, the Cuban government could hardly be blamed for believing that the current rationale for the sanctions reflects ongoing U.S. hostility based on domestic politics—a hostility that would not diminish even if, for example, the Castro regime were to end the imprisonment of political dissenters.

I also will avoid considering the case of the Federal Republic of Yugoslavia. The question of U.S. sanctions was first raised in 1990, when Yugoslavia was still united, on human rights grounds: the persecution of ethnic Albanians in Kosovo by Serbia under the leadership of President Slobodan Milosevic. The Nickles Amendment required the United States to terminate aid unless abuses ended within six months. However, a few days after the law went into effect on May 5, 1991, the United States rescinded sanctions because Secretary of State James Baker certified that Yugoslavia was in compliance with the Helsinki Accord. Six months later, however, President George Bush imposed sanctions by executive order on what had become a rump Yugoslavia, as punishment for its role in the wars in Slovenia and Croatia. In May 1992 the United States took the lead in the United Nations (UN) Security Council in getting that body to impose multilateral sanctions because of the Milosevic regime's aggression in Bosnia. Trade sanctions were lifted at Christmas 1995 as a reward for Milosevic's signing of the Dayton Accords, but an "outer wall" of sanctions was maintained that excluded the Federal Republic of Yugoslavia from membership in international organizations, including the World Bank and the International Monetary Fund. The conditions for removing the remaining sanctions blended concerns for human rights (i.e., cooperation with the International Criminal Tribunal for the Former Yugoslavia) and concerns about aggression (i.e., promotion of a peaceful resolution of the status of Kosovo). Thereafter, however, when war broke out in Kosovo at the end of February 1998, and Milosevic's armed forces responded by systematically attacking and destroying civilian villages, the Security Council imposed new sanctions. As of late summer 1999, a peace agreement for Kosovo leaves the outer wall of sanctions in place.

Plainly, human rights considerations loom large in the sanctions that have been imposed on Yugoslavia. However, they are thoroughly intertwined with concerns about limiting and punishing aggression. Accordingly, it seems impossible to disentangle the factors that prompted the imposition and maintenance of sanctions and to measure the results solely from the standpoint of what was or was not achieved for human rights.

CHINA

The Bush administration imposed sanctions on China following the crackdown on protests in Beijing's Tiananmen Square on June 3-4, 1989, which was marked by the killing of hundreds of demonstrators in the vicinity of the square and the arrest and imprisonment of thousands more. The United States suspended diplomatic exchanges, stopped military exchanges and technology and arms transfers, and ceased supporting loans to China by international financial institutions. However, none of these measures—each of which was later lifted— aroused great public debate. Rather, the issue that aroused debate was the question of whether, in 1994, the United States should revoke China's eligibility for most-favored nation (MFN) trading status.

Although now largely forgotten, the MFN issue arose due to an accident of timing. Because China was considered a "nonmarket economy," it required an annual presidential waiver to be eligible for MFN status under the Jackson-Vanik Amendment to the 1974 Trade Act, a law originally intended to bring pressure on the Soviet Union to permit Jews to emigrate. In its preamble, however, the Amendment provides that its purpose is "to assure the continued dedication of the United States to fundamental human rights." It was on this slender basis that human rights proponents called on President Bush not to provide a waiver to China. Normally, it was possible for a U.S. president to claim that concerns about human rights had nothing to do with China's policies on emigration. But, by coincidence, the date by which a presidential waiver was required for China happened to be June 3, the anniversary of the Tiananmen Square massacre. Moreover, because Jackson-Vanik permits Congress to override a presidential waiver by an affirmative vote, the mechanics of the law made it necessary for both the executive and the legislative branches of government to take a stand on whether it would be more important to maintain normal trade relations with China (which is all that is provided by MFN) or to impose trade sanctions because of China's abuses of human rights.

As is now recognized, there was never a realistic possibility that China would lose MFN status. The country is too big, the economic and political interests at stake are too important, and the sanction is too sweeping in its impact to be overridden by human rights concerns. Hundreds of major corporations and prominent foreign policy spokespersons such as Henry Kissinger and Cyrus Vance lobbied the Clinton administration to ensure that it would not follow through on the president's 1993 executive order, which provided that MFN would be extended in June 1994 only if China made certain human rights improvements. While the debates about MFN were underway in the period from 1990 to 1994, and when Beijing was attempting to convince the International Olympic Committee to designate it the site for the year 2000 Olympics, China released a relative handful of its most prominent political prisoners, allowing them to emigrate or, as with Wei Jingsheng, expelling them to the West.[2]

Thus the debates over MFN did shine the spotlight of international public attention on some of China's human rights abuses, notably its long prison sentences for peaceful dissenters and the appalling conditions of confinement they endured. Ultimately, however, the debate over MFN for China also did significant damage to the human rights cause. That became apparent on May 26, 1994, when President Clinton reversed the stand he had taken a year earlier and announced the "delinkage" of MFN from China's human rights practices. This delinkage sent a harmful signal that, while the United States was prepared to pay lip service to the promotion of human rights, it would not give precedence to human rights in its foreign policy when matters of real weight were at stake. This retreat not only nullified the effectiveness of the MFN stick, which had become the main weapon for promoting human rights in China, but it also undercut the human rights movement by demonstrating that it lacked the power to prevail when important economic interests were arrayed against it.

Delinkage indicated that the United States had adopted a new double standard not unlike that of the cold war era. Then the United States had held countries aligned with the Soviet Union to a much tougher standard on their abuses of human rights than it did those noncommunist states considered to be on the U.S. side. Countries such as China that were being courted by both sides largely escaped criticism or scrutiny on human rights grounds, even as they committed crimes of the magnitude of China's disastrous "Cultural Revolution," under way even while President Nixon's celebrated opening to China took place. Following the end of the cold war, the United States began reporting abuses more even-handedly, as exemplified by the State Department's annual *Country Reports* on human rights.[3] However, with delinkage, Clinton demonstrated that although human rights concerns might affect U.S. policy toward countries of no great economic or geopolitical significance, they would not influence the United States in its relations with countries or interests of first-rank importance. Sanctions would be reserved for "less important" countries such as Burma; if China engaged in similar abuses, these could not be allowed to interfere with normal trade relations.

Apprehensive of just such a result, Human Rights Watch had proposed in 1992 that, rather than eliminate MFN, tariffs should be imposed selectively on China and adjusted according to the way its human rights situation developed. Government-owned industries would be the targets for particular penalties. Legislation embodying this approach was introduced and adopted by Congress, but President Bush vetoed it on September 28, 1992. The House of Representatives voted to override, but the Senate vote of 59 to 40 fell just short of the two-thirds majority required to enact the measure into law. Had this approach succeeded, it would have avoided the all-or-nothing approach of denying China MFN and might have staved off a severe setback for the human rights cause.

In retrospect, it would have been better if a proposal for sanctions against China from the outset had been more modest and more focused on a particular abuse, such as denial of access to Chinese prisons by the International Committee of the Red Cross. If less drastic sanctions were put in place, they could have toughened over time if no headway was made on the issue on which they focused. By starting with a proposal for sweeping sanctions, the human rights movement picked a fight it could not win. Of course, that proposal was offered in the emotional aftermath of Tiananmen Square; at that moment, it was difficult to get consideration of a more nuanced approach. But with the advantage of hindsight, it seems clear that a proposal for limited sanctions would have been more realistic and, in the long run, would have achieved better results.

BURMA

In 1988 large-scale public demonstrations urged an end to Burma's long-term military dictatorship but were crushed by troops who turned machine guns on the protestors. Thousands were killed. That September a new military junta was established that called itself the State Law and Order Restoration Council (SLORC) and promised that elections would be held after order was restored. The opposition National League for Democracy (NLD), led by Aung San Suu Kyi, was allowed scant access to the media in the period leading up to the elections of May 1990, but it nevertheless captured more than 80 percent of the seats in Parliament. SLORC responded by canceling the results of the election and arresting and imprisoning many victorious candidates for office, including Aung San Suu Kyi. It has ruled ever since by decree. In addition, the SLORC generals changed the country's official name in English to Myanmar, a transliteration of the country's Burmese language name. This change, done by decree and without public consultation, has been rejected by Burma's democratic opposition.

The United States reacted to the events in Burma by imposing sanctions by degrees. In 1988–1989 it terminated direct U.S. economic aid, withdrew trade preferences, imposed an arms embargo, and blocked loans from international financial institutions. In 1990 it downgraded diplomatic representation in Rangoon (Yangon) from ambassador to the level of a chargé d'affaires; in 1996 it prohibited visas for senior members of the Burmese military and their families; and, most significantly, in 1997 it prohibited any new investments by U.S. companies in Burma. Other states also have imposed sanctions in varying degrees. Japan cut off aid; Canada's sanctions resemble those of the United States; and Britain's Labor government has said it is actively discouraging investments. In December 1997 the European Union invoked the human rights provisions of its Generalized System of Preferences (GSP) for the first time, cutting off Burma's low-tariff access to the European Union market because of Burma's use of forced labor. The largest foreign investor in Burma is Singapore, but the Asian financial collapse dashed SLORC's hopes that investments by other Association of Southeast Asian Nations (ASEAN) countries (which accepted Burma for membership in 1997) would replace those from Western democracies that imposed sanctions.

Despite this array of sanctions against Burma and the fact that some have been in place for a decade, they have had little visible result. Burma remains one of the most tightly controlled dictatorships in the world, lacking any freedom of speech, of assembly, or of the press; completely denying due process of law; and continuing to practice such abuses as arbitrary political imprisonment, torture, mass forced relocations, and forced labor. Whatever tiny space for dissent exists in what is otherwise a totalitarian system is due to the unique leadership of Aung San Suu Kyi. International public attention to the country is primarily attributable to her efforts and only secondarily to debates over sanctions.

Nevertheless, like most human rights proponents, I would argue that economic sanctions against Burma are serving valuable purposes. Their main impact is on the country's rulers rather than on its impoverished population. With close to a half-million men in service, Burma's swollen armed forces require a substantial flow of funds if soldiers are to be paid. The military has made it clear that if Burma had more money, much of it would be used to purchase military equipment from China and other suppliers. The economy is not organized in a manner that would make poor Burmese citizens the main beneficiaries of any increases in trade.

Sanctions are also responsible for focusing international attention on Burma, and they have the effect within the country—where radio broadcasts from outside its borders are the main source of popular information—of signifying that the international community opposes the military regime and sides with Aung San Suu Kyi and other pro-democracy Burmese. Over time the sanctions could force the government to seek an accommodation with the National League for Democracy. Though the Burmese military leaders have thus far resisted pressure for negotiations with Aung San Suu Kyi and her NLD colleagues over such an accommodation, the economic pressures on the regime have intensified recently with the U.S. ban on new investments, with state and local laws in the United States that prohibit transactions with firms doing business in Burma, and with the regime's realization that its Southeast Asian neighbors are not in a position to help it economically.[4] It seems unlikely that the military rulers of Burma will be able to hold out indefinitely against the sanctions that are now in place.

The Burma case makes it clear that sanctions imposed to promote human rights may have to be kept in place for an extended period to achieve their ultimate aim. A repressive regime is unlikely to collapse because of sanctions. It has many ways of attempting to circumvent or overcome the difficulties that result from sanctions, and it may well have a tolerance for economic hardship that enables it to endure their consequences for a long time. As indicated, the sanctions imposed on Burma already have achieved substantial positive results, but it is not possible to predict how long it might take before they achieve their ultimate aim of transforming Burma into a country where human rights are respected.

SOUTH AFRICA

There is widespread agreement that sanctions played a part in the transformation that took place in South Africa in the 1990s, though how large a part is a matter of dispute. Sanctions were imposed by many countries, including the United States, during the 1980s; Margaret Thatcher's Britain was an exception, and President Ronald Reagan also attempted to resist sanctions. However, in 1985, in the face of proposed legislation that otherwise seemed certain of adoption even over his veto, Reagan signed an executive order that was considerably weaker than the congressional bill. It prohibited computer and nuclear exports; it suspended loans; it banned imports of gold Krugerrands; and it provided measures to persuade U.S. companies doing business in South Africa to use their power and influence in compliance with the "Sullivan principles," drafted by the Reverend Leon Sullivan in 1977 to guide U.S. firms in promoting integration and equal opportunity in South Africa.[5] In an effort to suggest that the executive order did not entail a shift in policy, Reagan labeled it "active constructive engagement" and coupled its issuance with an announcement of the return to Pretoria of the U.S. ambassador, who had been withdrawn a few months earlier to protest cross-border military raids by the South African armed forces into Botswana and into Angola from the South African–ruled territory that has since become Namibia. Thereafter, however, in October 1986, Congress imposed much tougher sanctions in an act adopted over President Reagan's veto. Even before the United States imposed official sanctions, opponents of the apartheid system brought economic pressure against the South African government by launching a "disinvestment" campaign. The campaign persuaded many institutional investors, such as pension funds, universities, and private charities, not to hold shares in companies doing business in South Africa. In addition, debates on college campuses and elsewhere about disinvestment provided an ongoing forum for those eager to call attention to the suffering that resulted from the enforcement of apartheid.

Richard N. Haass, director of Foreign Policy Studies at the Brooking Institution, is one of those who has questioned the significance of sanctions in bringing apartheid to an end. "To be sure," he argues, "sanctions may have contributed to change in that instance. But the rapidity of change within South Africa cannot be connected to any meaningful ratcheting up of sanctions, which suggests that factors other than sanctions mattered as much or more."[6]

As one who has visited South Africa frequently in the last two decades, I believe this view misconstues the manner in which sanctions had an impact. It was unmistakably clear to visitors how much it mattered to white South Africans to see their country and themselves as an outpost of Western civilization. From this standpoint, the sanctions not only had an economic impact but, in combination with the international sports boycott, they signified that South Africa was rejected by the West. In the late 1980s, the South African economy went into a tailspin, and sanctions were considered to be partly responsible.

More important, however, this was the period in which Mikhail Gorbachev's reforms in the Soviet Union were reducing cold war tensions. Those reforms led to the revolutions of 1989 in Eastern Europe that ended an era in which the world had been divided into two camps. The impact in South Africa was to eliminate any remaining prospect that the West would reconcile with the apartheid regime simply because it was aligned against a communist enemy. With no ready ally, white South Africans saw that their country's isolation would only deepen unless they ended apartheid. Accordingly, on February 2, 1990, President F. W. DeKlerk, who had been elected the previous September, announced that Nelson Mandela and hundreds of other opponents of apartheid would be released from prison; that such organizations as the African National Congress, the Pan-Africanist Congress, and the South African Communist Party would be legalized; and that he was ready to begin negotiations over the adoption of a new national constitution, under which all, regardless of race, would enjoy equal rights.

By themselves, sanctions did not bring South Africa to this point. To look for some "ratcheting up" that suddenly made them more effective is to look in the wrong place. What did happen, however, is that historical events unfolded in a manner that suddenly made the impact of sanctions, and the fear of even greater isolation from the West, far greater in February 1990 than they had been five years earlier.

The South African case demonstrates—as in varying degree is true else-where—that it is a mistake to measure the impact of sanctions exclusively or predominantly in terms of their economic consequences. Often identification as a pariah state is of comparable significance. In South Africa, that was the main way that sanctions contributed to the end of apartheid.

POLAND

On December 13, 1981, the government of General Wojciech Jaruzelski declared martial law; it banned Solidarity, the labor union that had become a social movement and that had enrolled an astonishing ten million members during the previous sixteen months; and it arrested some 30,000 people. (The majority were released after a few months, but about 2,000 remained in prison at the end of 1993, and several hundred were held in prison for more extended periods.) Shortly thereafter, in early 1982, the Reagan administration imposed economic sanctions including denial of most-favored nation trading status, credit purchasing of grain, financial aid, transfer of high technology, fishing rights, airline landing rights, and, most important, the cancellation of talks on rescheduling the Polish debt and denial of access to the International Monetary Fund (IMF).

Prior to the imposition of martial law, Poland had enjoyed warmer ties to the Untied States than other Soviet bloc states. As a country in which the Catholic church always had maintained a significant measure of independence and where the important agricultural sector had resisted collectivization, it was not regarded by the West in the same light as the other "satellites." In addition, a large Polish immigrant population in the United States that maintained ties to the homeland was a factor in American foreign policy. The economic ties that developed between Poland and the United States left the country more vulnerable to American sanctions than other Warsaw Pact states.

Reagan announced that the sanctions would remain in place until martial law was lifted, until all the political prisoners were freed, and until Jaruzelski's government began a new dialogue with Solidarity and the Catholic church. In June 1983 the Reagan administration modified its condition: The reference to Solidarity was dropped, and the administration said the sanctions would be eased if Poland "took meaningful liberalizing measures."[7]

A month after the Reagan administration modified its stand, the Polish regime formally lifted martial law and declared an amnesty for most, but not all, of the political prisoners. In response, the Reagan administration lifted a few sanctions, including, most important, the exclusion of the Polish fishing fleet from American waters. In the next year, 1984, Warsaw declared a broader amnesty, reducing from 700 or 800 to about 30 the number of people held in prison for their activity in Solidarity. This action brought about a further relaxation of sanctions by the United States, which announced its readiness to renew landing rights for Lot Polish Airlines at New York's John F. Kennedy Airport and raised the possibility that objections to Poland's entry into the IMF would be withdrawn. With those incentives in view, the communist government released the last two Solidarity prisoners, Bogdan Lis and Piotr Mierzewski, both of whom had been charged with treason in December 1984 for their role in the banned union; shortly thereafter the United States announced that it would favor Poland's admission to the IMF.

In 1985 the Polish regime began rearresting some of those freed in 1984, including Bogdan Lis. Nevertheless, regular flights between Poland and the United States resumed that April, and Poland was admitted to the IMF, in a vote from which the United States abstained, because European governments feared that Poland would default on its debts. Washington did keep two sanctions in place: Poland did not get MFN trading status under the Jackson-Vanik Amendment, and the United States maintained its ban on government-guaranteed credits for investments. Then, in September 1986, the Jaruzelski regime announced yet another amnesty, freeing all the political prisoners arrested during the previous two years. After waiting a few months to see whether those released would be rearrested, the Reagan administration announced on February 19, 1987, that it would remove all remaining sanctions.

The sanctions against Poland are probably the clearest case in which incentives were offered for human rights improvements and adjustments were made to reward specific performance. Over a five-year period, these economic measures contributed significantly to a new political opening. They thus helped spawn new negotiations between the government and Solidarity, helping bring about a peaceful end to the communist regime, which paved the way for similar transitions throughout the region. Although other factors also contributed, sanctions played a larger role in promoting human rights in Poland than anywhere else. The clarity with which they were linked to performance on particular human rights issues and Poland's eagerness to regain its relatively favored relationship with the United States probably were key to the success of sanctions.

LATIN AMERICA

At the outset of his administration in 1977, President Jimmy Carter proclaimed his administration's commitment to making the promotion of human rights an important factor in U.S. foreign policy.[8] He stated early in his presidential campaign that his dream was "that this country set a standard within the community of nations of courage, integrity, and dedication to basic human rights and freedoms."[9] He applied that commitment more comprehensively and forcefully in Latin America than anywhere else. As a consequence, U.S. military and economic assistance to Chile and other military dictatorships in the region was cut drastically under Carter. U.S. aid had totaled $93.7 million in fiscal year (FY) 1975, the first full year that U.S. economic assistance reflected support by Presidents Nixon and Ford for the coup that brought General Augusto Pinochet to power in September 1973. In contrast, in FY1978, the first full year of the Carter administration, aid declined to $5.8 million, all except $200,000 under the Food for Peace Program. It is difficult to say whether this contributed to a slight easing of repression in 1977–1978, including replacement of the "state of siege" as of March 11, 1978, by a somewhat less restrictive "state of emergency."

However, when Ronald Reagan became president in 1981, his administration quickly signaled that it would pursue a different policy. Alexander Haig, Reagan's first secretary of state, told a Senate hearing that terrorism would replace human rights as a top priority in U.S. foreign policy. He declared that "international terrorism will take the place of human rights in our concern because it is the ultimate abuse of human rights."[10] Other administration officials, among them United Nations Ambassador Jeane Kirkpatrick, Assistant Secretary of State for Inter-American Affairs Thomas Enders, and Assistant Secretary of State for Human Rights Elliott Abrams, made it clear that the shift in U.S. policy would be especially dramatic in Latin America. The Reagan administration blamed Carter and his human rights policy for the fall of the regime of General Anastasio Somoza in Nicaragua in 1979 and its replacement by Daniel Ortega and the left-wing Sandinistas. The administration was determined that concerns about human rights abuses should not interfere with U.S. support for other Latin American military dictatorships. U.S. abandonment of those regimes, it believed, could allow left-wing governments aligned with the cold war enemy to gain additional footholds on the mainland of the Western Hemisphere. Jeane Kirkpatrick warned that "the deterioration of the U.S. position in the hemisphere has already created serious vulnerabilities . . . and threatens now to confront this country with the unprecedented need to defend itself against a ring of Soviet bases on and around our southern and eastern borders."[11]

As matters turned out, however, the Reagan administration was forced by Congress and by public concern for human rights to deny U.S. economic assistance to some Latin American military dictatorships. This policy thereby helped to promote a shift to civilian democratic government that, over the course of the 1980s, swept the continent. A key role was played by legislation adopted by Congress known as the International Security and Development Cooperation Act of 1981, which contained a number of country-specific provisions. Under provisions of the law, introduced by a small band of members of Congress who had identified themselves with the human rights cause, economic and military assistance, including arms sales, could not be provided to certain governments, including Argentina, Chile, and El Salvador, unless the U.S. president certified that they had complied with criteria that were written to deal specifically with human rights abuses associated with those countries.

One of the provisions of the law required the president to take into account "efforts by the Government of Argentina to provide information on citizens identified as 'disappeared.'" Disappearances had been at the heart of the repression by the Argentine military regime that took power in 1976. A Truth Commission that conducted an investigation after democracy was restored in 1983 documented 8,960 disappearances and said there were many more.[12] A central element of this crime was the government's denial of any knowledge of those who had been abducted, tortured, murdered, and then "disappeared," and therefore the certification requirement imposed a condition that the Argentine military regime could not meet. This placed the Reagan administration in a quandary: U.S. officials repeatedly manifested their eagerness to certify Argentina's compliance with the criteria, so that economic and military assistance would flow. However, human rights groups in Argentina and the United States worked together to demonstrate conclusively that the conditions for certification had not been met. Reagan administration spokespeople were unable to defend their proposal to certify when the issue became the focus of congressional hearings, and military aid was never provided before the military regime came to an end in December 1983.

The congressional requirements for certification presented an even greater difficulty in the case of Chile. One provision required the president to state that "the Government of Chile is not aiding or abetting international terrorism and has taken appropriate steps to cooperate to bring to justice by all legal means available in the United States or Chile those indicted by a United States grand jury in connection with the murders of Orlando Letelier and Ronni Moffitt," the former Chilean defense minister and his American aide who were killed by a car bomb on the streets of Washington, D.C., in 1976.[13] What made this especially troublesome for the Reagan administration was that certain attorneys in the Justice Department had worked on the murders of Letelier and Moffitt and had secured indictments by a federal grand jury of three Chilean military officers who were being sheltered by the Pinochet government. If Reagan were to certify Chile's compliance with the criteria, it was widely expected that a number of these Justice Department attorneys would publicly denounce him. It was a risk the administration was not eager to take in a case involving a terrorist bombing in the nation's capital.

Among the requirements for certifying El Salvador's compliance with the conditions of the law were that it demonstrate "full observance of internationally recognized human rights . . . an end to extremist violence . . . and control of all government security forces in this effort . . . free, fair, and open elections at the earliest date . . . [and] a complete and timely investigation of the deaths of all United States citizens killed in El Salvador since October 1979."[14] At this time, the Salvadoran security forces were using "death squads" to murder many thousands of suspected leftists, so it should not have been possible for Reagan to certify that El Salvador met the conditions for aid. However, El Salvador mattered most to the Reagan administration because it was a nearby neighbor of Sandinista Nicaragua and because a leftist insurgency posed a genuine threat to the country's military regime. Accordingly, it was the country in which the Reagan administration was determined to draw the line against further advances by forces aligned with Cuba, Nicaragua, and the Soviet Union in the Western Hemisphere.

The congressional act required certifications every 180 days if U.S. aid were to flow to El Salvador. The first certification was scheduled for January 1982. Americas Watch (one of the organizations that later became part of Human Rights Watch) helped to call attention to the certification issue by publishing a book-length report two days before certification was scheduled, documenting in great detail why it was not warranted. Americas Watch followed up by publishing additional reports of a similar nature every 180 days before each certification was due. These reports did not prevent certifications, but they brought pressure on the administration to curb abuses in El Salvador. Congressional hearings on each of the certifications also called attention to these issues, and the combined effect was to make the question of human rights abuses in El Salvador, and U.S. complicity in those abuses, a matter of national debate, even though the letter of the law was not followed, and aid continued to flow to El Salvador despite its human rights abuses.

In an effort to comply with the conditions for certification, the Reagan administration did require the Salvadoran military to hold elections, beginning in 1983, and also to prosecute and convict several low-ranking national guardsmen for the December 1980 murder of three U.S. nuns and a lay churchwoman.[15] For a long time, however, the Salvadoran regime did little to respond to death squad murders until, at long last, in December 1983, Vice President George Bush was dispatched to San Salvador for an unpublicized meeting with the military high command. Bush demanded that the death squad killings be curbed, and he named names of military officers who were known to be responsible for them. The effect was immediate: The number of death squad killings dropped dramatically, although many other severe abuses of human rights persisted throughout the decade.

The Reagan administration succeeded in certifying that El Salvador was entitled to U.S. economic and military assistance, which amounted to more than

$4 billion during the war years from 1980 to 1992. But its insistence on doing so made it all the more wary of the criticism it would have faced from human rights groups, Congress, and the media if it had certified Argentina and Chile as well. Accordingly, it never did so while the military held power in either country. As a result, U.S. arms were denied to Argentina in the period prior to its disastrous 1982 war with Britain over the Falklands/Malvinas, which hastened the military's downfall. In the case of Chile, the Reagan administration gradually distanced itself from General Pinochet's regime, becoming more critical in the annual *Country Reports,* abstaining in votes on World Bank loans, and, in 1988, denying Chile benefits under the Generalized System of Preferences because of its violations of labor rights. During Reagan's second term, the United States was represented in Santiago by Ambassador Harry Barnes, who played a leading role in promoting the restoration of democratic government. A consistent supporter of beleaguered Chilean human rights groups, Barnes intervened at a crucial moment to prevent the last-moment cancellation of the 1988 plebiscite that, a year and a half later, would bring Pinochet's rule to an end. The effect of sanctions on Chile was to keep the United States and the Pinochet regime at arm's length from each other, making it possible for diplomatic pressure to play a significant part in helping eventually to end a repressive regime.

Broadly speaking, the effect of the certification requirements enacted in 1981 was to promote an end to repressive military regimes in the region and a transition to democratic governments that have been largely respectful of human rights.

THE IMPACT OF SANCTIONS

Sanctions are not a magic bullet: In particular, advocates of human rights have not been able to get the United States to impose sweeping economic sanctions in circumstances where major U.S. interests are at stake. The Bush and Clinton administrations have not allowed their concerns about pervasive, severe abuses in human rights in China to outweigh their interest in maintaining normal trade relations, and when the Reagan administration considered El Salvador a leading battleground in its worldwide struggle with the Soviet Union, it certified the country's compliance with human rights standards even in the face of thousands of death squad murders. In such circumstances, the most that human rights proponents can achieve, I believe, is certain modest gains for human rights by small-scale sanctions that are narrowly targeted. An example is the prosecution of the national guardsmen in El Salvador for the murders of the four U.S.

churchwomen, which was spurred at one point by a measure in Congress that specifically conditioned $19 million in U.S. aid on progress in the case.

But much can be achieved for human rights where interests of lesser geopolitical significance do not overwhelm human rights issues. Even in such circumstances, however, the more targeted the incentives, the better the likely results, as the case of Poland shows: Sanctions were relaxed and tightened directly in response to specific changes on the ground. Argentina and Chile also illustrate this point because the specificity of the human rights conditions in the 1981 law on U.S. aid focused attention on particular abuses and made it possible to measure reliably whether they had complied. Although neither government improved its human rights record enough to meet these conditions while the military held power, the denial of U.S. assistance ultimately became a factor in spurring the transitions to democratic government and a consequent dramatic improvement in respect for human rights.

It is important not to claim too much for sanctions. It is rarely, if ever, possible to demonstrate a one-to-one cause-and-effect relationship between their imposition and a particular advance for human rights. At most, they are one factor among many that may combine for positive effect. Frequently, as happened in South Africa when the cold war ended, and in Burma when the Southeast Asian financial collapse dashed hopes for regional investments, unanticipated events heighten the impact of sanctions at particular moments. Thus, even as we recognize that they do not provide a magic bullet, it is important also to recognize sanctions' symbolic significance: Their effect on the international standing of the target countries, their demonstration of support for local human rights victims and activists, and their importance in calling attention to abuses, are benefits that may considerably outweigh their actual economic consequences.

NOTES

1. See *Burma Debate,* a quarterly publication of the Open Society Institute, New York, available online at <www.soros.org/burma/>. See especially the backgrounder to the recent debates over the Massachusetts Burma Selective Purchasing Law, "David and Goliath— Sanctions Style," *Burma Debate,* Summer 1999, <http://www.soros.org/burma/burmadebate/bdsummer99.html>.
2. See chapter 2 in this volume.
3. Such reports, which have been publicly issued annually since 1977, review human rights developments in the previous year worldwide. See chapter 12 in this volume.
4. See "An act regulating state contracts with companies doing business with or in Burma (Myanmar)," *Commonwealth of Massachusetts Selective Purchasing Law* (signed by Governor William F. Weld, June 25, 1996), <http://metalab.unc.edu/freeburma/boycott/sp/mass.html>; "Prohibiting New Investment in Burma—Message from the President of the

United States," *Burma and the U.S. Congress* (H. Doc. 105-85) (House of Representatives, May 20, 1997); and related news articles: Steven Mufson, "High Court Considers Mass. Anti-Burma Law," *Washington Post,* March 23, 2000; Joan Biskupic "High Court to Review Mass. Law on Burma," *Washington Post,* November 30, 1999; Associated Press, "State Attorney General Seeks Review of Burma Trade Ruling," *Boston Globe,* July 13, 1999.

5.   There were seven "Sullivan Principles": desegregation; equal and fair employment practices; equal pay; training programs for nonwhites; increased numbers of nonwhites in supervisory positions; improvements in employees' circumstances outside the work environment; and efforts to eliminate laws and customs impeding social justice. The Reverend Leon Sullivan is a prominent African American clergyman who served on the board of General Motors.

6.   Richard Haass, "Introduction," in Haass, ed., *Economic Sanctions and American Diplomacy* (New York: Council on Foreign Relations, 1998), p. 4.

7.   Quoted in Michael Getler, "Brzezinski, West Berlin Mayor Urge Quick U.S. Nod to Poland," *Washington Post,* June 26, 1983, p. A21.

8.   See chapter 3 in this volume.

9.   Jimmy Carter, *Keeping Faith: Memoirs of a President* (New York: Bantam Books, 1982), p. 143.

10. Lawrence Knutson, "Haig Sounds Anti-Terrorism Foreign Policy Emphasis," Associated Press, January 29, 1981.

11. Jeane Kirkpatrick, "U.S. Security in Latin America," *Commentary,* January 1981.

12. *Nunca Mas,* Report of the National Commission on Disappeared Persons (Sabato Commission), Buenos Aires, 1984. See also chapter 6 in this volume.

13. John Dinges and Saul Landau, *Assassination on Embassy Row* (Pantheon: New York, 1980); Taylor Branch and Eugene Propper, *Labyrinth* (New York: Viking, 1982).

14. There had been seven Americans killed in El Salvador during that period: four church-women, two labor advisors, and a journalist.

15. The four guardsmen were eventually freed in 1993 under one of the periodic amnesty laws enacted in the country. In 1998 the guardsmen said for the first time that they had "orders from above" to murder the four churchwomen. In 1993 a UN Truth Commission had accused a former Minister of Defense and a former commander of the National Guard of organizing a cover-up. Larry Rohter, "Four Salvadorans Say They Killed US Nuns on Orders of Military," *New York Times,* April 3, 1998.

FOURTEEN

Human Rights and Humanitarian Intervention in the Twenty-First Century

Kofi Annan

Kofi Annan of Ghana is the seventh Secretary-General of the United Nations. The first Secretary-General to be elected from the ranks of United Nations staff, he began his term on January 1, 1997. Before being appointed Secretary-General, Mr. Annan served as Assistant Secretary-General for Peacekeeping Operations (March 1993–February 1994) and then as Under Secretary-General (February 1994–October 1995; April 1996–December 1996). His tenure as Under Secretary-General coincided with unprecedented growth in the size and scope of United Nations peacekeeping operations, with a total deployment, at its peak in 1995, of almost 70,000 military and civilian personnel from 77 countries. From November 1995 to March 1996, following the Dayton Peace Agreement that ended the war in Bosnia and Herzegovina, Mr. Annan served as Special Representative of the Secretary-General to the former Yugoslavia, overseeing the transition in Bosnia and Herzegovina from the United Nations Protection Force (UNPROFOR) to the multinational Implementation Force (IFOR) led by the North Atlantic Treaty Organization (NATO).

At the dawn of the twenty-first century, the United Nations (UN) has become more central to the lives of more people than ever before. Through our work in development, peacekeeping, the environment, and health, we are helping nations and communities to build a better, freer, more prosperous future. Above all, however, we have committed ourselves to the idea that no individual—regardless of gender, ethnicity, or race—shall have his or her human rights abused or ignored. This idea is enshrined in the Charter of the United Nations and the Universal Declaration of Human Rights. It is the source of our greatest inspiration and the impulse for our greatest efforts. Today we know more than ever that without respect for the rights of the individual, no nation, no community, no society can be truly free. Whether our task centers on advancing development, or emphasizing the importance of preventive action, or intervening—even within the boundaries of a state—to stop gross and systematic violations of human rights, the individual has been the focus of our concerns.

The Emerging UN Commitment to Human Rights

The promotion and defense of human rights is at the heart of every aspect of our work and every article of the UN Charter. The United Nations is an association of sovereign states, but the rights it expounds in its Charter belong to peoples, not governments. When civilians are attacked and massacred because of their ethnicity, as in Kosovo, the world looks to the United Nations to speak up for them. When civilians are assaulted and their limbs hacked off, as in Sierra Leone, here again the world looks to the United Nations. When women and girls are denied their right to equality, as in Afghanistan, the world looks to the United Nations to take a stand. Above all, I believe human rights are at the core of our sacred bond with the peoples who make up the member states of the United Nations.

Perhaps more than any other aspect of our work, the struggle for human rights resonates with our global constituency and is deeply relevant to the lives of those most in need—the tortured, the oppressed, the silenced, the victims of ethnic cleansing and injustice. If, in the face of such abuses, we do not speak up and speak out, if we do not act in defense of human rights and advocate their lasting universality, how can we answer that global constituency? In a world where globalization has limited the ability of states to control their economies, regulate their financial policies, and isolate themselves from environmental damage and human migration, the last right of states cannot and must not be the right to enslave, persecute, or torture their own citizens.

Emerging slowly, but, I believe, surely, is an international norm against gross violations of human rights that will and must take precedence over concerns of state sovereignty. It is a principle that protects minorities—and majorities—from gross violations. And let me therefore be very clear: Even though we are an organization of member states, the rights and ideals the United Nations exists to protect are those of peoples. Thus in April 1991, the late François Mitterrand congratulated the Security Council on its decision to intervene in the internal affairs of Iraq, in order to save the Kurds. "For the first time," President Mitterrand declared, "noninterference has stopped at the point where it was becoming failure to assist a people in danger." No government has the right to hide behind national sovereignty in order to violate the human rights or fundamental freedoms of its peoples. Whether a person belongs to the minority or the majority, that person's human rights and fundamental freedoms are sacred.

Two Concepts of Sovereignty

Parallel to this development in the consciousness of human rights as central to the relations among states has been a transformation in the role and responsibilities of the state in international affairs. State sovereignty, in its most basic sense, is being redefined by the forces of globalization and international cooperation. The state is now widely understood to be the servant of its people, not vice versa. At the same time, individual sovereignty—and by this I mean the human rights and fundamental freedoms of each and every individual as enshrined in our Charter—has been enhanced by a renewed consciousness of the right of every individual to control his or her own destiny.[1]

These parallel developments—remarkable and in many ways welcome—do not lend themselves to easy interpretations or simple conclusions.

They do, however, demand of us a willingness to think anew: about how the United Nations responds to the political, human rights, and humanitarian crises affecting so much of the world;[2] about the means employed by the international community in situations of need; and about our willingness to act in some areas of conflict while limiting ourselves to humanitarian palliatives in many other crises whose daily toll of death and suffering ought to shame us into action. Above all, we need to think anew about the perils and promise of intervention in the face of extreme human suffering.

We all applaud the police officer who intervenes to stop a fight, or the teacher who prevents a bigger boy from bullying a smaller one. And medicine uses the word "intervention" to describe the act of the surgeon, who saves life by "intervening" to remove malignant growths or to repair damaged organs. Of course, the most intrusive methods of treatment are not always to be recommended. A wise doctor knows when to let nature take its course. But a doctor who *never* intervened would have few admirers, and probably even fewer patients.

So it is in international affairs. Why was the United Nations established, if not to act as a benign police officer or doctor? Our job *is* to intervene: to prevent conflict where we can, to put a stop to it when it has broken out, or—when neither of those things is possible—at least to contain it and prevent it from spreading.

On the face of it, there is a simple distinction between international conflict, which is clearly the United Nations' business, and internal disputes, which are not. The very phrase "domestic dispute" sounds reassuring. It suggests a little local difficulty that the state in question can easily settle if only it is left alone to do so.

We all know that in recent years these distinctions have fallen away.[3] Most wars nowadays are civil wars. Or at least that is how they start. And these civil wars are anything but benign. In fact they are "civil" only in the sense that *civilians*—that is, noncombatants—have become the main victims. In the First World War roughly 90 percent of those killed were soldiers, and only 10 percent civilians. In the Second World War, even if we count all the victims of Nazi death camps as war casualties, civilians made up approximately half of all those killed. But in many of today's conflicts, civilians have become the main targets of violence. It is now conventional to put the proportion of civilian casualties somewhere in the region of 75 percent.[4] The victims of today's brutal conflicts are not merely anonymous but literally countless.

Sometimes in concert with internal conflict comes genocide. The tragic irony of this age of human rights—where greater numbers of people are enjoying human rights than perhaps at any other time in history—is that it has been repeatedly darkened by outbursts of genocidal violence and organized mass killings. For example, in Cambodia, in the 1970s, up to 2 million people were killed by Pol Pot's regime. And in the 1990s, from Bosnia to Rwanda, thousands upon thousands of human beings were massacred for belonging to the wrong ethnicity.

Each time, though, the world says "never again." And yet it happens. The vicious and systematic campaign of "ethnic cleansing" conducted by the Serbian authorities in Kosovo appeared to have one aim: to expel or kill as many ethnic Albanians in Kosovo as possible, thereby denying a people their most basic rights to life, liberty, and security. The result was a humanitarian disaster throughout the entire region. We all deeply regret that the international community, despite months of diplomatic efforts, failed to prevent this disaster. What gives me hope—and should give every future "ethnic cleanser" and every state-backed architect of mass murder pause—is that universal outrage led to the eventual return of the Albanian population to Kosovo.

Yet so long as the conflict rages within the borders of a single state, the old orthodoxy would require us to let it rage. It would dictate that we leave it even to escalate, regardless of human consequences, at least until the point when its effects spill over into neighboring states, so that it becomes, in the words of so many Security Council resolutions, "a threat to international peace and security."

INTERVENTIONS PAST AND FUTURE

In reality, this "old orthodoxy" was never absolute. The Charter, after all, was issued in the name of "the peoples," not the governments, of the United Nations.[5] Its aim is not only to preserve international peace—vitally important though that is—but also "to reaffirm faith in fundamental human rights, in the dignity and worth of the human person." The Charter protects the sovereignty of peoples. It was never meant as a license for governments to trample on human rights and human dignity. Sovereignty implies responsibility, not just power.

The Universal Declaration of Human Rights (UDHR) was not meant as a purely rhetorical statement.[6] The General Assembly that adopted it also decided, in the same month, that it had the right to express its concern about the apartheid system in South Africa. In this case, the principle of international concern for human rights took precedence over the claim of noninterference in internal affairs.

And the day before it adopted the Universal Declaration in 1948, the General Assembly had adopted the Convention on the Prevention and Punishment of the Crime of Genocide, which puts all states under an obligation to "prevent and punish" this most heinous of crimes. It also allows them to "call upon the competent organs of the United Nations" to take action for this purpose.[7] Since genocide is almost always committed with the connivance, if not the direct participation, of state authorities, it is hard to see how the United Nations could prevent it without intervening in a state's internal affairs.

State frontiers should no longer be seen as a watertight protection for war criminals or mass murderers. The fact that a conflict is "internal" does not give the parties any right to disregard the most basic rules of human conduct. Besides, most "internal" conflicts do not stay internal for very long. They soon spill over into neighboring countries.

The most obvious and tragic way this happens is through the flow of refugees.[8] Other spillover effects include a rapid spread of small arms, destabilized state borders, and the subsequent strengthening of organized crime and terrorist networks. Moreover, today's conflicts do not spread only across existing frontiers. Sometimes they actually give birth to new states, which of course means new frontiers.

The process is seldom as smooth and trouble-free as the famous "velvet divorce" between Czechs and Slovaks. Even when new states emerge peacefully, as in the former Soviet Union, the initial separation may be largely nonviolent, and yet it soon gives rise to new conflicts, which pose new problems to the international community. It is best to avoid waiting until the conflict eventually becomes so dangerous that the international community finds itself *obliged* to intervene. By then it can only do so in the most intrusive and expensive way, which is military intervention.[9]

The most effective interventions are not military. It is much better, from every point of view, if action can be taken to resolve or manage a conflict *before* it reaches the military stage. Sometimes this action may take the form of "carrots," such as economic advice and assistance; sometimes of "sticks," targeted sanctions. [10]

In recent years, there has been an increasing emphasis on the UN's political work, as the size, though not the number, of peacekeeping operations has shrunk since their peak in the early 1990s.[11] Early diplomatic intervention, at its best, can avert bloodshed altogether. The United Nations is more than happy if disputes can be dealt with peacefully at the regional level, without the UN needing to be involved. For example, when the Organization of American States (OAS) lent its support to Guatemalan civil society in its resistance against the government's suspension of the constitution, judiciary, and legislature in 1993, it provided key international diplomatic support to the opposition and helped to end the coup threat. We must assume, however, that there will always be some tragic cases where peaceful means have failed, where extreme violence is being used, and where only forceful intervention can stop it.

ENSURING THE EFFECTIVENESS AND LEGITIMACY OF INTERVENTION

Even during the cold war, when the UN's own enforcement capacity was largely paralyzed by divisions in the Security Council, there were cases where extreme violations of human rights in one country were a factor in facilitating military intervention by one of its neighbors. In 1971, for example, Indian intervention ended the civil war in East Pakistan, halting atrocities by the army and leading to the birth of Bangladesh. In 1978 Vietnam intervened in Cambodia, putting an end to the genocidal rule of the Khmer Rouge. In 1979 Tanzania intervened to overthrow Idi Amin's dictatorship in Uganda.

In all three of those cases the intervening states cited refugee flows across the border as the reason why they had to act. But what made their action more legitimate in the eyes of the world was the internal character of the regimes they acted against. And history has by and large ratified that verdict. Few would now deny that in those cases intervention was a lesser evil than allowing massacre and extreme oppression to continue.

Most of us would prefer, especially now that the cold war is over, to see such decisions taken collectively, by a fully international institution with undisputed legal authority. And the only institution competent to assume that role is the Security Council of the United Nations. The Charter clearly assigns responsibility to the Council for maintaining *international* peace and security. I would argue that the Council has the full legal authority to decide that the *internal* situation in any state is so grave as to justify forceful intervention.

While the genocide in Rwanda will define for our generation the conse-quences of inaction in the face of mass murder,[12] the more recent conflict in Kosovo has prompted important questions about the consequences of action in the absence of complete unity on the part of the international community. It has cast in stark relief a dilemma: on one side, the question of the legitimacy of an action taken by a regional organization without a UN mandate; on the other, the universally recognized imperative of effectively halting gross and systematic violations of human rights with grave humanitarian consequences.

The inability of the international community in the case of Kosovo to reconcile these two equally compelling interests—universal legitimacy *and* effectiveness in defense of human rights—can only be viewed as a tragedy.[13] It has revealed the core challenge to the Security Council and the United Nations as a whole in the next century: to forge unity behind the principle that massive and systematic violations of human rights—*wherever* they may take place—should not be allowed to stand.

The Kosovo conflict and its outcome have prompted a wide debate of profound importance to the resolution of conflicts, from the Balkans, to Central Africa, to East Asia. And to each side in this critical debate, difficult questions can be posed.

To those for whom the greatest threat to the future of international order is the use of force in the absence of a Security Council mandate, one might ask—not in the context of Kosovo—but in the context of Rwanda: If, in those dark days and hours leading up to the genocide, a coalition of states had been prepared to act in defense of the Tutsi population, but did not receive prompt Council authorization, should such a coalition have stood aside as the horror unfolded?

To those for whom the Kosovo action heralded a new era when states and groups of states can take military action outside the established mechanisms for enforcing international law, one might ask: Is there not a danger of such interventions undermining the imperfect, yet resilient, security system created after the Second World War, and of setting dangerous precedents for future interventions without clear criteria to decide who might invoke these precedents and in what circumstances?

In response to this turbulent era of crises and interventions, there are those who have suggested that the Charter itself, with its roots in the aftermath of global interstate war, is ill-suited to guide us in a world of ethnic wars and intrastate violence. I believe they are wrong.

The Charter is a living document, whose high principles still define the aspirations of peoples everywhere for lives of peace, dignity, and development. Nothing in the Charter precludes a recognition that there are rights beyond borders. Indeed, its very letter and spirit are an affirmation of those fundamental human rights. In short, it is not the deficiencies of the Charter that have brought us to this juncture, but our difficulties in applying its principles to a new era, an era when strictly traditional notions of sovereignty can no longer do justice to the aspirations of peoples everywhere to attain their fundamental freedoms.

Four Principles for Intervention

The sovereign states that drafted the Charter over a half century ago were dedicated to peace but experienced in war. They knew the terror of conflict but knew equally that there are times when the use of force may be legitimate in the pursuit of peace. That is why the Charter's own words declare that armed force shall not be used save in the common interest. But what is that common interest? Who shall define it? Who shall defend it? Under whose authority? And with what means of intervention? These are the monumental questions facing us as we enter a new century. While I will not propose specific answers or criteria, I shall identify four aspects of intervention that I believe hold important lessons for resolving future conflicts.

First, it is important to define intervention as broadly as possible, to include actions along a wide continuum, from the most pacific to the most coercive. A tragic irony of many of the crises that continue to go unnoticed and unchallenged today is that they could be dealt with by far less perilous acts of intervention than the one we witnessed recently in Yugoslavia. And yet the commitment of the international community to peacekeeping, to humanitarian assistance, to rehabilitation and reconstruction varies greatly from region to region and crisis to crisis.[14]

It is also necessary to recognize that any armed intervention is itself a result of the failure of prevention. As we consider the future of intervention, we must redouble our efforts to enhance our preventive capabilities—including early warning, preventive diplomacy, preventive deployment, and preventive disarmament. A recent powerful tool of deterrence has been the actions of the Tribunals for Rwanda and the Former Yugoslavia.[15] In their battle against impunity lies a key to preventing future crimes against humanity. With these concerns in mind, in my 1999 Annual Report, I stressed the importance of moving from a culture of reaction to a culture of prevention.[16] Even the costliest policy of prevention is far cheaper, in lives and in resources, than the least expensive use of armed force.

Second, conceptions of national interest must change. It is clear that sovereignty is not the only obstacle to effective action in human rights or humanitarian crises. No less significant are the ways in which the member states of the United Nations define their national interest in any given crisis. Of course, the traditional pursuit of national interest is a permanent feature of international relations and of the life and work of the Security Council. But while the world has changed in profound ways since the end of the cold war, I believe our conceptions of national interest have failed to follow suit.

A new, more broadly defined, more widely conceived definition of national interest in the new century would, I am convinced, induce states to find far greater unity in the pursuit of such basic Charter values as democracy, pluralism, human rights, and the rule of law. A global era requires global engagement. Indeed, in a growing number of challenges facing humanity, the collective interest *is* the national interest.

Third, a revitalization of the effectiveness and relevance of the Security Council must become a cornerstone of our efforts to promote international peace and security in the next century. Since the end of the cold war, the world has witnessed important instances in which the Council rose to the challenge and legitimized both peacekeeping operations and the use of force when they were just and necessary. Central America and the reversal of the Iraqi aggression against Kuwait are prime examples of the Security Council playing the role envisioned for it by its founders.

However, more recently, there has been a regrettable tendency for the Security Council not to be involved in efforts to maintain international peace and security. If states apply a more broadly defined national interest, which acknowledges the Charter's demand that the UN defend common interests, the Security Council can ensure its central role in promoting peace.

The case of Kosovo casts into sharp relief the fact that member states and regional organizations sometimes take enforcement action without Security Council authorization. The choice, as I said during the Kosovo conflict, must not be between Council unity and inaction in the face of genocide—as in the case of Rwanda, on the one hand; and Council division, with regional action, as in the case of Kosovo, on the other. In both cases, the member states of the United Nations should have been able to find common ground in upholding the principles of the Charter and acting in defense of our common humanity. A parallel trend has been the flouting of international sanctions imposed by the Security Council by individual member states and even regional organizations. In addition, states have failed to cooperate with the Security Council in a variety of areas, from disarmament and nonproliferation, to cooperation with the International Tribunal for the Former Yugoslavia and with United Nations investigative human rights missions.

Unless the Security Council is able to assert itself collectively where the cause is just and the means available, its credibility in the eyes of the world may well suffer. The Security Council must address this noncooperation in areas of common global interest. To help renew its effectiveness and relevance, the Council must become more representative, reflecting current realities rather than the realities of 1945. It also must improve the quality and speed of its decisions. Humanity is ill-served when the Council is unable to react quickly and decisively in a crisis. But lack of progress toward reform must not be allowed to detract from the Council's current authority and responsibility. The Charter requires the Council to be the defender of the common interests, and unless it is seen to be so—in an era of human rights, interdependence, and globalization—there is a danger that other forces could seek to take its place.

Finally, after the conflict is over, it is vitally important that the commitment to peace be as strong as was the commitment to war. In this situation, too, consistency is essential. Just as our commitment to humanitarian action must be universal if it is to be legitimate, so our commitment to peace cannot end with the cessation of hostilities. The aftermath of war requires no less skill, no less sacrifice, no fewer resources in order to forge a lasting peace and avoid a return to violence.

Kosovo—and other UN missions currently deployed or looming over the horizon—presents us with just such a challenge. Unless the United Nations is given the means and support to succeed, not only the peace but the war too will have been lost. From civil administration, to policing, to the creation of a civil society capable of sustaining a tolerant, pluralist, prosperous society, the challenges facing our peacekeeping, peacemaking, and peace-building missions are immense.

But if member states provide the means—in Kosovo *and* in Sierra Leone, in East Timor *and* in Angola—we have a real opportunity to break the cycles of violence, once and for all.

Conclusion

If the collective conscience of humanity—a conscience that abhors cruelty, renounces injustice, and seeks peace for all peoples—cannot find in the United

Nations its greatest tribune, there is a grave danger that people will soon lose faith in the UN's ability to make a difference and look elsewhere for peace and for justice.

The critical challenge for the United Nations and the member states is to refuse to stand aside when gross and systematic violations of human rights are taking place. Intervention must be based on legitimate and universal principles if it is to gain the sustained support of the world's peoples. This emerging international norm in favor of intervention to protect civilians from wholesale slaughter will no doubt continue to pose profound challenges to the international community.

Any such evolution in our understanding of state sovereignty and individual sovereignty will, in some quarters, be met with distrust, skepticism, even hostility. But it is an evolution that we should welcome. Why? Because, despite the UN's limitations and imperfections, its evolution is testimony to a humanity that cares more—not less—for the suffering in its midst, and a humanity that will do more—and not less—to end it. This is a hopeful sign at the end of the twentieth century.

NOTES

1. See Kofi Annan, "Two Concepts of Sovereignty" *The Economist,* September 18, 1999.
2. There is an increasing emphasis on finding methods to improve international cooperation and collaboration during the international community's responses to crises. For example, at the United Nations, the sharpening of the focus of the Department of Humanitarian Affairs in the creation of the Office for the Coordination of Humanitarian Affairs (OCHA) in 1998 was done to facilitate more interagency cooperation and a streamlining of procedures for the support of field coordination during complex emergencies.
3. See my report to the Security Council on the protection of civilians in armed conflict, *Report of the Secretary-General,* of September 8, 1999 (S/1999/957) and the subsequent Security Council resolution, Resolution 1265 (1999), adopted by the Security Council on September 17, 1999.
4. See chapter 15 in this volume.
5. Witness the eloquent Preamble to the UN Charter: "We the peoples of the United Nations, determined to save succeeding generations from the scourge of war, which twice in our lifetime has brought untold sorrow to mankind, and to reaffirm faith in fundamental human rights, in the dignity and worth of the human person, in the equal rights of men and women and of nations large and small, and to establish conditions under which justice and respect for the obligations arising from treaties and other sources of international law can be maintained, and to promote social progress and better standards of life in larger freedom, and for these ends to practice tolerance and live together in peace with one another as good neighbors, and to unite our strength to maintain international peace and security, and to ensure, by the acceptance of principles and the institution of methods, that armed force shall not be used, save in the common interest, and to employ international machinery for the promotion of the economic and social advancement of all peoples, have resolved to combine our efforts to accomplish these aims."

6.   For the work that went into creating the Declaration by members of nongovernmental organizations, see William Korey, *NGOs and the Universal Declaration of Human Rights: "A Curious Grapevine"* (New York: St. Martin's Press, 1998).

7.   Convention of the Prevention and Punishment of the Crime of Genocide, adopted December 9, 1948, entered into force January 12, 1951, available in 78 *United Nations Treaty Series* 277.

8.   The total number of people of concern to the United Nations High Commissioner for Refugees rose from 17 million in 1991 to a record 27 million in 1995. The number dropped to around 22 million in 1999. Despite the overall fall, this figure still represents one out of every 280 people on Earth. They include refugees, returnees, and people displaced within their own countries.

9.   For one of the first academic studies to document the increasing use of military intervention by the international community, see Lori Fisler Damrosch, ed., *Enforcing Restraint: Collective Intervention in Internal Conflicts* (New York: Council on Foreign Relations Press, 1993).

10.   See chapter 13 in this volume where Aryeh Neier discusses economic sanctions. See also chapter 3, where Jimmy Carter stresses the important role of the United States as a donor and contributor to international economic development and political stability.

11.   The cost of UN peacekeeping personnel and equipment peaked at almost $4 billion in 1993, reflecting the expense of operations in the former Yugoslavia and Somalia. In the year 2000, the UN peacekeeping budget will be over $2 billion with major peacekeeping operations in Kosovo, East Timor, the Democratic Republic of the Congo, and Sierra Leone. Since 1948 there have been fifty-three United Nations peacekeeping operations. As of November 1999, there were seventeen under way.

12.   See the United Nations' *Report of the Independent Inquiry into the Actions of the United Nations during the 1994 Genocide in Rwanda* (New York: United Nations, December 15, 1999).

13.   To reconcile these interests, some have even proposed providing the United Nations with more adequate means of military intervention. Sir Brian Urquhart, former UN Under Secretary, was an early and key proponent of a UN rapid reaction force. See Urquhart, "For a UN Volunteer Military Force," *New York Review of Books,* No. 10, June 1993.

14.   For the first time, the consolidated United Nations interagency appeals were launched simultaneously (in December 1998 for 1999). As of July 31, 1999, the response to the appeals was about 49 percent of the amount sought. Excluding southeastern Europe, however, the response was 31.6 percent, only marginally better than in 1998. The geographical and sectoral commitment of funds has been extremely uneven. Not even minimum levels of assistance could be guaranteed in certain sectors and some countries were left critically underfunded. The poor response to crises in Africa, at a time when many donor countries are enjoying a period of prolonged prosperity, was particularly distressing.

15.   See chapter 9 in this volume. Also, for an account of the tribunals that places them in historical context and discusses their efforts to provide accountability, see Aryeh Neier, *War Crimes: Brutality, Genocide, Terror, and the Struggle for Justice* (New York: Times Books, 1998).

16.   See *Report of the Secretary-General on the Work of the Organization, United Nations Official Records,* Supplement No. 1 (A/54/1), August 31, 1999.

FIFTEEN

Human Rights and Warfare:
An Ounce of Prevention Is
Worth a Pound of Cure

DAVID HAMBURG

David Hamburg is the Co-Chair and President Emiritus of the Carnegie Corporation of New York, where he was President from 1983 to 1997. He has served as Co-Chair of the Carnegie Commission to Prevent Deadly Conflict; he has held academic posts at Stanford and Harvard University; and he served as the President of the Institute of Medicine, National Academy of Sciences, and the Chairman and President of the Board of the American Association for the Advancement of Science. He has served on the Chief of Naval Operations Executive Panel, and currently serves on the Defense Policy Board of the United States Department of Defense. Dr. Hamburg is also a member of the President's Committee of Advisors on Science and Technology. He has a long-standing interest in the issues of human aggression and violence and has published many articles on these subjects.

One of the most striking paradoxes of the twentieth century, and particularly of the postwar world, is that the tremendous explosion in human rights awareness and law described by Louis Henkin and Kenneth Roth in chapters 1 and 10 has been coupled with an even more pronounced expansion of deadly conflict. Even as more citizens around the world enjoy economic, social, civil, and political rights, this greater freedom is increasingly vulnerable to recent trends in warfare.

The impact of war on civilians grew worse in the twentieth century. Civilians have been made pawns and objects of warfare: The forcible expulsion of hundreds of thousands Albanians from Kosovo in spring 1999 is a recent example. The stresses of the modern world are in part to blame for this increase in organized violence against civilians. The frustrations and uncertainties in a complex, rapidly changing world can trigger scapegoating of highly visible groups, such as minorities, immigrants, and government officials, who become targets of irrational, hateful, and extremist responses. Severe social stress, manipulated by a hate-filled and fanatical leadership, can lead to mass killing, even genocide. Incitements to hideous atrocities are proffered by the likes of Hitler, Stalin, Pol Pot, and their murderous successors; indeed, they can be spread more efficiently and vividly now by advanced telecommunications.

Thus despite the advances in recognition of human rights and the international laws to protect them, the technology and practices of twentieth-century warfare have increased the danger to civilians and the risk of new and ever greater human rights catastrophes. A people's seemingly indelible memory of violations of their human rights by others can lead to further war and human rights violations, as victims seek retribution and vengeance through violent means. A recent example is the killings of Hutu refugees fleeing Rwanda across Zaire by Rwandan Tutsi forces, after the Hutus' genocide against the Tutsis in Rwanda in 1994.

Civilization struggles to find ways to interrupt this chain of violence, but successes are, as yet, few and far between: South Africa's Truth and Reconciliation Commission and similar "truth commissions" in other countries are efforts in this direction, as are international war crimes tribunals (described by Richard J. Goldstone in chapter 9). The breakdown of civilized values that is war creates the conditions under which more war and more human rights violations may proliferate endlessly. The bloody connection between war and human rights violations is truly a case in which an ounce of prevention—the prevention of deadly conflict—is worth a pound of cure. Thus prevention is the focus of this chapter.

Prevention consists not only of averting confrontations and avoiding the escalation of a crisis into warfare, but also of creating a durable basis for peaceful alternatives. In the long run, we can be most successful in interrupting the chain of human rights violations of which ethnic, religious, and international wars are a part by promoting democracy, market economies, and the creation of civil institutions that protect human rights. Preventive strategies rest on three orientations: early responses to signs of trouble; a comprehensive, forward-looking approach to counteract the factors that raise the risk of violent conflict; and an extended effort to resolve the underlying causes of violence. Thus I conclude this chapter with a detailed review of specific proposals toward these ends.[1] First, however, I outline some of the hopeful indicators of advances in human rights and their more sobering counterpart, the evidence of increasing war–related human rights abuses. I explore some of the causal connections between war and human rights violations, because these causes suggest potential areas for cures. The concluding section of the chapter reviews proposals for improvements in international law and institutions that would facilitate actions by the international community in the areas of early warning, response, and prevention of human rights violations and deadly conflict; and proposals to foster domestic initiatives to improve human rights and peaceful security, including democratization, the rule of law, and human rights protections.

TWENTIETH CENTURY
HUMAN RIGHTS: STEPS FORWARD AND BACK

Most citizens in most countries today live longer, healthier lives in generally better circumstances than did their parents. Although the number of people living below the poverty line has increased by 39.7 percent since 1965,[2] life expectancy worldwide has risen as much as nine years since 1970,[3] infant mortality rates have been cut by more than half since 1975,[4] and adequate nutrition is more widely available than it was twenty years ago.[5] People in developing countries also enjoy far greater access to education than two decades ago: The literacy rate in developing countries has increased from less than 45 percent to 70 percent between 1970 and 1995, while enrollment in primary education worldwide has risen from 48 percent to 77 percent between 1960 and 1991.[6] Concern for the condition of the planet has led to unprecedented international cooperation to combat many environmental problems, including global warming, environmental pollution, and the movement and disposal of hazardous waste.[7]

Respect for human rights has become widely recognized as an important responsibility of governments and civil society. The number of countries that routinely carry out extrajudicial executions has decreased since the mid-1990s, but the number of countries in which the authorities torture or mistreat detainees has not decreased.[8] There are signs of hope. Even China, which is notorious for resisting the demands of international human rights organizations on grounds of "cultural relativity" and opposition to interference in its internal affairs, signed the two major Covenants that comprise the International Bill of Rights, thereby exposing its internal human rights record to international scrutiny.[9] Today 117 countries, more than twice as many as in the 1970s, are either democracies or in the process of democratizing. In Latin America 18 countries have made the transition from military to democratic governments since 1980.[10] In Africa nearly 30 multiparty presidential elections have been held since 1990.[11] The percentage of women in national legislatures ranges from 9 percent in developing countries to 12 percent in developed countries, and the global average rose from 7.4 percent in 1975 to 11 percent in 1995.[12]

Yet in spite of these advances in the human condition, grave violations of human rights, including torture, expulsion, and genocide, were seen to be increasing in the twentieth century. Deadly conflicts, including civil wars and interstate wars, are deeply implicated in this horror, as anyone with access to international mass media can see. The very changes that contribute to advances in human health and safety also may contribute to raising the risk of war and its dangers.

While the changing world holds great promise for improvements in the human condition, the very process of rapid change also creates new stresses, especially when accompanied by increased social and economic disparity. During the 1990s nearly a quarter of the world's states underwent political transformations. People and ideas have become more mobile within and between states. New technology has generated immense wealth, but those left behind are increasingly aware that their prospects of sharing this new wealth are dim. Thus many of the changes now underway could result in even greater risk of violent conflict and the concomitant jeopardy to the human rights of large numbers of people.

Violence can grow out of a number of root causes, and many factors heighten its likelihood, including the political and economic legacies of colonialism or of the cold war, problematic regional relationships, religious or ethnic differences sustained by systematic cultural discrimination, political or economic repression, weak or illegitimate government institutions, and corrupt or collapsed regimes. Rapid population growth and drastic economic changes can generate social and economic frictions; shortages of vital resources can exacerbate feelings of deprivation, alienation, hatred, and fear. Other factors can worsen the situation, including sudden changes of regime, rapid economic deterioration, disturbances in neighboring areas, and the ready availability of weapons and ammunition.

Modern technology and the geopolitics of the twentieth century also made war more dangerous for more civilians. Civilians are eight times more likely to be killed in an armed conflict now than at the beginning of the twentieth century.[13] The patterns of deadly conflict—who does the fighting, and who gets killed, injured, impoverished, or displaced—have altered in recent decades. In World War II, for example, the warring parties were sovereign states from all over the world: the Allies on one side and the Axis powers on the other side. Of the estimated 36.7 million casualties from the war, 47 percent were civilians; that is, people not involved in active combat.[14] In contrast, 95 of the 101 wars between 1989 and 1996 were internal wars,[15] and some estimates put the percentage of civilians killed during those conflicts as high as 90 percent.[16] The methods of warfare also have changed, with increases in guerrilla fighting and the targeting of women and children; it is estimated, for example, that 40 percent of the Rwandan population has been killed or displaced since 1994.[17] In Kosovo, estimates by the U.S. State Department put the number of ethnic Albanians who were internally and externally displaced between March and June 1999 at more than 90 percent of the total population of Kosovo, or 1.5 million people.[18]

War is more dangerous for civilians, in part, because warfare now is no longer waged by conventional armies of opposing states on battlegrounds far from home. Instead, conflicts are fought in and around inhabited villages by irregular armies, and the distinction between civilian and combatant is often blurred. Such guerrilla-style warfare exposes civilians more to crossfire, deliberate violence, and suffering due to the denial of food, shelter, and dignity.[19]

THE RELATIONSHIP BETWEEN
DEADLY CONFLICT AND HUMAN RIGHTS

The linkage between war and human rights violations, including the loss of recent gains in health, education, nutrition, and safety, has become increasingly, and horrifyingly, evident. Before the wars in the former Yugoslavia and Rwanda, for example, women there had achieved greater access to education and political participation and decreased rates of maternal mortality. Yet prior to the conflicts, many of those gains were negated by brutal political oppression, inflammatory uses of the mass media, and widespread human rights abuses. During the conflicts, a genocidal rape strategy was employed.

The circular relationship between human rights violations and deadly conflicts has long been recognized. Not only do wars cause human rights abuses; such abuses also may signal the imminence of deadly conflict. The recognition of this link and the resultant pairing of the goals of preventing deadly conflict and advancing human rights have a long history. The original decision to enshrine a commitment to uphold human rights in the UN Charter reflected more than a humanitarian or idealist impulse of member governments. The founders of the United Nations were interested primarily in preventing another world war, and many had concluded that the Nazis' terrible human rights abuses were the early warning signs of aggression. They believed that if the international community had acted early and firmly to deter or to stop Hitler and his followers from committing *internal* human rights abuses, it might have been possible to prevent World War II.

Moreover, governments that do not respect the rights of their own citizens may not respect the rights of weaker neighbors. Even when such behavior is not a precursor of broader aggression against neighboring countries, it may warn of the imminence of unwelcome refugee flows and other troubles that could spiral into a costly humanitarian emergency. The UN High Commissioner for Refugees often reminds governments that today's human rights abuses may result in tomorrow's refugee movements.

Yet there has never been any consensus on the best means of averting conflict. Whatever their postwar resolve, few could agree in the aftermath of World War II on how to prevent wars in the future. With the onset of the cold war, prevention reverted to more traditional strategies of deterrence and balance of power, instead of focusing on strengthening human rights protection and collective security. Although a vast body of international human rights norms and laws has emerged in the last fifty years—from the Universal Declaration and the Helsinki Accords to the Covenants—human rights protection requires more; it requires the active and unceasing engagement of individual governments and nongovernmental organizations (NGOs). The guidelines, political will, and international capacity for such engagement are developing only very slowly in the absence of a consensus among states that it is in their national interest. However, currently, states face new problems of collective security that are giving human rights greater political salience. Protection of human rights is thus becoming an instrument of preventive diplomacy and collective security.

PREVENTING DEADLY CONFLICT: BREAKING THE CHAIN OF VIOLENCE

Given the impact of war on human rights, prevention of deadly conflict may well be the most important possible contribution to protection of human rights. The proposals of the Carnegie Commission on Preventing Deadly Conflict suggest how the international community might take further steps both to prevent deadly conflict and to protect human rights worldwide. In brief, it can do so by strengthening existing international law to meet the challenges of deadly conflict and developing international law to set standards aimed at deterring its occurrence; by targeting and integrating UN efforts to facilitate preventive reform and to develop an early warning system of conflict and associated human rights violations; and by funding efforts to advance the rule of law, democratization, and national human rights efforts.

International law

Strengthening humanitarian law—the norms themselves and also their dissemination and acceptance by states—so that more combatants abide by it would decrease the effects of deadly conflict on civilians. Prohibitions against certain types of violence within states—such as genocide and torture—apply irrespective of whether the conflict is internal or international in character. However (apart from the Genocide Convention[20] and more general prohibitions contained in international human rights instruments), there is no specific international legal provision prohibiting *internal* violence corresponding to Article 2(4) of the UN Charter, which prohibits the use of force between states, nor is there any widely accepted principle that the use of force within a state should be prohibited. International provisions specifically governing (although not prohibiting) internal violence, found in Common Article 3 of the Geneva Conventions (1949) and Additional Protocol II to the Geneva Conventions (1977), have remained untested and largely ignored by the international community from the time of their adoption.[21] The principles embedded in those instruments were acknowledged by the United Nations in 1993, when it made them the basis for prosecution of international crimes by incorporating them into the Statutes establishing the ad hoc International Criminal Tribunals for Rwanda and the former Yugoslavia.[22] Despite this official endorsement, debate continues over whether the instruments, especially Additional Protocol II dealing with noninternational conflicts, constitute "customary international law" that is binding on all states, or whether instead they are binding only on the states that have ratified them. Thus our first recommendation for helping make international law a more effective basis for the prevention and punishment of internal violence is for the international community to codify and develop the principles of Common Article 3 and Additional Protocol II.

Common Article 3 of the Geneva Convention is a building block for promulgating humanitarian norms that is especially important to internal conflict. This Article applies to all armed conflicts of a "noninternational" character occurring in the territory of a signatory state. It calls for the humane treatment of noncombatants and others who do not take up arms, and prohibits violence of any type against these people. The world has not yet had time to assess the impact of the two war crimes Tribunals' development of humanitarian norms on the prevention of deadly conflict at either the international or the internal level. While the Tribunals have convicted people under the provisions of the Statutes, which incorporate Common Article 3, it is unclear whether these convictions are sufficient to raise the provision to the status of customary international law, binding on all states.

Numerous less institutionalized approaches under international law also have their place. Arbitration and mediation can help broker resolutions to disputes. Arbitration, while effective under conditions of defined legal relationships—such as in treaties or charters—is limited in impact as it takes place in a defined and confrontational framework within a judicial or quasi-judicial environment, which may be difficult to achieve in cases of impending or ongoing conflict. Mediation, on the other hand, enjoys a higher rate of success in international settings. It requires no advance commitment, allows parties to communicate directly, and has as its goal simply to settle the conflict to the satisfaction of all parties. It has been used extensively as a tool for settling both interstate and internal conflicts. For example, the civil wars in El Salvador and Mozambique and the dispute between Greece and the former Yugoslav Republic of Macedonia were resolved through mediation.[23] Therefore, international efforts to strengthen the availability and effectiveness of alternative dispute resolution can help prevent deadly conflict and human rights abuses.

Institutional Reform

Strengthening institutions, particularly the United Nations, early warning systems, and local government institutions, can contribute to peace, security, and adherence to human rights.

The United Nations   The UN commitment to helping prevent deadly conflict resides in its central purposes of promoting peace and security, fostering sustainable development, inspiring widespread respect for human rights, and developing the regime of international law. Three major documents combine to form a working program for the UN to fulfill these roles: *An Agenda for Peace,* published in 1992; *An Agenda for Development,* published in 1995; and *An Agenda for Democratization,* published in 1996.[24] Each report focuses on major tasks essential to help reduce the global epidemic of violence, preserve global peace and stability, prevent the spread of weapons of mass destruction, promote sustainable economic and social development, advance the cause of human rights and fundamental freedoms, and alleviate massive human suffering. The current Secretary-General, Kofi Annan, has emphasized human rights in speeches all over the world. He has greatly strengthened the office of the UN High Commissioner for Human Rights.[25]

UN action to promote democratic practices rests on the principles outlined in three core documents: the UN Charter, the Universal Declaration of Human Rights, and the Declaration on the Granting of Independence to Colonial Countries and Peoples. The United Nations, together with its member states, offers a wide range of assistance to help build the political culture necessary to sustain democratic practices. The United Nations International Children's Fund (UNICEF), the UN Development Program (UNDP), and the UN High Commissioner for Refugees (UNHCR) recently have begun to emphasize prevention. In 1996, for example, UNICEF launched its Anti-War Agenda to lessen the suffering of children due to mass violence.[26] The agenda's top priority is prevention, and it emphasizes the importance of education to promote tolerance and peaceful means of dispute resolution. These organizations should integrate their efforts with a more activist UN High Commissioner for Human Rights to strengthen the UN's role in early warning, the protection of human rights, and conflict prevention. The Office of the Secretary-General can play a crucial role in facilitating this integration, primarily through its "good offices," by providing neutral grounds for discussing and resolving disputes.

Early warning The circumstances that give rise to violent conflict usually can be foreseen. Mass violence is almost invariably due to the deliberately violent response of determined leaders and their associates to social, economic, and political conditions that, although they provide the environment for violent conflict, do not themselves independently spawn violence. Prevention strategies should be tailored to address these predisposing factors and to neutralize the violence-prone leadership. Doing this requires an international focus on early warning and early response.

Early indicators of trouble include widespread human rights abuses, increasingly brutal political oppression, inflammatory use of the media, the accumulation of arms, and sometimes a rash of organized killings and expulsions. Such developments, especially when combined with chronic deprivation and increasing scarcity of basic necessities, can create an extremely volatile situation. Successful prevention of mass violence therefore will depend on slowing and then reversing the development of such circumstances. In hindsight, we can see that that there was ample early warning of the catastrophe of Rwanda: Hutu militants committed a spate of "practice massacres" of hundreds of people in the early 1990s, prior to the sustained violence of April, May, and June 1994 that killed some 800,000 Tutsis and moderate Hutus.[27]

Human rights are gaining significance not only as a moral imperative but also as a tool of analysis and policy formation; their violation gives early warning of worse problems to come. Thus strengthening the monitoring of human rights can serve as an early warning system for deadly conflict, and preventing human rights abuses may help prevent deadly conflicts from taking place at all. One step in the right direction was announced by President Clinton on December 10, 1998, the fiftieth anniversary of the signing of the Universal Declaration of Human Rights:

The United States established an early warning center on genocide to focus American intelligence on uncovering potentially genocidal situations around the world. Located in the intelligence and research division of the State Department, it was announced as part of a package aimed at strengthening the protection and promotion of human rights in general.[28]

However, the problem is not solved by early warning alone, as amply illustrated by the Rwandan genocide; it also requires early action. A rapid reaction force therefore is needed to help fulfill the Security Council's mandate to uphold international peace and security. The core of this force should be contributed by sitting members of the UN Security Council. Its nucleus would be a well-trained, cohesive infantry brigade with its own organic weapons, helicopters for in-country transportation, and compatible logistical and communication support. The force would need the ability to react rapidly in potentially violent intrastate situations or in certain types of interstate crises. It would not, however, be a substitute for the normal range of UN peacekeeping operations. The operational integrity of such a force requires that it not be assembled piecemeal or in haste; a standing force may well be a necessity for effective prevention.

Domestic Reform

While international initiatives have a crucial role to play in preventing deadly conflict, the key to long-term prevention on an international scale is to foster preventive reform on a domestic level, most urgently within states where troubles are brewing. These reforms should focus on initiatives that establish the rule of law in place of arbitrary or violent coercion, aid the peaceful transition to democratic systems of government, and help develop national human rights policies and organizations.

Rule-of-Law Initiatives An understanding of and adherence to the rule of law is crucial for a healthy system of social organization, both nationally and internationally. Any effort to create and maintain such a system must itself rest on the rule of law. The rule of law is both a goal—it forms the basis for the just management of relations between and among people—and a means. A sound legal regime helps ensure the protection of fundamental human rights, political access through participatory governance, mutual accommodation of diverse groups, and equitable economic opportunities.

Democratization The international community should aid the transition to democracy, because a state's internal political system influences its dealings with other states. It is now commonplace to note that democratically organized states tend not to fight one another.[29] Although democratic states may disagree, their habits of negotiation and tolerance of domestic dissent tend to lead them to resolve conflicts without resort to organized violence. Indeed, democracy may provide its most powerful contribution to peace by moderating relationships between democratic states so as to prevent the onset of serious disputes in the first place.[30] In their dealings with each other, democratic states sometimes create new institutions and processes to meet new demands, such as the dispute resolution mechanisms in global economic organizations.[31]

There is perhaps no more fundamental political right than that of citizens to have a say in how they are governed. Healthy political systems reflect a shared contract between the people and their government that, at its most basic, ensures the ability to survive free from fear or want. Beyond basic survival, however, widespread political participation—democracy—assures all citizens the opportunity to better their circumstances while managing the inevitable clashes that arise in the process. Democracy achieves this goal by accommodating competing interests through regular, widely accessible, transparent processes at many levels of political interaction. It also requires a functioning and fair judicial system, a military that is under civilian control, and a police and civil service that are competent, honest, and fundamentally accountable to the electorate.

Effective participatory government based on the rule of law reduces the need for people to take matters into their own hands and resolve their differences through violence. The institutions and processes to ensure widespread political participation can vary widely, but it is important that all groups within a society can trust that they have real opportunities to influence the political process.

Pressure for national human rights policies and organs Although outside powers can help detect looming conflict and help supply resources to nurture civil society and to fortify democratic governance and legal institutions, the international community should not lose sight of the fact that it is *national* governments that must take the lead in establishing and fortifying domestic institutions devoted to the promotion and protection of human rights.

The World Conference on Human Rights, held in Vienna in 1993, emphasized the important role that national human rights institutions could play. While recognizing the right of each state to choose the framework that most suits its needs at the national level, the World Conference encouraged the establishment and strengthening of national institutions based on the "Paris Principles" that had been elaborated at the first international meeting of national human rights institutions in October 1991.[32]

According to those principles, a national human rights institution should have as broad a mandate as possible clearly set forth in a constitutional or legislative text that specifies the institution's composition and sphere of competence. The responsibilities of such institutions should be to:

- Submit recommendations, proposals, and reports to the government, parliament, and any other competent body on any matter relating to human rights (including legislative and administrative provisions and any situation of violation of human rights)
- Promote conformity of national laws and practices with international human rights standards
- Encourage ratification and implementation of international standards
- Contribute to the reporting procedure required under international instruments
- Assist in formulating and executing human rights teaching and research programs and in increasing public awareness of human rights through information and education
- Cooperate with the United Nations, regional institutions, and national institutions within the country.

Because some national institutions have jurisdiction to receive and act on individual complaints of human rights violations, the Paris Principles suggest that the functions of such national institutions may include:

- Seeking an amicable settlement of the matter through conciliation, binding decision, or other means
- Informing the complainant of his or her rights and of available means of redress, and promoting access to such redress
- Hearing complaints and referring them to a competent authority
- Making recommendations to the competent authorities, including proposals for amending laws and regulations that obstruct the free exercise of human rights. [33]

The Paris Principles also include detailed guidelines on the composition of national institutions and the appointment of members; on guarantees of independence and pluralism; and on methods of operation, including the need to cooperate with other entities responsible for protecting human rights, such as the ombudsman and nongovernmental organizations active in the field. The principles were endorsed by the United Nations Commission on Human Rights in 1992 and by the General Assembly in 1993.

CONCLUSION

The twentieth century showed us the terrible link between human rights abuse and war, both as cause of and as effect on one another. In the early 1930s, there were unmistakable signs that there would be a reign of terror if the Nazis came to power in Germany. Far from hiding his brutality from the sight of the world, Adolf Hitler proclaimed his foreign policy views in speeches and made his view on war especially clear in *Mein Kampf* as early as 1924. There were opportunities during Hitler's rise to power and in the years following when the international community could have taken effective preventive action. The atrocities of Hitler's storm troopers in his first months in office should have been a powerful warning: A regime that massively violates domestic law and egregiously violates human rights will create a similarly lawless foreign policy. Hitler's Germany proved, if proof were needed, that human rights are linked both within and beyond a country's borders. In a fundamental sense, the protection of human rights is not only intrinsically valuable; it is the key to preventing the massive violence that can endanger the future of humanity.

The twentieth century witnessed some of the bloodiest, most destructive wars in recorded history. At the dawn of the third millennium, many unresolved intergroup and interstate conflicts continue to fester, taking a toll in human lives, in suffering, and in resources. For too long now the international community, and especially the developing world, has deluded itself with the complacent belief that the events in faraway lands are not the whole world's concern, that the problems of other peoples do not have consequences for all. This shortsighted view has left the international community ill-prepared to deal with conflicts when they occur, leaving it to muddle through from crisis to crisis, applying emergency first aid. Instead, more fundamental solutions are urgently needed: Prominent among these must be the protection of human rights, firmly embedded in democratic institutions with the protection of national and international law.

The record of this century also provides a compelling basis for hope. The decline of tyranny and the extension of representative and responsive government, the protection of human rights, and the promotion of social justice and economic well-being—imperfect and incomplete though they are—suggest what human ingenuity, decency, and dedication can accomplish.

NOTES

1. For these proposals, and much else that underpins this chapter, I draw heavily on the work of the Carnegie Commission on Preventing Deadly Conflict, established in 1994, of which

I was co-chair with Cyrus Vance. See publications of the Carnegie Commission on Deadly Conflict, and especially *Preventing Deadly Conflict* (New York: Carnegie Corporation of New York, 1997).

2.   Mayra Buvinic, "Women in Poverty: A New Global Underclass," *Foreign Policy*, No. 38 (Fall 1997), p. 43.

3.   Ibid., p. 42.

4.   World Health Organization, *World Health Report 1998*, "Progress in Achieving Targets for Health for All by the Year 2000," <http://www.who.int/whr/1998/file1e.jpg>.

5.   Buvinic, "Women in Poverty," p. 42.

6.   Carnegie Commission, *Preventing Deadly Conflict*, p. 13.

7.   For example, as of April 15, 2000, eighty-four countries had signed the Kyoto Protocol, a 1998 agreement aimed at curbing the emission of greenhouse gases to reduce global warming.

8.   In 1995, confirmed or possible extrajudicial executions were carried out in 63 countries; by 1998, that number had decreased to 47. In 1995, 114 countries subjected detainees to torture or ill treatment; by 1998, while 125 countries tortured or ill-treated detainees, there were resultant deaths in 41 countries. *Amnesty International Reports 1996, 1997, 1998, 1999* available from <http://www.amnesty.org/ailib/aireport>.

9.   The Universal Declaration of Human Rights, which covers the spectrum of rights, bans all forms of discrimination, slavery, torture and other cruel, inhuman, or degrading treatment or punishment, and guarantees every human's right to life, liberty, nationality, freedom of movement, religion, marriage, assembly, and many other fundamental rights and freedoms. One hundred thirty states have signed on to the Universal Declaration since its adoption by the UN General Assembly on December 10, 1948. The International Covenant on Economic, Social and Cultural Rights (ICESCR) and the International Covenant on Civil and Political Rights (ICCPR), with its two Optional Protocols, together form the International Bill of Rights, the cornerstone of the "worldwide human rights movement" foreshadowed in the UN Charter. Many regional organizations incorporate the International Bill of Rights in their charters and proceedings, and some include additional human rights provisions. For example, the Helsinki Accords (the founding documents of the Conference on Security and Cooperation in Europe [CSCE, now OSCE]) provide, as does the Universal Declaration, for freedom of thought, conscience, religion, and belief. China signed the ICESCR on October 27, 1997, and the ICCPR on October 5, 1998.

10. Carnegie Commission, *Preventing Deadly Conflict*, p. 13. See also UN Development Program (UNDP), *Human Development Report 1999* (New York: Oxford University Press, 1999); and Freedom House Survey Team, *Freedom in the World* (New York: Freedom House, 1999).

11. Carnegie Commission, *Preventing Deadly Conflict*, p. 13.

12. Jane S. Jaquette, "Women in Power: From Tokenism to Critical Mass," *Foreign Policy*, No. 23 (Fall 1997), p. 26.

13. See the Carnegie Commission, *Preventing Deadly Conflict*, p. 11.

14. Weekly Review, "The Human Cost: V-E day 1945–1995," *Montreal Gazette*, May 6, 1995, p. B3.

15. Interdisciplinary Research Program on Root Causes of Human Rights Violations (PIOOM), *World Conflict and Human Rights Map 1998* (Leiden: PIOOM, 1998).

16. Carnegie Commission, *Preventing Deadly Conflict*, p. 11.

17. Ibid.

18. U.S. State Department Report, "Ethnic Cleansing in Kosovo: An Accounting" (U.S. Department of State, December 1999), available online at <http://www.state.gov/www/global/human_rights/kosovoii/homepage.html >.

19. Kofi Annan, "Peacekeeping and National Sovereignty," in Jonathan Moore, ed., *Hard Choices: Moral Dilemmas in Humanitarian Intervention* (Lanham, MD: Rowman and Littlefield, 1998), p. 56.

20. The Convention on the Prevention and Punishment of Genocide (1948) defines genocide (Article II) as "any of the following acts committed with the intent to destroy, in whole or in part, a national, ethnical, racial or religious group, as such: (a) Killing members of the group; (b) Causing serious bodily or mental harm to members of the group; (c) Deliberately inflicting on the group conditions of life calculated to bring about its physical destruction in whole or in part; (d) Imposing measures intended to prevent births within the group; and (e) Forcibly transferring children of the group to another group."

21. Together, the four Geneva Conventions and the two Additional Protocols form the network of international law governing the treatment of people, both combatants and civilians, during an armed conflict (*jus in bello*). The Conventions deal with, respectively: wounded and sick members of the armed forces on the ground; wounded, sick, and shipwrecked members of the armed forces at sea; protection of prisoners of war; and treatment of civilians. The two Additional Protocols deal with similar issues, the first covering international conflicts, and the second covering non-international conflicts.

22. The Statute for the International Criminal Tribunal for Rwanda can be found at <http://www.ictr.org/statute.html>; and the Statute for the International Criminal Tribunal for the former Yugoslavia at <http://www.un.org/icty/basic/i-bencon.htm>.

23. For a general discussion of mediation, its use, success, failure, and advantages over arbitration, see John Burton, *Conflict: Resolution and Prevention* (New York: St. Martin's Press, 1990); Gareth Evans, *Cooperating for Peace: The Global Agenda for the 1990s and Beyond* (Sydney: Allen and Unwin, 1993); and I. William Zartman and Saadia Touval, "International Mediation in the Post–Cold War Era," in Chester A. Crocker and Fen Osler Hampson, eds., *Managing Global Chaos: Sources of and Responses to International Conflict* (Washington, DC: United States Institute of Peace [USIP] Press, 1996).

24. Boutros Boutros-Ghali, *An Agenda for Peace, 1995: With New Supplement and Related UN Documents*, 2nd ed. (New York: United Nations, 1995); Boutros-Ghali, *An Agenda for Development, 1995: With Related UN Documents* (New York: United Nations, Department of Public Information, 1995); Boutros-Ghali, *An Agenda for Democratization* (New York: United Nations Department of Public Information, 1996).

25. See chapter 14 in this volume.

26. The statistics of children in armed conflicts tell a horrifying story. According to UNICEF, 300,000 children under eighteen are serving as regular soldiers, guerrilla fighters, spies, porters, cooks, sexual slaves, and suicide commandos in conflicts in fifty countries. Over the past ten years, as the result of war, more than 2 million children have died, 6 million have been maimed, 1 million are orphans, 10 million have serious psychological trauma, and wars have also resulted in children constituting half the world's 24 million refugees. Statistics from Judith Miller and Paul Lewis, "Fighting to Save Children from Battle," *New York Times,* August 8, 1999, p. A8.

27. See, for example, Philip Gourevitch, *We Wish to Inform You that Tomorrow We Will Be Killed with Our Families: Stories from Rwanda* (New York: Farrar, Straus, and Giroux, 1998).

28. The Center is a joint program involving the CIA and the State Department. Dana Priest and John M. Goshko, "Genocide Warning Center Established," *Washington Post,* December 11, 1998, p. A52.

29. While democratic states have been involved in conflicts—such as the 1998–1999 American and British strikes against Iraq and Yugoslavia—no dispute or crisis between states has ever escalated into an international war unless at least one of the states involved was not democratic. The foundation article of "the democratic peace" argument is Michael Doyle, "Kant, Liberal Legacies, and Foreign Affairs," Parts 1 and 2, *Philosophy and Public Affairs,* Vol. 12, No. 3 and No. 4 (Summer and Fall 1983), pp. 205-54 and 323-53 respectively; and Doyle "Liberalism and World Politics," *American Political Science Review,* Vol. 80, No. 4 (December 1986), pp. 1151-69. See also Bruce Russett, *Grasping the Democratic Peace* (Princeton, NJ: Princeton University Press, 1993); Miriam Fendius Elman, ed., *Paths to*

Peace: Is Democracy the Answer? (Cambridge, MA: The MIT Press, 1997); and James Lee Ray, "The Democratic Path to Peace," *Journal of Democracy,* Vol. 8, No. 2 (1997), pp. 49, 50.

30.   Ray, "The Democratic Path to Peace," p. 57.

31.   However, the *transition* to democracy carries its own dangers. Jack Snyder points out that weak and imperfect democratic institutions may facilitate the spread of the kind of demagogic ethnic slander that Slobodan Milosevic purveyed to keep himself in power, and the result there was "ethnic cleansing" and war. See Edward D. Mansfield and Jack Snyder, "Democratization and War," *Foreign Affairs,* Vol. 74, No. 3 (May-June 1995); Jack Snyder and Karen Ballentine, "Nationalism and the Marketplace of Ideas," *International Security,* Vol. 21, No. 2 (Fall 1996), pp. 5-40; V. P. Gagnon, "Ethnic Nationalism and International Conflict: The Case of Serbia," *International Security,* Vol. 19, No. 3 (Winter 1994-95), pp. 130-66; and Jack Snyder, *From Voting to Violence: Democratization and Nationalist Conflict* (New York: Norton, 2000).

32.   The first of a series of UN-sponsored meetings of representatives of national institutions, convened to clarify the concept of a "national institution" and its role in the promotion and protection of human rights, was held in Paris in October 1991; it was followed by workshops in Tunis in 1993 and Manila in 1995. See Center for Human Rights, *National Human Rights Institutions: A Handbook on the Establishment and Strengthening of National Institutions for the Promotion and Protection of Human Rights,* Professional Training Series No. 4 (Geneva: United Nations, 1995).

33.   Carnegie Commission, *Preventing Deadly Conflict,* p. 99.

"Conscience Trigger": The Press and Human Rights

Anna Husarska

Anna Husarska is a Polish-born, French-educated journalist. Over the last dozen years she has worked on the staff of the *Buenos Aires Herald, Gazeta Wyborcza, The New Yorker,* and *The New Republic.* She has reported from many conflict zones, including Afghanistan, Algeria, Bosnia, Cambodia, East Timor, El Salvador, Guatemala, Iraq, Kashmir, Kosovo, and Nicaragua. From 1996 to 1998 she served as a political analyst with the International Crisis Group (ICG) in Bosnia and was responsible for the ICG's Kosovo project. Most recently, she taught a postgraduate course on political transitions at the Ecole Nationale des Sciences Politiques in Paris.

We live in an age when the media's interest in itself is turning into an obsession. The mirror seems to be taking precedence over the pencil, the microphone, and the camera. Journalists appreciate their own work on a continuum from self-flagellation to self-congratulation. It should not be surprising, then, that a journalist chooses to discuss the relationship between media and human rights. A whole body of recent literature discusses what the various media can or cannot do about foreign policy and foreign disasters, man-made or otherwise.[1] But none of these works address the media's capacity to affect human rights abuses. There is a powerful and underexplored connection. Whereas reports on foreign trade wars, cultural crusades, or international monetary disasters do not necessarily compel the audience to be personally moved and to act or call for action, with human rights it is different. Learning—through the media—about a violation often translates into a moral imperative to do something. So when it comes to human rights, the media constitute a "conscience trigger" as nowhere else. The function of "conscience trigger" is at the heart of the connection between the media and the protection of human rights.

In this chapter I explore the role of the media in altering—for better or for worse—a variety of situations in which human rights have been under attack. Framing the question in a slightly different way might be more encouraging: What would human rights be without the media? To say that it would be only old ladies writing postcards to "His Excellency Mr. Dictator" to tell him that he is naughty would be an exaggeration, but such an image helps one to imagine how powerless human rights advocates would be if they were stripped of the power of the media.[2]

As the subject is vast and this chapter could be a book in itself, I have limited my focus to situations in which this particular relationship is the most pertinent and the most inspiring. Here are some of the parameters of the discussion that follows:

First, as it is better to speak about a subject a person knows or has directly experienced, I describe mostly situations that I know firsthand.[3] These examples should be treated as exactly this—examples—and not as anything more general.

Second, because interaction between the media and the human rights communities is most desperately needed in developing countries and those countries that are in a state of civil war, I draw on examples from these areas. I do not discuss stable countries that suffer from long-standing, isolated human rights abuses. These abuses usually have already become the subject of scrutiny by lobbying groups, specialized media, and other mechanisms.

Third, although some conflicts generate heavy media coverage, I focus here on situations when a human rights case is *not* already big news. In these circumstances, the media have the opportunity to influence the human rights agenda in a more powerful way.

Fourth, I do not discuss specialized legal, human rights, and political journals that play a completely different role from that of daily news or weekly magazine reporting. These publications can supply an invaluable record to those interested, but they usually preach to the converted, and constitute less of a tool for the advancement of human rights than a trade literature.

Finally, since the role of foreign media covering human rights abuses is very different from that of local media, I bring examples only from the media that are foreign to the problems they describe. Countries in which human rights violations are notorious usually lack a free media, so the local media are not a great help in promoting human rights, and indeed often themselves need outside help. A few courageous outlets may hang on and, because they operate in the local language with local journalists and newsreaders, occasionally they can reach the local population. Belgrade's Radio B-92, Minsk's Radio 101.2, Port-au-Prince's Radio Soleil, and the Algerian newspapers *El Watan* and *La Nation* are examples.[4] However, for every brave voice of independence, we can find a counterexample in which local media incite their audiences to commit acts in violation of human rights. Here I am thinking in particular of Radio Mille Collines in Rwanda and radio and television in Republika Srpska, the Serb part of Bosnia.[5]

Working within these parameters, I show how, in situations where human rights violations occur, the media have it in their power to describe and investigate cases, to protect human rights workers, to publicize the issues, and to advocate and propose solutions or even preventive measures. The success with which journalists, their editors, and their producers take on and perform these tasks is another matter. I review each of these tasks and offer some examples from my own experience. I conclude by looking in more detail at the lessons learned from media coverage of the recent human rights disaster in Kosovo.

DESCRIBING HUMAN RIGHTS CASES

The media fulfills an educational role every time it describes a human rights violation. Simply by presenting the facts and naming the violation, the media often point to an action that needs to be taken. If, for example, the public reads, hears, or sees that rape may be considered a war crime and that the perpetrator may be hauled up before a war crimes tribunal, then its awareness of the gravity of this human rights violation has been raised, which is a step in the right direction.

Here is an example of the concrete power of simple journalistic description. In the summer of 1992 in Moscow, I came across a group of Cuban émigrés who had been sent on scholarships to the Soviet Union. At that time they preferred to remain in post-perestroika Russia rather than return to Cuba, which was less free. Caught in the middle, they lacked the right to stay outside Cuba but were fearful to return. Fascinated by this irony, I described their predicament in print.[6] Later one of those students told me that the Canadian immigration authorities at Gander Airport, Newfoundland (where Cubana Airline makes a technical stop on the way from Moscow to Havana and often "loses" many of its passengers) had been persuaded, in part by my article, to grant those Cubans temporary asylum. A simple description of the plight of several Cuban students-in-exile helped in this particular situation to protect the human rights of these individuals.

The power of description also can achieve other goals: For example, human rights education can be advanced through the media. In Cuba, I once saw a collection of translated journalistic texts about the Polish Solidarity movement in the hands of a prominent leader of the Cuban human rights movement. The sight of this greasy, dog-eared copy, falling into pieces, scribbled all over in several different pencils and pens, as read as read can be, moved me profoundly. The Cuban dissidents did not know how to pronounce the names of the rebellious towns of Jastrzebie or Szczecin (indeed, hardly anyone knows), but because they had this book, they could recount the events there that had advanced the human rights cause in Poland, and they could imagine how they might do the same in Cuba.

I suspect that the organizers of the protests in Serbia in the aftermath of the North American Treaty Organization (NATO) air strikes had read ten-year-old press reports about the media-friendly tactics employed by Eastern Europeans in their struggle for human rights. It is easy to imagine that such stories inspired them. Similarly, Albanians in Kosovo explain that it was media coverage of the 1989 revolutions in Poland, Czechoslovakia, and the Baltics that awakened their hopes for change at home.

INVESTIGATING HUMAN RIGHTS CASES

Investigation takes the journalist a step further than simple description. These investigations can do far more than descriptions to advance human rights because of the power of the media, both in resources and in reach. When investigating human rights violations, journalists from major media outlets usually have the advantage of knowing that if the story is judged to be "big" (an assessment not necessarily tied to the gravity of the abuse), no means will be spared to cover it. The most powerful human rights organization in the world cannot match the impact of a major newspaper or television network. Media outlets are likely to have regional offices staffed by people who are familiar with the territory, possess good communication equipment, and have the financial means to hire the right people, secure transportation, and devote the time necessary to dig out the story.

A textbook example of such a media investigation involved the case of a Nazi officer who was hiding in Argentina. Here is what the Simon Wiesenthal Center has to say about it: "No one ever anticipated that . . . S.S. Captain Erich Priebke would be located and extradited for trial. . . . But, thanks to ABC-TV's Sam Donaldson, that's just what happened."[7] In the mid-1990s Donaldson went to

Argentina and confronted Priebke; the material was aired on the television news show *Primetime.* As a result, Priebke was brought to trial, and is now serving a sentence in an Italian prison.

I was personally involved in a story that shows the effects of description and investigation by media and their potential for impact on human rights protection. In February 1995, rather by accident, I happened upon a journalistic scoop, the case of Captain Lawrence Rockwood of the U.S. Army.[8] Rockwood had served in an intelligence unit during the peace mission in Haiti in September 1994. His concern for human rights led him to undertake a solitary inspection of the Port-au-Prince prison, notorious for its appalling conditions. He believed that the U.S. Army should have been present in the prison from the very beginning of the intervention. Although his deed exposed the army's reluctance to put soldiers' lives at risk, his unauthorized trip to the prison exceeded his mandate, and his act met with the disapproval of his superiors. Ultimately, Rockwood was court-martialed. After my longish but merely descriptive piece, other journalists and television news and magazine shows, including (oh, the ultimate consecration!) CNN, launched their own investigations, digging out additional details and confronting the military brass and the Department of Defense. The court-martial became a cause célèbre. In the end, Rockwood was found guilty on most counts; as his penalty, he was dismissed from the army. Largely as a result of this case and the attention it received, enforcement of human rights standards by soldiers on peacekeeping missions became a topic of discussion in human rights circles, in military academies, and even in the political arena.[9]

During the Bosnian war, media investigations of human rights violations often had a major impact on policy, or at least on policy rhetoric. Take the most prominent example: The world knew that Bosnian Serbs committed a massacre against Muslims in Srebrenica in July 1995. David Rohde, reporting for the *Christian Science Monitor,* proved to be the most dogged investigator: He discovered evidence of the mass graves containing the remains of the Srebrenica victims.[10] Rohde's initial story was corroborated by aerial photographs taken by U.S. spy planes. Ten days after the story ran, and one day after another mortar killed thirty-seven people in Sarajevo, NATO planes launched air strikes on Bosnian Serb positions. The impact of Rohde's reporting cannot be established precisely, but public knowledge of this massacre, and the outrage that followed, pushed policymakers in the NATO countries finally toward punishing those who were committing genocide.

Investigative reporting is, of course, not new. In November 1969 Seymour Hersh filed the first story about the My Lai massacre perpetrated by American soldiers in Vietnam in March 1968.[11] Hersh's investigation was instrumental in exposing the case, a major embarrassment to the U.S. Army, which to this day has not fully come to terms with the idea that American soldiers could be guilty of war crimes.

In January 1982 the U.S. Army was embarrassed again: Two American journalists exposed the massacre of civilians in El Mozote, El Salvador, by the Salvadoran Army's special U.S.-trained Atlacatl Battalion.[12] Their investigation resulted in stories in the *Washington Post* and the *New York Times;* those stories were vehemently denied by the U.S. administration, which was providing military aid to the Salvadoran government at the time. We cannot know if the Salvadoran military planned and abandoned similar armed raids, but we can surmise that the possibility of publicity may well have served as a deterrent to future abusers.

PROTECTING HUMAN RIGHTS ACTIVISTS

Although it sounds counterintuitive, media exposure and publicity sometimes can offer protection to human rights activists. I came to understand this in Haiti in 1992. I set out to interview a man who had written about violence against journalists. Although his office was cool and quiet, he insisted that we conduct the interview on the hot and noisy terrace outside. When I inquired, he explained that he wanted to be seen speaking to a foreign reporter, because this might protect him from reprisals for his human rights activities.

A few years later I set out to interview a human rights activist in Kashmir, Jalil Andrabi. Instead, however, I interviewed his widow: Jalil was murdered shortly before I arrived in Srinagar. His two brothers, who were trying to see justice done in his case, insisted that I include their names and details about their families in my story. Again, they believed that the publicity offered by journalistic recognition could serve as protection against attack by the paramilitaries or government-paid thugs.

In 1984 the smuggled picture of human rights activist Yuri Orlov, emaciated and visibly exhausted in a Soviet labor camp, was published in *Newsweek* next to a picture of Orlov in good health before he entered the camp.[13] As Susan Osnos of Human Rights Watch has said, when a media outlet, using the material provided by a human rights group, stages a full-fledged "free this person" campaign, the impact is absolutely unmatched.

There are, however, occasions in which people living under totalitarian regimes get into trouble because they speak to foreigners. Journalists must exercise extreme discretion and should always allow the interviewee to decide whether to publicize the meeting. Generally, human rights activists and famous dissidents get better protection by having contacts with foreigners, whereas less prominent people may be punished for the same contacts. All too often, however, the outside media report only on human rights activists and on the independent journalists in countries under totalitarian regimes, because such people are usually more media-savvy and more likely to meet with foreign journalists and to speak foreign languages. Although they are important carriers of the message about human rights violations, it is crucial for journalists to make it clear they are not the *only* victims of the regimes.

PUBLICIZING HUMAN RIGHTS CASES

Sometimes a journalist neither describes from firsthand knowledge nor investigates; often he or she simply reports on the work of human rights organizations that have released a study or report. This approach publicizes both the specific human rights case and the general issue of human rights protection.[14] Such a news story typically begins something like this: "In a report published today, a human rights organization documented the execution of so-and-so. . . ." Journalists who have themselves gathered information on human rights violations sometimes cannot "sell" their story to editors and must rely instead on the release of such reports as a news peg on which to hang their own stories. The resulting article could tell the tale of a particular human rights violation or could describe the whole human rights scene, placing one particular case in a larger context; it is the human rights organization's documentation that nudges editors toward publication.

This relationship between journalists and human rights organizations can be mutually beneficial. Journalists learn about human rights standards or about specific cases of violation from the human rights monitors and from their reports, while human rights groups count on journalists to publicize their work and to draw public and governmental attention to concrete cases of human rights violations. A good journalist dealing with countries in conflict considers the reports of respectable human rights groups as "must-read" literature before landing, and he or she carries a well-prepared list of relevant Web site addresses on the road.[15]

Due to their financial means and their institutional credibility, major media outlets usually can gain better access to stories of abuses than sole journalists or human rights organizations. But this is not always the case. Sometimes discreet work by a human rights group can harvest more fruit. An example is Human Rights Watch's October 1998 report on Kosovo, which enumerated abuses committed by the Kosovo Liberation Army that the media had previously missed or ignored.[16] Many journalists shone their first spotlight on the not-so-clean record of the Kosovo Liberation Army when they reported on the release of this report.

Unfortunately, if there are constant or repeated violations in the same circumstances against the same group of people—Serbs mistreating Albanians in Kosovo, Albanians mistreating Serbs in Kosovo, Indians mistreating Muslims in Jammu-Kashmir, Hispanics mistreating indigenous groups in Guatemala— it becomes far more difficult for human rights organizations or activists to get media coverage. These abuses are vastly underreported, because the story is deemed already "done." Unless a journalist can introduce new elements, or offer a novel analysis, it is difficult to get the editors interested: "So? What else is new?" they say.[17] We journalists must struggle constantly to find a fresh approach that brings the world's attention to the places it is most needed.

ADVOCATING HUMAN RIGHTS VALUES
AND PROPOSING SOLUTIONS

By writing about cases of abuse and investigating them, journalists keep the status of human rights in the public eye. In so doing, they are the allies of human rights advocates. In one example, countless journalists made calling for the arrest of indicted war criminals in Bosnia their personal crusade. This effort has, unfortunately, been futile, as the major war criminals remain at large, but perhaps occasionally we have managed to spoil the breakfast of the decision makers who refuse to order the arrests. Unfortunately, commercial factors often drive journalists away from human rights stories, which are seldom considered "sexy." There is not much appeal in the stench of mass graves, the silhouette of a woman speaking about how she was raped, or the fuzzy shot of a distant labor camp. Compassion fatigue quickly kicks in.

Moreover, most of my colleagues, especially those from the U.S. media, have the myth of "journalistic neutrality" very strongly implanted within them. This stated commitment to neutrality almost stands in their way of bringing compassion to the story. Of course, their opinions filter through in the ways they stress certain themes or in their choices of whom to interview. But their declared attitude of neutrality precludes any overt advocacy. The op-ed pages are designated forums for prescription, but they are off-limits to professional correspondents, those who have the very field experience that is *needed* to prescribe wisely. To the extent that journalists advocate human rights, they do so through their editorial boards, but the editorial space is scarce and is filled mostly by headquarters staff who seldom travel. As a result, the insight, the exposure, and the compassion that come from direct contact are rarely translated into direct and concrete prescription. The exceptions are the traveling columnists or reporters for journals of opinion, rare birds indeed.

This kind of opinionated journalism seems to be most efficient when it proposes concrete solutions and precise policy recommendations. The impact one can have with a policy-oriented advocacy op-ed was brought home to me in 1994, when I wrote an opinion piece in the *New York Times*. I argued that President Clinton should not isolate Cuba after a wave of refugees left the island. Although the suggestion was not taken, I did get invited to the National Security Council (NSC) to be debriefed about my idea in greater detail. This alarmed my mother in Poland, who spent most of her adult life under a Stalinist regime and for whom the "National Security Council" sounded dangerously like the KGB, the "Committee for National Security." She was sure that the NSC would cut off my electricity as a punishment. (Clearly there is a significant need for more human rights education in my homeland.) I still have hopes that my arguments concerning Cuba will be recalled and will eventually have some effect.

PREVENTING HUMAN RIGHTS VIOLATIONS

Prevention is probably the most frustrating aspect of media involvement with human rights issues. It is next to impossible to gauge the impact of journalists in helping prevent or curb human rights violations. However, it is safe to say that the mass media are not good at providing early warning of human rights violations. Until the situation gets really ugly, editors tend to resist coverage.

For example, anyone who tuned in to the 1999 human rights disaster in Kosovo probably asks why the world did not do something to prevent it. Did the foreign correspondents not know it was coming? Why did nobody warn us? But in fact, every self-respecting foreign correspondent covering the region probably had filed at least one story about the deterioration of the human rights situation in Kosovo. Without new elements on the scene, it was impossible to get the editors interested. The response was predictable: Our audience already has been outraged over this before. And indeed the reporter had difficulty finding new elements to add. The story of Serb repression and Albanian radicalization got old before it got new again. The Serbian forces may have intensified their mistreatment, beatings, and arrests of ethnic Albanians, but the pattern of behavior remained consistent, and only the names of the localities and the number and names of victims changed. "More of the same," we know, does not sell advertising.

The arrival of the media on the Kosovo scene was "late" if one dates their arrival according to human rights abuses, but from the perspective of editors with their concerns, the coverage was right and timely. Indeed, as soon as there was a major massacre, there was major coverage. Here I am not being ironic; I am just stating a fact.

We journalists and many others knew that Kosovo would be "the next Bosnia;"[18] to say so was almost a cliché. Each of us had knowledge of some compelling human rights story from Kosovo that had moved us personally, but because it was more of the same, we did not manage to enlist our editors to the cause. *Our* consciences were triggered, but we were unable to get the word out to the audience we would have needed if we hoped to change policy.

I had a very sobering firsthand experience of this: I have closely followed the situation in Kosovo since 1996, I traveled there often, and I could see what was coming. I wrote a very long political analysis report that was about to go to print in March 1998.[19] When I informed my editors that I wanted to write an op-ed, they leaned in with anticipation, but as soon as they heard the word "Kosovo," their eyes glazed over and—their voices overcome with boredom—they asked if there was really anything *new* in Kosovo. They refused to print my early warning calls. This particular occasion was just two days before the first massive killing of ethnic Albanians in Drenica. Once the bloodshed had started, of course, the very same media became very excited, and my phone rang off the hook with requests for information and for a copy of the report I had written.

NEW APPROACH:
THE INTERNATIONAL CRISIS GROUP

Many journalists who report from countries where human rights are still an abstract concept and where violations are anything but abstract often dream, "If only I could write what I feel," or "If only I could write pieces as long as the subject demands," or "If only I was sure that my piece would reach those I am trying to reach." In this sense, the International Crisis Group (ICG) is a journalist's dream.[20]

The ICG is a multinational private organization founded in 1995 and chaired for its first four years by former U.S. Senator George Mitchell (D-Maine). The idea of the indefatigable former Assistant Secretary of State Morton Abramowitz was to create an organization that would provide analysis of potential and breaking crises and offer preventive policy options; that would advocate actions at international, regional, and local levels; and that also would provide assistance to local initiatives. Although ICG is neither exclusively nor even primarily a human rights group, by trying to anticipate and contain conflicts, it is very much a tool of human rights protection in the most effective way because it focuses on prevention. ICG does not pretend to play the role of media in this or any other field, although many of its members are journalists (along with lawyers, diplomats, humanitarian workers, and others). By providing political analysis to inform journalists about the wider context, complete with local color and a deep understanding of the local situation, the organization has managed to establish itself as an authority on human rights for journalists and as a source of journalism expertise for human rights activists. Journalists working for ICG as political analysts have put human rights issues on the map by writing innumerable op-ed articles with analyses and recommendations for the crisis-stricken regions and for some of those regions where conflicts are brewing. The organization thus urges its staff—people in the know—to circulate ideas for conflict prevention or suppression and for postconflict reconciliation. Because of the staff's knowledge and independence, ICG analysis is trusted. Because of the board's prominence, ICG's recommendations are read. Because the analysts are on ICG's payroll, they can supply a form of news coverage, analysis, and prescription without asking for support from mainstream media, which wait for the bloodbath before they expend resources to pay for coverage.

The ICG was an instant success in Bosnia, where it started by monitoring the Dayton Peace Agreement. It made a significant difference in Cambodia and in the Great Lakes region in Africa.[21] It began offering field-based insights into the brewing conflict in Kosovo back in 1997 and at the beginning of 1998. I joined ICG in May 1996 to cover Bosnia, and relished my role as analyst and reality check. For example, in September 1996 I monitored the elections in Bosnia for ICG and enjoyed the opportunity to conduct lengthy and deep political investigation and analysis while also retaining independence to criticize policy. At that time, I filed a weeklong diary for *Slate,* an online magazine, where I described the pressure from Washington on international institutions to hold an election even though it could be neither free nor fair. I had the time and resources to detail the electoral fraud, along with the freedom to publicly assail the decision of U.S. policymakers. In the *Slate* piece, I wrote that I had "developed something of a reputation as a party-pooper. But a party-pooper with a cause."[22]

CONCLUSION

How do we make the interaction between the media and the human rights community more fruitful, so that by describing, investigating, and publicizing human rights violations, the media can trigger more consciences? Ensuring that the early warning calls make it into the media and that the human rights abuses stay in the headlines requires a commitment from editors, producers, publishers, and, ultimately, the general public. The catch is that it is only when the media covers these events that the general public gets interested in these issues in the first place. This interest, reflected in the ratings, generates more coverage.

Because human rights stories are predominantly sad and grim, they make it to the news only when they are somehow extreme: big numbers, heartbreaking drama, ghastly sights, sobbing protagonists. This is a very cynical concept but an effective one: A tearjerker on one particular case of misery, written, recorded, or filmed, often triggers an interest in a pattern of human rights violations that may be multiplied if other journalists follow the lead and make it into a bigger story. Not surprisingly, the best understanding of this interaction comes from people who have worked in both fields: When human rights groups employ former journalists, they know how to produce effectively for print or broadcast. When media outfits employ former human rights advocates or regional experts, they do not leave their consciences behind and usually push to get better exposure for human rights issues. On the whole, however, it is frustrating to reflect upon the potential power that journalists could leverage in advancing the cause of human rights and to note how little they do achieve. Commercial demands reduce editorial interest in human rights stories until massive violations have become the story. By then, however, it is usually too late for warnings or prevention.

It is not the job of journalists to stop all the world's human rights violations, but they should not be ashamed to commit themselves to that cause, an urgent and potentially ennobling one.

NOTES

1. *Does It Pressure or Distort Foreign Policy Decisions?* Working Paper 94-1 (Cambridge, MA: Joan Shorenstein Barone Center on the Press, Politics and Public Policy, John F. Kennedy School of Government, Harvard University, June 1994); Johanna Neuman, *Lights, Camera, War* (New York: St. Martin's Press, 1996); Warren P. Stroebel, *Late-Breaking Foreign Policy* (Washington, DC: United States Institute of Peace Press, 1997); and Susan Moeller, *Compassion Fatigue: How the Media Sell Disease, Famine, War and Death* (New York: Routledge, 1998). These works are excellent, but they all deal more or less exclusively with ongoing conflicts or peace operations where the television cameras have already arrived. Gowing and Neuman limited their studies to technologically advanced media; Stroebel describes only peace operations, that is, cases where the U.S. government already has seen and somehow acknowledged the seriousness of the situation; and Moeller's book deals with situations so well-known that "fatigue" kicks in. Indeed, one of the criticisms of human rights organizations is that they have done little to build domestic constituencies apart from those triggered in an ad hoc fashion by press coverage.

2. David Rieff, "The Precarious Triumph of Human Rights," *New York Times Magazine*, August 8, 1999, p. 41. "So far, what power the human rights movement has obtained derives not from an evolution in popular sentiment—as occurred, for example, with regard to civil rights or the environment—but from the press and the political elite."

3. A disclaimer: I have worked as a journalist and as a humanitarian officer and political analyst. Although I have never done strictly human rights work, I can think of very few articles I have written that could not have been footnoted with a quotation from the Universal Declaration of Human Rights.

4. After the Yugoslav authorities hijacked Radio B-92 at the beginning of NATO air strikes on April 2, 1999, the journalists and editors launched a new incarnation of the same station and named it B2-92.

5. On Radio Mille Collines, see Philip Gourevitch, *We Wish to Inform You that Tomorrow We Will Be Killed with Our Families* (New York: Farrar, Straus, and Giroux, 1998). On the spread of hate in media in the Balkans, see Mark Thompson, *Forging War: The Media in Serbia, Croatia and Bosnia-Herzegovina* (Avon: The Bath Press, 1994); and see also the International Crisis Group report, *Media in Bosnia-Herzegovina: How International Support Can Be More Effective*, March 18, 1997, available on ICG's Web site, <http://www.cri-sisweb.org>.

6. Anna Husarska, "Little Havana," *New Republic*, June 15, 1992.

7. Simon Wiesenthal Center Press Release, "Simon Wiesenthal Center Commends Decision in Argentina Today to Extradite Nazi War Criminal Erich Priebke to Italy," May 1995.

8. Anna Husarska, "Duty to Disobey; One GI's Haiti Crusade," *Washington Post*, February 5, 1995, p.C01; "Conduct Unbecoming: The Army Captain Who Faces Court-Martial for Doing the Right Thing, " *Village Voice*, April 11, 1995, p. 21. See also Steven Wrage, "A Question of Duty," *Newsweek*, November 22, 1999, p. 52.

9. I used Rockwood's case to criticize a similar U.S. military policy in Bosnia, which emphasized "force protection" above all other goals, in Husarska, "A Larger Mission in Bosnia," *Washington Post*, February 13, 1996, p. A19. For a discussion of Rockwood in a study published by the Army War College, see Warren D. Hall, III. *The Obligation to Protect Human Rights: A New Legal Requirement for Commanders?* (Carlisle Barracks, PA: Army War College, 1996).

10. See, for example, several of the Pulitzer Prize–winning articles by David Rohde in *Christian Science Monitor*: "Evidence Indicates Bosnia Massacre," August 18, 1995, p. 1; "Bosnian Muslims Were Killed by the Truckload," October 2, 1995, p. 1; "Graves Found That Confirm Bosnia Massacre," November 16, 1995, p. 1. See, in addition, Rohde's book *Endgame: The Betrayal and Fall of Srebrenica* (New York: Farrar, Straus, and Giroux, 1997); and Chuck Sudetic, *Blood and Vengeance: One Family's Story of the War in Bosnia* (New York: Norton, 1998).

11. See Seymour M. Hersh, *Cover Up: The Army's Secret Investigation of the Massacre at My Lai 4* (New York: Random House, 1972).

12. Alma Guillermoprieto reported for the *Washington Post* and Raymond Bonner did so for the *New York Times*. Mark Danner later described the same events in a series of articles in *The New Yorker* that were later turned into the book, *The Massacre at El Mozote: A Parable of the Cold War* (New York: Vintage Books, 1994).

13. The photos were published in "A Siberian Exile Gets a Phone Call," *Newsweek*, December 10, 1984, p. 57. Orlov was released to the West in October 1986 as part of a deal made between Reagan and Gorbachev at the Iceland Summit.

14. During the second Chechnya war, for instance, the *New York Times'* Michael R. Gordon wrote: "Human Rights Watch reported Thursday that many civilians are pinned down in basements and that the conflict has overwhelmed Chechnya's hospitals" in "Russia Opens Chechen Border to Flood of Refugees Fleeing Bombs," *New York Times*, November 5, 1999, p. A18. The same day Daniel Williams of the *Washington Post* wrote: "Russia launched the ground offensive against Chechnya five weeks ago. After weeks of muted commentary, Western governments have stepped up criticism of Russia's bombing of civilian targets and treatment of refugees. Amnesty International and Human Rights Watch expressed alarm; Human Rights Watch estimated that 40,000 refugees were stuck at the border;" "Russia Eases Blockade for Fleeing Chechens," *Washington Post*, p. A25.

15. See, for example, Amnesty International, <http://www.amnesty.org/>; Human Rights Watch, <http://www.hrw.org>; International Rescue Committee, <http://www.intrescom.org/>; the University of Minnesota Human Rights Library links page, <http://www.umn.edu/humanrts/links/links.htm>; the International Federation of Human Rights Leagues, <http://www.fidh.imaginet.fr/uindex.htm>; UN Human Rights, < http://www.un.org/rights/>; the Hague Tribunal, <http://www.un.org/icty/>; International Criminal Tribunals, <http://www.cij.org>; the International Crisis Group, <http://www.crisisweb.org/>; and the U.S. State Department Country Reports on Human Rights Practices, <http://www.state.gov/www/global/human_rights/hrp_reports_mainhp.html>.

16. Human Rights Watch, *Federal Republic of Yugoslavia: Humanitarian Law Violations in Kosovo* (New York: Human Rights Watch, October 1998).

17. See Moeller, *Compassion Fatigue.*

18. I wrote as much in an article actually entitled "Dateline Pristina: The Next Bosnia." This appeared in *The New Republic* on November 15, 1993, and was later republished in Nader Mousavizadeh, ed., *The Black Book of Bosnia* (New York: Basic Books, 1996). My reportage from East Timor's capital Dili published in February 1999 in the Polish weekly *Tygodnik Powszechny* is entitled "Kosovo on the Pacific."

19. "Kosovo Spring," published in March 1998 by the International Crisis Group.

20. The Web site of the International Crisis Group (ICG) is <http://www.crisisweb.org>.

21. See, for example, the International Crisis Group (ICG) Press Release, *ICG Calls for an Honest Assessment of the Cambodian Poll,* July 26, 1998; ICG Report, *Towards a Crisis Prevention Plan for Central Africa,* December 6, 1996; and ICG Report, *Why the Bosnian Elections must be Postponed,* August 14, 1996.

22. See <http://www.slate.com/Diary/96-09-09/Diary.asp>.

PART IV

Afterword:
The Challenges Ahead

The Challenges Ahead:
Analysis and Integration

Mary Robinson

Mary Robinson, former President of Ireland (1990–1997), became UN High Commissioner for Human Rights in 1997.

The beginning of a new century prompts us to assess progress made on human rights, to ask how close our achievements have come to our aspirations. A variety of evaluations and diagnoses have been made by governments and civil society, international and nongovernmental organizations, and religious communities and individuals, as well as by United Nations bodies. The challenge now is to draw practical lessons from these analyses and the critical material, lessons that can help us do better at championing and defending human rights in this new era. The chapters in this book underscore the crucial importance of reflecting on the institutional mechanisms and policy tools at our disposal. Gleaning from their lessons, I see five key challenges ahead: prevention, monitoring, enforcement, development, and integration.

PREVENTION: STRENGTHENING NATIONAL INSTITUTIONS

The United Nations, its members, and nongovernmental organizations must emphasize prevention by establishing and supporting national human rights capacities and structures. Another powerful prevention force is found in regional and subregional cooperation, which enables governments to build on the experiences and best practices of nearby countries, to cooperate with their neighbors, and to use available resources efficiently. One of the major changes in the UN approach to human rights has stemmed from the recognition that outside review and commentary on a country's human rights records, although vital, is not enough. Without national institutions to promote and protect human rights, critical comments by international human rights bodies simply hang in the air. Unless justice systems and democratic procedures function at the domestic level, human rights cannot be addressed in a sustainable way. We must all focus on supplying assistance to countries to strengthen their national capabilities.

While the need to develop strategies for prevention is neither controversial nor new, making it operational requires great commitment from all actors, including member states, regional organizations, and the United Nations system as well as civil society as a whole. Acting collectively to prevent human-made disasters is not a luxury but rather a necessity, not least because the preventive approach makes the most efficient (if not always the most glamorous) use of scarce public resources.

The UN also has made the prevention of abuses the chief rationale behind our rapidly growing range of technical cooperation programs with individual countries. Ten years ago the UN technical cooperation program in the field of human rights was able to offer only a small number of seminars per year, whereas today it includes approximately forty projects in some thirty countries. They are financed mainly from voluntary contributions by states, which amounted to $5.7 million in 1999. It is encouraging that the demand for technical assistance in the field of human rights is growing so rapidly. One can see this as an indicator of increasing commitment to human rights and also of confidence in the services the UN can provide. However, a truly effective response will require coordinated involvement by UN partners. A recent review of technical assistance provided by the UN system indicated that there is considerable potential: Many agencies and programs already have included human rights components into their respective technical cooperation projects. Making the best use of this potential, however, requires basic coordination of efforts and information.

I believe that effective national structures ultimately can take over many of the responsibilities that are, at present, on the agenda of international organizations. Our goal should be domestic self-sufficiency in human rights implementation, without the necessity for international assistance.

MONITORING

Monitoring is crucial to give an objective and impartial picture of the worldwide implementation of human rights. Effective monitoring is indispensable for identifying needs and emerging threats, for extrapolating trends in the state of human rights at all levels, and, on this basis, for determining priority areas and methods of work. For the United Nations, monitoring provides the basis for the appropriate orientation of policies and activities, in particular confidence-building and technical cooperation at the national level. The Office of the High Commissioner for Human Rights (OHCHR) and the UN Commission on Human Rights, treaty-based bodies, and other parts of the human rights machinery regularly monitor situations involving high risks to human rights. Our aim is to contribute to early warning mechanisms as well to provide expert advice on training, legislation, and institution-building in human rights, democracy, and the rule of law.

Just ten years ago, the human rights program had no staff in the field; today more field staff work on the ground than at UN headquarters. Twenty-two human rights field presences have been deployed around the world, from Cambodia to Colombia, from the Great Lakes of Africa to the former Yugoslavia and Mongolia. From the beginning, these groups have had the mission of applying impartial, independent, and objective monitoring of the human rights situation on the ground and making direct contact with victims, witnesses, and authorities. Over time, this function has evolved to include technical assistance as well. For example, field presences provide electoral assistance in Cambodia, train educators in human rights in Abkhazia/Georgia, and strengthen national institutions such as the Office of the Ombudsman in Colombia. More recently, building national human rights capacities is becoming the most prominent part of our work on the ground. Regional human rights presences also play a leading role in helping to build local monitoring capabilities. One such office has already been established by the OHCHR in Pretoria. The implementation of the Framework for Regional Technical Cooperation in the Asia-Pacific region, which was adopted by the governments of the region in Tehran in 1998, should also lead to the establishment of such human rights presences.[1]

Analytical information coming from the UN human rights organs and bodies can play a particularly important role in early warning of violations that threaten to increase the risk of open conflicts. It is essential, however, that UN member states and other relevant bodies respond appropriately and promptly to such information. Several months before the tragedy in Rwanda, a report by the Special Rapporteur on Extrajudicial, Summary or Arbitrary Executions warned against a possible outbreak of an ethnic conflict in that country, a report that was not heeded.[2] Warnings about the fragile human rights situation in Kosovo also were coming through loud and clear, long before the conflict there erupted. We must learn the lessons of these tragic missed opportunities.

ENFORCEMENT

Enforcement is also key to the drive to consolidate human rights: Those who abuse human rights must be held accountable for their actions. There must be no impunity for those who commit human rights abuses or crimes against humanity. If we are to address cases where human rights are grossly abused and to deter further abuses, effective international enforcement measures must be put in place. In July 1998 an important element of such a strategy was agreed upon by the international community, namely, the rejection of impunity inherent in the institutionalization of international criminal justice. The Security Council had set the precedent in this respect by establishing the International Criminal Tribunals for the former Yugoslavia and Rwanda.[3] The Statute of the International Criminal Court in Rome now awaits sixty ratifications to establish the first permanent international court of criminal justice. This is an important test of political will: If the international community is serious in its desire to prevent acute human rights violations, states must reiterate their rejection of impunity and ratify the Statute without delay. All individuals, regardless of official rank or capacity, are legally bound to refrain from committing such horrific crimes as genocide, war crimes, and crimes against humanity; the international community must make it clear to all that, if they do commit such crimes, they will be pursued and brought to justice.

DEVELOPMENT

Development is also crucial to securing an international human rights system. We must pay as much attention to economic, social, and cultural rights as we do to civil and political rights. Poverty and social exclusion are contemporary plagues affecting many countries. Even in resource-rich countries, the gap between rich and poor is growing. It is evident that over the long term, poverty and social imbalance can only undermine democracy and stability. Bridging the gap between rich and poor and between ruler and ruled should be seen not just as a moral imperative but also as a practical central program for our societies and the international community. The danger to be avoided is described with bitter irony in writer Anatole France's famous comment: "The Law, in its majestic equality, forbids the rich, as well as the poor, to sleep under the bridges, to beg in the streets, and to steal bread."[4]

Recognizing this challenge, the 1986 Declaration on the Right to Development stated that "every human person and all peoples are entitled to participate in, contribute to, and enjoy economic, social, cultural and political development, in which all human rights and fundamental freedoms can be fully realised."[5] Much of the agenda of the 1999 meeting of the World Economic Forum in Davos, Switzerland, was devoted to problems inseparably linked to human rights: common global values, global justice, and responsibility. Human rights–related considerations permeated debates on markets, technologies, and economic cooperation. In his address to the Forum, Secretary-General Kofi Annan defined the basic challenges encountered by leaders of the world economy:

> We have to choose between a global market driven only by calculations of short-term profit, and one which has a human face; between a world which condemns a quarter of the human race to starvation and squalor, and one which offers everyone at least a chance of prosperity, in a healthy environment; between a selfish free-for-all in which we ignore the fate of the losers, and a future in which the strong and successful accept their responsibilities, showing global vision and leadership.[6]

The global distribution of wealth is becoming increasingly skewed. According to a recent United Nations Development Programme (UNDP) "Human Development Report," eighty-nine countries are now worse off economically, despite global economic growth, than they were ten or more years ago. A quarter of the world's population lives in extreme poverty; one child in four is unable to attend school; and 250 million children work in conditions harmful to their health and development. Recognizing that extreme poverty and social exclusion are human rights issues implies that not only governments, but international financial institutions and the private sector at all levels, have a legal and moral duty to accept responsibility and become accountable for these challenges.

Central is the question of debt, especially as it relates to developing countries, where it has taken on crippling dimensions. The costs of indebtedness, measured in terms of human welfare and economic inefficiencies, have been enormous: lost opportunities for health, education, and employment, and increased vulnerability to illness, illiteracy, and poverty. Without determined international action, many poor countries will continue to suffer chronic underdevelopment. International human rights organs and bodies, therefore, have recommended initiatives aimed at resolution of the debt problem. Examples can be seen in the

Heavily Indebted Poor Countries Initiative recently been adopted by the Group of Eight major industrialized nations. The measures taken are not as generous as I would wish, but they show that the international financial community is waking up to the human rights dimension of development and the need to build cooperative alliances between debtors and creditors with the active participation of civil society, donors, and NGOs.

The debt relief initiative is an example of how the problem of extreme poverty can be helped by looking at it from a human rights perspective; national and regional initiatives also provide useful models. An important example can be seen in the South African Human Rights Commission, which, together with the Gender Commission, a national institution and independent body created by the state, and a coalition of NGOs, brought together more than 10,000 people for public hearings on how to address issues of poverty in practical ways. Benchmarks were set that reflect the particular needs of South Africa and its people, such as a target date by which all citizens will have access to safe water within 200 meters.

It would be illogical to expect civil societies to flourish where access to education, health care, food, and water is denied. It has sometimes been contended that the negative consequences of contemporary economic trends are unavoidable because the process of globalization cannot be mitigated: Decision makers claim that globalization ties their hands. Others continue to push the view, popular in the 1970s, that intensive development requires that limits be imposed on democracy, not only through restrictive measures but also by the transfer of decision making to multilateral institutions lacking democratic legitimization. I believe such arguments are wrong. The powerful cannot be relieved of their responsibility, especially for those who are vulnerable. We cannot demand that people bear the costs of economic adjustment without participating in the decision making process. We cannot simply hope that, without democratic controls, those who govern can satisfy the people they govern. We cannot expect that people will suffer acute economic hardships with unending patience when they are deprived of their fundamental human rights and of influence on the decisions that affect them.

The right attitude toward human rights and development acknowledges that the purpose of both is to empower individuals and communities. By taking the integrated approach to human rights and development, we can change this "lawless development" into human rights–oriented development, through which people are protected against alienation from economic, social, and political life. To that end, development programs, whether at the international or the national level, should be based on a "rights approach" that orients activities not simply in terms of human needs, nor exclusively in terms of development requirements, but in terms of society's obligations to respond to the inalienable rights of individuals. A human rights approach tells people at the grass-roots level that security, economic opportunity, and a better life for their children are not vague or undefined entitlements, nor favors bestowed by a government or an international agency, but rather essential rights to which each individual is entitled in order to develop fully and live a life of dignity.

INTEGRATION

The final lesson is integration: It affects all of the others. It is essential that we coordinate human rights policies better at all levels, finding methods to facilitate interaction among international, regional, national, and nongovernmental institutions so they work together and learn from each other. These organizations must join together to analyze the instruments they have deployed to promote and protect human rights. Integration also demands that institutions and individuals who have never viewed their mandates in human rights terms begin to do so: to factor human rights into their daily decisions and their overall missions. Constructing an integrated approach is important because human rights violations do not limit their impact to the individuals directly affected; they have global relevance. Martin Luther King, Jr., summed it up well: "Injustice anywhere is a threat to justice everywhere. We are caught in an inescapable network of mutuality, tied in a single garment of destiny. Whatever affects one directly, affects all indirectly."[7] The peace on which global prosperity hinges is also dependent on respect for human rights. As long ago as 1957, Secretary-General Dag Hammarskjold said: "We know that the question of peace and the question of human rights are closely related. Without recognition of human rights we shall never have peace, and it is only within the framework of peace that human rights can be fully developed."[8] This insight teaches us that while building the world of the future, we must ensure that basic human values and the well-being of individuals frame the process of globalization.

The UN reform effort launched in 1997 offers one example of how human rights can become part of an integrated approach. Human rights are no longer seen as the responsibility of just one part of the United Nations Secretariat. In a program of reforms to enhance the effectiveness of the United Nations, Secretary-General Kofi Annan organized the work of the United Nations into four central fields—peace and security, economic and social affairs, development cooperation, and humanitarian affairs—with human rights as the issue that cuts across all four of these program fields. Accordingly, the Office of the UN High Commissioner for Human Rights (UNHCHR) is now represented in all management structures of the United Nations, including the four Executive Committees of the Secretariat that deal with peace and security, development, social, and humanitarian matters. The UN human rights program thus is integrated into the entire range of UN activities. In September 1997, just after I assumed office, the Office of the UNHCHR and the Center for Human Rights were consolidated into a single office. This merger creates a solid institutional basis for a systemwide integration of human rights activities.

The human rights integration effort also should be broadened to embrace partners inside and outside intergovernmental and governmental institutions. Addressing the General Assembly on the occasion of the fiftieth anniversary of the Universal Declaration of Human Rights in 1998, I proposed a renewed effort to translate the words of the Declaration into action with the following immediate objectives:

- That all states, within the next five years, sign and ratify the International Covenant on Civil and Political Rights, the International Covenant on Economic, Social and Cultural Rights, and the four principal Conventions: the 1965 International Convention on the Elimination of All Forms of Racial Discrimination; the 1979 Convention on the Elimination of All Forms of Discrimination against Women; the 1984 Convention against Torture and Other Cruel, Inhuman or Degrading Treatment or Punishment; and the 1989 Convention on the Rights of the Child
- That all states make the Universal Declaration on Human Rights known to every one of their citizens, starting by introducing it to all primary education curricula
- That all states implement the Declaration on Human Rights Defenders, which provides a legal framework for the establishment of an international set of principles and norms to protect human rights defenders, not just formally but in a true spirit of support for human rights defenders everywhere[9]
- Most important, that all states redouble their efforts to implement the thirty Articles of the Universal Declaration of Human Rights in full.

We have begun to see the shape of a consistent, integrated approach to human rights that involves a range of actors playing a multiplicity of roles. Our goal must be to bring together all of the actors into a global partnership for human rights. I do not regard this an unrealistic objective; on the contrary, it seems to me that the growing interest in human rights worldwide and the increased appreciation of its importance make this an ideal time to turn rhetoric into action and make human rights really work.

NOTES

1. This framework was designed to develop: national plans of action for the promotion and protection of human rights and the strengthening of national capacities; human rights education; national institutions for the promotion and protection of human rights; and strategies for the realization of the right to development and economic, social and cultural rights.

2. Report on the Mission to Rwanda, from April 8-17, 1993, issued on August 11, 1993, UN Doc. E/CN.4/1994/7 Add. 1.

3. These Tribunals are described in chapter 9 of this volume.

4. Anatole France, *The Red Lily* (London: World Distributors, 1961), Chapter 7.

5. *Human Rights: A Compilation of International Instruments,* Vol. I, Part 2 (New York: United Nations, 1994), pp. 501-14.

6. Statement on February 1, 1999; UN Doc. SG/SM/6881.

7. "Letter from the Birmingham Jail" (April 16, 1963), Martin Luther King, Jr., *I Have a Dream: Writings and Speeches that Changed the World,* ed. James Melvin Washington (San Francisco: HarperSanFrancisco, 1992), p. 88.

8. Dag Hammarskjold, Address on Human Rights and the Work for Peace at the Fiftieth Dinner of the American Jewish Committee, New York, April 10, 1957, *in Public Papers of the Secretaries-General of the United Nations, Vol. III: Dag Hammarskjold, 1956–1957,* selected and edited with commentary by Andrew W. Cordier and Wilder Foote (New York: Columbia University Press, 1973), p. 555.

9. The Declaration on Human Rights Defenders is a historic achievement in the struggle toward better protection of those at risk for carrying out human rights activities. It is officially called the Declaration on the Right and Responsibility of Individuals, Groups and Organs of Society to Promote and Protect Universally Recognized Human Rights and Fundamental Freedoms and was adopted by the UN General Assembly on December 9, 1998.

ABOUT THE EDITORS

SAMANTHA POWER

Samantha Power is the executive director of the Carr Center for Human Rights Policy of the John F. Kennedy School of Government. From 1993 to 1996 Power covered the wars in the former Yugoslavia as a reporter for the US News and World Report and the Economist. She is a frequent contributor to the New Republic and is currently writing a book, *The Quiet Americans* (Random House, 2001), which examines U.S. responses to genocide since the Holocaust. She is a graduate of Yale University and Harvard Law School, and she moved to the United States from Ireland in 1979.

GRAHAM ALLISON

Graham Allison is Director of the Belfer Center for Science and International Affairs at Harvard's John F. Kennedy School of Government, and Douglas Dillon Professor of Government. From 1977 to 1989 Dr. Allison served as Dean of the School. In the first term of the Clinton Administration, Dr. Allison served as Assistant Secretary of Defense for Policy and Plans where he coordinated DOD strategy and policy toward Russia, Ukraine, and the other states of the former Soviet Union. Dr. Allison's publications include: *Essence of Decision: Explaining the Cuban Missile Crisis* (1971), which was recently released in an updated and revised second edition (1999) and ranks among the best-sellers in political science with more than 250,000 copies in print; and *Avoiding Nuclear Anarchy: Containing the Threat of Loose Russian Nuclear Weapons and Fissile Material* (1996).

INDEX